Contents at a Glance

Table of Contents

Marc J. Wolenik

Rajya Vardhan Bhaiya

Microsoft Dynamics CRM 4 Integration

UNLEASHED

800 East 96th Street, Indianapolis, Indiana 46240 USA

Microsoft Dynamics CRM 4 Integration Unleashed

ISBN-13: 978-0-672-33054-4
ISBN-10: 0-672-33054-7

Library of Congress Cataloging-in-Publication Data

Wolenik, Marc J.

 Microsoft Dynamics CRM 4 integration unleashed / Marc J. Wolenik, Rajya Vardhan Bhaiya.

 p. cm.

 Includes index.

 ISBN-13: 978-0-672-33054-4 (pbk.)

 ISBN-10: 0-672-33054-7

 1. Customer relations—Management—Computer programs. 2. Management information systems. I. Bhaiya, Rajya Vardhan. II. Title.

 HF5415.5.W634 2010

 658.8'12028553—dc22

                                                        2009030419

Printed in the United States of America

First Printing, October 2009

Trademarks

All terms mentioned in this book that are known to be trademarks or service marks have been appropriately capitalized. Sams Publishing cannot attest to the accuracy of this information. Use of a term in this book should not be regarded as affecting the validity of any trademark or service mark.

Warning and Disclaimer

Every effort has been made to make this book as complete and as accurate as possible, but no warranty or fitness is implied. The information provided is on an "as is" basis. The authors and the publisher shall have neither liability nor responsibility to any person or entity with respect to any loss or damages arising from the information contained in this book.

Bulk Sales

Sams Publishing offers excellent discounts on this book when ordered in quantity for bulk purchases or special sales. For more information, please contact

U.S. Corporate and Government Sales

1-800-382-3419

corpsales@pearsontechgroup.com

For sales outside of the U.S., please contact

International Sales

international@pearson.com

Associate Publisher
Greg Wiegand

Senior Acquisitions Editor
Loretta Yates

Development Editor
Kevin Howard

Technical Editor
Barry Givens

Managing Editor
Patrick Kanouse

Full-Service Production Manager
Julie B. Nahil

Copy Editor
Keith Cline

Indexer
Cheryl Lenser

Proofreader
San Dee Phillips

Publishing Coordinator
Jennifer Gallant

Cover Designer
Gary Adair

Compositor
Jake McFarland

Graphics
Tammy Graham

About the Authors

Marc J. Wolenik, MCP, PMP, and MBS CRM certified professional, is the founder and CEO of Webfortis, a consulting company based in northern California. Webfortis specializes in solutions around Dynamics CRM and is a Microsoft Gold Certified Partner. He has extensive experience with CRM implementation, integration, and migration for companies of all sizes and is heavily involved in vertical solutions around the Dynamics platform.

Rajya Vardhan Bhaiya is the software practice manager at a Microsoft Gold Certified Partner consulting company in Northern California. Rajya is certified in MCPS, MCSD, MCAD for .NET, MCNPS, and MCTS in SharePoint. His primary focus is .NET development focused specifically in SharePoint and CRM development. Rajya has extensive experience working with technologies such as SharePoint, VoIP systems, Office Communicator, and specifically how they integrate with the Microsoft Dynamics CRM system. Rajya's working experience spans the gamut, from simple out-of-the-box environments, to complex projects with various integration points and complex customizations.

Dedication and Acknowledgments

I want to thank the crew at Webfortis for helping to carry part of the load while this book was being written—they went above and beyond in my absence. Additionally, I want to recognize the support we received from Microsoft—Barry Givens (also our TE), Menno te Koppele, Stefan Burak, Josh Lingerfelt and Hany Solimon. They provided valuable help and resources, and continually impress me with their professionalism and dedication. Our chapters on Scribe would not have happened without the support of and efforts by the Scribe team, specifically, Tom O'Brien, and the production team at Sams, including Loretta, Julie, Kevin, Patrick, and San Dee, who were extremely supportive when we leaned on them. Finally, I'd be remiss without acknowledging both Nicole, Adam, and now Ethan, as without their support, the long nights and early mornings would not have been possible.

—Marc

I want to thank my friends and family for moral support. Especially Harsh Bhaiya, Yash Bhaiya, Abhishek Kakani, and Mayur Attawar for providing valuable help and resources. Thanks also go to Marc for initially approaching me to work on a book together. I want to thank the entire team at OSIsoft and especially Bernard Morneau, president at OSIsoft, for initially introducing me to Microsoft CRM. I want to thank the ExtraTeam for providing moral support during this project.

—Rajya

We Want to Hear from You!

As the reader of this book, *you* are our most important critic and commentator. We value your opinion and want to know what we're doing right, what we could do better, what areas you'd like to see us publish in, and any other words of wisdom you're willing to pass our way.

You can email or write me directly to let me know what you did or didn't like about this book—as well as what we can do to make our books stronger.

Please note that I cannot help you with technical problems related to the topic of this book, and that due to the high volume of mail I receive, I might not be able to reply to every message.

When you write, please be sure to include this book's title and author as well as your name and phone or email address. I will carefully review your comments and share them with the author and editors who worked on the book.

E-mail: consumer@samspublishing.com

Mail: Greg Wiegand
Associate Publisher
Sams Publishing
800 East 96th Street
Indianapolis, IN 46240 USA

Reader Services

Visit our website and register this book at informit.com/register for convenient access to any updates, downloads, or errata that might be available for this book.

Introduction

Microsoft Dynamics CRM 4.0 was introduced in early January 2008, and with it came the desire and greater ability for organizations to modify it to fit their particular needs.

This book covers not only how to leverage Microsoft Dynamics CRM as an application that can be integrated with other applications and extended and customized to fit your organizational needs, but also how to think about Microsoft Dynamics CRM as a platform that you can use for almost any purpose.

Feature enhancements to version 4.0, including the following, position it as a truly enterprise application:

- ▶ Support for SQL 2008

- ▶ Compatibility with 64-bit architectures

- ▶ Multitenancy and support for connecting without a virtual private network (VPN) via the Internet Facing Deployment (IFD) option

- ▶ Integration with Office 2007

- ▶ Upgraded and updated software development kit (SDK)

- ▶ Upgraded support for multilanguage and currency uses

- ▶ Many GUI feature enhancements (smart lookup, email smart tracking, most recently used [MRU] lists, and Report Wizard, among others)

As previously mentioned, one of the best features of Microsoft Dynamics CRM 4.0 is the ability to truly position the application as a platform and not just an application. What this means is that organizations can implement Microsoft Dynamics CRM 4.0 and use the business rules, security, and related foundation to drive custom applications. Microsoft has touted this approach of development as xRM (X relationship management), where the X stands for *any* kind of relationship (not just customer relationships), including the following:

- ▶ Vendors

- ▶ Distributors

- ▶ Users/employees

- ▶ Affiliates

- ▶ CRM relationships (integrations with other CRM systems)

- ▶ Events

Our goal in writing this book is not to address every possible option for integration, but to use our experience with integrations to highlight the use of Microsoft Dynamics CRM as a platform by which you can leverage both custom code and add-ons to extend functionality of your Microsoft Dynamics CRM deployment.

Among other things, this book covers internal extensions (for example, Silverlight, SharePoint, and Performance Point) and how to extend CRM externally (for example, via CRM accelerators and public web services). In addition, you also learn how to use one of the best-of-breed (in our opinion) applications to bridge two systems together: Scribe Software components.

In this book, you also learn about cloud computing. Azure was first officially announced at Microsoft PDC in Las Vegas in late 2008, and since then we can hardly go a day without seeing another option for cloud computing that involves Microsoft Dynamics CRM.

The examples in this book can help you extend your Microsoft Dynamics CRM deployment to gain new efficiencies and productivity that you might have wanted to realize in the past but just weren't certain how.

This book also examines the use of Microsoft Dynamics CRM Online versus an On Premise deployment. Restrictions apply when considering either option (Microsoft currently forbids running code of any kind on their servers, for example), and therefore be sure to check which deployment you are targeting with the solutions mentioned in this book.

> **NOTE**
>
> Without exception, the examples included within this book are for the On Premise deployment of Microsoft Dynamics CRM. This doesn't mean they won't work with a hosted solution (usually a partner-hosted solution will make or have a provision to allow some/all of the customizations included), but be sure to check with the hosting provider (either Microsoft or the hosting partner) before engaging in the customizations mentioned; you might find that there is a limitation with the platform (not the examples include herein).

Finally, where possible, this book includes notes that indicate the CRM and development platform or version to which the text refers. The default development platform for this book (and recommended for Microsoft Dynamics CRM 4.0) is Microsoft Dynamics CRM On Premise and Microsoft Visual Studio Professional 2005 or later, using SQL Server 2005 and/or SQL Server 2008.

While Microsoft has indicated that the next version of CRM (currently referred to as CRM v.Next or CRM 5.0) is right around the corner (with the goal of a new release every 18 to 24 months), Microsoft has continued to add functionality to Microsoft Dynamics CRM 4.0. To date they have announced the following:

- ▶ Accelerators

- ▶ Mobile Express

- ▶ Update Rollups (version 6 just released in Q3, 2009)

- ▶ New Outlook client with increased performance and reliability (available early Q4, 2009)

This development schedule truly indicates what CRM means to Microsoft and highlights its commitment to making it a robust and easy-to-extend application.

Extending Microsoft Dynamics CRM Explained

When we consider what *extending* Microsoft Dynamics CRM means, it is important to understand what Microsoft Dynamics CRM is and how it is configured to work upon initial installation.

Unlike earlier versions of Microsoft CRM (prior to v3.0), where each functional area (Sales, Marketing, and Service) was available separately, all are installed and made available for use (provided you have the necessary permissions). If your organization does not have permission to use, or does not need, the Service area, for example, it can be hidden or removed. However, what if the Service area doesn't provide enough features for what you want to do? You can modify the application forms and add script to enhance the functionality. If that doesn't work, however, you need to consider alternative methods.

This chapter helps you create a model to show what extending Microsoft Dynamics CRM means and when and where you want to extend it.

Platforms

Microsoft Dynamics CRM introduces one of the most exciting prospects from a software standpoint in a long time: the ability to receive 100% of the software as a service. Of course, we're referring to CRM Online, but this concept isn't limited to just renting it from Microsoft via CRM Online. Instead, it can be hosted on your organization's internal servers and can be accessed from the Internet as a fully functional application.

Although this concept isn't a new one (think of your online banking transactions, viewing which seat you want to sit in for an airline flight, and so on), it is one of the first endeavors by Microsoft to rent software, instead of selling it.

What really makes the prospect of working with Microsoft Dynamics CRM exciting is the fact that regardless of which way organizations decide to use the software, it is the same code base.

This has fantastic ramifications for developers in that they can develop applications against a common code base, and with only a few limitations, they can deploy their applications regardless of how the users have selected to use the software.

An additional component is the ability for both developers and nondevelopers to build against it.

A rich development software development kit (SDK) available from Microsoft allows for extensive customization and integration options, and provides an easy-to-use interface for modifying forms and creating new fields.

SDK Explanation

The Microsoft Dynamics SDK is a supported development toolkit that can be used to develop against Microsoft Dynamics CRM. It includes code samples, methods, and recommendations for how to work with the data, business process, and related objects.

You can download the SDK from Microsoft.com. Just search for "CRM SDK."

> **NOTE**
>
> Be sure to check for updates to the SDK. As of this writing, the current version is 4.0.9, and there are new updates about every 3 to 4 months.

Extending via the Platform (xRM)

While CRM stands for *customer relationship management*, xRM stands for *anything relationship management* and is the idea that Microsoft Dynamics CRM can be used as a platform from which to extend other applications that manage relationships beyond the standard "customer" definition.

This idea of anything management came about when trying to define what a customer actually is. The classic definition is someone who conducts business in some way with your organization. However, because Microsoft Dynamics CRM already tracks noncustomers (in the form of leads, or prospective customers, and relationships, such as vendors), why can't it be extended to track other relationships?

Common examples of xRM deployments include the following:

▶ Managing events

▶ Vendors or suppliers

- Grant management

- Resource management

- Membership management

- Constituents

- Sports management (teams, schedules, equipment)

xRM deployments can consist of anything that uses the CRM platform for building a line-of-business application and might consist of regular Microsoft Dynamics CRM, a custom application embedded within CRM that exposes new/different ways of working with the data or application, or a custom application that doesn't use any of the existing Microsoft Dynamics CRM forms at all. It may be a .NET web application, a Silverlight application, or something else entirely. What it will use as the base development platform is Microsoft Dynamics CRM and the programming methods described in this book.

Extending CRM Methods

When extending Microsoft Dynamics CRM, there are typically two main approaches:

- Customizing or extending Microsoft Dynamics CRM with the native Microsoft Dynamics CRM tools

- Modifications via code (plug-ins and custom workflow activities)

Using the native Microsoft Dynamics CRM tools is largely limited to items such as modifications to the site map, creating workflows with the workflow GUI, and creating form-level scripting events.

When working with code creation, there are typically two methods: external extension via web services and internal DLL manipulation via plug-ins.

When you are extending Microsoft Dynamics CRM, the approaches above may be used jointly or independently. Dedicated software companies (independent software vendors [ISVs]) have typically established their own dedicated toolkits to work with Microsoft Dynamics CRM, whereas .NET programmers or companies with a Microsoft Dynamics CRM deployment might not need a standardized methodology for working on a Microsoft Dynamics CRM project and can create their code on-the-fly.

NOTE

Toolkits are typically pretested and standardized code that interacts with Microsoft Dynamics CRM.

Companies that create solutions for Microsoft Dynamics CRM have a dedicated and trained development staff that focuses primarily on either add-on or integrated solutions for Microsoft Dynamics CRM to extend functionality. Alternatively, they can be ISVs, which create specific applications that interact with Microsoft Dynamics CRM.

They can create the following types of components for Microsoft Dynamics CRM:

▶ Add-ons

▶ Integration components (frequently utilizing plug-ins)

▶ ISV applications

It is important to understand that a toolkit that may exist for any one company might be completely different for another company. Further, companies that develop these kinds of solutions also usually have a series of best practices that they use when approaching both project definition and deployment that extend beyond just the creation and usage of the code base.

> **NOTE**
>
> *Best practices* is a common term used to describe the recommended way to perform a series of actions. The recommended method can either derive from the vendor (such as reviewing Microsoft documentation for the creation of a component), be mandated by company policy (such as always doing load testing on a component, regardless of the use), or it can be a combination of both.

It is not uncommon to have a base class developed in Visual Studio that is specifically for interacting with CRM. The Microsoft Dynamics SDK includes several samples for how to interact with data using a variety of methods and can serve as a base toolkit for companies that haven't developed one yet. In addition, the Microsoft Dynamics CRM Engineering for Enterprise (CRM E2) has made a Developer Toolkit available for download and use.

Although the Developer Toolkit is closed source and supports only On-Premise deployments, it does offer a great development tool that is integrated into Visual Studio.

You can download the Microsoft Dynamics CRM Developer Toolkit from http://code.msdn.microsoft.com/E2DevTkt.

Standardization is hugely important when deploying solutions across multiple organizations or when there are many people working varying solutions, as it can drastically reduce troubleshooting and decrease development time (by reusing existing code).

Standardized methods a toolkit might include are as follows:

▶ Validating CRM credentials

▶ Caching the CRM credentials so that re-authentication doesn't have to occur on every request (established by the creation of the `CrmAuthenticationToken`).

▶ Standardized exception handling

▶ Creating, updating, or deleting entities

When considering extending CRM, you need to consider four areas:

- ▶ Web service programming
- ▶ Plug-ins
- ▶ Workflow
- ▶ Client-side programming

Programming against the Microsoft Dynamics CRM web service allows users to interact with CRM and enforce CRM business rules, information, and security roles.

This level of interaction is usually the result of external (that is, not Microsoft Dynamics CRM) data needing to perform some action with the Microsoft Dynamics CRM data. Common examples of this include synchronization with an integrated enterprise resource planning (ERP; accounting) system and updating a SharePoint dashboard or an external website with Microsoft Dynamics CRM data (such as customer or case management information).

When Microsoft Dynamics CRM needs to interact within the platform (for example, directly with other Microsoft Dynamics CRM data), a plug-in would be used. Plug-ins are compiled .NET assemblies that subscribe to Microsoft Dynamics CRM events and run when the event occurs. They allow developers to trigger actions based on the same event pipeline as other CRM internal logic, such as save, update, and delete actions.

A common scenario for a plug-in might be after the save event of a new order. After the order is saved, the plug-in might fire and update the Account record to show the total number of orders incremented by one.

Workflow is used to incorporate business logic and processes into the application. Supported events for workflow include when a record is created, when the record status changes, when a record is assigned, when a record is deleted, and when any of the attributes on a record are changed. Workflow is commonly used to create activities against a business rule. For example, when an opportunity has a contract received date that gets populated, we might fire a workflow to create a new activity for the account manager with a task of calling the account to schedule an implementation date.

Because Microsoft Dynamics CRM forms cannot be modified directly, other than by using the customization functions that CRM provides (there is no direct editing of the underlying HTML code), client-side programming via JavaScript is the method for performing the following:

- ▶ Form modifications
- ▶ Form events
- ▶ User alerts
- ▶ Validating data
- ▶ Querying the Microsoft Dynamics CRM database

Except for when a client-side script is created (and then referenced) in a customization file, all client-side programming is stored as part of the Microsoft Dynamics CRM metadata database in the form of entity customizations, allowing for portability of the modifications. Metadata is covered later in this chapter.

In Figure 1.1, the Telephone field has been set to read-only by some client-side script that sets the field to disabled status.

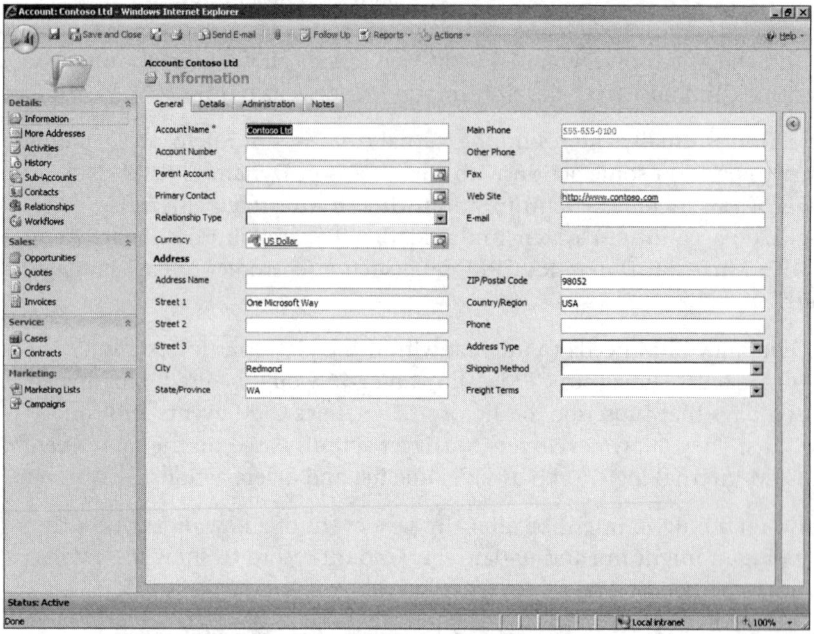

FIGURE 1.1   Account form with disabled Telephone field.

Figure 1.2 shows the script in the XML code that makes up the Account entity.

If you are so inclined, you can perform client-side programming tasks directly on the exported XML files for the entities. Once imported and published, they will execute if properly formatted.

NOTE

This method is prone to errors that can be hard to detect, and you lose the ability to quickly and easily check the configurations by using the Preview option you have in the form designer.

Metadata

The term *metadata* refers to "data about data" and is a concept utilized by Microsoft Dynamics CRM extensively to store the data for all form modifications, including client-side code and for other entities such as the site map.

When extending Microsoft Dynamics CRM, you need to be familiar with the options associated with each entity, and using the Metadata browser is recommended for this (see Figure 1.3).

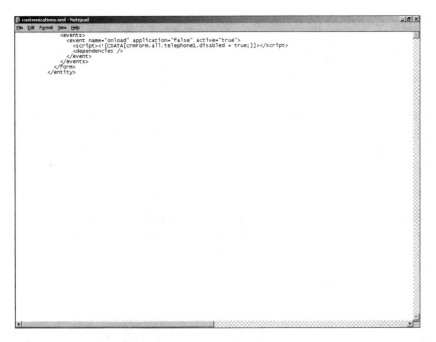

FIGURE 1.2   Exported Account customization file.

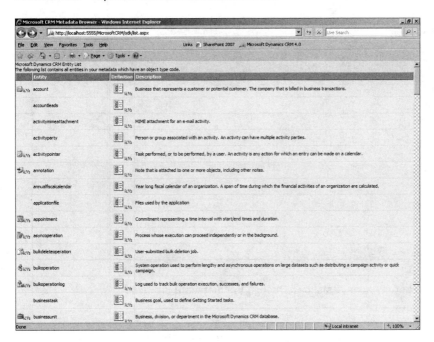

FIGURE 1.3   Metadata browser.

To access the Metadata browser, navigate to http://<<servername>>/sdk/list.aspx.

NOTE

Metadata is specific for the organization you're working with. In multitenant organizations, modify the Metadata browser URL to include the name of the organization. (As with most operations involving Microsoft Dynamics CRM, the default organization is used when no organization is explicitly selected.)

To view the Metadata browser for CRM Online, navigate to https://<<organization name>>.crm.dynamics.com/sdk/list.aspx, where <<organization name>> is your chosen CRM organization name. (To check this, log on to CRM Online and check the URL value when logged on.)

With the Metadata browser, you can easily navigate through each entity in the system and query on the metadata associated with it. Figure 1.4 shows the Account entity, and you can see how easy it is to check for information such attributes, attribute names, attribute type, length, and so forth.

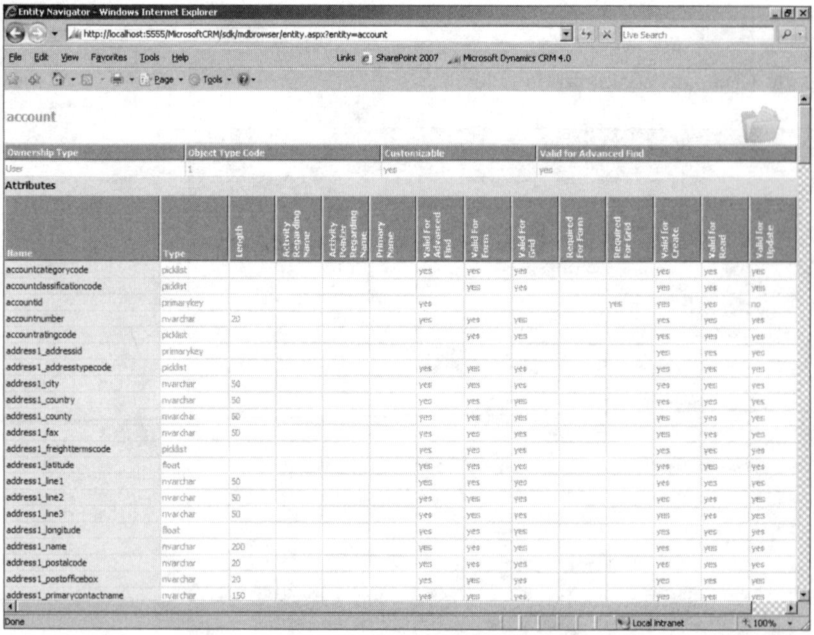

FIGURE 1.4   Account metadata as shown through the metadata browser.

The concept of a "metadata-driven user interface" is the idea that how the form is presented to users, including code and navigation options and language options, is driven by this metadata.

Layer Access

When considering extending Microsoft Dynamics CRM, where to access the data is an important consideration.

Microsoft Dynamics CRM has three distinct layers:

- ▶ Application
- ▶ Database
- ▶ Platform

Extending within the Application Layer

The application layer is the actual web application, and it is here where the actual graphical user interface (GUI) lives in the form of the application forms and navigation options.

You need a basic understanding of the forms and their type when accessed programmatically using the crmForm object. Table 1.1 shows the form types.

TABLE 1.1   CRM Form Types

Form Value	Type
1	Create
2	Update
3	Read-Only
4	Disabled
6	Bulk Edit
0	Undefined

When programming against the forms, you always want to validate the form type. If you fail to do so, your code may have unintended consequences.

When working with forms, you also want to validate other items, such as whether the form is online or offline and which client the user is accessing. Often this is done to check whether the user is working with the Outlook offline client.

The following example illustrates a check of both the form type codes and a client check:

```
//Check if user is online
if (IsOnline())
{
//check if using outlook client
//they are online
```

```
if (IsOutlookClient())
{
        //perform some action
}
//Not using the client
else
{
        //New CRM Form
        if (crmForm.FormType = 1)
        {
        //perform some action
        alert('You are not using the Outlook client, but you are online currently');
        }
}
}
else
{
//display or do something else because client is offline
}
```

Beyond the scripting examples previously mentioned, there is the possibility to modify the forms and navigation by either the site map or the Isv.Config files.

The site map is a global XML customization that modifies the application's main navigation options. The Isv.Config files can be used to modify the form navigation options.

Extending within the Database Layer

Within the database layer, the actual database structure, data, and stored procedures live. In addition, filtered views (which support security roles) are available and are the only thing that should be accessed on this layer when extending Microsoft Dynamics CRM. Because the filtered views are SQL-based, they return tabular data. The reason for this is that any direct access with the database is unsupported and may not be compatible with upgrades to the system.

> **NOTE**
>
> Access to this layer is not available when working with CRM Online.
>
> The warning about working directly with the database applies here, too, because not only is it unsupported, but it can also place the entire application into an unworkable state.

There are two (or more if working with a multitenant implementation) databases as part of this layer:

- ▶ <<organization name>>_MSCRM
- ▶ MSCRM_Config

The <<organization name>>_MSCRM is the database that contains all the metadata and data for the selected organization. In multitenant implementations, you see multiple <<organization name>>_MSCRM databases for each organization. (You can match the names in the Deployment Manager.) Each database is completely isolated from the other, allowing for disparate levels of data storage, form configurations (via the metadata configurations stored in the database), and integrations.

The MSCRM_Config database houses implementation data and other information relevant to the usage of all the <<organization name>>_MSCRM databases.

Extending within the Platform Layer

The platform layer includes one of the most powerful features for extending Microsoft Dynamics CRM: web services.

Web services are the mechanism by which any application that supports Simple Object Access Protocol (SOAP) access Microsoft Dynamics CRM data and business rules and can perform updates and basically use Microsoft Dynamics CRM programmatically. Web services are the foundation upon which xRM is modeled and allows for any kind of application to be built and to leverage CRM.

MetadataService Web Service   Now that we have reviewed what metadata is and how Microsoft Dynamics CRM works with it, and have covered the different layers, specifically web services, let's take a look at the use of both via the MetadataService web service because it is this web service that provides access to the metadata database.

Using this web service is particularly important when extending Microsoft Dynamics CRM as an ISV. Consider this example: Values associated with a particular customer's implementation may be unexpected or unusual and need to be validated before installing your custom code or product. Perhaps they have renamed one of the attributes, or maybe you want to set a drop-down value for a pick list that is necessary for your solution.

You would use the MetadataService to validate this before performing an install.

The MetadataService is located at

- ▶ **Active Directory:** http://<<server name>>/mscrmservices/2007/metadataservice.asmx.

- ▶ **CRM Online:** https://<<organization name>>.crm.dynamics.com/mscrmservices/2007/metadataservice.asmx

CrmDiscoveryService   Similar to the MetadataService web service, the CrmDiscoveryService web service enables you to query the CRM installation for organization and URL information.

You need to understand that this web service provides the mechanism for deploying solutions where the URLs for necessary web services, such as the MetadataService, are unknown. If you build a solution for your implementation, you don't need to use the CRMDiscoveryService.

The CrmDiscoveryService is located at

- ▶ **Active Directory:** http://<<server name>>/mscrmservices/2007/ad/ crmdiscoveryservice.asmx

- ▶ **CRM Online:** https://<<organization name>>.crm.dynamics.com/MSCRMServices/ 2007/Passport/ CrmDiscoveryService.asmx

CrmService   When extending Microsoft Dynamics CRM programmatically, you will make significant use of the CrmService web service, because this service extends the core functionality of CRM to the calling application.

The CrmService is located at

- ▶ **Active Directory:** http://<<server name>>/MSCRMServices/2007/CrmService.asmx

- ▶ **CRM Online:** https://<<organization name>>.crm.dynamics.com/MSCRMServices/ 2007/ Passport/CrmDiscoveryService.asmx

Of all the web services, the CrmService will be the main service used to work with Microsoft Dynamics CRM programmatically.

NOTE

Because the goal of this book is to describe how to extend Microsoft Dynamics CRM, we do not provide in-depth examples of the methods or usages of the web services; however, they are used in the examples contained within this book. They are covered at great length in our other book, Microsoft Dynamics CRM Unleashed.

Summary

This chapter highlighted the platforms and the programming methods and options involved when extending Microsoft Dynamics CRM.

We reviewed the platforms that Microsoft Dynamics CRM has and the different mechanisms for access.

A prerequisite to building any custom application for the first time is to download and thoroughly review the SDK available from Microsoft. The SDK has all the essentials for you to start.

Integration methods you may consider based on what you learned in this chapter include the following:

- ▶ Mashups across the enterprise consisting of compositing
- ▶ Consuming web services to enforce business logic and using parameterized plug-ins to query, update, and return data
- ▶ Data synchronization with disparate systems
- ▶ Workflow and process integration
- ▶ Data integration options with Microsoft Office
- ▶ SharePoint compositing with CRM web parts or integrated analytics

CHAPTER 2

Infrastructure Design Considerations

When you deploy Microsoft Dynamics CRM with other applications, you must make several design decisions. This chapter examines several possible deployment scenarios.

In today's world, typically a number of applications specialize in specific LOB functions. Therefore, considerably large demand exists for integrating between these specialized platforms. To increase end-user productivity, software architects need to establish seamless integration bridges between these systems. In this chapter, we highlight the different deployment methods and demonstrate the different architectures for the end users. This chapter examines small, medium, and large architecture designs. The scalability decisions focus on end-solution availability and performance.

Of the design considerations, determining performance needs (and the related hardware solutions) is a critical step in planning a Microsoft Dynamics CRM and Microsoft Office Server deployment. Unfortunately, it is often difficult to establish clear, detailed performance and scalability requirements for portal site deployments because it can be hard to predict use levels. To complicate matters further, use levels often change over time. Nevertheless, you can often use throughput measured as pages per second as a guideline for measuring performance.

In addition to pages per second or load time, you can use a number of other metrics to measure performance, such as the following:

▶ Server/client resource usage

▶ SQL database seek time

▶ Network hops or latency

To measure pages per second or load time, the recommended tool is Fiddler. Fiddler is a great tool to analyze the HTTP traffic that is being served to the end users. Fiddler exposes the timeline and sequence of all the page components (Auth requests, CSS, JS, and the actual HTML). You can download Fiddler from http://www.fiddler2.com. It provides an easy-to-use graphical interface for measuring page load. Figure 2.1 shows what to expect on a well-functioning network. If your Fiddler shows anything different, you might need to delve further to optimize the application.

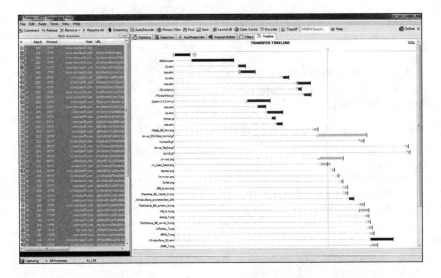

FIGURE 2.1   Fiddler showing a trace from a well-functioning network.

Hardware Requirements

There is no simple formula to determine the hardware requirements for a given solution because the requests made on its servers are the result of a complex interaction involving several factors. However, here are some questions to consider:

- ▶ How many users will this solution serve at peak?
- ▶ How much throughput is needed from the system (pages per second)?
- ▶ How much CRM content will the solution contain?
    - ▶ Tabs
    - ▶ Reports
    - ▶ SharePoint integration
- ▶ How much data will exist for Reporting Services to present in this solution contain?
    - ▶ Complexity of reports (processor intensive).

► Has a data warehouse been created to solve the performance problem but will require capacity on disk?

  ► Number of reports running concurrently?

► How much content will exist for SharePoint collaboration?

  ► Number of documents

  ► Average size of documents

  ► Lists and libraries

► How much email transaction do you foresee for this solution?

  ► Number of users *x* average mailbox size

► Is high availability needed?

► What is the performance impact of customizations?

In this chapter, we review some of the design factors important to consider when planning a typical CRM deployment.

.NET Framework

The .NET Framework, the Microsoft standard for building applications, provides a variety of benefits, such as the following:

► **Common Language Runtime (CLR):** The virtual machine component of the .NET Framework. All .NET applications execute under the supervision of the CLR, thus allowing the standard behaviors, memory, and process management, and having the same baseline for security.

► **Interoperability:** This is a crucial module because this provides interactions between new and older applications, which are commonly required. The .NET Framework also provides a means to access functions that are implemented in applications outside the .NET environment.

► **Language independence:** One of the biggest benefits, allowing different application developers to coexist.

► **Base Class Library (BCL):** Part of the Framework Class Library (FCL), The BCL is a library of functionality available to all languages using the .NET Framework.

► **Security:** An inherited feature of the .NET runtime that provides features such as buffer overflows and contention against other system components.

► **Portability:** Last but one of the most important features, portability allows platform independence (as long as the same version is installed on the systems).

Microsoft Dynamics CRM is built on top of the .NET Framework, which allows various organizations to customize it on the standard development platform provided by Microsoft. Because Microsoft Dynamics CRM and Microsoft SharePoint Server are built on the same technology, the integration uses the .NET platform, which allows seamless portability of data between the two applications.

.NET has several different versions:

▶ **.NET 2.0**

In the 2.0 release of .NET, Microsoft introduced a new hosting API that gives a fine-grain control on the behavior of the runtime with regard to multithreading, memory allocation, assembly loading, and much more. This control enables developers to precompile and precache the application in memory before the user attempts to use the application.

This is the first time there was full support between the x64 and i386 architecture, allowing developers to choose between the different instruction sets.

In addition, they added new data controls with declarative data binding.

All the examples in this book use languages later than .NET 2.0.

▶ **.NET 3.0**

.NET 3.0 primarily optimized the functions in .NET 2.0 and added the following features:

▶ Windows Presentation Foundation (WPF), a new user interface subsystem and API based on XML and vector graphics, which uses 3D computer graphics hardware and Direct3D technologies.

▶ Windows Communication Foundation (WCF), a service-oriented messaging system that allows programs to interoperate locally or remotely similar to web services.

▶ Windows Workflow Foundation (WF) allows for building of task automation and integrated transactions using workflows.

▶ Windows CardSpace, a component that stores a person's digital identities and provides a unified interface for choosing the identity for a transaction, such as logging in to a website.

▶ **.NET 3.5**

.NET 3.5 introduced the following new features:

▶ Adds support for expression trees and lambda methods.

▶ Expression trees to represent high-level source code at runtime.

▶ Language Integrated Query (LINQ), along with its various providers (for example, LINQ to Objects, LINQ to XML, and LINQ to SQL).

▶ Paging support for ADO.NET.

- ▶ ADO.NET synchronization API to synchronize local caches and server-side datastores.

- ▶ Asynchronous network I/O API.

- ▶ Peer-to-peer networking stack, including a managed PNRP resolver.

- ▶ Managed wrappers for Windows Management Instrumentation and Active Directory APIs.

- ▶ Enhanced WCF and WF runtimes, which let WCF work with POX and JSON data and expose WF workflows as WCF services. WCF services can be made stateful using the WF persistence model.

- ▶ Support for HTTP pipelining and syndication feeds.

- ▶ ASP.NET AJAX is included

- ▶ New System.CodeDom namespace.

▶ .NET 4.0

This release will have improved support for parallel computing, which targets multi-core or distributed systems. Microsoft will have extensions such as PLINQ (Parallel LINQ), a parallel implementation of the LINQ engine, and Task Parallel Library, which exposes parallel constructs via method calls.

Deployment Scenarios

In this section, we look at deployment scenarios for organizations that want to deploy all of the following:

- ▶ Microsoft Dynamics CRM

- ▶ Microsoft Office SharePoint Server

- ▶ Office Communication Server

- ▶ Microsoft Exchange Server 2007

Because different organizations' deployments, hardware requirements, and infrastructure arrangements differ significantly, the recommendations included here might not apply to you. Aware of this, we present the information here as "best practices" for an organization.

Organizations can deploy Microsoft Dynamics CRM, SharePoint, Office Communication Server, and Exchange Server in several different configurations. This integration between the environments can provide a powerful and flexible business infrastructure that meets the demanding scale, performance, and extensibility needs of the very largest organizations.

Table 2.1 lists some recommendations to help choose the most appropriate server deployment strategy for your organization (and shows where your organization might fall in size). The deployment details for the topology are described in detail.

TABLE 2.1   Recommended Server Topology

Number of Users	Recommend Topology
< 50	Small business deployment
50–100	Small server deployment
100–1,000	Medium server deployment
> 1,000	Large server deployment

* These are suggested deployment strategies. If your organization uses one application more aggressively, you can always scale that application independently.

Small Business Deployment

Microsoft Small Business Server 2008 allows small organizations to install all the applications on one server. This deployment strategy works really well for companies that are small, or have a very low interaction with the CRM system.

Because all the services are on one server, we recommend the following hardware specifications:

▶ **Processor:** Dual Core Intel Xeon, 6MB cache, 1.86GHz, 1066MHz FSB

▶ **RAM:** 8GB

▶ **Hard Disk:** 2x 500GB

A system built with the hardware described in the preceding table should perform adequately and support the following minimums:

▶ **Exchange**

    ▶ Hosts up to 50 users with a mailbox of 400MB per user

▶ **Office Communication Server**

    ▶ Hosts up to 50 users for concurrent chat sessions

▶ **Microsoft Dynamics CRM**

    ▶ Maintain up to 200 accounts

    ▶ Manage up to 1,000 contacts

    ▶ Pursue up to 200 opportunities per user

    ▶ Pursue up to 200 leads per user

- ▶ Manage up to 20 marketing campaigns
- ▶ Manage up to 400 cases
- ▶ Organize 400 active service activities

▶ **SharePoint**

- ▶ Store up to 100,000 documents
- ▶ Host up to 50 SharePoint sites and personal sites
- ▶ Host up to 10 collaboration sites

Small Server Deployment

Many smaller organizations can address all their capacity requirements with three servers (provided high availability is not required) running Microsoft Dynamics CRM, SharePoint, Office Communication Server, and Exchange Server.

Figure 2.2 illustrates a typical small server deployment.

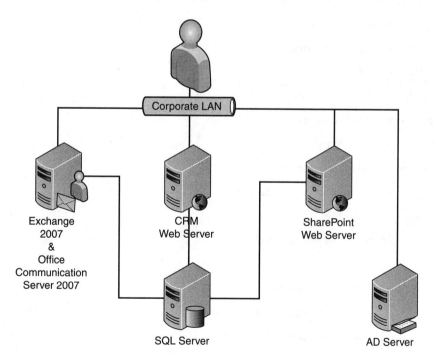

FIGURE 2.2   Small server deployment.

Table 2.2 has the recommended minimums for each of the listed servers in Figure 2.2.

TABLE 2.2   Small Server Deployment

Server Type	RAM	Logical Hard Disk	CPU
Exchange 2007 and Office Communication Server 2007	4GB	200GB	Dual Core Intel Xeon 1.86GHz
Database Server	4GB	500GB	Dual Core Intel Xeon 1.86GHz
SharePoint Server	2GB	100GB	Dual Core Intel Xeon 1.86GHz
CRM Web Server	2GB	100GB	Dual Core Intel Xeon 1.86GHz

A system built with the hardware described in the preceding table should perform adequately and support the following minimums:

▶ **Exchange**

    ▶ Host up to 200 users with a mailbox of 400MB per user

▶ **Office Communication Server**

    ▶ Host up to 100 users for concurrent chat sessions

▶ **Microsoft Dynamics CRM**

    ▶ Maintain up to 200 accounts

    ▶ Manage up to 1,000 contacts

    ▶ Pursue up to 200 opportunities per user

    ▶ Pursue up to 200 leads per user

    ▶ Manage up to 20 marketing campaigns

    ▶ Manage up to 400 cases

    ▶ Organize 400 active service activities

▶ **SharePoint**

    ▶ Store up to 0.5 million documents

    ▶ Host up to 1,000 SharePoint sites and personal sites

    ▶ Host up to 25 collaboration sites

NOTE

If you deploy a small server large farm, it is recommended to build redundancy for the database servers so that SharePoint and CRM data is protected.

Medium Server Deployment

This is the most common scaled-out deployment method used by most medium and large organizations. Most organizations have this logical infrastructure primarily for ease of management rather than for scalability reasons.

The key benefit of this deployment strategy is for the system administrators to perform server maintenance in the middle of business hours without impacting the business. There is a hot standby and an alternate path for every application (except Office Communication Server) in this suggested architecture.

Figure 2.3 illustrates a typical medium server deployment.

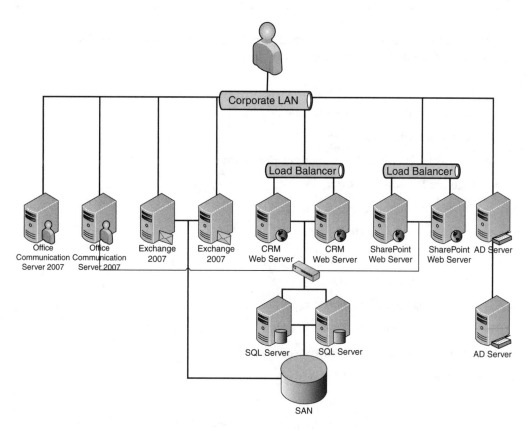

FIGURE 2.3   Medium server deployment.

Table 2.3 has the recommended minimums for each of the listed servers in Figure 2.3.

TABLE 2.3   Medium Server Deployment

Server Type	RAM	Logical Hard Disk	CPU
2x Exchange 2007	2GB	100GB	Dual Core Intel Xeon 1.86GHz
1x Office Communication Server 2007	2GB	100GB	Dual Core Intel Xeon 1.86GHz
2x Database Server	8GB	100GB	Dual Core Intel Xeon 1.86GHz
2x CRM Web Server	2GB	100GB	Dual Core Intel Xeon 1.86GHz
2x SharePoint Web Server	2GB	100GB	Dual Core Intel Xeon 1.86GHz
SAN		2TB	

A system built with the hardware described in the preceding table should perform adequately and support the following minimums:

▶ **Exchange**

  ▶ Host 1,500 users with a mailbox of 400MB per user

▶ **Office Communication Server**

  ▶ Host 1,000 users for concurrent chat sessions

▶ **Microsoft Dynamics CRM**

  ▶ Maintain up to 2,000 accounts

  ▶ Manage up to 10,000 contacts

  ▶ Pursue up to 2,000 opportunities

  ▶ Pursue up to 2,000 leads

  ▶ Manage up to 200 marketing campaigns

  ▶ Manage up to 4,000 cases

  ▶ Organize up to 4,000 active service activities

▶ **SharePoint**

  ▶ Store up to 1 million documents

  ▶ Host up to 10,000 SharePoint sites and personal sites

  ▶ Host up to 250 collaboration sites

NOTE

If you deploy a medium or large farm, equip your servers with more than one network card for better throughput.

Large Server Deployment

The key benefit of using the large server farm is for scalability concerns. You can distribute the middle tier further and separate the applications in the middle tier to increase application performance.

Figure 2.4 illustrates a typical large server deployment.

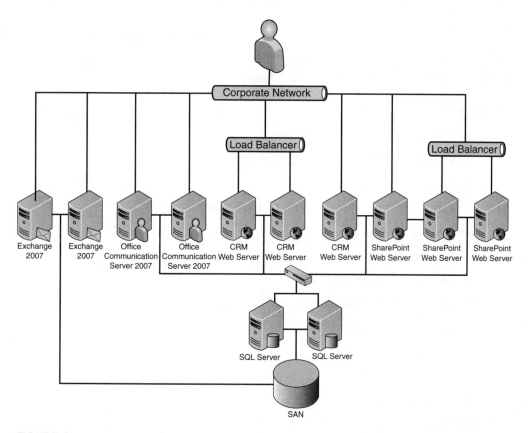

FIGURE 2.4   Large server deployment.

Table 2.4 has the recommended minimums for each of the listed servers in Figure 2.4.

TABLE 2.4   Large Server Deployment

Server Type	RAM	Hard Disk	CPU
2x Exchange	2GB	200GB	Quad Core E7310 Xeon, 1.6GHz
2x Office Communication Server	2GB	100GB	Dual Core Intel Xeon 1.86GHz
2x Database Server	32GB	100GB	Quad Core E7310 Xeon, 1.6GHz

TABLE 2.4   Large Server Deployment

Server Type	RAM	Hard Disk	CPU
2x CRM Web Server	2GB	100GB	Dual Core Intel Xeon 1.86GHz
2x CRM Application Server	2GB	100GB	Dual Core Intel Xeon 1.86GHz
2x SharePoint Web Server	2GB	100GB	Dual Core Intel Xeon 1.86GHz
SAN		4TB	

A system built with the hardware described in the preceding table should perform adequately and support the following minimums:

▶ **Exchange**

  ▶ Host 15,000 users with a mailbox

  ▶ 400MB per user mailbox

▶ **Office Communication Server**

  ▶ Host 12,000 users for concurrent chat sessions

▶ **Microsoft Dynamics CRM**

  ▶ Manage 20,000 accounts

  ▶ Manage 100,000 contacts

  ▶ Manage 20,000 opportunities

  ▶ Manage 20,000 leads

  ▶ Manage 2,000 marketing campaigns

  ▶ Manage 40,000 cases

  ▶ Manage 40,000 active service activities

▶ **SharePoint**

  ▶ Store up to 10 million documents

  ▶ Host up to 10,000 SharePoint sites and personal sites

  ▶ Host up to 2500 collaboration sites

NOTE

If you deploy a medium or large farm, equip your servers with more than one network card for better throughput. For more information, see the paper titled "Microsoft Solution Accelerator for Intranets." You can download this from the Microsoft website directly at http://technet.microsoft.com/en-us/office/sharepointserver/bb310655.aspx.

Authentication

Authentication, a most crucial aspect of deployment, is often overlooked, but it is a necessary overhead task that requires an advanced understanding of your network configuration. This is one of the most important aspects of a deployment and should be carefully considered. Authentication awareness allows architects to design with the following considerations in mind:

▶ User authentication passed to the back-end system. Users have access to all back-end systems.

▶ Users authenticate only with the front-end web servers. Then, the front-end servers use service accounts to authenticate against back-end systems.

Authentication decisions allow a variety of options, as shown in Table 2.5.

TABLE 2.5   Authentication Types

Authentication Type	Pro	Con
NTLM (Windows NT LAN Manager)	Simple CRM deployment.	Cannot access reports based on user credentials Cannot connect to a SharePoint infrastructure as the user
Hybrid authentication	None really. This is a common deployment we have seen at client locations.	Usually considered a "complex deployment" Cannot access reports based on user credentials Cannot connect to a SharePoint infrastructure as the user Adds a layer of network overhead when the servers process Kerberos authentication, and the web servers accept only NTLM
Basic Kerberos authentication	Allows user credentials to access reports (allows data-level security). Allows user credentials to access the SharePoint document library.	Allows the server to delegate to any back-end system
Constrained Kerberos delegation	Allows user credentials to access reports (allows data-level security). Allows user credentials to access the SharePoint document library. Data secured at all levels of the application tiers (for administrators for higher security).	Some complexity in deployment

There are many different authentication scenarios in Windows operating systems. The two authentications used are Windows NT LAN Manager (NTLM) and Kerberos. Kerberos authentication features delegation, which enables impersonation of user identity across multiple servers. The delegation feature was introduced in Windows Server 2003. Delegation provides a different method for authentication than the challenge-response method provided by NTLM. The following sections examine the differences between NTLM and Kerberos authentications. We also examine the three different delegation scenarios involving Kerberos authentication.

What Is Delegation?

Kerberos provides the fundamental security services required for a distributed environment: authentication, data integrity, and data privacy. But there's more to this technology.

For example, the user has already authenticated herself to Server A. Server A can now impersonate the user and attempt to access something on its local system, such as a file. In this case, the access checking is built in to the local Windows installation and will grant or deny the access based on the file's ACL (access control list).

In a distributed environment, however, if user authenticates to Server A, and Server A requires information from Server B on behalf of the user, we need to delegate the security. Even though Server A is requesting access to Server B directly, the access requested will be on behalf of the original user. For this to work correctly, the user needs some way to pass its identity to Server A, allowing Server A to make further remote requests on its behalf. Kerberos supports this concept through delegation.

NTLM Authentication

NTLM (NT LAN Manager) is a popular authentication mechanism and is still widely used. As illustrated in Figure 2.5, in the NTLM protocol, the client sends the request with the username to the server. The server generates and responds with a challenge to the client. The client encrypts that challenge using the user's password and responds to the server. The authentication option varies based on whether the account is a local or a domain user account:

▶ **Local user account:** The server will look into its local Security Accounts Manager (SAM) and authenticate the end user.

▶ **Domain user account:** The server forwards the challenge, along with the client's response, to the domain controller. The domain controller validates the response and sends it directly to the server.

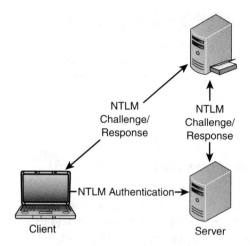

FIGURE 2.5   Integrated NTLM authentication.

Authentication to Back-End Servers with NTLM

Typical deployment requires a service account on the front-end server (servers that interact with the end users) to authenticate against a back-end server (in a multi-tiered environment, this is usually the one holding the data or responsible for certain application roles), as shown in Figure 2.6.

> ▶ **Pro**
>
>> ▶ Required to manage security for one account in the back-end server
>
> ▶ **Con**
>
>> ▶ The service account will require access to all data/resources from the back-end server.
>
>> ▶ The access to data needs to be managed at the front server level.

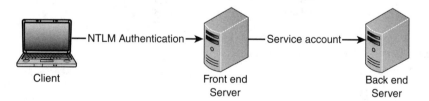

FIGURE 2.6   NTLM authentication using a service account to access the back-end server.

> **NOTE**
>
> When the service account is not specified, the request will be made as a null userAuthentication to back-end servers with NTLM. This usually means that the user cannot access the back-end data (reports, document library, and so on). This is the most common error people get in their deployments.

Hybrid Authentication

Many organizations use Kerberos authentication for the front-end server and use NTLM authentication for the backend server.

Kerberos authentication can enhance security because it provides additional features such as auditing and accountability. With the additional features, you can potentially add extra load (perhaps authenticating thousands of unique users). Alternatively, NTLM does not need additional authentication after the first request.

Having this hybrid authentication is not recommended. This will increase the load on the front-end server and will not provide the impersonation to the back-end server. This is similar to the previous scenario, with additional load to the front-end servers.

Figure 2.7 illustrates a typical hybrid authentication deployment.

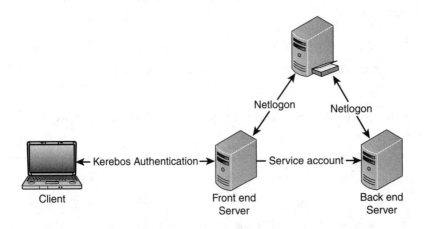

FIGURE 2.7   Kerberos and NTLM hybrid authentication.

Kerberos Authentication

In the Windows environment, authentication delegation is possible only with the Kerberos protocol. Therefore, all systems involved in delegation scenarios must use the Kerberos protocol. There are two main delegation scenarios:

▶ Basic Kerberos delegation

▶ Kerberos authentication using constrained delegation

Basic Kerberos Delegation

As illustrated in Figure 2.8, when using the basic Kerberos authentication, the user authenticates to the front-end server; the server requests data from the back-end server using the user's account.

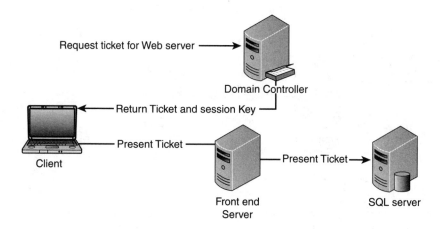

FIGURE 2.8   Basic Kerberos delegation.

Delegation enables the user's credentials to be passed from one server to another and preserves the user identity. This will allow you to have multiple front-end servers. This enables you to scale the middle tier for growth.

▶ **Pro**

  ▶ Security controlled at the data layer, so there is no way security can be compromised.

▶ **Con**

  ▶ Big security management overhead because all security is managed on the back-end systems.

  ▶ The middle tier is allowed to access any back-end data source based on the user credentials.

NOTE

Kerberos authentication passes a Kerberos token provided by the Kerberos Ticket Granting service only after the initial authentication. At no point are the user's credentials passed within the server farms.

Kerberos Authentication Using Constrained Delegation

This can allow you to enforce a limit that applies to which network resources an account trusted for delegation can access. This feature is supported in Windows 2003 domain functional level and up. Figure 2.9 shows Kerberos authentication using constrained delegation.

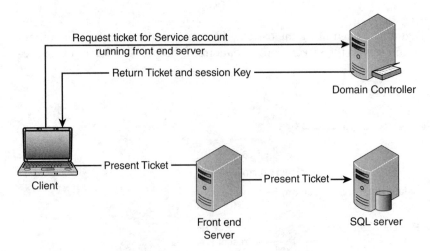

FIGURE 2.9   Kerberos authentication constrained to a service.

To limit the resources that services can access on behalf of a user, you can configure constrained delegation by listing services to which account can present delegated credentials. This list is in the form of SPNs (service principle names). Impersonating to any nontrusted back end will fail authentication.

This is the most common deployment of Kerberos authentication.

Setting Up Kerberos

To use Kerberos completely, you must configure a number of things, including the following:

- ▶ Client settings
- ▶ Front-end tier, typically an IIS server
- ▶ Back end
- ▶ Active Directory

Figure 2.10 shows the Kerberos flow.

Client Configuration

Before setting up or debugging Kerberos, client settings need to be verified.

> **NOTE**
>
> To ensure consistency with the client settings, it is recommended to use Group Policy (GPO) to enforce the settings on client machines.

The following steps ensure that integrated authentication is enabled on the client:

1. In Internet Explorer, click Tools, Internet Options, Advanced, and scroll to Security.

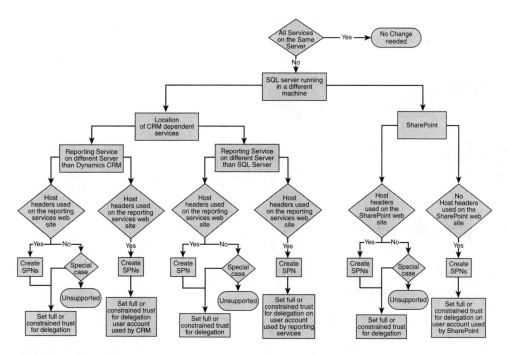

FIGURE 2.10   Kerberos flow.

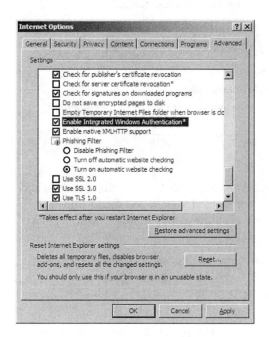

FIGURE 2.11   Enable integrated Windows authentication.

2. Ensure Automatic Logon is enabled in the appropriate zone on the client. (In Internet Explorer, click Tools, Internet Options, Security.)

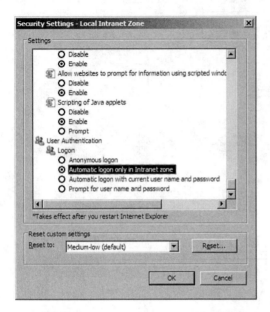

FIGURE 2.12   Enable the Automatic Logon Only in the Intranet Zone option.

NOTE

▶ Client needs to be a member of a trusted domain.

▶ Ensure the URL is part of the client's local intranet sites.

▶ The domain user must have the Account Is Sensitive and Cannot Be Delegated option unselected in Active Directory.

IIS Settings

The web servers containing the web applications (Dynamics CRM, Reporting Services, and SharePoint) will all need to be set up to enable Kerberos. However, you might find that this is not necessary if the web server is the same machine as the domain controller (such as in a small business deployment).

The IIS Metabase needs to be configured for "enabling editing" to ensure that the Metabase attempts to pass credentials using Kerberos. To enable editing in the IIS v6.0 Metabase, right-click the server name and select Properties. Check the Enable Direct Metabase Edit check box.

This will enable you to configure the Metabase without stopping IIS. This can be done in a few ways.

Before performing either, you need to determine the identifier of the site. This can be found by navigating to IIS and viewing the Identifier column. (If you don't see the column, select View from the Management Console and be sure that the Identifier column is shown.) Figure 2.13 shows the identifiers of two websites.

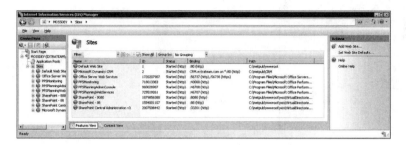

FIGURE 2.13   IIS identifier.

The first method is by updating the Metabase using admin scripts:

1. At the command prompt, navigate to C:\Inetpub\Adminscripts.

2. Type the following command (Where xx is the identifier of the website you want to change authentication type):

   ```
   cscript adsutil.vbs set w3svc/xx/NTAuthenticationProviders "Negotiate,NTLM"
   ```

Figure 2.14 shows the output of the adstuil.

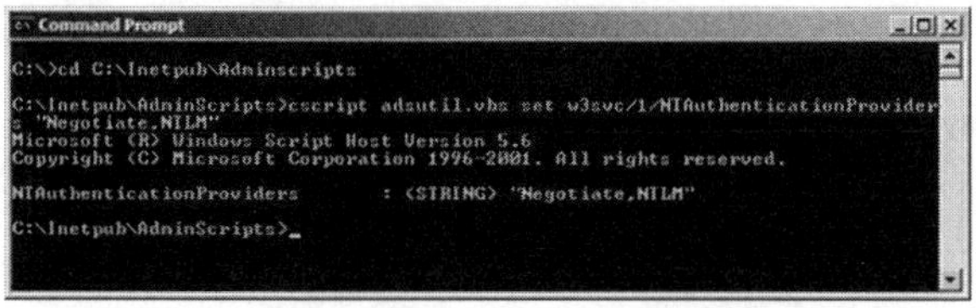

FIGURE 2.14   Configure authentication using the command line.

For more advanced users, you can modify Metabase.xml directly, as follows:

1. Navigate to the Metabase.xml file. This is typically found at the following location: <root drive name>\System32\Inetsrv.

2. Set all existing instances of NTAuthenticationProviders="NTLM" to NTAuthenticationProviders="Negotiate,NTLM".

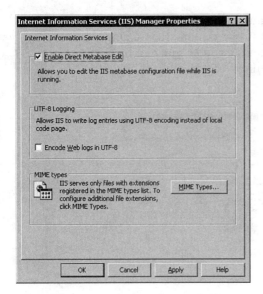

FIGURE 2.15   Enable Metabase XML updates.

Before you can make changes to that file, you will have to enable the changes in the inetmgr, as shown in Figure 2.15.

3. You can use PowerShell to make changes to the WMI. Use set-wmiobject for IISWebService.

NOTE

After making these changes, you must restart IIS.

In IIS 6.0, the application pools under which the relevant websites/applications run should be set to run as either a system account (Network Service or Local System) or as a user account configured correctly in Active Directory (as shown in Figure 2.16).

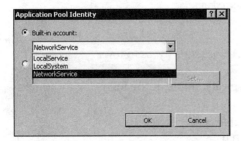

FIGURE 2.16   Application pool setting.

AD Configuration

All SPNs must be defined in Active Directory.

All relevant computers accessing data from a different machine need to be set to Trusted for Delegation. To access this setting, follow these steps:

1. Open Active Directory Users and Computers.

2. Search for the relevant account (computer/user) that needs to be trusted for delegation.

3. Right-click each object, and then check the Trusted for Delegation option on the Properties dialog box (as shown in Figure 2.17).

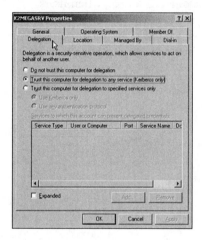

FIGURE 2.17   Configure Active Directory delegation.

If the Microsoft CRM website is in the application pool that is running under a specific user account (that is, not Network Service/Local System), that account will require an SPN.

To acquire an SPN, perform the following steps:

1. Download and install the setspn tool on any machine on the domain. For Windows 2003 SP2, you can find this tool at http://go.microsoft.com/fwlink/?LinkId=100114. For Windows 2008, this tool is built in to the operating system.

2. Open a command prompt window. For Windows 2003, navigate to the directory in which this tool has been installed.

3. Enter the following command for each account on each web server. You must use the name that the users will be using to access the system:

```
setspn -A HTTP/computer Domain\User
setspn -A HTTP/computer.domain.local Domain\User
setspn -A HTTP/CRMalias Domain\User
setspn -A HTTP/CRMalias.domain.local Domain\User
```

> **NOTE**
>
> The Delegation tab will not appear in the Active Directory Computer/User property screen. To enable the Delegation tab, enable the SPN settings as described earlier.

Debugging Kerberos

One of the hardest things to debug in the organization is security, especially when the security is passed through several middle-tier applications and the system administrator does not have access to intercept the request in the middle.

However, the most common problems users experience is that the front application will load, but there may be some areas that may be missing data. For example, when users open the Microsoft CRM Dynamics application and click the Reports section, they will be able to view the list of the reports. When they click it, they will be allowed to choose the filter criteria. When they try to run the report, however, they will get a CRM authentication failure (as shown in Figure 2.18).

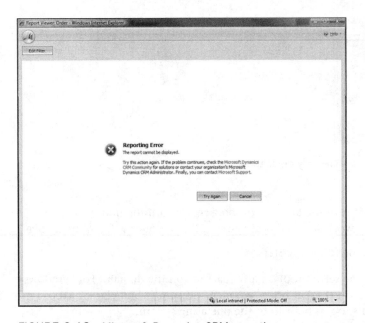

FIGURE 2.18   Microsoft Dynamics CRM reporting error.

See the next section, "SQL Server Reporting Services Integration," for more information about debugging this type of installation.

To debug Kerberos, you have to start debugging on the server side first and then move to the client. Microsoft has created a variety of tools to help facilitate this. Here is a list of some server-side tools (further details in the next section):

▶ IIS utilities

- ▶ Windows Resource Kit

- ▶ Kerberos logging

To complete the investigation/debugging, here are some client-side tools (detailed later):

- ▶ wFetch

- ▶ kList

- ▶ KerbTray

IIS Utilities (Installed on the Server)

You can find the IIS utility Authentication and Access Control Diagnostics 1.0 (x86) at http://www.microsoft.com/downloads/details.aspx?FamilyId=E90FE-4A21-4066-BD22-B931F7572E9A&displaylang=en.

This utility must be installed on the web server. You can save the output as an XML file and review it for configuration problems (as shown in Figure 2.19).

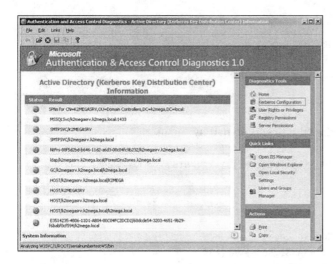

FIGURE 2.19   Graphical view of settings (AD, IIS, user and computer accounts).

This tool helps highlight misconfigured SPNs quickly.

Windows Resource Kit

The Resource Kit contains a couple of very useful utilities to debug Kerberos. In this section, we demonstrate the KerbTray and the kList tools specifically. You can download the Windows Resource Kit from the Microsoft website at http://www.microsoft.com/windows2000/techinfo/reskit/tools/existing/kerbtray-o.asp.

- ▶ **KerbTray** (client-side tool)

  This tool runs in the system tray and displays the active tickets issued to the client computer and user.

▶ **kList**

This tool lets you view the tickets in a command-line console. You can also purge specific tickets to debug reenrollment of tickets.

You can also view the ticket-granting service (TGS).

The following code sample shows via kList the ticket-granting authority to which the user is connected):

```
C:\Program Files\Windows Resource Kits\Tools>klist tgt
Cached TGT:

ServiceName: krbtgt
TargetName: krbtgt
FullServiceName: rbhaiya
DomainName: Domain.Local
TargetDomainName: Domain.Local
AltTargetDomainName: Domain.Local
TicketFlags: 0x40e00000
KeyExpirationTime: 0/40/4 0:00:10776
StartTime: 10/8/2008 16:57:52
EndTime: 10/9/2008 2:57:52
RenewUntil: 10/15/2008 16:57:52
TimeSkew: 10/15/2008 16:57:52
```

The next code sample shows via kList the tickets owned by the user:

```
C:\Program Files\Windows Resource Kits\Tools>klist tickets


Cached Tickets: (2)

    Server: krbtgt/Domain.Local@Domain.Local
      KerbTicket Encryption Type: RSADSI RC4-HMAC(NT)
      End Time: 10/9/2008 2:57:52
      Renew Time: 10/15/2008 16:57:52


    Server: HTTP/webserver.Domain.Local@Domain.Local
      KerbTicket Encryption Type: RSADSI RC4-HMAC(NT)
      End Time: 10/9/2008 2:57:52
                        Renew Time: 10/15/2008 16:57:52
```

Kerberos Logging

To enable Kerberos event logging, change the following Registry value and restart the computer:

```
HKEY_LOCAL_MACHINE\SYSTEM\CurrentControlSet\Control\Lsa\Kerberos\Parameters
```

```
Registry Value: LogLevel
Value Type: REG_DWORD
Value Data: 0x1
```

This will give verbose logging in the event logs.

You can find a description of the messages in KB article 837361.

SQL Server Reporting Services Integration

SQL Server Reporting Services is a crucial integration component that often causes Microsoft Dynamics CRM administrators frustration. No other aspect of Microsoft Dynamics CRM caused more problems related to Kerberos than the Reporting Services integration. Lucky for us, the main problem (the double-hop authentication problem) was largely fixed in Microsoft Dynamics CRM 4.0 with the aid of MS CRM SSRS Connector, and now only incorrect configuration causes SQL Server Reporting Services to fail.

By default, some basic integration enables you to run some reports stored in SQL Server. In addition, users can create custom RDL files and display the reports through the integrated view in CRM. To ensure that the IIS authentication is configured properly, you should run the IIS Authentication and Access Control Diagnostics (as shown in Figure 2.20).

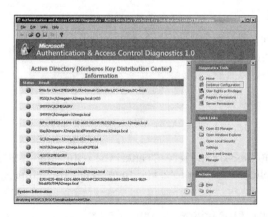

FIGURE 2.20   Authenticated Diagnostics

Additional integration points are available when using CRM, SharePoint, and SQL Reporting Services. In the later chapters, we demonstrate how to have prerendered reports and dashboards using SQL Server Reporting Services (as described in Chapter 5, "SharePoint Integration"). For now, we describe how to set up the infrastructure to facilitate these features.

You may consider three possible deployment scenarios. Choosing the appropriate deployment depends on the number of requests for reporting.

Install the Reporting Server on the Same Server as the Microsoft Dynamics CRM Server

► Pro

  ► Simple deployment.

  ► The reporting server is the same server as CRM server (see Figure 2.21).

  ► You can use NTLM or Kerberos authentication to get user-specific data.

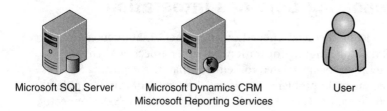

Microsoft SQL Server   Microsoft Dynamics CRM   User
                            Miscrosoft Reporting Services

FIGURE 2.21   Reporting server on the same server as the CRM server.

► **Con**

  ► Puts extra load on the CRM web servers.

The installation steps are as follows:

1. Log in to the CRM front-end web server.
2. Navigate to the Microsoft SQL installation setup.
3. Launch the setup.
4. Click Next to install the prerequisites.
5. Click Next on the Welcome screen.
6. Click Next on the Prerequisite Check.

   If IIS and ASP.NET are not installed/configured on the server, cancel the setup and configure IIS and ASP.NET using the application server role, and then restart the setup.

7. Enter the product key and click Next.
8. On the Components to Install screen, select the following components:

   a. Reporting Services

   b. Workstation components, Books Online, and development tools (recommended)

9. Click Advanced.
10. In the Documentation, Samples, and Sample Databases screen, deselect Sample Databases and Sample Code and Applications (recommended).
11. Click Next.

12. On the Instance Name screen, you can specify an instance name for Reporting Services and database engine. If you want to install it on the default instance instead, select Default Instance (MSSQLSERVER).

13. On the Service Account screen, do the following:

   Specify a domain user account. (Refer to the "Authentication" section in this chapter for guidelines about choosing a service account.)

14. Click Next.

15. Select the appropriate collation. If unsure, use default values.

16. Click Next.

17. On the Report Server Installation Options screen, select Install the Default Configuration.

18. Click Next to begin installation.

The following configuration steps are required only if you did not configure at the time of installation:

1. Click Start.

2. Click Microsoft SQL Server 2005.

3. Click Configuration Tools.

4. Click Reporting Services Configuration (see Figure 2.22).

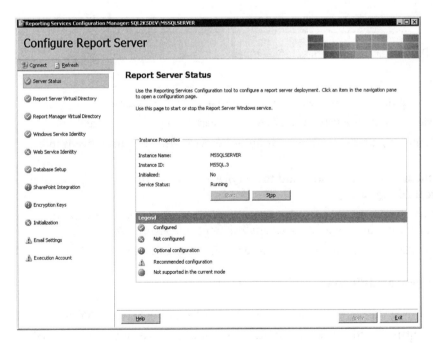

FIGURE 2.22   Reporting server status.

5. Start the Reporting Service if not started already (see Figure 2.22).

6. Create a virtual directory for report storage (by default, it is ReportServer) (see Figure 2.23).

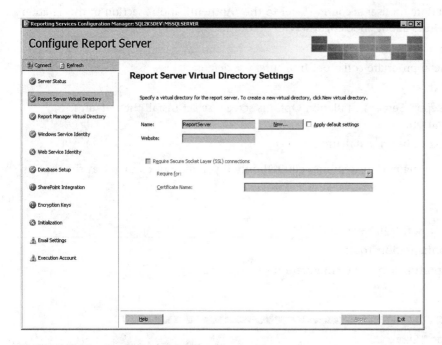

FIGURE 2.23 Report server virtual directory settings.

7. Create a virtual directory (by default, it is Reports) (see Figure 2.24).

8. Select the appropriate identity (as chosen in the earlier steps) (see Figure 2.25).

   This has to be either NTLM authentication or Kerberos authentication needs to be enabled.

9. Confirm the web service identity and the service accounts running the application (see Figure 2.26).

10. Select the database location of the report server. This is a required configuration for running the service in a load-balanced environment (see Figure 2.27).

11. On the Initialization screen, select Initialize the Reporting Server.

The verification steps are as follows:

1. Before beginning the configuration, verify whether Reporting Services is running.

2. Navigate to http://localhost/reports or https://localhost/reports (if you enabled SSL on your server). You should see the Report Manager home page.

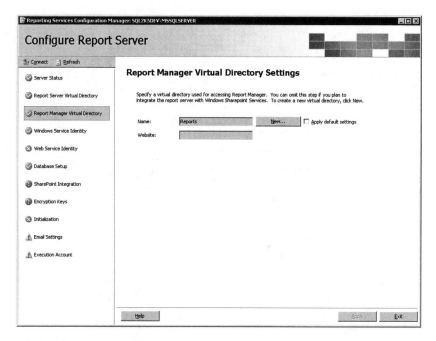

FIGURE 2.24   Report Manager virtual directory.

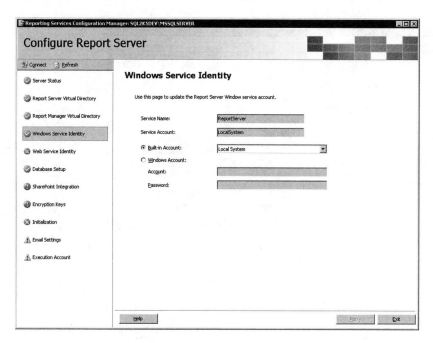

FIGURE 2.25   Windows service identity.

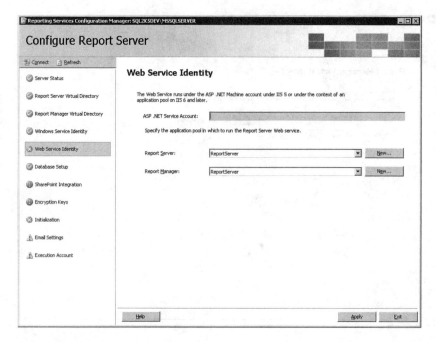

FIGURE 2.26   Web service identity.

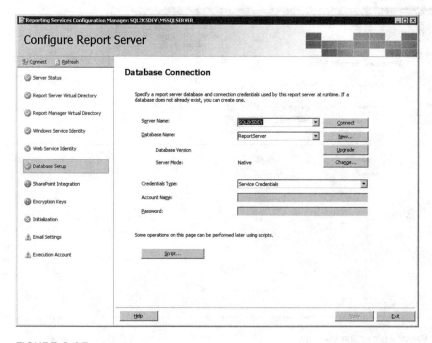

FIGURE 2.27   Database setup.

> **NOTE**
>
> It is possible to use SharePoint Integrated Report Manager to manage the SQL reports inside SharePoint.

Install the Reporting Server on the Same Server as the Microsoft SQL Server

Figure 2.28 shows a deployment that has SQL Server and Reporting Services on the same machine.

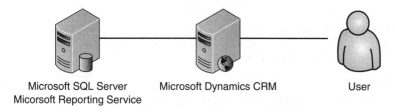

Microsoft SQL Server   Microsoft Dynamics CRM   User
Micorsoft Reporting Service

FIGURE 2.28   Reporting server on the same server as SQL Server.

▶ **Pro**

  ▶ Simple deployment.

  ▶ The reporting server is the same server as the SQL server.

  ▶ You can use a service account or Kerberos authentication to get user-specific data.

  ▶ If the SQL server is clustered, Reporting Services can be load balanced.

▶ **Con**

  ▶ Adds additional load on the SQL server.

  ▶ Usually database administrators are very strict about the applications that run on the SQL server.

The installation steps are as follows:

1. Log in to the SQL server.
2. Navigate to the Microsoft SQL installation setup.
3. Launch setup.
4. Click Next to install the prerequisites.
5. Click Next on the Welcome screen.
6. Click Next on the Prerequisite Check.

If IIS and ASP.NET are not installed/configured on the server, cancel the setup and configure IIS and ASP.NET using the application server role, and then restart the setup.

7. Enter the product key and click Next.

8. On the Components to Install screen, select the following components:

   a. SQL Server Database Services

   b. Reporting Services

   c. Workstation components, Books Online, and development tools (recommended)

9. Click Advanced.

10. On the Documentation, Samples, and Sample Databases screen, deselect Sample Databases and Sample Code and Applications (recommended).

11. Click Next.

12. On the Instance Name screen, you can specify an instance name for Reporting Services and database engine. If you want to install it on the default instance instead, select Default Instance (MSSQLSERVER).

13. On the Service Account screen, do the following:

    Specify a domain user account. (Refer to the "Authentication" section in this chapter for guidelines about choosing a service account.)

14. Start SQL Agent as Automatic Startup.

15. Click Next.

16. Specify Windows Authentication on the Authentication Mode screen (recommended).

17. Click Next.

18. Select the appropriate collation. If unsure, use default values.

19. Click Next.

20. On the Report Server Installation Options screen, select Install the Default Configuration.

21. Click Next to begin installation.

The following configuration steps are required only if you did not configure at the time of installation:

1. Click Start.

2. Click Microsoft SQL Server 2005.

3. Click Configuration Tools.

4. Click Reporting Services Configuration.

5. Start Reporting Services (if not started already; see Figure 2.29).

6. Create a virtual directory (by default, ReportServer), as shown in Figure 2.30.

7. Create a virtual directory for report storage (by default, Reports), shown in Figure 2.31.

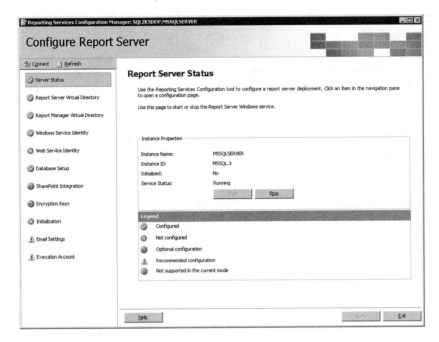

FIGURE 2.29   Report server status.

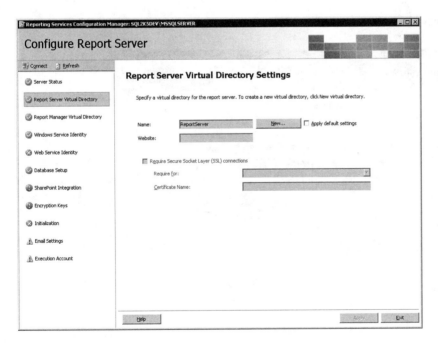

FIGURE 2.30   Report server virtual directory settings.

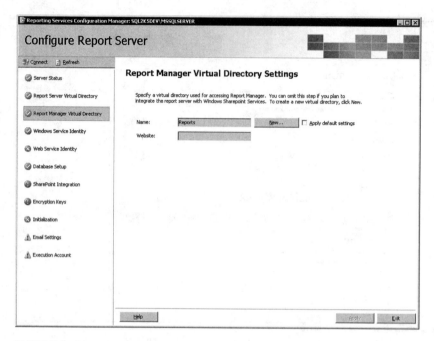

FIGURE 2.31   Report Manager virtual directory.

8. Select the appropriate identity (as chosen in the earlier steps), see Figure 2.32.

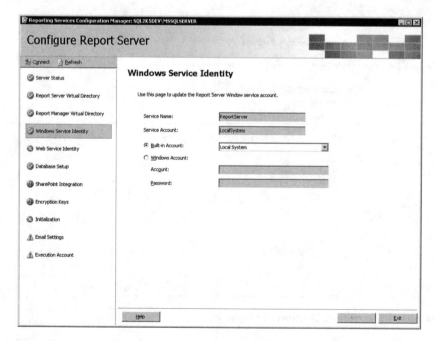

FIGURE 2.32   Windows service identity.

9. Confirm the web service identity (Figure 2.33) and the service accounts running the application. This needs to be either a service account accessing the data source or Kerberos authentication needs to be enabled.

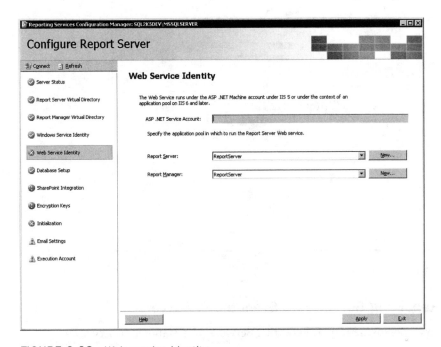

FIGURE 2.33   Web service identity.

10. Select the database location of the report server, as shown in Figure 2.34. This is a required configuration for running the service in a load-balanced environment.

11. On the Initialization screen, select Initialize the Reporting Server.

The verification steps are as follows:

1. Before beginning the configuration, verify whether the following services are running:

   a. SQL Server

   b. Reporting Services

   c. SQL Server Agent

2. Navigate to http://localhost/reports or https://localhost/reports (if you enabled SSL on your server). You should see the Report Manager home page.

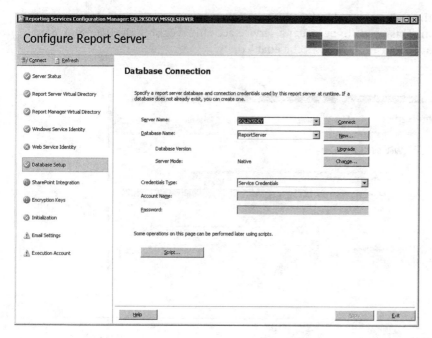

FIGURE 2.34   Database setup.

Install the Reporting Server on a Standalone Server

Figure 2.35 shows a deployment with Reporting Services on a standalone server.

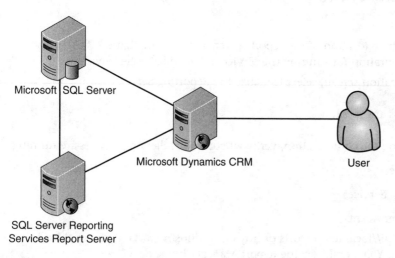

FIGURE 2.35   Reporting server on a standalone server.

- ▶ **Pro**

    - ▶ The reporting server is on a standalone server, not impacting load on any other server.

    - ▶ You can use a service account or Kerberos authentication to get user-specific data.

- ▶ **Con**

    - ▶ Complex deployment.

The installation steps are as follows:

1. Log in to the CRM front-end web server.
2. Navigate to the Microsoft SQL installation setup.
3. Launch setup.
4. Click Next to install the prerequisites.
5. Click Next on the Welcome screen.
6. Click Next on the Prerequisite Check.
7. If IIS and ASP.NET are not installed/configured on the server, cancel the setup and configure IIS and ASP.NET using the application server role, and then restart the setup.
8. Enter the product key and click Next.
9. On the Components to Install screen, select the following components:

    a. Reporting Services

    b. Workstation components, Books Online, and development tools (recommended)
10. Click Advanced.
11. On the Documentation, Samples, and Sample Databases screen, deselect Sample Databases and Sample Code and Applications (recommended).
12. Click Next.
13. On the Instance Name screen, you can specify an instance name for Reporting Services and database engine. If you want to install it on the default instance instead, select Default Instance (MSSQLSERVER).
14. On the Service Account screen, do the following:

    Specify a domain user account. (Refer to the "Authentication" section in this chapter for guidelines about choosing a service account.)
15. Click Next.
16. Select the appropriate collation. If unsure, use default values.
17. Click Next.
18. On the Report Server Installation Options screen, select Install the Default Configuration.
19. Click Next to begin installation.

The following configuration steps are required only if you did not configure at the time of installation:

1. Click Start.

2. Click Microsoft SQL Server 2005.

3. Click Configuration Tools.

4. Click Reporting Services Configuration (Figure 2.36).

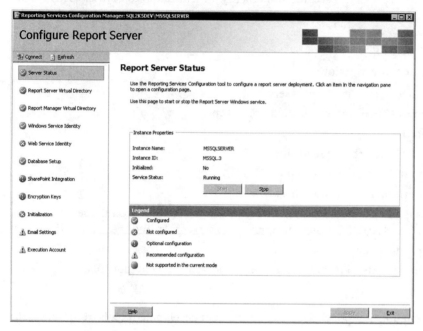

FIGURE 2.36   Reporting server status.

5. Start Reporting Services (if not started already).

6. Create a virtual directory (by default, ReportServer), as shown in Figure 2.37.

7. Create a virtual directory (by default, Reports), as shown in Figure 2.38.

8. Select the appropriate identity (as chosen in the earlier steps), see Figure 2.39.

9. Confirm the web service identity and the service accounts running the application (Figure 2.40). This needs to have either a service account accessing the data source or Kerberos needs to be enabled.

10. Select the database location of the report server (Figure 2.41). This is a required configuration for running the service in a load-balanced environment.

11. On the Initialization screen, select Initialize the Reporting Server.

The verification steps are as follows:

1. Before beginning the configuration, verify whether the following services are running:

    a. SQL Server

    b. Reporting Services

    c. SQL Server Agent

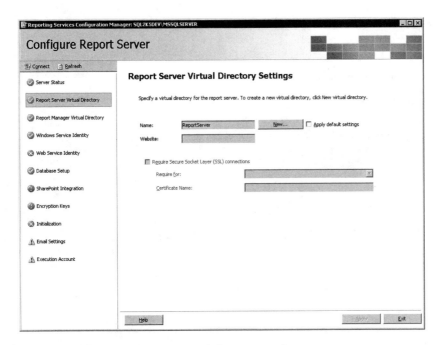

FIGURE 2.37   Report server virtual directory settings.

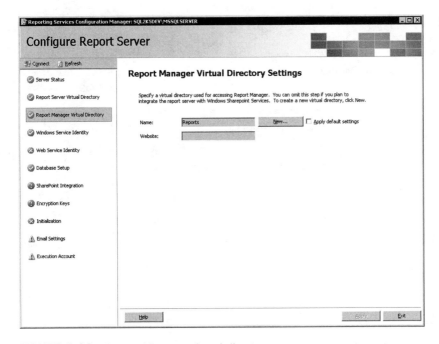

FIGURE 2.38   Report Manager virtual directory.

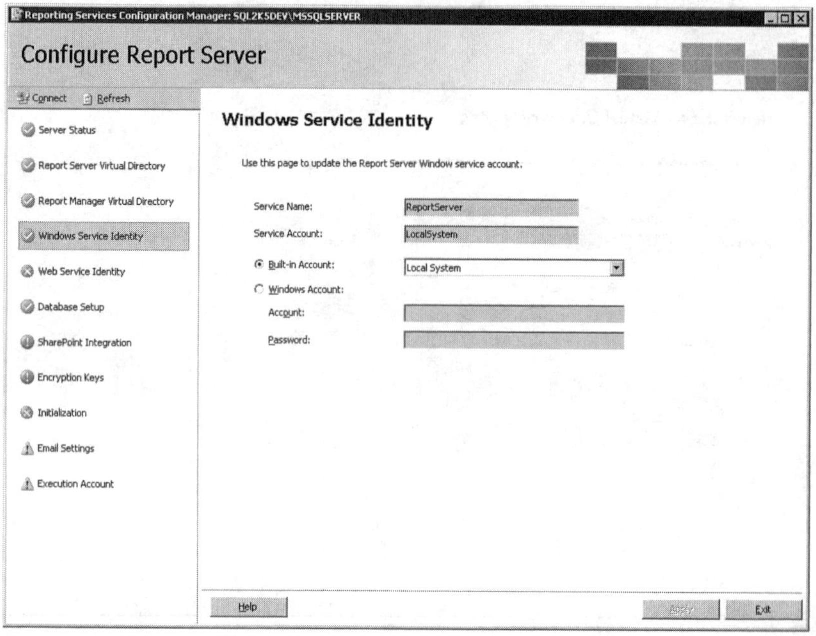

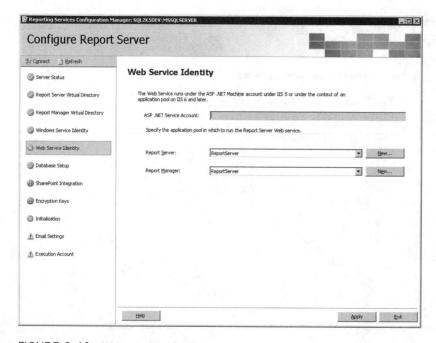

FIGURE 2.39   Windows service identity.

FIGURE 2.40   Web service identity.

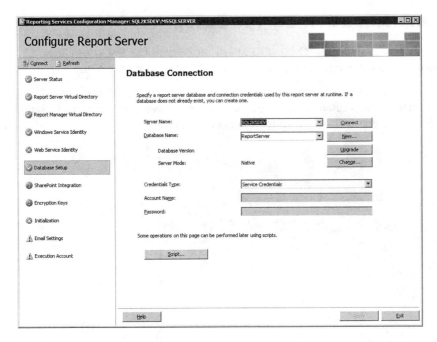

FIGURE 2.41   Database setup.

2. Navigate to http://localhost/reports or https://localhost/reports (if you enabled SSL on your server). You should see the Report Manager home page.

Reporting Services Connector

The Connector needs to be installed on the same server as SSRS.

Installing this Reporting Services Connector eliminates the need to configure Kerberos for Microsoft Dynamics CRM for both the built-in reports and the reports accessed from within the CRM application. If you have any reports that are not being accessed through CRM, however, you will need to configure Kerberos on the servers accessing Reporting Services.

> **NOTE**
>
> The SSRS Connector does not allow you to access reports running HTTPS using trusted certificates.

Office Communication Server Setup

Using Office Communication Server (OCS) with Microsoft Dynamics CRM allows users to view the presence of other users in the organization for ease of communication.

This integration also enables users to interact with each other from the Presence icon. Users can view someone else's calendar and free/busy times and can send email or instant messages with one click. Figure 2.42 illustrates a person "in office."

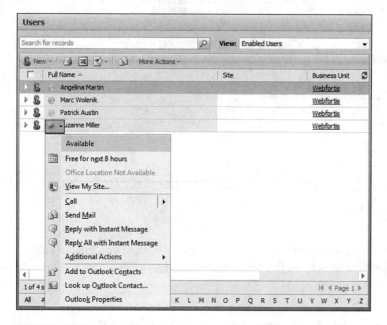

FIGURE 2.42   Sample OCS options.

The installation steps are as follows:

1. Log on the server where you want to install OCS Standard edition as a domain admin.
2. Locate the set for Microsoft Office Communications Server 2007.
3. Click Deploy Standard Edition Server.
4. At Deploy Server, click Run.
5. Select the location to install on the Location for Server Files screen.
6. On the Main Service Account for Standard Edition Server screen, enter the username and password for the service account that will run the service.
7. Click Next.
8. On the Component Service Account for this Standard Edition Server screen, enter the server name and the service account that will run the audio/video conferencing server and the web conferencing server.
9. Click Next.

10. On the Web Farm FQDNs screen, specify the internal URL that will be used by users to download client for web conferencing content, distribution group expansion, and the address book.

11. Click Next.

12. On the Location for Database Files screen, specify the location for the database transaction log files.

13. Click Next.

14. Review the summary and click Next to begin installation.

The configuration steps are as follows:

1. Log on to the server running OCS.

2. Locate the installer for Microsoft Office Communications Server and start the setup to launch the Deployment Tool.

3. In the Deployment Tool, select Deploy Standard Edition Server.

4. Click Run.

5. Select the server from the list on the Server or Pool to Configure screen.

6. Click Next.

7. Verify the SIP domain on the SIP Domains screen.

8. Click Next.

9. On the Client Logon Settings screen, ensure the DNS SRV records are configured properly so that the clients in your organization will automatically sign in.

10. Click Next.

11. Select the check box for the domains that will be supported by the server for automatic sign in.

12. Click Next.

13. On the Ready to Configure Server or Pool screen, review the settings that you specified.

14. Click Next to finish the setup.

To have fine-grain control on the group policy, you have the options shown in Figure 2.43.

You can find the Group Policy template (conf.adm) at http://www.microsoft.com/downloads/details.aspx?FamilyID=92759d4b-7112-4b6c-ad4a-bbf3802a5c9b&displaylang=en.

If you are still using the previous version of Microsoft Communication Server, Office Communicator, you can still have access to this feature. To enable this feature on Microsoft Live Communication Server 2005, you need to push the following group policy:

```
;;;;;;;;;;;;;;;;;;;;;;;;;;;;;;;
CLASS USER ;;;;;;;;;;;;;;;;;;;
;;;;;;;;;;;;;;;;;;;;;;;;;;;;;;;;
CATEGORY !!RTCPOLICY_TOP_CAT
```

```
CATEGORY !!RTCPOLICY_MESSENGERONLY_CAT
KEYNAME "Software\Policies\Microsoft\Office\11.0\Outlook\IM"

 POLICY !!PolicyEnabled
 EXPLAIN !!ExplainText_Enabled
  VALUENAME "Enabled"
  VALUEON   NUMERIC  1
  VALUEOFF  NUMERIC  0
 END POLICY

 POLICY !!PolicyEnablePresence
 EXPLAIN !!ExplainText_EnablePresence
  VALUENAME "EnablePresence"
  VALUEON   NUMERIC  1
  VALUEOFF  NUMERIC  0
 END POLICY

END CATEGORY ; RTCPOLICY_MESSENGERONLY_CAT

CATEGORY !!RTCPOLICY_MESSENGERONLY_CAT
KEYNAME "Software\Policies\Microsoft\Office\11.0\Common\PersonaMenu"

 POLICY !!PolicyQueryServiceForStatus
 EXPLAIN !!ExplainText_QueryServiceForStatus
  PART !!PolicyQueryServiceForStatus DROPDOWNLIST NOSORT
  VALUENAME "QueryServiceForStatus"
  ITEMLIST
  NAME !!QueryServiceForStatus0   VALUE NUMERIC  0
  NAME !!QueryServiceForStatus1   VALUE NUMERIC  1
  NAME !!QueryServiceForStatus2   VALUE NUMERIC  2 DEFAULT
  END ITEMLIST
  END PART
 END POLICY

END CATEGORY ; RTCPOLICY_MESSENGERONLY_CAT
END CATEGORY; RTCPOLICY_TOP_CAT


[strings]
RTCPOLICY_TOP_CAT="Microsoft Office Communicator Policy Settings"
RTCPOLICY_MESSENGERONLY_CAT="Microsoft Office Communicator Feature Policies"
```

PolicyEnabled="Enable the person Names Smart Tag"
ExplainText_Enabled="Enable the pawn guys to be displayed on the clients computer.\n\nIf you enable this policy setting, users can See the pawn guy next to people's names.\n\nIf you disable or do not configure this policy setting, users cannot
See the pawn guy next to people's names.\n\n"

PolicyEnablePresence="Display Messenger Status in the Form field"
ExplainText_EnablePresence="This displays the status of the users on the icon itself.\n\nIf you enable this policy setting, users can See the status of other users.\n\nIf you disable or do not configure this policy setting, users cannot see the
status of other users on the pawn.\n\n"

PolicyQueryServiceForStatus="Configure status information queries"
ExplainText_QueryServiceForStatus="A registry value is available to configure how
Outlook queries for a contact's presence information. You can configure this registry value to determine how Outlook retrieves the online status for contacts who are
not on your Windows Messenger contact list. \n\n 0 - If you type a value of zero,
you receive status information only about people who are on your contact list. In
this scenario, Outlook does not request status information about people who are not
on your contact list. \n\n 1 - If you type a value of one, Outlook requests status
information from the Microsoft Exchange Instant Messaging (IM) service about people
who may or may not be on your contact list. \n\n 2 - If you type a value of two,
Outlook requests status information from the Real-Time Communications (RTC) service
about people who may or may not be on your contact list. \n\n Note You cannot configure this registry value to cause Outlook to request status information from the
Exchange Instant Messaging service and the Real-Time Communications IM service at
the same time. Additionally, the .NET Messenger Service together with a Microsoft
.NET Passport account does not allow status information queries for people who are
not on your "buddy" list."

QueryServiceForStatus0 = "If you type a value of zero, you receive status information only about people who are on your contact list. In this scenario, Outlook does
not request status information about people who are not on your contact list."
QueryServiceForStatus1 = "If you type a value of one, Outlook requests status information from the Microsoft Exchange Instant Messaging (IM) service about people who
may or may not be on your contact list."
QueryServiceForStatus2 = "If you type a value of two, Outlook requests status information from the Real-Time Communications (RTC) service about people who may or may
not be on your contact list. "

FIGURE 2.43   Group policy options.

Live Communication Server and OCS are tightly integrated with Windows Messenger. This group policy can also enable you to integrate with your phone system through the IM client directly. You can download this group policy file from Microsoft's website. Integration between chat logs and Microsoft Dynamics CRM is described in Chapter 3, "Extending Microsoft Dynamics CRM 4.0."

Outlook Infrastructure Optimization

Microsoft Dynamics CRM is tightly coupled with Outlook to bring a single screen as the dashboard for the user. Outlook is the standard work desk for a lot of companies.

Optimization techniques include the following:

▶ Set the crawl items from 1,000 to 25.

Because it is the work desk, most users typically have very large mailboxes. For large email mailboxes, it is recommended to deploy the following Registry settings:

```
[HKEY_CURRENT_USER\Software\Microsoft\MSCRMClient]
"TagMinItemsForCrawl"=dword:00000000
"TagAllowedItemsForCrawl"=dword:00000025
```

This setting requires a restart and will only crawl (or inspect) the first 25 items in a user's mailbox. This settings increases the user performance drastically, because every time the asynchronous "tagging engine" wakes up, it looks for only the last 25 emails that came into Outlook, instead of scanning every email located in the Inbox and Sent Items folders. However, the downside to this setting is that it will not automatically go through older emails and change the icon appropriately; this might be a little misleading and confusing for some users.

▶ Ensure adequate memory on the client exists.

This is typically overlooked, but minimum memory on a client is 1GB (using the online version). We recommend 2GB for the client and 4GB if using the offline version. (The offline version has a subset copy of the Dynamics CRM database synchronized with the server.)

▶ Ensure service packs are installed for both Windows and for Microsoft Dynamics CRM.

▶ Microsoft Dynamics CRM has many service packs depending on a variety of conditions. If your organization has deployed any of the service packs, be sure that *both* the server and client service packs are deployed.

To force a client deployment, system administrators can configure the updates as mandatory in the CRM Client AutoUpdate, as follows:

1. The first time you run AutoUpdate, go to \InetPub\wwwroot and create a new folder named `crmpatches`.

NOTE

If this is a load-balanced environment, create this folder on each subsequent web server in the same location.

2. Ensure that all clients have the following Registry settings:

   Location: `HKEY_LOCAL_MACHINE\Software\Microsoft\MSCRMClient`

   Key: `AutoUpdateDownloadUrl` (string)

   `http://[servername]/crmpatches/` (remember the closing /)

NOTE

If this Registry is not set, the clients will not get any updated for the clients. To set up the updates for clients, you should follow the instructions available from http://technet. microsoft.com/en-us/library/dd979062.aspx.

3. Download the hotfix to your server (each CRM web server) and extract the contents to the \InetPub\wwwroot\crmpatches folder.

4. Extract the contents of the client patch on your server. Locate the PatchId value, which is required for the XML file configuration.

     a. Open a command prompt, and type
`[DownloadedLocation]\[CRMPatchFileName].exe /x`.

     b. Enter the location (`\InetPub\wwwroot\crmpatches`) when prompted.

     c. Open config.xml and copy the ParchId to configure the next steps.

5. Create/modify your configuration XML file:

```
<ClientPatches>
    <Create>
        <ClientPatchInfo>
            <PatchId>[Enter PatchId Guid]</PatchId>
            <Title>[Patch Specific Title]</Title>
            <Description>[Patch Description]</Description>
            <IsMandatory>true</IsMandatory>
            <IsEnabled>true</IsEnabled>
            <ClientType>OutlookDesktop,OutlookLaptop</ClientType>
            <LinkId>[CRMPatchFileName].exe</LinkId>
        </ClientPatchInfo>
    </Create>
</ClientPatches>
```

NOTE

You can add multiple `<ClientPatchInfo>` to post multiple hotfixes at one time.

The title and description are for display only.

The `IsMandatory` option dictates whether a user is required to install the hotfix in order to continue using CRM.

The `ClientType` can be either `OutlookDesktop` or `OutlookLaptop` or `OutlookDesktop,OutlookLaptop` depending on which clients require the updates.

---

6. In a command prompt, locate ClientPatchConfigurator.exe, usually located in [ServerInstallDir]\Tools.

7. Run microsoft.crm.tools.clientpatchconfigurator.exe [configfile].xml.

When this is properly configured, users will receive the update screen shown in Figure 2.44.

Depending on the `IsMandatory` switch used, the user can either install or elect to not install.

By navigating to your CRM options, you can set which records you want to synchronize. Figure 2.45 shows the standard synchronization options.

Ensure that you only have the records synchronized to your local computer that you own. In addition, this can be changed to other criteria that may decrease the amount of data that needs to be synchronized from/to the server.

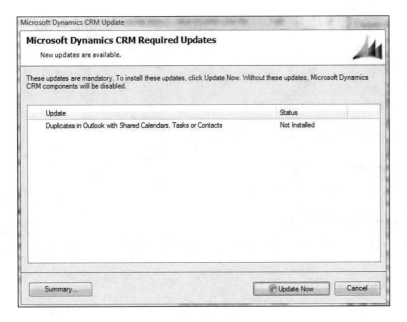

FIGURE 2.44 Install updates from the CRM server.

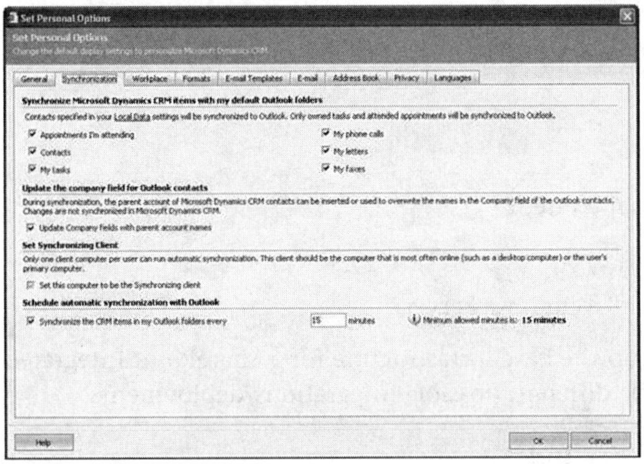

FIGURE 2.45 CRM synchronization options.

Windows SharePoint Integration

Windows SharePoint Services is primarily used to provide document management for Microsoft Dynamics CRM. SharePoint document management capabilities are far superior to the ones in CRM, and therefore it is suggested to integrate the two technologies when working with or considering document management requirements that exceed the out-of-the-box functions of Microsoft Dynamics CRM. These requirements may include the following:

▶ Full text searching

▶ Document archiving

▶ Document versioning

There are two different versions of Windows SharePoint:

▶ Windows SharePoint Services v3 (WSS)

▶ Microsoft Office SharePoint Server (MOSS)

Windows SharePoint Services v3

Windows SharePoint Service v3 (WSS) differs from Microsoft Office SharePoint Server (MOSS) as follows:

▶ **Windows SharePoint Services**

   ▶ Collaboration sites

   ▶ Wiki and blogs

   ▶ Simple search engine

▶ **Microsoft Office SharePoint Server**

   ▶ All the services from WSS

   ▶ Published portals

   ▶ My Sites

   ▶ Enterprise search for external content

   ▶ Business intelligence

Finally, WSS is a free component (part of Windows Server).

In this section, we explain how to set up the base infrastructure for a SharePoint integrated environment. In Chapter 5, we describe different possible integrations/deployments.

Install Windows SharePoint Services

If installing this on a farm, you need to follow these steps on all servers.

1. Run setup on the first server.
2. Locate the installation files and run WSSv3.exe.
3. Accept the terms of agreement on the Read the Microsoft Software License Terms screen.
4. Click Continue.
5. On the Choose the Installation screen, select Advanced.
6. On the Server Type tab, select Web Front End.

7. Review the selections, and click Install Now.

8. When setup is complete, run the SharePoint Products and Technologies Configuration Wizard to configure the service. If you are installing this on additional servers, install the Windows SharePoint Services before configuring the service.

To add servers to the farm, follow these steps:

1. Locate the installation files and run WSSv3.exe.

2. Select the agreement terms on the Read the Microsoft Software License Terms screen.

3. On the Choose the Installation screen, select Advanced.

4. On the Server Type tab, Select Web Front End.

5. Review the selections, and click Install Now.

6. When setup is complete, run SharePoint Products and Technologies Configuration Wizard to configure the service.

To configure Windows SharePoint Services, follow these steps:

1. On the Welcome to SharePoint Products and Technologies screen, click Next.

2. Select Yes in the dialog box confirming that some services might need to be restarted during the configuration.

3. On the Connect to a Server Farm screen, if this is the first server in the farm, select No, I Want to Create a New Server Farm.

4. Click Next.

5. Enter the database server name on the Specify Configuration Database Settings screen.

6. Enter the appropriate database name to host the configuration database. The default name is SharePoint_Config.

7. In the User Name and Password box, enter the username and password that will run the SharePoint Services.

8. Click Next.

9. On the Configure SharePoint Central Administration Web Application screen, you can specify the port number if you want, and then select the appropriate option and enter the port number. Otherwise, you can let the system generate a random port.

10. On the Configure SharePoint Central Administration Web Application screen, select the authentication method, as chosen from the earlier section.

11. Click Next and finish the wizard.

Microsoft Office SharePoint Server 2007

Integrating Microsoft Dynamics CRM with Microsoft Office SharePoint Server (MOSS) gives you the same document management features. As explained previously, MOSS provides the following additional features:

▶ Enterprise portal

▶ Enterprise content management

- ▶ Business process forms
- ▶ Business intelligence
- ▶ Enterprise search

In Chapter 5, we demonstrate how to use the following services with CRM:

- ▶ Enterprise content management
- ▶ Business process forms
- ▶ Business intelligence
- ▶ Enterprise search

NOTE

Unlike WSS, MOSS is a separately licensed server application. Be sure to check your licensing requirements when considering a deployment.

As explained in the previous section, we are going to explain how to set up the base infrastructure for a SharePoint integrated environment. In Chapter 5, we describe different possible integrations/deployments.

To install MOSS, follow these steps:

1. Locate the installation files and run setup.
2. Enter the product key in the dialog box.
3. Click Continue.
4. On the Read the Microsoft Software License Terms screen, review the terms and conditions and accept the terms.
5. Click Continue.
6. On the Choose the Installation You Want screen, select Advanced.
7. On the Server Type tab, select either Application Server or Web Server and an Application Server, based on the role the server will host.
8. Click Install Now.

To run the SharePoint Products and Technologies Configuration Wizard, follow these steps:

1. On the Welcome to SharePoint Products and Technologies screen, click Next.
2. Select Yes in the dialog box confirming that some services might need to be restarted during the configuration.
3. On the Connect to a Server Farm screen, if this is the first server in the farm, select No, I Want to Create a New Server Farm.

4. Click Next.

5. Enter the database server name on the Specify Configuration Database Settings screen.

6. Enter the appropriate database name to host the configuration database. The default name is SharePoint_Config.

7. In the User Name and Password box, enter the username and password that will run the SharePoint Services.

8. Click Next.

9. On the Configure SharePoint Central Administration Web Application screen, you can specify a port number if you want, and then select the appropriate option and enter the port number. Otherwise, you can let the system generate a random port.

10. On the Configure SharePoint Central Administration Web Application screen, select the authentication method, as chosen from the earlier section.

Configure 2007 Office SharePoint Server Services

To take advantage of the search and indexing servers, you first need to start and configure the Office SharePoint Server Search service on at least one of your front-end servers. This service will query and display the content indexed by the indexing services.

To start and configure the Search service, follow these steps:

1. Launch the SharePoint Central Administration home page.

2. Click the Operations tab.

3. Click Servers in Farm.

4. Select the server on which you want to configure the Search service on.

5. Select Start next to Office SharePoint Server Search.

6. On the Office SharePoint Server Search Settings page, do the following:

    a. In the Query and Indexing section, verify that this server is listed for Use This Server for Indexing Content and ensure that the Use This Server for Serving Search Queries is selected.

    b. In the Default Catalog Location section, enter the path to a physical folder to store the index files.

    c. In the Contact E-Mail Address section, specify a valid email address to send any administration emails to.

    d. In the Service Account section, enter the username and password for the service account to run the farm.

7. In the Web Front End and Crawling section, do one of the following:

    a. If the Search service is on the same server as the web server and the server is responsible for rendering web content, select No Dedicated Web Front-End Computer for Crawling.

    b. If the Search service is on a server that is a standalone search server, which does not provide web services and render web content, select Use a Dedicated Web Front-End Computer for Crawling, and then in the Select a Web Front End Computer section, select the server you want to use for crawling.

8. Click Start.

Install and Configure Excel Calculation Services

To integrate SharePoint, PerformancePoint, and Microsoft CRM, you need to enable Excel Calculation Services, as follows:

1. Launch the SharePoint Central Administration home page.
2. Click the Administrative Tasks link.
3. Click Add Excel Services Trusted Locations.
4. Click Add Trusted File Location.
5. Enter the location in Address field. It is recommended that the trusted file locations be stored in a SharePoint site.
6. Click Windows SharePoint Services.
7. Select Allow External Data, and select the trust level for external data sources that you want to enable by doing one of the following:

    a. Click None to prevent Excel Calculation Services from processing connections to any external data connection.

    b. Click Trusted Data Connection Libraries Only to prevent Excel Calculation Services from processing connections to external data sources that are embedded within workbooks.

    c. Click Trusted Data Connection Libraries and Embedded to permit Excel Calculation Services to process direct connections to external data sources that are embedded within workbooks.

Summary

In this chapter, we highlighted the different deployment topologies and covered the security considerations required to build a scalable infrastructure.

CHAPTER 3

Extending Microsoft Dynamics CRM 4.0

Extending Microsoft Dynamics CRM means many things. To some, it is simply using built-in features of Microsoft Dynamics CRM, such as onChange events (JavaScript events available on CRM forms) to format data a certain way after it has been input. To others, it is building complex systems that interact with the CRM platform for internal applications (such as backend human resources or enterprise resource planning [ERP]/accounting systems) via the creation of plug-ins and/or usage of middleware applications for managing synchronization (usually BizTalk or Scribe applications).

This chapter covers both options, but first we review what it means to extend Microsoft Dynamics CRM and examine some necessary factors you must consider before performing any of the included customizations.

As mentioned in Chapter 1, "Extending Microsoft Dynamics CRM Explained," extending Microsoft Dynamics CRM can be accomplished via any of the following:

▶ Custom logic via plug-in development

▶ Source-to-source integration (web services integration)

▶ Custom application integration using IFrames

▶ CRM JScript to extend across various forms

▶ Workflow

While a large portion of this chapter addresses how you can make modifications to Microsoft Dynamics CRM when you know the user base, browser version, and requirements, it is important to consider what it means when these environmental variables are unknown, or when the application needs to cross domains or be available to a wide array of users. If this is your situation, it is worthwhile to consider an xRM platform approach.

This chapter also includes customization examples that relate both to the client side and to the server end. And to show what it means to extend Microsoft Dynamics CRM with other internal applications (such as other CRM systems or other line-of-business applications), we also delve into some sophisticated models of integration within this chapter.

Limitations and Licensing Considerations

Microsoft Dynamics CRM 4.0 is licensed on either a per-named user or per-device model. (This is somewhat dissimilar from some of Microsoft's ERP offerings that have a licensing model of concurrency.) Therefore, each and every user who accesses Microsoft Dynamics CRM 4.0 must be identified and set up in Microsoft Dynamics CRM as a valid user with a valid role. End-user licensing is referred to as client access licenses (CALs). Figure 3.1 shows how users are administered in Microsoft Dynamics CRM 4.0.

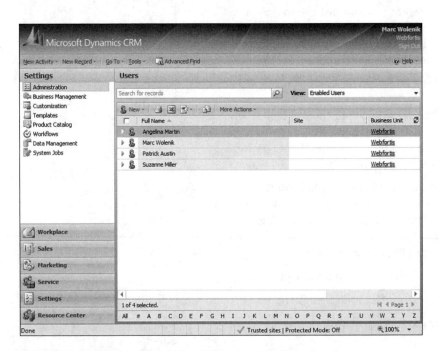

FIGURE 3.1   Microsoft Dynamics CRM administration of users.

Figure 3.2 shows the device model that is commonly used in call center and manufacturing organizations, where multiple users may use the same computer (but not at the same time).

In Figure 3.2, it is important to remember that all three users listed will need to be added to Microsoft Dynamics CRM as valid users (as shown in Figure 3.1). However, instead of purchasing three separate CALs, one for each user, only one CAL must be purchased.

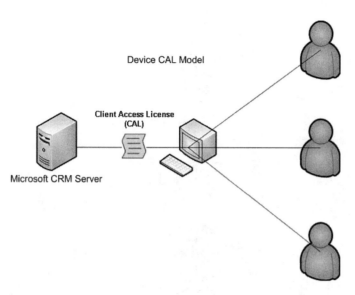

FIGURE 3.2   Microsoft Dynamics CRM with a single-device CAL.

> **NOTE**
>
> Be careful when considering your licensing requirements and evaluating the device CAL. If at any point any of the users access another computer that has not been identified as the device computer, the organization may be out of compliance.

Contrast Figure 3.2 with Figure 3.3, which shows three figures, and therefore requires three CALs.

> **NOTE**
>
> Microsoft Dynamics CRM 4.0 is not offered with fewer than five user CALs (either device or named user). The examples provided thus far are for illustrative purposes.

The end result from both of these examples is the following:

- ▶ From a licensing perspective, you will have either one CAL (a device CAL) or three named-user CALs.

- ▶ From a CRM administration perspective, you will have three users set up and configured with valid roles in Microsoft Dynamics CRM.

This example is included to show the extension of Microsoft Dynamics CRM when a valid user is required (which is often the case when building components that integrate with Microsoft Dynamics CRM).

A frequent mistake that amateur integrators make is to just take advantage of an existing user CAL and use that CAL as the hard-coded authentication/integration credentials. Although this is not necessarily a problem (and several of our examples include such a

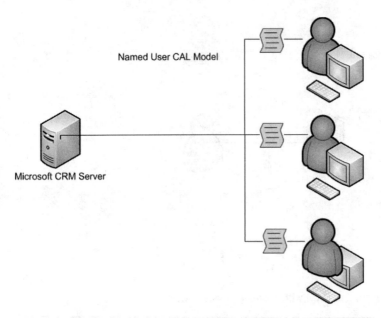

FIGURE 3.3   Microsoft Dynamics CRM with three named-user CALs.

method), it is important to realize that Microsoft recognizes such usage as a method of access, and it may therefore place the organization in license-compliance risk. This is especially true if the system is designed to perform any level of integration with any application that delivers data outside of the domain.

In addition, it is important to remember that Microsoft Dynamics CRM CALs are instance based, and with multiple on-premise servers (such as with a server farm), only the single-user CAL is required, regardless of the number of actual CRM servers.

As stated previously, Microsoft has positioned Microsoft Dynamics CRM as a platform and has therefore developed a licensing model for it that enables access to it without requiring a license for every user. But, a license is required if data is going to be accessed across the organizational domain; this method of access is referred to as using the connector model or connector licensing.

External Connector License

The Microsoft External Connector license allows organizations to extend Microsoft Dynamics CRM data both across disparate applications and across the domain.

Although it is nothing more than a licensing mechanism, it is important to understand and is included within the context of this book because it is a necessary license when performing several of the integration options mentioned.

> **NOTE**
>
> Although the External Connector license is purchased separately, there is no configuration made to Microsoft Dynamics CRM that reflects the existence of this license.

The External Connector license is available in two different formats for Microsoft Dynamics CRM:

- Full External Connector
- Limited External Connector

The intention of the Limited External Connector is to allow interaction on a read-only level with the Microsoft Dynamics CRM data, whereas the Full External Connector allows full read/write on the Microsoft Dynamics CRM data. (The cost of the license reflects the restriction levels; the Limited External Connector is approximately one-third the cost of the Full External Connector.)

Connection Options

Finally, it is appropriate to mention that the method of access is completely optional to the end user. There are three ways to interact with Microsoft Dynamics CRM data:

- Microsoft Dynamics CRM web services
- SQL Server CRM filtered views
- SQL Server CRM tables

> **NOTE**
>
> Although all three options are included, it is recommended to use only the first two options listed here.
>
> Any direct interaction directly with the SQL Server CRM tables is *highly* cautioned against and may place the modified records (if not the entire system) into an unstable state, and should be performed only by an experienced CRM partner.

Microsoft Dynamics CRM web services allow applications to consume CRM business rules and data directly from the CRM web server. In some cases, this is the preferred method, and creating a connection directly to the SQL Server database is impractical.

SQL Server CRM filtered views (see Figure 3.4) are similar to CRM web services in that they're designed to be used by end users who are performing integrations, because they enforce security roles, which are important when considering integration applications that can be used by a variety of users in an organization. In addition, the views can be used for read-only access, but should not be used for write access.

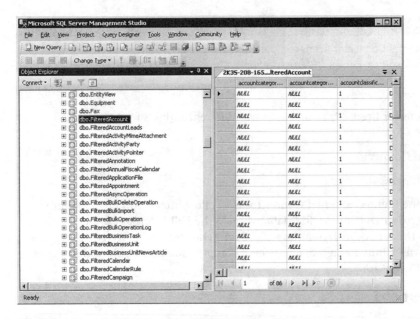

FIGURE 3.4   Microsoft Dynamics CRM SQL filtered views.

> **NOTE**
>
> It is important to remember that Microsoft Dynamics CRM can have user roles that are
> disproportionate from their Active Directory roles, and therefore a low-level CRM user
> may be a system administrator in Active Directory (and vice versa).

Although our discussion references all the methods listed previously, be sure to understand the implications of using one versus the other.

Customization Options by CRM Version

Because Microsoft Dynamics CRM comes in three different versions (On Premise, Partner
Hosted, and Microsoft Hosted [CRM Online]), some limitations apply to what you can do
within each version when considering customization.

Table 3.1 shows customization options by CRM version.

Customizing Navigation

Microsoft Dynamics CRM enables you to easily perform navigation customizations by
editing the site map. The site map is an XML file that is read and parsed by Microsoft
Dynamics CRM when it is first loaded and can be used to change what and how information displays in the navigation pane.

TABLE 3.1   Microsoft Dynamics CRM Customization Options

	Microsoft Dynamics CRM Version		
	On Premise	Partner Hosted	Microsoft CRM Online
Entity customization	X	X	X
Attribute customization	X	X	X
Form/view customization	X	X	X
Relationship customization	X	X	X
Workflow customization	X	X	X
BU, teams, and role configuration	X	X	X
Administration configuration	X	X	X
Business management configuration	X	X	X
Product catalog configuration	X	X	X
Relationship roles configuration	X	X	X
JScript events on forms and fields	X	X	X
Navigation options	X	X	X
User interface customizations	X	X	X
IFrame	X	X	X
Create new reports (Report Wizard)	X	X	X
Upload custom reports	X	Varies	–
Programmatically upload reports	X	X	–
Access to filtered views	X	X	–
Import/export and publish customizations	X	X	X
Import/export and publish workflow	X	X	X
Data import/migration	X	X	X
Plug-in usage	X	Varies	–
Workflow creation	X	X	X
Workflow creation using .NET assemblies	X	Varies	–
Access to Discovery web service	X	X	X

ω

TABLE 3.1   Microsoft Dynamics CRM Customization Options

	Microsoft Dynamics CRM Version		
	On Premise	Partner Hosted	Microsoft CRM Online
Access to CRMService web service	X	X	X
Access to MetaData web service	X	X	X
Access to Deployment web service	X	X	–
Active Directory (AD) authentication	X	–	–
Forms-based authentication	X	X	–
Windows Live authentication	–	–	X

Figure 3.5 shows a configuration that was made to the Resource Center that renames it from Resource Center to Help Area.

The site map consists of three primary elements:

▶ The Area element, which is used for the primary areas on the navigation pane (Workplace, Sales, Marketing, Service, Settings, and Resource Center).

▶ The Group element, which divides the Area elements into subareas. The workplace area has six default groups: My Work, Customers, Sales, Marketing, Service, and

FIGURE 3.5   Microsoft Dynamics CRM configured navigation option.

Scheduling. These are optionally shown, however, because users select which ones they will see.

▶ The SubArea element, which has the actual content links. All the links in the default site map point to the CRM application, with the exception being the Resource Center. In addition, the SubArea element can link to either CRM items or point to any hyperlink.

3

NOTE

A common use of the SubArea Resource Center element is to point to your organization's intranet site, instead of the Microsoft Internet site, for CRM resources.

You also have the option to edit the localized titles using the locale ID (LCID), to add descriptions to the primary elements, and to set the privilege level to view the subarea.

To edit the site map, it must be first exported, then modified, and then reimported.

To export the site map, navigate to Settings, Customizations, and then select Export Customizations. Locate the site map (see Figure 3.6) and select Export Selected Customizations. Save the resulting customizations.zip file to your desktop.

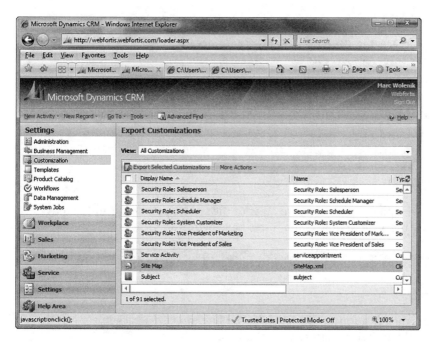

FIGURE 3.6   Microsoft Dynamics CRM configured navigation option.

When you are editing the site map, we highly recommend an environment that performs schema validation. Although Microsoft Dynamics CRM will perform validation on the schema during the upload, the editing environment will prevent you having to rework any applied edits.

A free application that supports schema validation is XML Notepad 2007, which you can download from http://www.microsoft.com/downloads/details.aspx?familyid=72d6aa49-787d-4118-ba5f-4f30fe913628&displaylang=en. In addition, you can use the Microsoft

demonstration tool available from http://www.microsoft.com/downloads/
details.aspx?FamilyID=634508DC-1762-40D6-B745-B3BDE05D7012&displaylang=en.
This application has a built-in site map editor that enables you to modify the site map
without having to work with it by hand.

In the preceding example in which we changed the Resource Center to Help Area, we're
using the Title element as follows:

Navigate to the Area element for ResourceCenter, and edit it from this

```
<Area Id="ResourceCenter" ResourceId="Area_ResourceCenter"
Icon="/_imgs/resourcecenter_24x24.gif"
➥DescriptionResourceId="ResourceCenter_Area_Description">
```

To this

```
<Area Id="ResourceCenter" ResourceId="Area_ResourceCenter"
Icon="/_imgs/resourcecenter_24x24.gif" Title="Help Area"
➥DescriptionResourceId="ResourceCenter_Area_Description">
```

A number of other options can be performed when working with the site map:

▶ Changing the shown icon

▶ Changing the order of the areas

▶ Adding or removing areas

▶ Adding groupings

In addition, you can apply security roles to areas of the site map to create an "adaptive
UI" and show only the areas and links that users have permission to view.

NOTE

Changes to the site map are global in nature.

Before making any modifications to the site map, be sure to make a backup copy of the
XML output in case you need to restore your changes.

Form Events

Two events are global in nature for all forms: the onLoad event and the onSave event.

The onLoad event fires after the form has completed loading, and is commonly used to
send an alert to the user, disable fields, or modify field values.

The onSave event fires when the Save or Save and Close buttons are accessed, and it is
important to note that it fires regardless of whether data on the form has been changed.
This event is commonly used to validate an entry because the onSave event can cancel the
save operation.

In addition to the form events, the onChange event is available for every field on a CRM form. To fire the onChange event, the field that has the event attached to it must have its value changed, and it must lose the focus (by the user selecting or tabbing elsewhere on the form).

These events are utilized by writing JavaScript, and our first two examples at the end of this chapter show these events in action.

IFrames

One of the easiest ways to perform an integration to an existing Microsoft Dynamics CRM deployment (both hosted or On Premise) is to use IFrames.

IFrames are "inline frames or windowless inline floating frames" and provide an easy mechanism for integrating data, because they can exist free form or easily pass data through them to the underlying source.

> **NOTE**
>
> Although this is one of the easiest ways to extend Microsoft Dynamics CRM, it does have one major limitation: You must have a connection to the underlying application. Therefore, if you're working offline or remotely and your application requires a VPN to access (because it is on your local intranet), you should consider an alternative solution.
>
> In addition, there is no built-in CRM reporting on any of the IFrame application data.

> **NOTE**
>
> Microsoft Dynamics CRM Online supports the creation of IFrames, but it doesn't support the hosting of the underlying page. Therefore, you must leverage your own (or someone else's) hosting services for an integration with CRM Online.

To create an IFrame, open the Form Designer, select Add an IFrame, and complete the information required. Figure 3.7 shows the basic information of a sample IFrame.

You want to pay special attention to two areas:

- ▶ Pass Record Object-Type Code and Unique Identifier as Parameters
- ▶ Restrict Cross-Frame Scripting

The first option (Pass Record Object-Type Code and Unique Identifier as Parameters) is actually six parameters in Microsoft Dynamics CRM 4.0 (only two in the previous version):

1. typename
2. type
3. id
4. orgname
5. UserLCID
6. OrgLCID

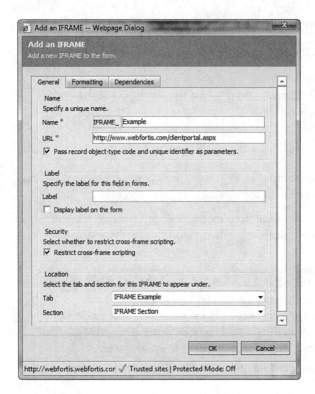

FIGURE 3.7   Microsoft Dynamics CRM IFrame creation example.

The typename is the name of the entity (Account, Contact, and so on). For custom entities, the customization prefix is prepended (normally new_; but if you've changed the customization prefix, which is always a good practice, that will be your prefix, followed by the entity name. For example, if we create a new entity called ProjectDescriptions, the typename will equal new_ProjectDescriptions or wf_ProjectDescriptions).

The type is an integer that uniquely identifies the entity. Table 3.2 shows the object codes for CRM.

TABLE 3.2   Microsoft Dynamics CRM Object Type Codes

Account	1	Invoice	1090
Activity	134	InvoiceDetail	1091
AppointmentActivity	142	Lead	4
EmailActivity	138	Opportunity	3
FaxActivity	136	OpportunityProduct	1083
LetterActivity	141	Organization	1019
PhoneCallActivity	137	PriceLevel	1022

TABLE 3.2   Microsoft Dynamics CRM Object Type Codes

TaskActivity	134	Product	1024
ActivityParty	135	ProductPriceLevel	1026
Annotation	5	Quote	1084
BusinessUnit	10	QuoteDetail	1085
Competitor	123	SalesOrder	1088
Contact	2	SalesOrderDetail	1089
CustomerAddress	1071	Subject	129
Discount	1013	SystemUser	8
DiscountType	1080	Territory	2013
Incident	112		

The id is the ObjectId, which is the unique identifier or GUID. This value is displayed in the URL of every form in the system (and is null until the form is created).

Figure 3.8 shows a GUID of a sample account in the address bar.

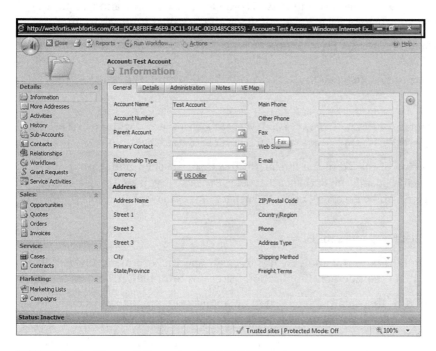

FIGURE 3.8   Microsoft Dynamics CRM GUID sample.

NOTE

Alternative methods of obtaining the GUID include adding a JavaScript onLoad event similar to "alert(document.location)" or a separate page that uses document.write to list out the query strings and their values.

The orgname is the unique name of the organization, the UserLCID is the language code in use by the current user, and the OrgLCID is the language code that represents the base language for the organization.

Both the UserLCID and the OrgLCID are four-digit codes. For a complete reference of language codes, see Appendix A, "Locale ID (LCID)."

NOTE

As counterintuitive as it sounds, best practices usually call for using the entity name (for example, Account, Contact) rather than the type code. The reason for this is that entity codes may differ between one Microsoft Dynamics CRM installation and another.

Consider this illustration of the effect that passing these parameters has. When the URL referenced in Figure 3.7 is called without Pass Record Object-Type Code and Unique Identifier as Parameters being selected, the following URL is called from the form:

http://www.webfortis.com/clientportal.aspx

When the Pass Record Parameters option is selected, the following URL is called from the form:

http://www.webfortis.com/clientportal.aspx?type=1&typename=account&id={5CA8FBFF-46E9-DC11-914C-0030485C8E55}&orgname=Webfortis&userlcid=1033&orglcid=1033

The page that is being displayed in the IFrame (in this case, the clientportal.aspx) can easily read the variables using the HttpRequest.QueryString. (If you are using an HTM page, the parameters can be accessing using the window.location.search property in JavaScript.)

Table 3.2 shows the object codes for CRM.

You can readily see how powerful and easy it is to create specific information related to the selected record on the underlying application using this information.

For an example of how this data is referenced in an application, see the last example in this chapter and see Chapter 5, "SharePoint Integration."

The second option, Restrict Cross-Frame Scripting, is selected by default to help protect the integrity of the CRM application. The effect of this selection is to basically place the application in the IFrame in restricted mode (as defined in Internet Explorer).

This option is unselected when you want to have a level of interaction between the application that is in the IFrame and CRM.

> **NOTE**
>
> The restriction also applies to applications contained within the IFrame that may need to read from the CRM application.

An example of this is a custom application that performs a background check on an account for credit-worthiness. When the credit check comes back, the custom application could reference a Boolean value on the account form and set the value of Background Check Cleared equal to true.

> **NOTE**
>
> The CRM Outlook laptop client has higher security restrictions in place, and in some cases it is not possible to programmatically update fields as described. Be sure to thoroughly test your solution in all environments before rolling out to production.

For more information about IFrames, be sure to thoroughly review the IFrame documentation on MSDN at http://msdn2.microsoft.com/en-us/library/ms535258.aspx.

We've included an example of how an underlying application might work using an IFrame with parameters; see the third example in the Examples section of this chapter.

Examples

The following examples represent some possibilities for customization or extending Microsoft Dynamics CRM when you don't need to worry about security outside of your domain.

Example One: Formatting the Phone Number

When entering a phone number into the system, no formatting logic/mask is applied to the entered number. Not having a formatting mask is helpful if you need to enter a phone number and an extension (such as 916-712-5451, ext: 001), but a properly formatted phone number adds to both human and integrated system readability.

Figure 3.9 shows a standard CRM Account form with a freely entered telephone in the Main Phone field.

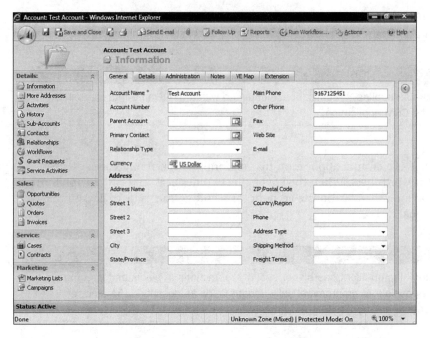

FIGURE 3.9   Microsoft Dynamics CRM with regular phone entry.

To add formatting to this field, place the following code in the Account form onLoad event. (Be sure the event is enabled.)

```
phoneFieldValidationFun = function (source)
{
    var oField = source;
    if (!IsNull(oField))
    {
        if(IsNull(oField.DataValue))
        {
            return;
        }

        var sUSPhone = oField.DataValue.replace(/[^0-9]/g, "");

        // Check the length and format as necessary
        switch (sUSPhone.length)
        {
            case "19167125451".length:
                oField.DataValue = "+1 ("+ sUSPhone.substr(1, 3) + ") " +
➡sUSPhone.substr(4, 3) + "-" + sUSPhone.substr(7, 4);
                break;
```

```
        case "9167125451".length:
            oField.DataValue = "("+ sUSPhone.substr(0, 3) + ") " +
➥sUSPhone.substr(3, 3) + "-" + sUSPhone.substr(6, 4);
            break;

        case "167125451".length:
            oField.DataValue = "(0"+sUSPhone.substr(0, 2)+") " +
➥sUSPhone.substr(2, 3) + "-" + sUSPhone.substr(5, 4);
            break;

        case "7125451".length:
            oField.DataValue = sUSPhone.substr(0, 3) + "-" +
➥sUSPhone.substr(3,4);
            break;
        }
    }
}
```

Now place the following code for each phone field (using the onChange event):

```
phoneFieldValidationFun(event.srcElement);
```

Applying the preceding code to the onChange event of the fields that need to be formatted with phone numbering will properly format the phone number entry, as shown in Figure 3.10.

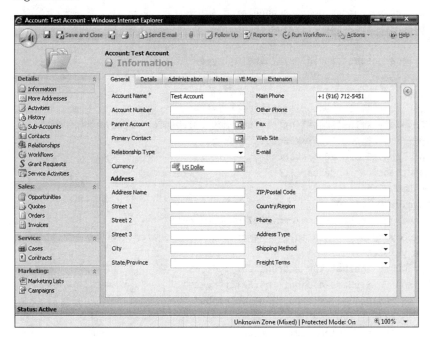

FIGURE 3.10   Microsoft Dynamics CRM with formatted phone entry.

This example clearly shows how to format data simply and easily on data entry. It would be a trivial matter to apply error handling and formatting for other fields by modifying the example shown.

Example Two: Validating Data Across the CRM Application

It is common to be working with Microsoft Dynamics CRM and need to query/validate entered data against another entity's data. A common example is when a Parent Customer or Primary Contact is selected for the Contact or Account records, but it could be used in a number of situations. Other common scenarios include the following:

▶ Populating data on the account for invoice quantities and/or amounts (if you wanted to use CRM to show total orders/amounts)

▶ Updating subordinate records such as Opportunities, Quote, Orders, or Invoices with information entered on the Account level

▶ Modifying Account data based on case status

This example shows how to check the related Account record of the Contact and validate phone numbers. If they differ, the system prompts the user as to whether the user wants to update the Contact record with the main phone number from the Account.

Place the following code on the Parent Customer field of the Contact entity using the JavaScript onChange event to call an asynchronous event to query the CRM database and update/validate a value based on a user selection:

```
//Check to see if the parentcustomer is populated
if(crmForm.all.parentcustomerid.DataValue != null)
{
    if(crmForm.all.parentcustomerid.DataValue[0].type == '1')
    {
        var xml = "" +
        "<?xml version=\"1.0\" encoding=\"utf-8\"?>" +
        "<soap:Envelope xmlns:soap=\"http://schemas.xmlsoap.org/soap/envelope/\"
xmlns:xsi=\"http://www.w3.org/2001/XMLSchema-instance\"
xmlns:xsd=\"http://www.w3.org/2001/XMLSchema\">" +
        GenerateAuthenticationHeader() +
        "  <soap:Body>" +
        "    <RetrieveMultiple
xmlns=\"http://schemas.microsoft.com/crm/2007/WebServices\">" +
        "      <query xmlns:q1=\"http://schemas.microsoft.com/crm/2006/Query\"
xsi:type=\"q1:QueryExpression\">" +
            //Query against the account entity
        "        <q1:EntityName>account</q1:EntityName>" +
        "        <q1:ColumnSet xsi:type=\"q1:ColumnSet\">" +
        "          <q1:Attributes>" +
            //Check the telephone1 attribute - this can be modified to
            //check any of the telephone fields that exist
```

```
"            <q1:Attribute>telephone1</q1:Attribute>" +
"          </q1:Attributes>" +
"        </q1:ColumnSet>" +
"        <q1:Distinct>false</q1:Distinct>" +
"        <q1:Criteria>" +
"          <q1:FilterOperator>And</q1:FilterOperator>" +
"          <q1:Conditions>" +
"            <q1:Condition>" +
"              <q1:AttributeName>accountid</q1:AttributeName>" +
"              <q1:Operator>Equal</q1:Operator>" +
"              <q1:Values>" +
"                <q1:Value xsi:type=\"xsd:string\">"+
"                    crmForm.all.parentcustomerid.DataValue[0].id +
"                </q1:Value>" +
"              </q1:Values>" +
"            </q1:Condition>" +
"          </q1:Conditions>" +
"        </q1:Criteria>" +
"      </query>" +
"    </RetrieveMultiple>" +
"  </soap:Body>" +
"</soap:Envelope>" +
"";


var xmlHttpRequest = new ActiveXObject("Msxml2.XMLHTTP");


xmlHttpRequest.Open("POST", "/mscrmservices/2007/CrmService.asmx", false);
xmlHttpRe-
quest.setRequestHeader("SOAPAction","http://schemas.microsoft.com/crm/2007/
➥WebServices/RetrieveMultiple");
xmlHttpRequest.setRequestHeader("Content-Type", "text/xml; charset=utf-8");
xmlHttpRequest.setRequestHeader("Content-Length", xml.length);
xmlHttpRequest.send(xml);


var resultXml = xmlHttpRequest.responseXML;
//alert(resultXml.xml);


var accountMainPhone = re
sultXml.selectSingleNode("//BusinessEntity/q1:telephone1");
if(accountMainPhone != null)
{
    var contactBusinessPhone = crmForm.all.telephone1;
```

```
                    //Validate the contact business phone against the account phone
            if(contactBusinessPhone.DataValue != accountMainPhone.text)
            {
                //If not equal then prompt to change it
                if(confirm("Account Main Phone is not equal to Contact Business
Phone. Would you like to change it?"))
                {
                            //User responded affirmatively, so let's update the contact
                            //phone with the account phone information
                    contactBusinessPhone.DataValue = accountMainPhone.text;
                }
            }
        }
    }
}
```

Figure 3.11 shows what happens when you try to set the Parent Customer of a Contact record. The code checks the Business Phone of the Contact against the Main Phone of the Account and prompts for updating of the Contact record.

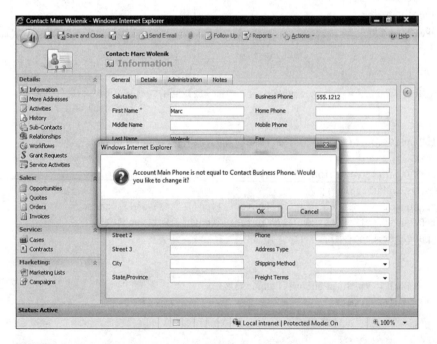

FIGURE 3.11   Microsoft Dynamics CRM with validation across multiple entities.

This example can easily be applied across other entities within the CRM system and is a common request to extend functionality internally.

Example Three: Extending a Form for IFrame Integration

As mentioned previously, there are several considerations when working with IFrames, including the fact that IFrames load asynchronously and are shared across all clients. This example checks whether the user is working offline, and if not, sets the target of the IFrame dynamically.

> **NOTE**
>
> It is important to note that when working with dynamically created IFrames, parameters are not passed to the new URL automatically and the query string parameters need to be appended before setting the src property.

To follow this example, create a new IFrame on the Contact entity, and set the URL on the IFrame URL equal to about:blank. This will open the IFrame to a blank page by default.

Modify the onLoad event for the form and add the following code:

```
Var sURLString = "";
        //Validate if the user is offline or not
        if(IsOnline())
        {
        //Check to see if the form is saved or just being created
        switch (crmForm.FormType)
                {
                //Form is being created - we can't pass anything yet
                case 1:
                //Set to our generic intranet site
                sURLString = "http://intranet";
                break;


                //Form is saved and we have data we can grab
                case 2:
                //Set to the intranet site with content specific to the contact
                sURLString = "http://intranet?contact=";
                //encode and add contact information
                sURLString += encodeURIComponent(crmFORM.all.name.DataValue);
                break;
                }
        }
        //User is not online
        else
        {
        //We can leave the URL as about:blank or change it to an
        //internal URL if we want
```

```
    }
```

```
//Finally set the IFrame URL (be sure to replace <<name>> with the name of
//your IFrame:
crmForm.all.IFRAME_<<name>>.src = sURLString;
```

If the user is online, the intranet site is displayed.

Summary

This chapter covered considerations that need to be given when performing customizations on Microsoft Dynamics CRM.

Our example of IFrame modification is probably the most common example of an internal integration. Because of the out-of-the-box functionality with CRM and its capability to pass parameters to an underlying application, it is incredibly easy to develop an extended platform for Microsoft Dynamics CRM without too much effort.

One consideration that is important when working with IFrames is that they must call an underlying application and, therefore, are limited to both Internet/LAN connectivity (depending on the application location).

Finally, our examples of manipulating data across the CRM application illustrated the flexibility inherent to the application at performing updates using JScript.

Extending Microsoft Dynamics CRM is not limited to the examples provided within this chapter, but the goal is to look at how to make customizations where a number of variables are known, such as your user base, browser version, and requirements.

CHAPTER 4

Silverlight

Introduction

In 2007, Microsoft released a "rich application platform" called Silverlight to allow end users to "light up the web." So what does that really mean? Adobe Flash was one of the first applications to allow web developers to have an interactive platform for the web. But the technology was restricted to client-side data interaction. Microsoft has released Silverlight 2.0 as a web browser plug-in; it is similar to Flash, but adds interaction with server-side technologies and enables control of client multimedia resources (images, movies, sound). Figure 4.1 shows the Silverlight controls and the compatibility between different systems. This extensive platform allows for a bridge between the dynamic data sources and the front-end multimedia experience.

Traditionally, obtaining data required a significant amount of work for client applications (JavaScript and HTML pages); to obtain new information, developers had to do post backs to the server. Because of this excessive work burden, the JavaScript community introduced Asynchronous JavaScript and XML (AJAX), which allows developers to obtain data asynchronously. However, AJAX and XML HTTP controls do not provide a rich interaction with multimedia resources. Microsoft Silverlight overcomes that drawback and allows a bidirectional communication foundation between the interactive multimedia user interface and the server-side data.

Silverlight 2.0 provides interactivity features and support for additional .NET languages. This technology delivers cross-platform experience, which enables developers and business units to provide a single interactive .NET application. Currently, this technology is supported on Windows 2000 and later, Mac OS X, Windows Mobile 6 devices, and

Symbian (Series 60) phones. Table 4.1 shows Silverlight's compatibility with different operating systems and browsers. Table 4.2 shows Silverlight's compatibility with mobile devices.

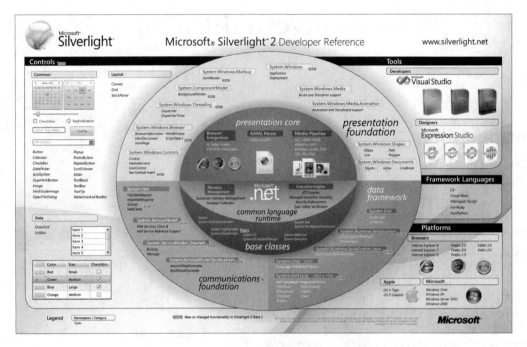

FIGURE 4.1   Developer reference for Microsoft Silverlight.

TABLE 4.1   Desktop Operating Systems and Browsers Supporting Different Versions of Silverlight

	Chrome	IE6	IE7	IE8	Firefox	Safari
Windows 2000	N/A	2.0	N/A	N/A	2.0	2.0
Windows XP	2.0	1.0, 2.0	1.0, 2.0	2.0	1.0, 2.0	1.0, 2.0
Windows Vista	2.0	NA	1.0, 2.0	2.0	1.0, 2.0	1.0, 2.0
Windows Home Server	2.0	NA	1.0, 2.0	2.0	1.0, 2.0	1.0, 2.0
Windows Server 2003	2.0	1.0, 2.0	1.0, 2.0	2.0	1.0, 2.0	1.0, 2.0
Windows Server 2008	2.0	N/A	1.0, 2.0	2.0	1.0, 2.0	1.0, 2.0
Mac OS X PowerPC	N/A	N/A	N/A	N/A	1.0	1.0
Mac OS X Intel	N/A	N/A	N/A	N/A	1.0, 2.0	1.0, 2.0

TABLE 4.2   Mobile Device Operating Systems and Browsers Supporting Different Versions of Silverlight

	Built-in Browser	Firefox Mobile	Opera Mini
Windows Mobile 6.1	2.0	N/A	N/A
Windows Mobile 6.5	2.0	N/A	N/A
Symbian (Series 60) Nokia S60	1.0	N/A	N/A
iPhone	N/A	N/A	N/A

Microsoft is thus attempting to make Silverlight a "people-ready" technology. Silverlight provides a web interface that can interact with the backend database through a service layer. Silverlight enables you to deliver multimedia videos and animation to a cross-browser platform. Silverlight also allows you to retrieve data from multiple sources and provide an integrated experience for end users. Silverlight can also increase team collaboration when integrating various components of Microsoft Dynamics CRM and other third-party systems in a unified location. A great early example of this Silverlight technology was a search engine called Tafiti. (It has been discontinued as of this writing, but the code for it can be found on codeplex.) Tafiti incorporated visuals with common web searches. Searches were presented through a graphic interface, with results appearing in a central column. The left side allowed users to select the type of media to search in (websites, news feeds, books, or images). Results can be dragged and saved on a "shelf" on the right side. Figure 4.2 shows a sample search application built with Silverlight. A number of sites have begun to adopt this technology, and you can view a showcase at http://silverlight.net/Showcase/.

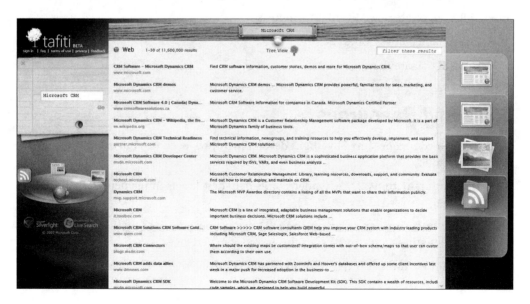

FIGURE 4.2   Sample search application built on Silverlight.

Some of the best uses of CRM and Silverlight are as follows:

- ▶ Custom dashboards
- ▶ Custom CRM GUI
- ▶ Accessing data from several other data sources
- ▶ As an add-on for external-facing systems

Recently, Microsoft announced the availability of Silverlight 3.0 for beta testing. Currently, Silverlight 3.0 contains the following additions to the existing platform:

- ▶ Support for spell checking
- ▶ Support to access PDF files
- ▶ Direct HTML rendering
- ▶ Print capabilities
- ▶ Offline storage (similar to Google Gears)
- ▶ Local database storage (similar to Google Gears)
- ▶ Database synchronization (similar to Google Gears)
- ▶ Access to local hard drive limited to My Documents
- ▶ Administrative access to all of hard drive
- ▶ Support for device access (such as USB)
- ▶ Can drag and drop from the desktop to Silverlight
- ▶ Ability to create new Silverlight windows
- ▶ Inverse kinematics/bones
- ▶ Some 3D capabilities

Tools and Resources

Before we can commence any Silverlight development, we need to understand two different kinds of tools:

- ▶ **Development tools:** Development tools help developers implement a designed solution.
- ▶ **Design and content-creation tools:** Designer tools are used by the graphic designers to design the look and feel of the end-user experience.

You can find these tools at http://www.microsoft.com/silverlight/resources/tools.aspx.

Development Tools

Microsoft Silverlight Tools for Visual Studio 2008 is an add-on for the Visual Studio 2008 development environment that enables the development of Silverlight directly within Visual Studio. You can leverage several features of the Visual Studio tools when creating applications in Silverlight. The Silverlight tools designer support is a subset of the features in the Windows Communication Foundation (WCF) Designer. You can download this from http://www.microsoft.com/downloads/details.aspx?familyid=C22D6A7B-546F-4407-8EF6-D60C8EE221ED&displaylang=en.

Microsoft has a software development kit (SDK) available for Silverlight. This SDK resembles the form and content of most of their technologies and highlights the recommended development methods. This Microsoft Silverlight SDK contains documentation, tools, Silverlight ASP.NET controls, and the libraries required to build Silverlight applications. You can download the SDK from http://msdn.microsoft.com/en-us/silverlight/bb187452.aspx. (The SDK is included in the installation of Microsoft Silverlight Tools for Visual Studio 2008.)

Microsoft has also provided an array of learning mechanisms to help you master Silverlight, which you can access at http://silverlight.net/Learn/.

Design and Content-Creation Tools

Microsoft Expression Studio enables web designers to create the Silverlight interface. Expression tools enable designers to fully apply their creativity while collaborating with developers who are using Microsoft Visual Studio.

Expression Studio comes in many versions and is available as an off-the-shelf product, just like Microsoft Office:

- ▶ Expression Web for building websites
- ▶ Expression Blend for illustration and graphic design
- ▶ Expression Design for creating Silverlight and Windows Presentation Foundation (WPF)-based sites
- ▶ Expression Media for assets management and media encoding
- ▶ Expression Encoder for transcoding video content
- ▶ Expression Studio, which includes all the previously listed functions

Deep Zoom Composer

The Deep Zoom Composer prepares images for use with the Deep Zoom feature in Silverlight 2. The new Deep Zoom technology in Silverlight enables users to see images on the web like never before. The smooth in-place zooming and panning that Deep Zoom allows is a true advancement and raises the bar on what image viewing should be. High-resolution images need to be prepared for use with Deep Zoom, and this tool enables the user to create Deep Zoom composition files that control the zooming experience and then export all the necessary files for deployment with Silverlight 2. Figure 4.3 shows an example of the Deep Zoom interface with three images at different sizes and image control.

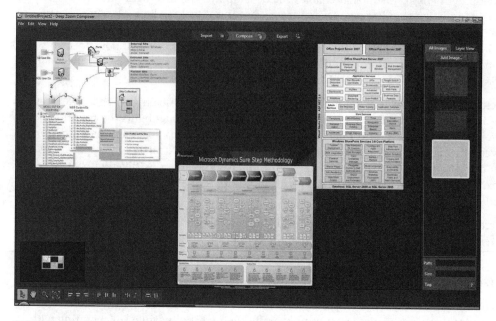

FIGURE 4.3   Deep Zoom Composer application user interface.

Kaxaml

Kaxaml is a lightweight XAML editor that provides a split-screen view of the XAML and the rendered content (as shown in Figure 4.4). This powerful tool enables rapid development of user controls and Silverlight applications. You can find this tool at http://www. kaxaml.com/.

Developing a Basic Silverlight Application

This section walks you through the basic steps necessary to create a project inside Microsoft Visual Studio 2008, using Microsoft Dynamics CRM data and then displaying within Microsoft Dynamics CRM. In this project, we use the Visual Studio add-in for Silverlight. This project is used as a building block for later sections of this chapter. In this foundation project, we build a UI component using a VS.NET project and a data access component using WCF:

1. Open Visual Studio 2008.
2. Select File, New, and then Project.
3. In the Project selection window, select Silverlight Application (as shown in Figure 4.5).
4. Click OK.

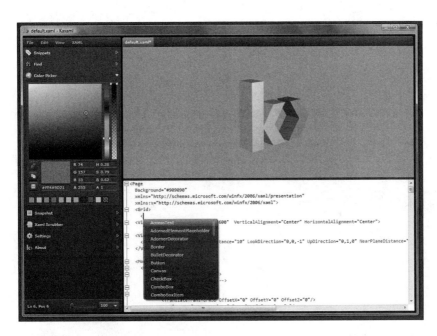

FIGURE 4.4   Kaxaml application user interface.

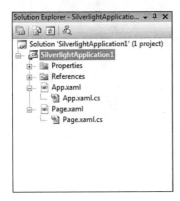

FIGURE 4.5   Project selection in Visual Studio 2008.

5. In the Add Silverlight Application dialog box, select Automatically Generate a Test Page to Host Silverlight at Build Time. For production release, you can attach this to an existing ASP.NET application. By default, this will create two files in the Solution Explorer:

▶ App.xaml is a file used to declare shared resources such as data grids and various style objects. The code behind this file is used for handling global events such as Application_Startup, Application_Exit, and Application_UnhandledException (see Figure 4.6).

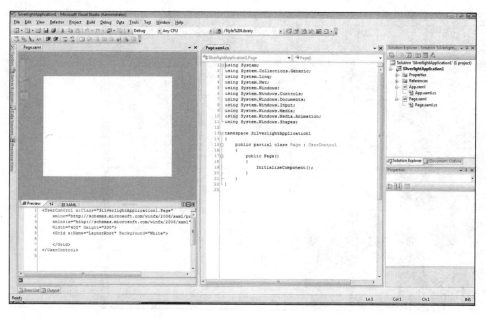

FIGURE 4.6   Show sample app.xaml.

▶ Page.xaml is the default file created. Typically, this is replaced with the new Silverlight page (see Figure 4.7).

FIGURE 4.7   Show sample page.xaml.

Create a WCF project in the same solution. WCF is used as the communication layer for the Silverlight application. WCF supports asynchronous connections between the Silverlight application and the backend data sources. Figure 4.8 shows the communication sequence between the client and the backend when a user is viewing CRM notes on the Account page using Silverlight and all the steps in between.

FIGURE 4.8   Sample of the process to extract data for Silverlight.

1. Right-click the solution and create a new WCF project.
2. Click Add.
3. Select New Project.
4. Select WCF Service Application, as shown in Figure 4.9.

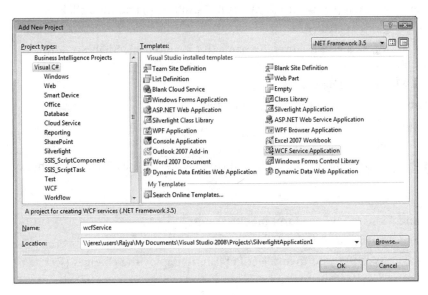

FIGURE 4.9   Select WCF Service Application.

Once the new project is attached to the solution, build the necessary connection to the CRM system, whether it is using web services or direct SQL access. Some organizations prefer direct SQL access for reading, whereas other organizations prefer to use the web services.

NOTE

It is recommended to use Microsoft Dynamics CRM web services to read and write data. However, if your application is only reading data, you can access the SQL views and access data very easily.

Deploying Silverlight Using IFrames

The most common way to integrate the Silverlight application is by using IFrames, which are located either in the main screen of the CRM (possibly used as dashboards) or inside the entity (such as an account summary, a rich note entity, and many others). To set up this feature in Microsoft Dynamics CRM, follow these steps:

1. Open Microsoft Dynamics CRM.
2. Click Customizations on the navigation menu on the left.
3. Click Customize Entities.
4. Open the Accounts entity.
5. Click Forms and Views.
6. Open the form.
7. Click Add a Tab from the Common Tasks list located on the right side.
8. Give it a name (for example, Silverlight Account Dashboard), and then click OK.
9. Navigate to the new tab created.
10. Click Add a Section and give it a friendly name (for example SilverlightSection). Then click OK.
11. Select the newly created IFrame.
12. Click Add an IFrame with the following properties:

    Name: SilverlightIFrame

    URL: http://<<siteURL>>
13. Check the Pass Record Object-Type Code and Unique Identifier as Parameters check box.
14. Click OK.
15. Click Save and Close to save the form modifications.
16. Click Save and Close to save the entity modifications.
17. Click the Accounts entity, and then select Publish, to deploy the changes (see Figure 4.10).

Notes Entity

The built-in notes entity for Microsoft Dynamics CRM stores only the raw text with a date and timestamp. In addition, the notes entity is difficult to search, and you can't copy and

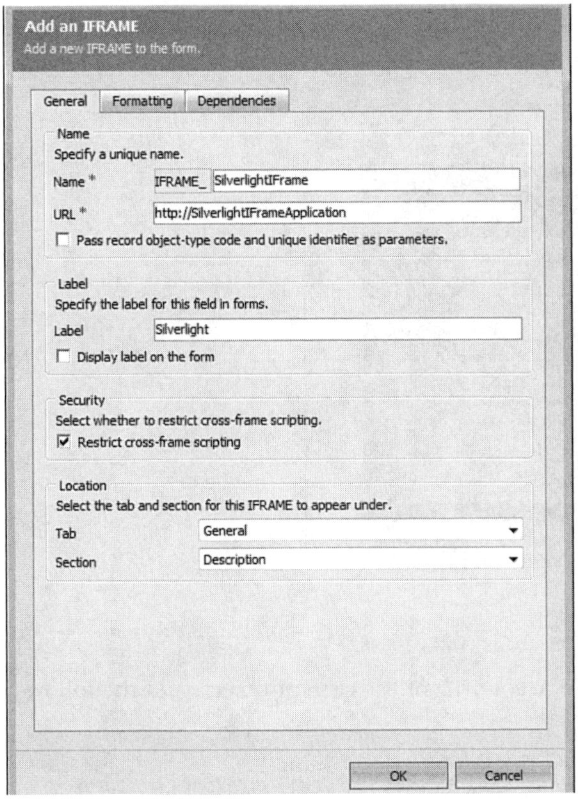

FIGURE 4.10   IFrame Properties page.

paste more than one note at a time. Silverlight can add a multimedia mask on top of the notes entity, which can potentially unlock other features, such as searching, copying and pasting, rich text formatting, inserting images, and much more. Silverlight can also provide a user-friendly interface for end users to view the notes and organize them graphically (see Figure 4.11).

In any Silverlight application, there are two necessary components:

▶ Access to the any data from the Microsoft Dynamics CRM system

▶ A WCF web service layer

Then you build the Silverlight XAML file to add the snazzy user interface.

Building a WCF web service is like building a standard web service. All you need to do is declare a public function called `GetNotesAsync`, which will be located in the WCF template we created earlier in this chapter. The `GetNotesAsync` function is responsible for

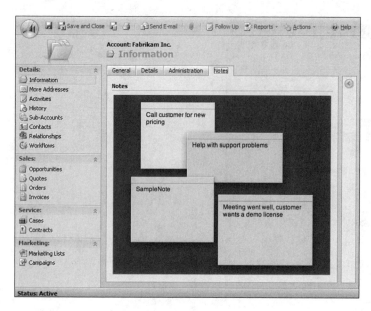

FIGURE 4.11   Sample notes customization.

accessing the related notes based on the AccountID of the current object. Add the following piece of code inside that function:

```
CrmSdk.CrmAuthenticationToken authToken = new CrmAuthenticationToken();
authToken.OrganizationName = "MicrosoftCRM";


CrmSdk.CrmService crmService = new CrmSdk.CrmService();
crmService.Credentials = System.Net.CredentialCache.DefaultCredentials;
crmService.CrmAuthenticationTokenValue = authToken;


QueryExpressionHelper qeHelper = new QueryExpression-Helper
➥(EntityName.annotation.ToString());
qeHelper.Columns.AddColumn("subject");
qeHelper.Criteria.Conditions.AddCondition("objectid", ConditionOperator.Like,
➥Request.QueryString["ObjectId"]);


BusinessEntityCollection annotationRetrieved =
➥service.RetrieveMultiple(qeHelper.Query);


foreach (annotation annotationItem in annotationRetrieved.BusinessEntities)
    writer.Write(annotationItem.nptetext + "<BR>");
```

Add the following lines in page.xaml:

```
<UserControl x:Class="CRMSL2B2.Page"
    xmlns="http://schemas.microsoft.com/winfx/2006/xaml/presentation"
    xmlns:x="http://schemas.microsoft.com/winfx/2006/xaml"
    Width="800" Height="600">
    <StackPanel x:Name="LayoutRoot" Background="White">
        <Button Width="240" Height="25" x:Name="btnGetNotes"
Click="btnGetNotes_Click" >
            <TextBlock>List Notes</TextBlock>
        </Button>
        <ListBox Height="500" Width="500" x:Name="dlNotes"/>
    </StackPanel >
</UserControl>
```

The "code behind" for button will look like this:

```
        System.Windows.Browser.HtmlPage.Window.Alert("Loading...");



        BasicHttpBinding bind = new BasicHttpBinding();
        EndpointAddress endpoint = new EndpointAddress
➥("http://<server>/CRMData/CRMWCF.svc");
        DSvc.CRMWCFDataServiceClient client = new DSvc.CRMWCFClient(bind,
➥endpoint);
        client.getNotesCompleted += new EventHandler
➥<CRMSL2B2.WDS.ListAccountsCompletedEventArgs>(client_getNotesCompleted);
        client.GetNotesAsync();
```

> **NOTE**
>
> It is recommended to add an additional web service layer for security and reliability reasons. Also, it is recommended to build applications loosely coupled and highly cohesive.

After the code has been compiled and deployed, you can integrate that into the CRM using IFrames.

Dashboards

Dashboards represent the number one request of most customers, because there is a huge need to show preaggregated data in a single user interface. You can choose from a number of solutions to accomplish this. Chapter 5, "SharePoint Integration," shows an example of using SharePoint Business Data Catalog (BDC) connections and IFrames to enable this concept, but for now we focus on a couple of easier solutions to show the power of an integrated Silverlight environment. Chapter 5 describes how to build dynamic dashboards.

You can leverage OLAP features of preaggregated data, and use Silverlight to show the data. You can build a custom solution to achieve this in a number of ways, including the following:

- Use off-the-shelf products
- Dundas charts
- Business objects
- Panorama Software
- Cognos
- MicroStrategy
- Build a custom solution

Custom development is inevitable in any company. Every company is run uniquely, and there is always a set of custom attributes for dashboarding.

NOTE

It is recommended to use a product like Dundas Chart for .NET OLAP Services 6.2 (http://www.dundas.com) to help reduce the development and deployment time. This web part can be installed on SharePoint and can communicate with an OLAP cube to allow end users to slice and dice the data in a web browser; they just have to drag and drop the necessary components onto the charts (see Figure 4.12).

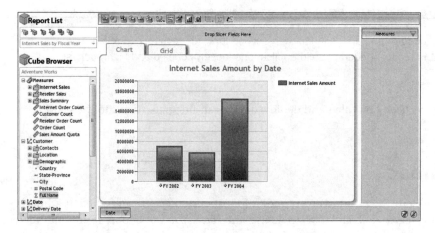

FIGURE 4.12   Sample dashboard built using Dundas web parts.

Summary

This chapter focused on what you need to consider when performing customizations on Microsoft Dynamics CRM for internal use and what that means. Silverlight is a new up-and-coming technology that provides a rich multimedia-based user interface while integrating with multiple data sources.

The example of IFrame modification in this chapter is probably the most common example of an internal integration. Because of the out-of-the-box functionality of CRM and its capability to pass parameters to an underlying application, it is incredibly easy to develop an extended platform for Microsoft Dynamics CRM.

SharePoint Integration

In this chapter, we explain the two main ways that Microsoft Dynamics CRM and Microsoft SharePoint can be integrated and provide a number of examples.

It is important to understand that both Microsoft Dynamics CRM and Microsoft SharePoint are considered enterprise applications and are by no means meant (or able) to replace each other. Instead, because they have such powerful complementary functions, an integrated solution leverages the "best of" offerings that they have.

Introduction

Microsoft SharePoint is both a product and a technology that is used by organizations for collaboration and managing business processes. It provides the following benefits to an organization:

▶ Enterprise search

▶ Workflow

▶ Document management

▶ Auditing

▶ Business intelligence

Microsoft SharePoint can be used as either a platform or as a service (although you can use the services without the platform, the services are required for platform use), and consists of the following products:

▶ Windows SharePoint Services 3.0 (WSS)

▶ Microsoft Office SharePoint Server 2007 (MOSS)

The application product, MOSS 2007, delivers the services that use WSS and has to be paid for, whereas the WSS 3.0 services are free. (They come either with or as an add-on to Windows Servers.)

Microsoft SharePoint uses the following technology:

- ASP.NET 2.0
- Windows Workflow Foundation
- Internet Information Services (IIS)
- SQL Server
- 32- or 64-bit technology

Because of the common technological backbone that exists between SharePoint and Microsoft Dynamics CRM, integration can be achieved with relative efficiency, bringing the kind of functionality described earlier into the Microsoft Dynamics CRM environment.

This chapter guides you through the different ways you can leverage Microsoft SharePoint to deliver a rich, user-friendly, and scalable application that is integrated with Microsoft Dynamics CRM.

Many different integration points exist between SharePoint and Dynamics CRM. A few of the most common are as follows:

- Using SharePoint to retrieve data from the CRM application and display it as a standard table.
- Using SharePoint to retrieve data from the CRM application and display it as a pivot table.
- Using SharePoint to display graphs and charts to present a dashboard.
- SharePoint can also be used as a data repository to store attachments (instead of using the CRM attach feature as part of the notes entity).
- Implementation of a portal solution whereby users interact with SharePoint and CRM data through one interface.

> **NOTE**
>
> The last option (implementation of a portal solution) is partially covered in Chapter 11, "Microsoft CRM Accelerators," because several of the accelerators use an integrated SharePoint environment to deliver functionality.

The following lists show how and when you would use either WSS versus MOSS:

- **WSS**
  - Display data using the Microsoft SharePoint List web part
  - IFrame integration

▶ Store attachments in SharePoint

▶ Custom web parts to display data

▶ Custom solution to store attachments

▶ **MOSS**

  ▶ Display data in the Report Center with key performance indicators (KPIs)

  ▶ Display data using Business Data Catalog (BDC)

  ▶ Search the CRM database using the Search Center in Microsoft Office SharePoint Server

MOSS has many add-on components to complete the Office suite of products. The following servers can be purchased and used independently and added to the Microsoft Office SharePoint Server Standard edition:

▶ Microsoft Office Excel Services

▶ Microsoft Office InfoPath Server

MOSS comes in several different versions, but the most common are these:

▶ Standard

▶ Enterprise

The Enterprise version includes all the options in the Standard version and the add-on components as part of the Microsoft Office Server suite. With all the components combined, the Microsoft Office SharePoint Server Enterprise edition can provide the following functions:

▶ BDC

▶ InfoPath Forms Server

▶ Excel Services

▶ Report Center

▶ Dashboarding

▶ Performance Point Services

See the "Licensing for SharePoint" section later in this chapter for more information about the versions and licensing requirements that may be necessary.

It is important to understand the difference between CRM and SharePoint. Each one of the applications provides complementing technologies:

▶ CRM is focused on structured data; SharePoint is focused on unstructured data.

▶ CRM uses a "top-down" structure requiring a planned hierarchy. CRM is a strategic application that will use the structure year after year.

▶ CRM provides a highly relational datastore. SharePoint provides a flat structure so that it can be used as a list.

▶ CRM is a datastore for business information. SharePoint is a presentation layer for business information and for aggregating business information; SharePoint also provides document management.

Microsoft SharePoint Versions

Microsoft SharePoint is one of the first of a few products that enables end users to collaborate, search, follow business processes, and analyze business data all within the same application. Before choosing the SharePoint product to purchase, you need to understand the features that are part of it.

Table 5.1 lists features of the various SharePoint products.

TABLE 5.1   SharePoint Features

Feature	Windows SharePoint Services 3.0	Search Server 2008 Express	Forms Server 2007	MOSS 2007 Standard	MOSS 2007 Enterprise
Collaboration	X	X	X	X	X
Portals	–	–	–	X	X
Enterprise search	–	X	–	X	X
Enterprise content management	–	–	–	X	X
Forms-driven business processes	–	–	X	–	X
Business intelligence	–	–	–	–	X

Each feature is helpful in its own way and they can increase team productivity collectively or used together to enhance user productivity.

Collaboration

Collaboration refers to a team keeping all the documents in a central location and working together on the task at hand using the centralized documents. SharePoint enables users to store documents, tasks, wikis, blogs, calendars, issue lists, and more in a single location, and all users can subscribe to Really Simple Syndication (RSS) to receive updates on the progress of the current task.

The SharePoint tools for document management are superior to the ones built into Microsoft Dynamics CRM, so Microsoft SharePoint could replace/augment some of the features inside the CRM application to enable more features for the end user.

You could easily replace CRM functionality and instead use SharePoint in the following CRM areas:

- ▶ Announcements

- ▶ Sales literature

- ▶ Account/contact contextual attachments

- ▶ Knowledge base

Table 5.2 shows collaboration features available in the various versions of SharePoint.

TABLE 5.2   SharePoint Collaboration Features

Features	Windows SharePoint Services 3.0	Search Server 2008 Express	Forms Server 2007	MOSS 2007 Standard	MOSS 2007 Enterprise
Real-time presence (available when integrated with Office Communication Server 2007)	X	X	X	X	X
Social networking web parts (public My Site pages to help establish connections between colleagues with common interests)	–	–	–	X	X
Standard site templates	X	X	X	X	X
Wikis	X	X	X	X	X
Blogs	X	X	X	X	X
Calendars (which can synchronize to Outlook)	X	X	X	X	X
Email integration (SharePoint lists can be enabled to receive new postings via email address.)	X	X	X	X	X
Task lists (which can synchronize to Outlook)	X	X	X	X	X
Surveys	X	X	X	X	X
Document library	X	X	X	X	X
Issue tracking template	X	X	X	X	X

Enterprise Search

This feature can index content across multiple data sources, and can provide the search results in a single location with relevance ranking. An example of this is the ability to view customer information along with any related documents, such as running projects, legal agreements, and more.

Table 5.3 lists the search features available with the various versions of SharePoint.

TABLE 5.3   SharePoint Search Features

Features	Windows SharePoint Services 3.0	Search Server 2008 Express	Forms Server 2007	MOSS 2007 Standard	MOSS 2007 Enterprise
Simple user interface (with industry-standard query syntax support)	X	X	X	X	X
Simple search results	X	X	X	X	X
Can search through more than 200 file types, including file shares, websites, SharePoint sites, Exchange public folders, and Lotus Notes databases out of the box (and custom IFilters are possible)	–	X	–	X	X
Relevance (ranking algorithm)	–	X	–	X	X
Granular indexing controls for inclusion and exclusion of certain content	–	X	–	X	X
People search	–	–	–	X	X
Business data search (using the BDC to search data from other data sources)	–	–	–	–	X
Ability to use third-party search products (such as BA-Insight, http://www.ba-insight.net)	–	X	–	X	X

Forms-Driven Business Processes

The Forms Server feature helps streamline business processes. Forms Server enables you to publish InfoPath forms so that they can be used through a web browser.

Forms Server optimizes any business process and enhances tracking possibilities while reducing the need for manual paperwork. For example, one common focal point of almost every organization is Master Data Management (MDM). A workflow can be published through the Forms Server to help manage MDM as follows:

1. There is a single entry point for all changes for the customer record.
2. Multiple sets of approvers can validate different pieces of the information provided. (For example, accounting can verify any purchase order information change, or the shipping department can validate shipping addresses.)
3. When all approvals are complete, the information can then be automatically written to the backend enterprise resource planning (ERP) system.
4. After the ERP has been updated, Forms Server can also update Microsoft Dynamics CRM.

This implementation of business processes helps provide a central location for all customer data management, reduces manual labor in multiple systems, reduces typos, and increases efficiency.

Table 5.4 shows the forms features of the various SharePoint versions.

TABLE 5.4   SharePoint Forms Features

Features	Windows SharePoint Services 3.0	Search Server 2008 Express	Forms Server 2007	MOSS 2007 Standard	MOSS 2007 Enterprise
Browser-based InfoPath forms.	–	–	X	–	X
Centralized forms management.	–	–	X	–	X
InfoPath forms conversion. (Forms designers can design their forms in InfoPath, and SharePoint Forms Server will automatically convert it into ASP.NET web forms.)	–	–	X	–	X
Form Import Wizard (converts forms designed in Excel and Word into InfoPath 2007 forms).	–	–	X	–	X
InfoPath 2007 can publish forms that have no managed code.	–	–	X	–	X
Compatibility Checker (helps forms designers validate those features before deploying the forms).	–	–	X	–	X

Business Intelligence

Microsoft has embedded a lot of new business intelligence (BI) features across multiple applications. In fact, the new buzzword is *BI everywhere*. Access to higher-quality data enables better business decisions. The BI features of Office SharePoint Server 2007 can access data from a vast number of data sources and aggregate them into a single location. Detailed information is available in Chapter 6, "Business Intelligence."

For example, via these features, a user can view the data from a backend ERP system, Microsoft Dynamics CRM, and a home-grown technical support system in a single view. This can reduce time to aggregate the results and decreases the manual work required to aggregate the data. With integration of forms-driven business processes, some business workflows can automatically be triggered, to increase the company's response time.

Table 5.5 shows the BI features in the various versions of SharePoint.

TABLE 5.5   SharePoint BI Features

Features	Windows SharePoint Services 3.0	Search Server 2008 Express	Forms Server 2007	MOSS 2007 Standard	MOSS 2007 Enterprise
Spreadsheet publishing from within Excel 2007 to the Excel Services in SharePoint.	–	–	–	–	X
Share sensitive spreadsheets and preserve the granular security required for your company.	–	–	–	–	X
Excel Services enables end users to use the power of Excel on the web.	–	–	–	–	X
Data connection libraries are centralized document libraries to store Office data connections (ODC) to external data sources	–	–	–	–	X
BDC enables end users to view external data inside the SharePoint Server 2007 environment. Users can also perform other functions on that data.	–	–	–	–	X
Business data web parts enable viewing lists, entities, and related information provided through the BDC.	–	–	–	–	X

TABLE 5.5 SharePoint BI Features

Features	Windows SharePoint Services 3.0	Search Server 2008 Express	Forms Server 2007	MOSS 2007 Standard	MOSS 2007 Enterprise
Business data actions. (With no custom coding, easily create actions that can perform functions on the data—for example, open web pages, or launch InfoPath forms to start a business process.)	–	–	–	–	X
Integrated BI dashboards can provide a single view to many KPIs across the organization, to enable more informed business decisions.	–	–	–	–	X
Report Center is a site template that is the base framework to build a reporting dashboard.	–	–	–	–	X
KPIs can highlight the status of goals to drive faster results.	–	–	–	–	X
Performance Point Dashboard Designer.	–	–	–	–	X

All components mentioned here integrate with Microsoft Dynamics CRM. Several components can be extended, and these leverage the core components of SharePoint to provide an extensible end-user platform.

Using Microsoft Dynamics CRM with Microsoft SharePoint

Different from the previous sections in which we used Microsoft SharePoint as the primary application to display CRM data, this section illustrates how to use Microsoft Dynamics CRM to display data *from* SharePoint (which can contain CRM data if properly integrated).

IFrame Integration Using Static and Dynamic Data from SharePoint

As mentioned in Chapter 3, "Extending Microsoft Dynamics CRM," you can integrate Microsoft Office SharePoint Server and Windows SharePoint Services as an IFrame. There are two possible options for IFrame integration:

▶ Static IFrame integration

▶ Dynamic IFrame integration

Static IFrame Integration

Static IFrame integration is useful when you have to show some static information with each entity (for example, if you want to display, as a tab within the form for accounts, account-naming best practices, or if you want to show the standard opportunity management best practices on the Opportunity screen). Figure 5.1 shows a sample IFrame integration.

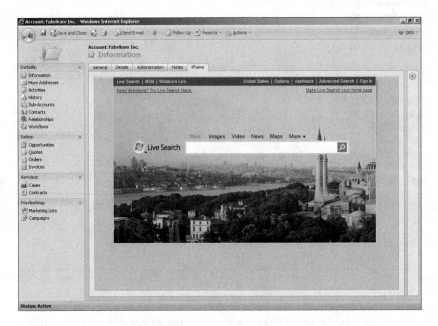

FIGURE 5.1   Sample IFrame integration with Microsoft Dynamics CRM.

You can also use static SharePoint integration to embed SharePoint Search in Microsoft Dynamics CRM (as mentioned earlier in this chapter).

Another common use for static SharePoint integration is for viewing dashboards made in SharePoint. You can build a dashboard using Excel Services, BDC, and PerformancePoint in SharePoint and display that as an integrated view in Microsoft Dynamics CRM.

In the following example, we show you how to integrate a dashboard. (Step-by-step instructions to build a PerformancePoint dashboard are included in Chapter 6, "Business Intelligence.") Once the Dashboard is ready and built in SharePoint, get the appropriate link to the dashboard.

To view the new dashboard, you need to customize Microsoft Dynamics CRM to include the dashboard, as follows:

1. Open the Microsoft Dynamics CRM application.
2. Select Customizations from the left navigation pane.
3. Select Export Customizations.

4. Select Site Map.

5. Select Export Select Customization, and save the file in an easy accessible location.

6. Unzip the recently saved file and extract customization.xml.

7. Open the customization.xml in Visual Studio 2008.

8. Add the following line under the kbarticle entity:

```
<SubArea Id="Dashboard" Title="Dashboard"
Url="http://SharePointServer/CRMDashboard" Icon="/_imgs/
bar_bottom_ico_reports.gif " />
```

9. Save and close the file.

10. Open the Microsoft Dynamics CRM application.

11. Select Customizations from the left navigation pane.

12. Select Import Customizations.

13. Select Browse, and locate the recently modified file.

14. Select Upload.

15. Select Import Selected Customizations.

Now when you refresh the CRM application, there will be a new link under Articles, as shown in Figure 5.2

FIGURE 5.2   Dashboard link in Microsoft Dynamics CRM.

Dynamic IFrame Integration

Dynamic IFrame integration is very similar to static IFrame integration with one major difference: The dynamic integration has a referential link between the two systems that enable users to view record-sensitive data.

For example, when a user opens an account screen, you can create some custom tabs to show additional information from a remote application in the same screen (shown in

Figure 5.3). In the following example, we show you how to open a SharePoint screen that has some web parts that are being filtered by a URL parameter.

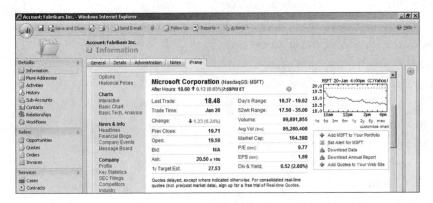

FIGURE 5.3   Account dashboard built using SharePoint available in Microsoft Dynamics CRM.

Before we begin this example, ensure that the SharePoint dashboard can accept URL parameters and can filter the data on the required web parts using the Connections feature in SharePoint. To set up this feature in Microsoft Dynamics CRM, follow these steps:

1. Open the Microsoft Dynamics CRM application.
2. Select Customizations from the left navigation pane.
3. Select Customize Entities.
4. Open the Accounts entity.
5. Select Forms and Views.
6. Open the form.
7. Select Add a Tab from the Common Tasks located on the right side.
8. Give it a name (for example, SharePoint Account Dashboard), and then click OK.
9. Navigate to the new tab created.
10. Select Add a Section, and give it a friendly name (for example, SharePointSection). Then click OK.
11. Select the new IFrame created.
12. Select Add an IFrame with the following properties:

    Name: SharePointIFrame

    URL: about:blank
13. Select Form Properties from the Common Tasks list located on the right side.
14. Select OnLoad.
15. Click Edit.

16. Enter the following code:

```
crmForm.all.tab4Tab.onclick = function()
{
if(crmForm.all.IFRAME_ SharePointIFrame.url.length < 15)
{
crmForm.all.IFRAME_iBASE.url =
"http://SharePointServer/CRMDashboard?AccountNumber=" +
crmForm.all.accountnumber.value;
}
}
```

17. Click OK.

18. Select Save and Close to save the form modifications. Select Save and Close to save the entity modifications.

19. Select the Accounts entity, and then select Publish, to deploy the changes.

The preceding steps will pass the Account Number value to the SharePoint site as a URL variable. The URL variable can be used to filter the data on web parts created using BDC connections (as mentioned earlier in this chapter).

NOTE

The preceding steps will dynamically set the URL property of the IFrame. Using this technique will help optimize initial page load times, and will help preserve end-user experience.

Using Microsoft SharePoint with Microsoft Dynamics CRM Functions

As previously stated, it is not uncommon for organizations to want to use Microsoft SharePoint as the primary application. They might want to for a number of reasons, including the following:

▶ CRM licensing constraints

▶ Existing application integration

▶ Portal usage

▶ Applications that don't need to use the CRM interface (but want to see/work with the CRM data)

For this reason, we have included the following examples to show how to get your data out of Microsoft Dynamics CRM and into Microsoft SharePoint.

Displaying Data in SharePoint Using the List Web Part for Microsoft Dynamics CRM 4.0

A web part is an ASP.NET server control that is used on a web part zone located within web part pages. Web parts can be programmed and can enable users to access the content, appearance, and behavior of the web page within a browser. SharePoint out of the box comes with a few web parts that are supported by Microsoft. Administrators can also either install third-party web parts or custom develop web parts in-house.

Using the Microsoft List web part for Microsoft Dynamics CRM is a way of displaying CRM data inside a SharePoint web part page. The List web part for Microsoft Dynamics CRM 4.0 provides a subset of the Microsoft CRM data and enables users to view it in a list format in a SharePoint dashboard (as shown in Figure 5.4). You can connect multiple web parts together to provide a richer dashboard.

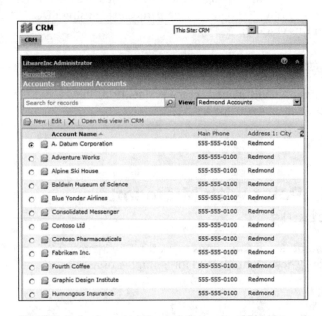

FIGURE 5.4   Sample Microsoft Dynamics CRM List web part.

Microsoft Dynamics CRM List web part was originally released for Microsoft CRM 3.0. This version allowed users to view the data in a simple data list format only, whereas the new version offers the following new features:

▶ Support for Multitenancy.

▶ Can authenticate against CRM Internet-facing deployment (IFD).

▶ Supports Secure Socket Layers (SSL) connections.

▶ Supports both 32-bit and 64-bit SharePoint servers.

▶ Enables users to open the current view in CRM to perform additional actions, such as running reports, creating Quick Campaigns, and more.

▶ Enables field-field connections between two CRM List web parts. This enables end users to select an account and be able to view all leads related to that account in one dashboard. (The Subscriber CRM List web part can automatically filter data using the provider's GUID).

▶ Allows row-row connections to provide data to third-party web parts.

You can download the List Web Part for Microsoft Dynamics CRM from http://www.microsoft.com/downloads/details.aspx?FamilyID=3b6eb884-ec15-4288-a2a3-d0b47e057458&DisplayLang=en.

To install web parts, follow these steps:

1. Log in to the SharePoint server as a farm administrator where you plan to install the List web part for Microsoft Dynamics CRM 4.0. A SharePoint farm can range from a single-server farm to a multiple set of servers. You must also have administrator privileges for the SharePoint Services server.

NOTE

The List web part for Microsoft Dynamics CRM 4.0 requires that Full Trust be enabled on the SharePoint servers.

2. Run the ListWebPart.msi that you downloaded from the link mentioned earlier.

3. On the license agreement page, select Agree.

4. Click Next after selecting the location for installation.

5. Click Finish.

To place web parts on the SharePoint web part page, follow these steps:

1. Navigate to the site where you want to display the web parts.

2. Select Site Actions.

3. Select Add WebPart.

4. Select the web part you want to display (as shown in Figure 5.5).

5. Click OK.

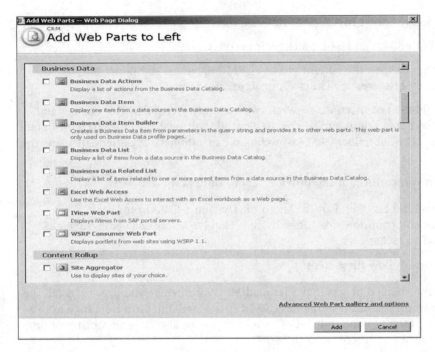

FIGURE 5.5   Adding the Microsoft Dynamics CRM List web part to a web part page.

NOTE

The Microsoft Dynamics CRM List web part can be installed on all versions of SharePoint. These web parts can be connected to each other or to other SharePoint or other web parts, which allows end users to be able to interact with two web parts together. For example, when a user clicks on a list item, the details Web Part will show information based on the user's selection.

Displaying Data Using BDC in Microsoft Office SharePoint Server

The BDC provides a platform layer between Microsoft Office SharePoint and disparate backend systems. This allows an administrator to build sites with data aggregated from multiple data sources and to enable SharePoint search of records in systems other than SharePoint.

For example, suppose that an organization needs a single dashboard to view the following:

▶ Average number of appointments needed to close an opportunity

▶ Average number of follow-up visits needed to close an opportunity

▶ Average number of phone calls needed to close an opportunity

▶ Summary of lead source efficiency

They might use the Analysis Services to consolidate the data and then use BDC to display the data in SharePoint so that the business units can make the necessary business decisions. In this example, it may help optimize the sales process.

Consider another example, for a technical support department in a company to analyze the call volume, resolution satisfaction, and agents' average idle time within a single screen. You can use the following KPIs:

▶ Technical support calls by product

▶ Ticket duration by line of support (first tier, second tier, and so on)

▶ Average ticket duration

▶ Cisco call volume for the technical support queue

▶ Customer satisfaction survey results stored in Microsoft Dynamics CRM

▶ Cisco agent idle time

▶ Schedule efficiency

▶ Self-service utilization and resolution (through the phone system options)

A standard BDC connection can be used to communicate to various data sources, including the following:

▶ SQL Server

▶ Web services

▶ ODBC connections to (Oracle, DB2, MySQL, and many other database systems)

> **NOTE**
>
> As indicated, you must have the Enterprise version of Microsoft Office SharePoint Server to take advantage of BDCs.

The following example demonstrates how to communicate to a Microsoft Dynamics CRM database and access the filtered views of Microsoft Dynamics CRM (discussed in Chapter 3) and shows how to retrieve the Customer list from Microsoft Dynamics CRM in SharePoint using the BDC connection.

> **NOTE**
>
> Microsoft best practices recommend the use of Microsoft Dynamics CRM filtered views when accessing Microsoft Dynamics CRM data, as filtered views enforce permissions (an enforcement unavailable when you access tables directly).
>
> The BDC definition enables SharePoint to retrieve information from Microsoft Dynamics CRM. (BDC is the communication layer between the two systems.)

Our first step is to create the BDC connection. Before we begin, however, you need to understand how the XML is structured for a BDC connection. The XML structure contains the following properties. (For a complete reference, visit http://msdn.microsoft.com/en-us/library/ms566019.aspx.)

▶ LobSystemInstance is where the authentication and connection string is provided.

▶ Entities are the definitions of the business objects that will be used by the end users.

▶ Identifier is used as the primary key for the entities.

▶ Methods are used to interact with the data. The most common methods are used to retrieve data (with names such as Get Customer List or Update Customer Record).

▶ Actions can be used to extend the data to other systems. For example, you can launch a stock research website based on the data from CRM.

▶ Association (optional) can be used to link related entities within a system. For example, you may want to link a Technical Support ticket number to a Cisco call queue.

Here is a standard skeletal structure of a BDC XML file:

```
<?xml version="1.0"?>
<LobSystem
xmlns:xsi="http://www.w3.org/2001/XMLSchema-instance"
xmlns:schemaLocation="http://schemas.microsoft.com/office/2006/03/
➥BusinessDataCatalog BDCMetadata.XSD"
Type="Database"
Version="1.0.0.0"
Name="ExtraTeam_MSCRMLOBSystem"
xmlns="http://schemas.microsoft.com/office/2006/03/BusinessDataCatalog">
  <Properties>...</Properties>
  <LobSystemInstances>
    <LobSystemInstance Name="DatabaseNameInstance">
<Properties>...</Properties>
    </LobSystemInstance>
  </LobSystemInstances>
  <Entities>
   <Entity>
    <Identifiers>...</Identifiers>
    <Methods>...</Methods>
    <Actions>...</Actions>
   </Entity>
  </Entities>
```

Using the connection in this example, we will enable various features, such as letting SharePoint index the Microsoft Dynamics CRM data. We will then use the index data to interact with other applications, such as the phone system and the email system.

In addition, after we have the connection built to the FilteredAccount view in the Microsoft Dynamics CRM database, we can perform the following:

▶ **Establish some method definitions**

    ▶ Get filtered accounts.

    ▶ Filtered-account-specific finder.

    ▶ Insert filtered accounts into the database directly (a function that can be performed through web services, too).

    ▶ Update filtered accounts to the database directly (a function that can be performed through web services, too).

▶ **Identify the custom actions we want to perform with the data**

    ▶ Search Google for the company name.

    ▶ Search MSN for the company address.

    ▶ Send email to the customer.

    ▶ SIC code lookup for the company.

    ▶ Ticker simple lookup.

    ▶ Launch customer website.

    ▶ Call customer's phone.

To create the connection, follow these steps:

1. Create a blank XML file, adding the following basic schema reference to the BDC XSD:

```
<?xml version="1.0"?>
<LobSystem
xmlns:xsi="http://www.w3.org/2001/XMLSchema-instance"
xmlns:schemaLocation="http://schemas.microsoft.com/office/2006/03/
➥BusinessDataCatalog BDCMetadata.XSD"
Type="Database"
Version="1.0.0.0"
Name="ExtraTeam_MSCRMLOBSystem"
xmlns="http://schemas.microsoft.com/office/2006/03/BusinessDataCatalog"
>...
</LobSystem>
```

2. Define any special properties required for the chosen data sources. For database connections, use the following properties.

Property	Type	Comments
WildcardCharacter **Default value, * (asterisk)** **(Not required)**	System.String	The remote-database-specific wildcard string. The wildcard filter replaces * in the search value with this string provided in this tag. This feature will ensure that the users will be trained to use * as a wildcard character, regardless of the backend system. For example, the wildcard in SQL Server is %. So if you input the % value for this property, it will replace all asterisks used in the end-user search with a % value. Note: This value cannot be null or an empty string.
WildcardCharacterEscapeFormat **Default value, \{0}** **(Not required)**	System.String	The wildcard filter escapes are also system-specific. This allows you to pass the asterisk character to the database system. To pass the * character to the database, the user must enter *. Note: This value cannot be null or an empty string.

For web service connections, use the following properties.

Property	Type	Comments
Bl	System.String	URL to a Web Service Discovery document or WSDL file.
WsdlFetch AuthenticationMode **Default value,** RevertToSelf **(Not required)**	Microsoft.Office. Server.Application Registry.System Specific. WebService. HttpAuthentication Mode	Authentication method used to retrieve the WSDL. The allowed values are as follows: PassThrough RevertToSelf Credentials WindowsCredentials
WsdlFetchSsoProvider Implementation **(Required if** WsdlFetch AuthenticationMode is either Credentials or WindowsCredentials)	System.String	Fully qualified type name of the ISsoProvider. Note: The SSO provider can be used to access other data sources such as SalesForce and SiebelOnDemand. For more information, view the connection details.

Property	Type	Comments
WsdlFetchSso ApplicationId **(Required if** WsdlFetch AuthenticationMode is either Credentials or WindowsCredentials)	System.String	Fully qualified type name of the ISsoProvider. Note: The SSO provider can be used to access other data sources such as SalesForce and SiebelOnDemand. For more information, view the connection details.
WebServiceProxy Namespace **(Required)**	System.String	Namespace to which to generate web service proxy classes.
WebServiceProxy Protocol **Default value,** Soap **(Not required)**	System.String	Proxy protocol used when calling the web service. The allowed values are as follows: Soap Soap12 HttpPost HttpGet HttpSoap
WebServiceProxyType **(Not required)**	System.String	This enables the developers to enter a fully qualified name of a type to use instead of automatically generating a web service proxy. If this property is set, a web service proxy will not be generated. This is useful when proxy generation fails, and it is simpler to manually compile the proxy and install it in the global assembly cache (GAC) and reference it with this property. This is really useful when accessing a system that is not developed by Microsoft. (This can be used with the Siebel On Demand web services.) Note: If you use the WebServiceProxyType property, the TypeDescriptor TypeNames need to be fully qualified type names. Note: The Assembly must be a subclass HttpWebClientProtocol.

5

For example, SQL Server uses the % character as a wildcard character. Add the following lines inside the LobSystem tags:

```
<Properties>
<Property Name="WildcardCharacter" Type="System.String">%</Property>
    </Properties>
```

3. Define the LobSystem instance (the communication string to the data source). For a database connection, use the following properties.

Property	Type	Comments
AuthenticationMode Default value, RevertToSelf (Not required)	Microsoft.Office.Server. ApplicationRegistry. SystemSpecific.Db. DbAuthenticationMode	Authentication method used to retrieve the data from the database. The allowed values are as follows: PassThrough RevertToSelf Credentials WindowsCredentials
DatabaseAccessProvider Default value, SqlServer (Not required)	Microsoft.Office.Server. ApplicationRegistry. SystemSpecific.Db. DbAccessProvider	Data provider required to gain access to the backend database. The allowed values are as follows: SqlServer OleDb Oracle Odbc
SsoProviderImplementation (Required if AuthenticationMode is Credentials or WindowsCredentials)	System.String	Fully qualified type name of the ISsoProvider. Note: This has to be Microsoft Single Sign-on provider.
SsoApplicationId (Not required)	System.String	Microsoft SharePoint Single Sign-on ID of the SSO enterprise application definition, which stores the credentials used to connect to the database.

Property	Type	Comments
RdbConnection Data Source RdbConnection Initial Catalog RdbConnection Integrated Security RdbConnection Pooling (Not required)	System.String	Properties prefixed with RdbConnection are automatically considered as a database connection properties. For example, the RdbConnection Data Source property is the same as the Data Source property in the database connection.
NumberOfConnections Default value, -1 (Not required)	System.Int32	Maximum number of concurrent connections to allow for this connection. -1 means unlimited connections are allowed. The allowed values are as follows: Either -1 or any positive integer
SecondarySsoApplicationId (Not required)	System.String	Microsoft SharePoint Single Sign-on ID of the SSO enterprise application definition, which stores the credentials used to connect to the database.

For web service connections, use the following properties.

Property	Type	Comments
WebServiceAuthenticationMode Default value, RevertToSelf (Not required)	System.String	Authentication mode used to invoke web service methods. The allowed values are as follows: PassThrough RevertToSelf Credentials WindowsCredentials
SsoProviderImplementation (Required if WsdlFetchAuthenticationMode is Credentials or WindowsCredentials)	System.String	Fully qualified type name of the ISsoProvider. Note: This has to be Microsoft Single Sign-on provider.

Property	Type	Comments
WebServiceSsoApplicationId (Required if WsdlFetchAuthenticationMode is Credentials or WindowsCredentials)	System.String	Microsoft SharePoint Single Sign-on ID of the SSO enterprise application definition, which stores the cred entials used to connect to the database.
WebProxyServerConfiguration (Not required)	System.String	Proxy server URL to send/receive the request for WSDL.
NumberOfConnections Default value, -1 (Not required)	System.Int32	Maximum number of concurrent connections to allow for this connec- tion. -1 means unlimited connec- tions are allowed. The allowed values are as follows: Either -1 or any positive integer
SecondarySsoApplicationId (Not required)	System.String	Microsoft SharePoint Single Sign-on ID of the SSO enterprise application definition, which stores the creden- tials used to connect to the data- base.
WebServiceUrlOverride (Not required)	System.String	Overrides the URL used to access the web service. This is useful when you are debugging against a devel- opment system.

NOTE

In this case, we are using pass-through authentication. Be sure to set the appropriate authentication mechanism required by your DBA.

Add the following lines after the Properties section:

```
<LobSystemInstances>
 <LobSystemInstance Name="ExtraTeam_MSCRMInstance">
  <Properties>
   <Property Name="DatabaseAccessProvider" Type="System.String">
   SqlServer
   </Property>
   <Property Name="AuthenticationMode" Type="System.String">
```

```
    PassThrough
    </Property>
    <Property Name="RdbConnection Data Source" Type="System.String">
    CRMSQL
    </Property>
    <Property Name="RdbConnection Initial Catalog" Type="System.String">
    ExtraTeam_MSCRM
    </Property>
    <Property Name="RdbConnection Integrated Security" Type="System.String">
    SSPI
    </Property>
    <Property Name="RdbConnection Pooling" Type="System.String">
    False
    </Property>
    </Properties>
   </LobSystemInstance>
  </LobSystemInstances>
```

4. Define the custom entities used for displaying data. Typically, each entity is related to a data set (for example, one entity for the Accounts list, a different entity for the Opportunity list).

   Add the following lines after defining the LobSystemInstances:

```
<Entities>
<Entity EstimatedInstanceCount="0" Name="dbo.FilteredAccount">
...
</Entity>
</Entities>
```

5. Define the identifiers for the entity. In the CRM database, the AccountId is the key identifier. If you have a complex database and would like to use a surrogate key, list multiple identifiers; the BDC subsystem will honor that request.

NOTE

All identifiers for entities in the CRM system are in the form of [EntityName]id.

Add the following lines inside the recently created entity:

```
<Identifiers>
 <Identifier TypeName="System.String" Name="[accountid]" />
</Identifiers>
```

6. Create a section for the methods required for this data source.

NOTE

The Methods section provides the end-user actions that can be performed on the items in a BDC list (for example, launch a search to an external source for the current row).

Add the following lines after defining the Identifiers sections:

```
<Methods>...</Methods>
```

7. Within the Methods section, list the methods and the properties associated with them. In our example, we are going to list the following for methods:

a. Get Filtered Accounts. This function will let you query the SQL view with a few SQL filters. The account name has been set up to accept wildcards in the search string, and the others are defined to use direct comparison to the data in SQL.

Add the following lines inside the Methods tags:

```
<Method Name="Getdbo.[FilteredAccount]">
  <Properties>
    <Property Name="RdbCommandText" Type="System.String">
Select
[accountid], [accountnumber], [address1_city], [address1_country],
[address1_line1], [address1_line2], [address1_line3], [address1_name],
[address1_postalcode] , [address1_telephone1], [address1_telephone2],
[createdbyname], [createdon], [emailaddress1], [emailaddress2],
[industrycodename], [modifiedbyname], [modifiedon], [name],
[owneridname], [parentaccountidname],[sic], [telephone1], [telephone2],
[telephone3], [tickersymbol], [websiteurl]
From dbo.[FilteredAccount]
Where
([owneridname] LIKE @OwnedBy)
and ([accountnumber] LIKE @AccountNumber)
and ([name] LIKE @AccountName)
    </Property>
    <Property Name="RdbCommandType" Type="System.Data.CommandType">Text
➥</Property>
  </Properties>
  <FilterDescriptors>
    <FilterDescriptor Type="Wildcard" Name="Account Name" />
    <FilterDescriptor Type="Comparison" Name="Account Number" />
    <FilterDescriptor Type="Comparison" Name="Owned By" />
  </FilterDescriptors>
  <Parameters>
    <Parameter Direction="In" Name="@OwnedBy">
      <TypeDescriptor
TypeName="System.String"
Name="owneridname"
```

```
AssociatedFilter="Owned By">
      <DefaultValues>
        <DefaultValue
  MethodInstanceName="dbo.[FilteredAccount]Finder"
  Type="System.String">
   Rajya Bhaiya
</DefaultValue>
       </DefaultValues>
      </TypeDescriptor>
     </Parameter>
     <Parameter Direction="In" Name="@AccountNumber">
      <TypeDescriptor
TypeName="System.String"
Name="accountnumber"
AssociatedFilter="Account Number">
      <DefaultValues>
        <DefaultValue
  MethodInstanceName="dbo.[FilteredAccount]Finder"
  Type="System.String">
   11111111
</DefaultValue>
       </DefaultValues>
      </TypeDescriptor>
     </Parameter>
     <Parameter Direction="In" Name="@AccountName">
      <TypeDescriptor
TypeName="System.String"
Name="name"
AssociatedFilter="Account Name">
      <DefaultValues>
        <DefaultValue
  MethodInstanceName="dbo.[FilteredAccount]Finder"
  Type="System.String">
   ExtraTeam
</DefaultValue>
       </DefaultValues>
      </TypeDescriptor>
     </Parameter>
     <Parameter Direction="Return" Name="dbo.[FilteredAccount]">
      <TypeDescriptor
TypeName="System.Data.IDataReader, System.Data, Version=2.0.3600.0,
➥Culture=neutral, PublicKeyToken=b77a5c561934e089"
IsCollection="true"
Name="dbo.[FilteredAccount]DataReader">
      <TypeDescriptors>
        <TypeDescriptor
```

5

```
      TypeName="System.Data.IDataRecord, System.Data, Version=2.0.3600.0,
➥Culture=neutral, PublicKeyToken=b77a5c561934e089"
   Name="dbo.[FilteredAccount]DataRecord">
       <TypeDescriptors>
         <TypeDescriptor TypeName="System.String" Name="accountid"
➥IdentifierName="[accountid]" />
         <TypeDescriptor TypeName="System.String" Name="accountnumber" />
         <TypeDescriptor TypeName="System.String" Name="address1_city" />
         <TypeDescriptor TypeName="System.String" Name="address1_country" />
         <TypeDescriptor TypeName="System.String" Name="address1_line1" />
         <TypeDescriptor TypeName="System.String" Name="address1_line2" />
         <TypeDescriptor TypeName="System.String" Name="address1_line3" />
         <TypeDescriptor TypeName="System.String" Name="address1_name" />
         <TypeDescriptor TypeName="System.String" Name="address1_postalcode" />
         <TypeDescriptor TypeName="System.String" Name="address1_telephone1" />
         <TypeDescriptor TypeName="System.String" Name="address1_telephone2" />
         <TypeDescriptor TypeName="System.String" Name="createdbyname" />
         <TypeDescriptor TypeName="System.String" Name="createdon" />
         <TypeDescriptor TypeName="System.String" Name="emailaddress1" />
         <TypeDescriptor TypeName="System.String" Name="emailaddress2" />
         <TypeDescriptor TypeName="System.String" Name="industrycodename" />
         <TypeDescriptor TypeName="System.String" Name="modifiedbyname" />
         <TypeDescriptor TypeName="System.String" Name="modifiedon" />
         <TypeDescriptor TypeName="System.String" Name="name" />
         <TypeDescriptor TypeName="System.String" Name="owneridname" />
         <TypeDescriptor TypeName="System.String" Name="parentaccountidname" />
         <TypeDescriptor TypeName="System.String" Name="sic" />
         <TypeDescriptor TypeName="System.String" Name="telephone1" />
         <TypeDescriptor TypeName="System.String" Name="telephone2" />
         <TypeDescriptor TypeName="System.String" Name="telephone3" />
         <TypeDescriptor TypeName="System.String" Name="tickersymbol" />
         <TypeDescriptor TypeName="System.String" Name="websiteurl" />
       </TypeDescriptors>
     </TypeDescriptor>
    </TypeDescriptors>
   </TypeDescriptor>
  </Parameter>
 </Parameters>


 <MethodInstances>
  <MethodInstance
Name="dbo.[FilteredAccount]Finder"
Type="Finder"
ReturnParameterName="dbo.[FilteredAccount]" ReturnTypeDescriptor
➥Name="dbo.[FilteredAccount]DataReader" ReturnTypeDescriptorLevel="0" />
```

```
  </MethodInstances>
</Method>
```

b. Get Specific Accounts. This function will be used by the action we will define as follows.

Add the following lines inside the Methods tags:

```
<Method Name="dbo.[FilteredAccount]SpecificFinder">
 <Properties>
  <Property Name="RdbCommandText" Type="System.String">
Select
[accountid], [accountnumber], [address1_name], [name], [owneridname],
[emailaddress1], [telephone1], [websiteurl], [tickersymbol], [sic]
From dbo.[FilteredAccount]
Where (accountid=@accountid)</Property>
  <Property Name="RdbCommandType" Type="System.Data.CommandType">
Text
  </Property>
 </Properties>
 <Parameters>
  <Parameter Direction="In" Name="@accountid">
   <TypeDescriptor
TypeName="System.String"
Name="[accountid]"
IdentifierName="[accountid]" />
  </Parameter>
  <Parameter Direction="Return" Name="dbo.[FilteredAccount]">
   <TypeDescriptor
TypeName="System.Data.IDataReader, System.Data, Version=2.0.3600.0,
➥Culture=neutral, PublicKeyToken=b77a5c561934e089"
IsCollection="true"
Name="dbo.[FilteredAccount]DataReader">
    <TypeDescriptors>
     <TypeDescriptor
TypeName="System.Data.IDataRecord, System.Data, Version=2.0.3600.0,
➥Culture=neutral, PublicKeyToken=b77a5c561934e089"
Name="dbo.[FilteredAccount]DataRecord">
      <TypeDescriptors>
       <TypeDescriptor
TypeName="System.String"
Name="accountid"
IdentifierName="[accountid]" />
       <TypeDescriptor TypeName="System.String" Name="accountnumber" />
       <TypeDescriptor TypeName="System.String" Name="address1_name" />
```

5

```
          <TypeDescriptor TypeName="System.String" Name="name" />
          <TypeDescriptor TypeName="System.String" Name="owneridname" />
          <TypeDescriptor TypeName="System.String" Name="emailaddress1" />
          <TypeDescriptor TypeName="System.String" Name="telephone1" />
          <TypeDescriptor TypeName="System.String" Name="websiteurl" />
          <TypeDescriptor TypeName="System.String" Name="tickersymbol" />
          <TypeDescriptor TypeName="System.String" Name="sic" />
        </TypeDescriptors>
      </TypeDescriptor>
    </TypeDescriptors>
  </TypeDescriptor>
 </Parameter>
</Parameters>
<MethodInstances>
 <MethodInstance
Name="dbo.[FilteredAccount]SpecificFinder"
Type="SpecificFinder"
ReturnParameterName="dbo.[FilteredAccount]"
ReturnTypeDescriptorName="dbo.[FilteredAccount]DataReader"
ReturnTypeDescriptorLevel="0" />
</MethodInstances>
</Method>
```

c. Insert Accounts. This function can insert data back into SQL Server.

NOTE

Inserting directly into the database is not supported, so consider using a web services connection instead.

Add the following lines inside the Methods tags:

```
<Method Name="insertdbo.FilteredAccount">
 <Properties>
  <Property Name="RdbCommandText" Type="System.String">
Insert into dbo.FilteredAccount) Values);
select SomethingToReturn = @@Identity
  </Property>
  <Property Name="RdbCommandType" Type="System.String">Text</Property>
 </Properties>
 <Parameters>
  <Parameter Direction="Return" Name="dbo.FilteredAccount">
   <TypeDescriptor TypeName="System.String" Name="SomethingToReturn" />
  </Parameter>
 </Parameters>
```

```
<MethodInstances>
 <MethodInstance
Name="dbo.FilteredAccountInserter"
Type="GenericInvoker"
ReturnParameterName="dbo.FilteredAccount" />
 </MethodInstances>
</Method>
```

d. Update Accounts. This function can update CRM data directly in the SQL Server. Add the following lines inside the Methods tags:

```
<Method Name="updatedbo.FilteredAccount">
 <Properties>
  <Property Name="RdbCommandText" Type="System.String">
Update dbo.FilteredAccount
SET WHERE([accountid]=@accountid);
select SomethingToReturn = @@Identity
   </Property>
  <Property Name="RdbCommandType" Type="System.String">Text</Property>
 </Properties>
 <Parameters>
  <Parameter Direction="In" Name="@accountid">
   <TypeDescriptor TypeName="System.String" Name="accountid" />
  </Parameter>
  <Parameter Direction="Return" Name="dbo.FilteredAccount">
   <TypeDescriptor TypeName="System.String" Name="SomethingToReturn" />
  </Parameter>
 </Parameters>
 <MethodInstances>
  <MethodInstance
Name="dbo.FilteredAccountUpdater"
Type="GenericInvoker"
ReturnParameterName="dbo.FilteredAccount" />
 </MethodInstances>
</Method>
```

8. Create a section for the actions required for this data source.

   Add the following lines after defining the Methods sections:

   ```
   <Actions>...</Actions>
   ```

9. Within the Actions section, list the actions and the properties associated with them.

   a. Perform an MSN search with the account name in a new window.

   Add the following lines inside the Actions tags:

   ```
   <Action Name="MSN Search" Position="1" IsOpenedInNewWindow="true"
   Url="http://search.msn.co.uk/results.aspx?q={0}" ImageUrl="">
   ```

```
<ActionParameters>
 <ActionParameter Name="name" Index="0" />
</ActionParameters>
</Action>
```

b. Perform a Google search with the account name in a new window.

Add the following lines inside the Actions tags:

```
<Action Name="Google Search" Position="2" IsOpenedInNewWindow="true"
Url="http://www.google.com/search?q={0}" ImageUrl="">
 <ActionParameters>
  <ActionParameter Name="name" Index="0" />
 </ActionParameters>
</Action>
```

c. Send an email to the primary email address listed.

Add the following lines inside the Actions tags:

```
<Action Name="Email Action" Position="3" IsOpenedInNewWindow="true"
Url="Mailto:{0}" ImageUrl="">
 <ActionParameters>
  <ActionParameter Name="emailaddress1" Index="0" />
 </ActionParameters>
</Action>
```

d. Open a website URL listed in the account entity in the current window, in a new window.

Add the following lines inside the Actions tags:

```
<Action Name="Launch Website" Position="4" IsOpenedInNewWindow="true"
Url="{0}" ImageUrl="">
 <ActionParameters>
  <ActionParameter Name="websiteurl" Index="0" />
 </ActionParameters>
</Action>
```

e. Look up SIC code description from the government site in the current window.

Add the following lines inside the Actions tags:

```
<Action Name="SIC Code lookup" Position="5" IsOpenedInNewWindow="false"
Url="http://www.osha.gov/pls/imis/sicsearch.html?p_sic={0}" ImageUrl="">
 <ActionParameters>
  <ActionParameter Name="sic" Index="0" />
 </ActionParameters>
</Action>
```

f. Show the stock ticker for the current company in a new window.

Add the following lines inside the Actions tags:

```
<Action Name="Google Stock lookup" Position="6" IsOpenedInNewWindow="true"
Url="http://finance.google.com/finance?q={0}" ImageUrl="">
 <ActionParameters>
  <ActionParameter Name="tickersymbol" Index="0" />
 </ActionParameters>
</Action>
```

g. Call the primary phone number listed in the account with a single click (as shown in Figure 5.6).

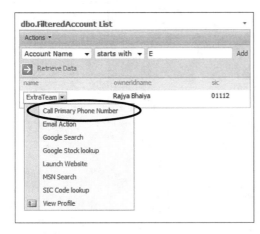

FIGURE 5.6   CTI integration between SharePoint, Dynamics CRM, Office Communication Server, and a Cisco phone system.

NOTE

This feature requires Office Communication Server 2007 be installed and integrated with the phone system.

Be sure to check Chapter 7, "Digital Phone Integration."

Add the following lines inside the Actions tags:

```
<Action Name="Call Primary Phone Number" Position="7" IsOpenedInNew
↪Window="false" Url="tel:{0};phone-context=dialstring" ImageUrl="">
 <ActionParameters>
  <ActionParameter Name="telephone1" Index="0" />
 </ActionParameters>
</Action>
```

After you have created the BDC connection file, import the application definition in the shared service provider to start consuming the data, as follows:

1. Log in to the SharePoint Service provider for the web application you want to display the data in.

2. Select Import Application Definition in the Business Data Catalog section, as shown in Figure 5.7.

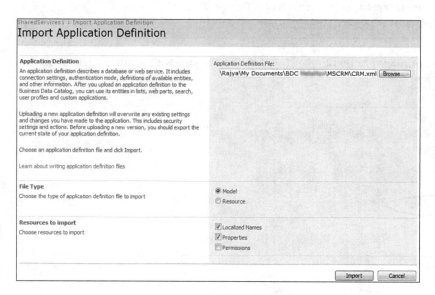

FIGURE 5.7   BDC configuration window, showing the import mechanism.

3. Browse and locate the file recently created.

4. Select Import.

After the application has been imported, you can navigate to the BDC Applications to manage the security for the newly created data set (as shown in Figure 5.8).

You can drill through and view the entity information, which shows the various methods, actions, and filters we created (as shown in Figure 5.9). Note that we have allowed content crawling. Therefore, the SharePoint indexing engine will index this data and provide the results in the Search Center.

Now to build the KPI dashboard, you will need to add the BDC on the user browser; there is one last step. We need to drop the web part on the user screens.

Microsoft offers the following web parts as part of the standard install of Microsoft Office SharePoint Server 2007 Enterprise edition:

▶ **Business Data List web part:** Displays a list of entity instances from a business application registered in the BDC.

▶ **Business Data Item web part:** Displays the details of an entity instance from a business application.

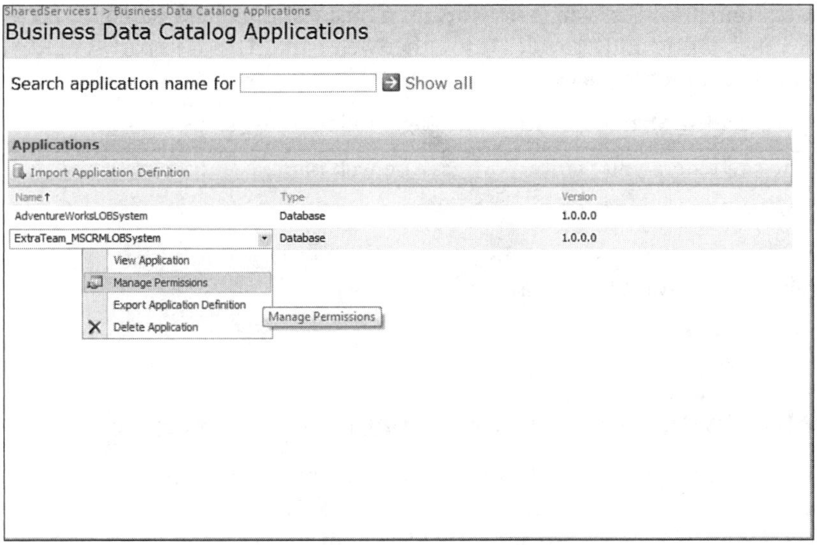

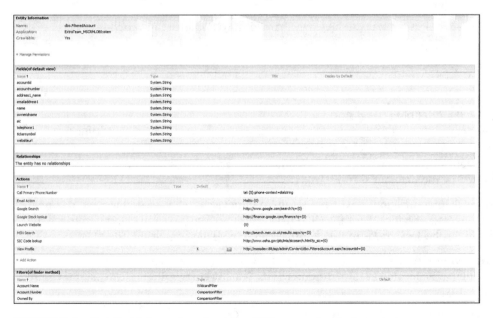

FIGURE 5.8   BDC configuration window, showing security control for the data sets.

FIGURE 5.9   Detailed information about the BDC connection just created.

▶ **Business Data Related List web part:** Displays a list of related entity instances from a business application.

▶ **Business Data Actions web part:** Displays a list of actions associated with an entity as defined in the BDC.

▶ **Business Data Item Builder web part:** Creates a business data item based on parameters in the query string and provides it to other web parts. This web part is used only on business data profile pages.

To place the web parts on the SharePoint web part page, follow these steps:

1. Navigate to the site where you want to display the web parts.

2. Select Site Actions.

3. Select Add WebPart.

4. Select the web part you want to display.

5. Click OK.

Content Searching with Microsoft Office SharePoint Server

The search feature in Microsoft Dynamics CRM provides only basic string matching against certain attributes, and cannot search document context, unless the content resides in CRM, such as CRM knowledge base articles. Using the built-in index and query services in Microsoft Office SharePoint Server Enterprise edition can empower users for a better search mechanism.

There are two possible ways to leverage SharePoint to enhance the search feature:

▶ Indexing the CRM data using BDC

▶ CRM Accelerator

Indexing the CRM Data Using BDC

To configure this, you have to first identify the entities and attributes you want to search using Microsoft Office SharePoint Server. After you have identified all the entities, you must establish the connection between SharePoint and Microsoft CRM using the BDC (as explained in the previous section).

After the BDC connections have been set up to retrieve data, it is recommended to configure a Search Center specifically for the CRM data. This uses a single connection to retrieve the data and display in SharePoint lists, for the search indexing engine and the KPIs.

Search Center is used to enter query requests. By default, the Search Center includes the following pages, located at /SearchCenter/Lists/SearchCenter/AllItems.aspx (as shown in Figure 5.10):

▶ **Default.aspx:** Default home for the Search Center

▶ **Advanced.aspx:** Customizable for adding custom properties to filter the search results

▶ **People.aspx:** To search for people in the SharePoint profile database

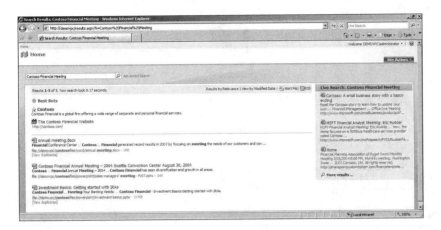

FIGURE 5.10   Microsoft SharePoint Search Center.

The Search Results list displays the results from the query requested in the Search Center pages. By default, this list includes the following pages, located at /SearchCenter/Lists/ SearchResults/AllItems.aspx:

▶ **Results.aspx:** Default page with best bets, keywords, and the actual results page

▶ **Peopleresults.aspx:** Results page for the people

Customize Search Center

Using the Search Center in a Microsoft SharePoint System is a fast way to get to the customer records efficiently. An example is an organization that uses SAP, Microsoft Dynamics CRM, BusinessObjects, and a home-grown software application. For end users to search everything about a customer, they will be required to go to all those locations to get the full history about the customer. The Search Center can provide a single interface to search across several systems, to increase end-user productivity (see Figure 5.11).

In this example, we create a page in the Search Center and the Search Results to filter the results to the data returned from the BDC connection to Microsoft Dynamics (in the current example, refining the results to the CRM accounts). This can be enhanced to include other data sources, too, if desired.

Create the SharePoint search page and tab, as shown in Figure 5.12:

1. Open the SharePoint List for the SearchCenter Tab control located at /SearchCenter/SearchCenter/AllItems.aspx.

2. Click the New link.

3. In the Tab Name field, enter `Microsoft Dynamics CRM`.

4. In the Page field, enter MSCRM.aspx.

5. Click OK.

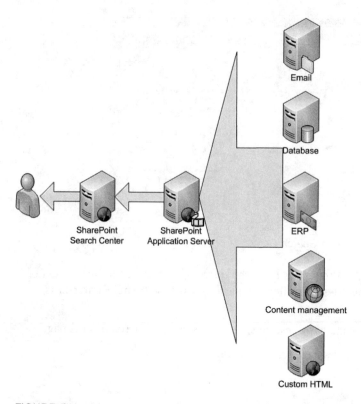

FIGURE 5.11   Microsoft SharePoint Search Center flow.

FIGURE 5.12   Tabs in Microsoft SharePoint Search Center.

Implement and customize the tabs on the search page as follows:

1. Open the Microsoft Dynamics CRM search page.
2. Click the Add a WebPart link in the top zone.
3. Select Search Box, and then click Add.
4. Select the drop-down arrow in the Search Box web part.
5. Select Modify Shared WebPart.
6. Expand the Scope Dropdown section in the tool pane.
7. In the Dropdown Mode list, select Do Not Show Scopes.
8. Expand the Miscellaneous section.

9. Select the Target Search Results Page URL Override field.

10. Click the ellipsis (...) button to open the Text Entry window for this field.

11. Replace the URL Results.aspx with `MSCRMResults.aspx`.

12. Click OK to save your changes.

After the Search Center has been created, we need to create the search results page:

1. Open the SharePoint List for the SearchResults tab control located at /SearchCenter/SearchResults/AllItems.aspx.

2. Click the New link.

3. In the Tab Name field, enter Microsoft Dynamics CRM Results.

4. In the Page field, enter MSCRMResults.aspx.

5. Click OK.

Now implement and customize the tabs on the search results page:

1. Open the Microsoft Dynamics CRM Results page.

2. Click the Add a WebPart link in the top zone.

3. Select Search Box, and then click Add.

4. Select the drop-down arrow in the Search Box web part.

5. Select Modify Shared WebPart.

6. Expand the Scope Dropdown section in the tool pane.

7. In the Dropdown Mode list, select Do Not Show Scopes.

8. Expand the Miscellaneous section.

9. Select the Target Search Results Page URL Override field.

10. Click the ellipsis (...) button to open the Text Entry window for this field.

11. Replace the URL Results.aspx with `MSCRMResults.aspx`.

12. Click OK to save your changes.

13. Click the Add a WebPart link in the middle left zone.

14. Select Search Core Results.

15. Click Add.

16. Select the drop-down arrow in the Search Core Results web part.

17. Select Modify Shared WebPart.

18. Expand the Results Query Options section in the tool pane.

19. Select the Selected Columns field.

20. Select the ellipsis (...) button to open the Text Entry window for this field.

21. Replace the existing XML for the Selected Columns property with the following:

```
<root xmlns:xsi="http://www.w3.org/2001/XMLSchema-instance">
  <SelectColumns>
    <Column Name="Rank"/>
    <Column Name="AccountName"/>
```

```
      <Column Name="AccountNumber"/>
      <Column Name="AccountTerritory"/>
      <Column Name="AccountAddress1Name"/>
      <Column Name="AccountModifiedDate"/>
      <Column Name="CollapsingStatus"/>
      <Column Name="HitHighlightedSummary"/>
      <Column Name="HitHighlightedProperties"/>
    </SelectColumns>
  </root>
```

22. Click OK to return to the tool pane.

23. Click Data Form WebPart to display the XSL Editor.

24. Click the Source Editor button to open the Text Entry window for the web part's XSL property.

25. Replace the contents of the XSL property with the following XSLT code:

```
<?xml version="1.0" encoding="utf-8" ?>
<!DOCTYPE xsl:stylesheet [
  <!ENTITY nbsp " ">
  <!-- white space in XSL -->
]>
<xsl:stylesheet version="1.0" xmlns:xsl="http://www.w3.org/1999/XSL/Transform"
>  <xsl:param name="ResultsBy" />
  <xsl:param name="ViewByUrl" />
  <xsl:param name="ViewByValue" />
  <xsl:param name="IsNoKeyword" />
  <xsl:param name="IsFixedQuery" />
  <xsl:param name="ShowActionLinks" />
  <xsl:param name="MoreResultsText" />
  <xsl:param name="MoreResultsLink" />
  <xsl:param name="CollapsingStatusLink" />
  <xsl:param name="CollapseDuplicatesText" />
  <xsl:param name="AlertMeLink" />
  <xsl:param name="AlertMeText" />
  <xsl:param name="SrchRSSText" />
  <xsl:param name="SrchRSSLink" />
  <xsl:param name="DisplayDiscoveredDefinition" select="True" />
  <!-- When there is a keyword to issue the search -->
  <xsl:template name="dvt_1.noKeyword">
    <span class="srch-description">
      <xsl:choose>
        <xsl:when test="$IsFixedQuery">        Please set the Fixed Query
➥property for the WebPartWebpart.  </xsl:when>
        <xsl:otherwise>        Enter one or more words to search for in the
search box.   </xsl:otherwise>
      </xsl:choose>
```

```
      </span>
    </xsl:template>
    <!-- When an empty result set is returned from search -->
    <xsl:template name="dvt_1.empty">
      <div class="srch-sort">
        <xsl:if test="$AlertMeLink and $ShowActionLinks">
          <img src="/_layouts/images/bell.gif" border="0" height="9" width="9" />
          <span class="srch-alertme" >
            <a href ="{$AlertMeLink}" id="CSR_AM1" title="{$AlertMeText}">
              <xsl:value-of select="$AlertMeText" />
            </a>
          </span>
        </xsl:if>
        <xsl:if test="string-length($SrchRSSLink) &gt; 0 and $ShowActionLinks">
          <xsl:if test="$AlertMeLink">      ¦   </xsl:if>
          <span class="ms-rssfeed">
            <a type="application/rss+xml" href ="{$SrchRSSLink}"
➥title="{$SrchRSSText}" id="CSR_SR">
              <xsl:value-of select="$SrchRSSText"/>
            </a>
          </span>
        </xsl:if>
      </div>
      <br/>
      <br/>
      <span class="srch-description" id="CSR_NO_RESULTS">
        No results matching your search were found.    <ol>
          <li>Check your spelling. Are the words in your query spelled
➥correctly?</li>
          <li>Try using synonyms. Maybe what you're looking for uses slightly
different words.</li>
          <li>Make your search more general. Try more general terms in place of
➥specific ones.</li>
          <li>Try your search in a different scope. Different scopes can return
➥different results.</li>
        </ol>
      </span>
    </xsl:template>
    <!-- Main body template. Sets the Results view (relevance or date)
➥options. -
->
    <xsl:template name="dvt_1.body">
      <div class="srch-results">
        <xsl:if test="$ShowActionLinks">
          <div class="srch-sort">
            <xsl:value-of select="$ResultsBy" />
```

```xml
          <xsl:if test="$ViewByUrl">
          ¦       <a href ="{$ViewByUrl}" id="CSR_RV" title="{$ViewByValue}">
              <xsl:value-of select="$ViewByValue" />
            </a>
          </xsl:if>
          <xsl:if test="$AlertMeLink">
          ¦       <img src="/_layouts/images/bell.gif" border="0" height="9"
width="9" />    <span class="srch-alertme" >
            <a href ="{$AlertMeLink}" id="CSR_AM2" title="{$AlertMeText}">
              <xsl:value-of select="$AlertMeText" />
            </a>
          </span>
          </xsl:if>
          <xsl:if test="string-length($SrchRSSLink) &gt; 0">
          ¦       <span class="ms-rssfeed">
            <a type="application/rss+xml" href ="{$SrchRSSLink}"
➥title="{$SrchRSSText}" id="CSR_SR">
              <xsl:value-of select="$SrchRSSText"/>
            </a>
          </span>
          </xsl:if>
        </div>
        <br />
      </xsl:if>
      <xsl:apply-templates />
      <br />
      <br />
    </div>
    <xsl:call-template name="DisplayMoreResultsAnchor" />
  </xsl:template>
  <!-- This template is called for each result -->
  <xsl:template match="Result">
    <xsl:variable name="id" select="id"/>
    <xsl:variable name="url" select="url"/>
    <span class="srch-Title">
      <xsl:value-of select="accountname"/>
      <br/>
    </span>
    <div class="srch-Description">
      <xsl:choose>
        <xsl:when test="hithighlightedsummary[. != '']">
          <xsl:call-template name="HitHighlighting">
            <xsl:with-param name="hh" select="hithighlightedsummary" />
          </xsl:call-template>
        </xsl:when>
        <xsl:when test="description[. != '']">
```

```
                      <xsl:value-of select="accountdescription"/>
                  </xsl:when>
               </xsl:choose>
           </div >
           <span class="srch-URL">
             <a href="{$url}" id="{concat('CSR_U_',$id)}" title="{$url}">
                 <xsl:choose>
                    <xsl:when test="hithighlightedhroperties/HHUrl[. != '']">
                       <xsl:call-template name="HitHighlighting">
                          <xsl:with-param name="hh"
select="hithighlightedhroperties/HHUrl" />
                       </xsl:call-template>
                    </xsl:when>
                    <xsl:otherwise>
                       <xsl:value-of select="url"/>
                    </xsl:otherwise>
                 </xsl:choose>
             </a>
           </span>
           <p class="srch-Metadata">
             <xsl:call-template name="DisplayString">
                <xsl:with-param name="str" select="AccountTerritory" />
                <xsl:with-param name="prop">Territory:</xsl:with-param>
             </xsl:call-template>
             <xsl:call-template name="DisplayString">
                <xsl:with-param name="str" select="AccountAddress1Name" />
                <xsl:with-param name="prop">Address Name:</xsl:with-param>
             </xsl:call-template>
             <xsl:call-template name="DisplayString">
                <xsl:with-param name="str" select="accountnumber" />
                <xsl:with-param name="prop">Account Number:</xsl:with-param>
             </xsl:call-template>
           </p>
       </xsl:template>
       <xsl:template name="HitHighlighting">
         <xsl:param name="hh" />
         <xsl:apply-templates select="$hh"/>
       </xsl:template>
       <xsl:template match="ddd">   &#8230;   </xsl:template>
       <xsl:template match="c0">
         <b>
           <xsl:value-of select="."/>
         </b>
       </xsl:template>
       <xsl:template match="c1">
         <b>
```

```
        <xsl:value-of select="."/>
      </b>
  </xsl:template>
  <xsl:template match="c2">
    <b>
        <xsl:value-of select="."/>
      </b>
  </xsl:template>
  <xsl:template match="c3">
    <b>
        <xsl:value-of select="."/>
      </b>
  </xsl:template>
  <xsl:template match="c4">
    <b>
        <xsl:value-of select="."/>
      </b>
  </xsl:template>
  <xsl:template match="c5">
    <b>
        <xsl:value-of select="."/>
      </b>
  </xsl:template>
  <xsl:template match="c6">
    <b>
        <xsl:value-of select="."/>
      </b>
  </xsl:template>
  <xsl:template match="c7">
    <b>
        <xsl:value-of select="."/>
      </b>
  </xsl:template>
  <xsl:template match="c8">
    <b>
        <xsl:value-of select="."/>
      </b>
  </xsl:template>
  <xsl:template match="c9">
    <b>
        <xsl:value-of select="."/>
      </b>
  </xsl:template>
  <!-- A generic template to display string with non zero (0) string length
(used for author and last-modified time) -->
  <xsl:template name="DisplayString">
```

```
    <xsl:param name="str" />
    <xsl:param name="prop" />
    <xsl:if test='string-length($str) &gt; 0'>
    ¦¦  <xsl:value-of select="$prop" />    <xsl:value-of select="$str"
/>
    </xsl:if>
  </xsl:template>
  <!-- document collapsing link setup -->
  <xsl:template name="DisplayCollapsingStatusLink">
    <xsl:param name="status"/>
    <xsl:param name="url"/>
    <xsl:if test="$CollapsingStatusLink">
      <xsl:choose>
        <xsl:when test="$status=1">
          <br/>
          <xsl:variable name="CollapsingStatusHref" select="concat(substring-
➡before($CollapsingStatusLink, '$$COLLAPSE_PARAM$$'), 'duplicates:&quot;',
$url,'&quot;', substring-after($CollapsingStatusLink,
➡'$$COLLAPSE_PARAM$$'))"/>
          <span class="srch-dup">
            [<a href="{$CollapsingStatusHref}">
              <xsl:value-of select="$CollapseDuplicatesText"/>
            </a>]
          </span>
        </xsl:when>
      </xsl:choose>
    </xsl:if>
  </xsl:template>
  <!-- The "view more results" for fixed query -->
  <xsl:template name="DisplayMoreResultsAnchor">
    <xsl:if test="$MoreResultsLink">
      <a href="{$MoreResultsLink}" id="CSR_MRL">
        <xsl:value-of select="$MoreResultsText"/>
      </a>
    </xsl:if>
  </xsl:template>
  <xsl:template match="All_Results/DiscoveredDefinitions">
    <xsl:variable name="FoundIn" select="DDFoundIn" />
    <xsl:variable name="DDSearchTerm" select="DDSearchTerm" />
    <xsl:if test="$DisplayDiscoveredDefinition = 'True' and string-
length($DDSearchTerm) &gt; 0">
      <script language="javascript">function ToggleDefinitionSelection()     {
var selection = document.getElementById("definitionSelection");          if
➡(selection.style.display == "none")       {          selection.style.display
➡="inline";       }       else       {          selection.style.display
➡="none";       }    }    </script>
```

```
      <div>
        <a href="#" onclick="ToggleDefinitionSelection(); return false;">
          What people are saying about <b>
            <xsl:value-of select="$DDSearchTerm"/>
          </b>
        </a>
        <div id="definitionSelection" style="display:none;">
          <xsl:for-each select="DDefinitions/DDefinition">
            <br/>
            <br/>
            <xsl:variable name="DDUrl" select="DDUrl" />
            <xsl:value-of select="DDStart"/>
            <b>
              <xsl:value-of select="DDBold"/>
            </b>
            <xsl:value-of select="DDEnd"/>
            <br/>
            <xsl:value-of select="$FoundIn"/>
            <a href="{$DDUrl}">
              <xsl:value-of select="DDTitle"/>
            </a>
          </xsl:for-each>
        </div>
      </div>
    </xsl:if>
</xsl:template>
<!-- XSLT transformation starts here -->
<xsl:template match="/">
  <xsl:variable name="Rows" select="/All_Results/Result" />
  <xsl:variable name="RowCount" select="count($Rows)" />
  <xsl:variable name="IsEmpty" select="$RowCount = 0" />
  <xsl:if test="$AlertMeLink">
    <input type="hidden" name="P_Query" />
    <input type="hidden" name="P_LastNotificationTime" />
  </xsl:if>
  <xsl:choose>
    <xsl:when test="$IsNoKeyword = 'True'" >
      <xsl:call-template name="dvt_1.noKeyword" />
    </xsl:when>
    <xsl:when test="$IsEmpty">
      <xsl:call-template name="dvt_1.empty" />
    </xsl:when>
    <xsl:otherwise>
      <xsl:call-template name="dvt_1.body"/>
    </xsl:otherwise>
  </xsl:choose>
```

```
        </xsl:template>
        <!-- End of Stylesheet -->
    </xsl:stylesheet>
```

26. Click OK to return to the tool pane.

27. Click OK to save the changes to the web part.

NOTE

All features mentioned are available in the Microsoft Office SharePoint Server and Microsoft Search Server. As mentioned in the first section of this chapter, the SharePoint search component can be purchased as a separate product called Microsoft Search Server 2008.

CRM Accelerators Inside SharePoint

Microsoft has recently released several CRM accelerators. Some of these accelerators can be used to extract and display information in SharePoint.

The available accelerators are as follows:

- ▶ Analytics

- ▶ eService

- ▶ Event Management

- ▶ Enterprise Search

- ▶ Sales Methodologies

- ▶ Extended Sales Forecasting

- ▶ CRM Notifications

- ▶ Business Productivity

Chapter 11, "Microsoft CRM Accelerators" describes these accelerators in greater detail.

Custom SharePoint Development

Microsoft has provided two very extendable frameworks: the Microsoft SharePoint and the Microsoft CRM APIs. The two systems have a lot of their APIs exposed (the details can be found on the MSDN site), which can allow developers to automate business processes for nearly every business permutation. (See, for example, Figure 5.13.) The APIs for both systems enable developers to accomplish numerous things. For example, an application can be created to trigger a forms-based workflow inside SharePoint when an attribute changes in Microsoft Dynamics CRM. The possibilities are endless via custom development.

FIGURE 5.13   Custom web part showing CRM data on Live Search Maps with Cisco integration.

The Microsoft Dynamics CRM (http://msdn.microsoft.com/en-us/library/bb928212.aspx) SDK contains architectural information about the entity and security model. The SDK also contains sample code for the following features:

▶ Server-side code

▶ Custom business logic

▶ Integration modules

▶ Workflow assemblies

▶ Customizing the web client using scripting

▶ Reference for the user interface style guide

The Microsoft SharePoint APIs (http://msdn.microsoft.com/en-us/library/ms441339.aspx) enable developers to create modules for the following components:

▶ The server-side object model allows developers to interact with the MOSS and WSS components directly (for example, populating data in Microsoft Dynamics CRM after a series of approvals on the data stored in a SharePoint list).

▶ The web services definition is the recommended mode of communication with Dynamics CRM and SharePoint.

▶ The Collaborative Application Markup Language (CAML) is an optimized way of retrieving data from SharePoint.

▶ You can use workflows to encapsulate business processes that can be attached to SharePoint lists in Windows SharePoint services.

▶ The Create Custom Field Types option is a way to store custom data types inside SharePoint for further integration (for example, creating a data type for a geographic information system (GIS), also known as a maps integration).

▶ Search APIs provide direct access to the query objects and Query web service to retrieve search results.

▶ Web part documentation elaborates the possibilities shown in this book with detailed examples.

To expedite web part development, Microsoft has provided a starter kit for the following development environments:

▶ **Visual Studio 2005, called Windows SharePoint Services 3.0 Tools:** Visual Studio 2005 extensions (available for download at http://www.microsoft.com/downloads/details.aspx?familyid=3E1DCCCD-1CCA-433A-BB4D-97B96BF7AB63&displaylang=en)

▶ **Visual Studio 2008, called Windows SharePoint Services 3.0 Tools:** Visual Studio 2008 extensions (available for download at http://www.microsoft.com/downloads/details.aspx?familyid=7BF65B28-06E2-4E87-9BAD-086E32185E68&displaylang=en)

Open Visual Studio and create a new project using the WebPart template. This will create a basic web part shell, with a deployment package. The basic WebPart template has the following code inside it:

```
using System;
using System.Runtime.InteropServices;
using System.Web.UI;
using System.Web.UI.WebControls;
using System.Web.UI.WebControls.WebParts;
using System.Xml.Serialization;


using Microsoft.SharePoint;
using Microsoft.SharePoint.WebControls;
using Microsoft.SharePoint.WebPartPages;


namespace WebPart1
{
    [Guid("e499bfed-b3d8-4bcf-9d03-642337145800")]
    public class WebPart1 : System.Web.UI.WebControls.WebParts.WebPart
    {
        public WebPart1()
        {
        }


        protected override void CreateChildControls()
        {
            base.CreateChildControls();


            // TODO: add custom rendering code here.
            // Label label = new Label();
```

```
        // label.Text = "Hello World";
        // this.Controls.Add(label);
    }
  }
}
```

Using the basic template, you can just enter the following lines of code inside the Render function. The following lines of code will show a list of accounts, where the account name starts with ExtraTeam (as shown in Figure 5.14):

```
CrmSdk.CrmAuthenticationToken authToken = new CrmAuthenticationToken();
authToken.OrganizationName = "MicrosoftCRM";


CrmSdk.CrmService crmService = new CrmSdk.CrmService();
crmService.Credentials = System.Net.CredentialCache.DefaultCredentials;
crmService.CrmAuthenticationTokenValue = authToken;


QueryExpressionHelper qeHelper = new
QueryExpressionHelper(EntityName.account.ToString());
qeHelper.Columns.AddColumn("name");
qeHelper.Criteria.Conditions.AddCondition("name", ConditionOperator.Like,
➥"ExtraTeam%");


BusinessEntityCollection accountsRetrieved =
service.RetrieveMultiple(qeHelper.Query);


foreach (account accountItem in accountsRetrieved.BusinessEntities)
    writer.Write(accountItem.name + "<BR>");
```

NOTE

It is recommended to separate the application into separate functions and classes based on the requirements.

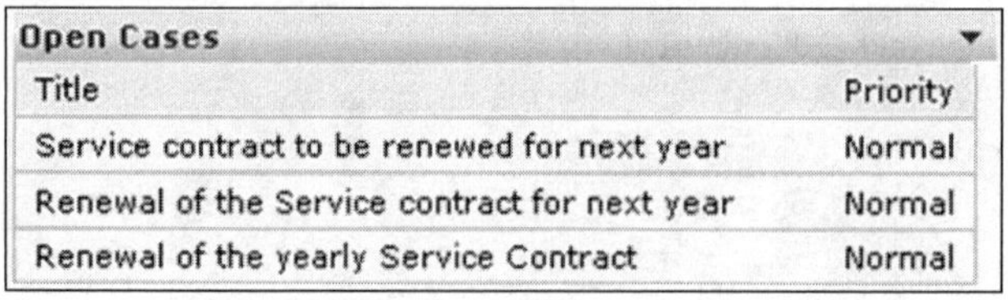

Open Cases	▼
Title	Priority
Service contract to be renewed for next year	Normal
Renewal of the Service contract for next year	Normal
Renewal of the yearly Service Contract	Normal

FIGURE 5.14   Custom web part showing CRM data.

Store Attachments in SharePoint Using a Custom Solution

SharePoint is one of the market leaders for a document management and collaboration solution. This feature can be used with Microsoft Dynamics CRM to increase team productivity in organizations. For example, although you can attach documents as notes in Microsoft Dynamics CRM, that capability has inherent limitations. You cannot, for instance, search the contents of the attachments using the built-in features. Therefore, there is a strong need to leverage the document management and search capabilities of SharePoint inside Microsoft Dynamics CRM because we are offloading the storage of document attachments to SharePoint.

In this example, we show you how to manage and access the documents stored in SharePoint. We create a separate entity in Microsoft Dynamics CRM that will allow us to have the same document linked to multiple entities in the CRM. For this example, you need to do the following:

- ▶ Create a custom button at the top of the entity in which you want to store the document integration.

   - ▶ Create a site to hold the document libraries.*

   - ▶ Create a document library to hold the documents.*

- ▶ Create a new entity in Microsoft Dynamics CRM to store the ID for the document.

   - ▶ Attribute for the OrganizationID

   - ▶ Attribute for the entity linked to the document in CRM

   - ▶ Attribute for the EntityID

   - ▶ Attribute for the SharePoint site URL storing the document library

   - ▶ Attribute for the SharePoint document library storing the document

   - ▶ Attribute for the SharePoint DocumentID

- ▶ Create a custom ASPX application to upload documents into SharePoint.

- ▶ Customize the isv.config inside the Microsoft Dynamics CRM to show a new attachments link.

- ▶ Add a new tab in the entity to show the documents for that entity using URL filtering inside SharePoint.

This can be automatic, to manage growth of the number of documents that will be stored.

To create a SharePoint site, follow these steps:

1. Open the SharePoint website in a web browser.
2. On the top navigation bar, select Sites to open the site directory.
3. On the Site Actions menu, click Create Site.
4. Enter the following information to create the site:

   Title: `CRM Document Store`

   Description: `To store documents for CRM attachments`

   URL: `http://<SharePoint Server>/SiteDirectory/CRMDocuments`

   Permissions: `Use the same permissions as the parent site`
5. Click the Show link on the top navigation bar.
6. Select the site categories in which to display the site directory.
7. Select a blank template to use as a basis for the site.

To create a document library, follow these steps:

1. Navigate to the new site.
2. On the top link bar, click Site Actions.
3. Select Create.
4. On the Create page, select Document Library, and enter the following informa-tion:

   Name: `CrmDocLib1`

   Description: `Document library to store attachments`
5. In the Navigation section, click Yes to put a link to this document library on the Quick Launch bar.

To create a column in a SharePoint document library, follow these steps:

1. Select the Settings drop-down.
2. Select Create Column.
3. Enter the following properties:

   Column name: `CRMRecordID`

   Type: `Single or multiple lines of text`

To create a new entity in Microsoft Dynamics CRM, follow these steps:

1. Open the Microsoft Dynamics CRM application.
2. In the navigation pane, click Settings.
3. Select Customization.
4. Select Customize Entities.
5. Click New and enter the following for the values:

   Display name: `CRMAttachment`

Plural name: `CRMAttachments`

Ownership: `Select organization`

Duplicate detection: `Ensure this is not selected`

Relationships: `Ensure that notes and activities are not selected`

Areas: `Select details`

6. Select the Primary Attribute tab, and enter the following values:

Display name: `AttachmentID`

Requirement level: `Set to No Constraint`

7. Click Save.

To create the custom attributes, follow these steps:

1. Open the Microsoft Dynamics CRM application.

2. In the navigation pane, click Settings.

3. Select Customization.

4. Select Customize Entities.

5. Open the newly created entity.

6. Under Details, click Attributes.

7. Select New and enter the following values:

Display name: `CRMRecordID`

`Name: CRMRecordID`

Requirement level: `Select No Constraint`

Searchable: `Select No`

Type: `Nvarchar`

IME mode: `Auto`

8. Select Save and Close to close the attribute form.

9. Repeat the steps 7 and 8 for the following attributes:

▶ Attribute storing the CRM organization name (useful when there are multiple organizations)

Display name: `OrganizationID`

`Name: OrganizationID`

Requirement level: `Select No Constraint`

Searchable: `Select No`

Type: `Nvarchar`

IME mode: `Auto`

▶ Attribute storing the name of the entity to which this attachment belongs

Display name: `EntityName`

Name: `EntityName`

Requirement level: `Select No Constraint`

Searchable: `Select No`

Type: `Nvarchar`

IME mode: `Auto`

▶ SharePoint URL hosting as the SharePoint repository (In this example, the value should be `http://<SharePoint Server>/SiteDirectory/CRMDocuments.`)

Display name: `SharePointURL`

Name: `SharePointURL`

Requirement level: `Select No Constraint`

Searchable: `Select No`

Type: `Nvarchar`

IME mode: `Auto`

▶ Document library for the document (In this example, the value should be CrmDocLib1.)

Display name: `DocumentLibraryName`

Name: `DocumentLibraryName`

Requirement level: `Select No Constraint`

Searchable: `Select No`

Type: `Nvarchar`

IME mode: `Auto`

▶ Attribute storing the SharePoint document ID (in case a reverse lookup is required)

Display name: `SharePointDocumentID`

Name: `SharePointDocumentID`

Requirement level: `Select No Constraint`

Searchable: `Select No`

Type: `Nvarchar`

IME mode: `Auto`

To create the ASPX file for uploading the documents, follow these steps:

1. Open Visual Studio (either 2005 or 2008).
2. Select File.
3. Select New.
4. Select Projects.
5. Select Visual C#.
6. Select ASP.NET Web Application, and enter the following values:

   Name: `SharePointCRMUploader`

   Solution name: `SharePointCRMUploader`
7. Click OK.
8. On the Solution Explorer, right-click the project and select Add Web Reference, with the following properties:

   URL dialog: `http://<SharePoint`
   `➥Server>/siteDirectory/CRMDocuments/_vti_bin/lists.asmx`

   Web service name: SharePointListsService
9. Select Add Reference, to close the dialog box.
10. Open the Default.aspx.cs file and enter the following lines of code for the Upload button click:

```csharp
protected void UploadButton_Click(object sender, EventArgs e)
        {
            SharePointListsService.Lists listService
= new SharePointListsService.Lists();


            listService.Credentials
= System.Net.CredentialCache.DefaultCredentials;
            listService.URL
= Request.QueryString["SharePointURL"];


            string fileName = Path.GetFileName(
fileAttachment.PostedFile.FileName);
            byte[] content;
            using (
Stream fileReader
= fileAttachment.PostedFile.InputStream)
            {
                content = new byte[fileReader.Length];
                fileReader.Read(
content,
0,
fileAttachment.PostedFile.ContentLength
```

```
);
        }
        listService.AddAttachment(
            Request.QueryString["DocumentLibraryName"],
            Request.QueryString["SharePointDocumentID"],
            fileName,
            content
            );
}
```

11. Follow the necessary steps to sign, build, and deploy the project according to Microsoft standards.

NOTE

This can be made into a web part rather than a standalone ASPX application. A web part is simpy an ascx control surrounded by a SharePoint framework. That SharePoint framework lets users interact with the web part to perform basic functions (such as Close web part, Audience targeting, and inheriting cascading style sheets). A web part framework will also allow developers to be able to create connectible web parts, with other objects on the site.

To customize the isv.config to add the custom attachment link example shown previously, follow these steps:

1. Open the Microsoft Dynamics CRM application.

2. In the navigation pane, click Settings.

3. Select Customization.

4. Select Export Customizations.

5. Select ISV Config.

6. Select Export Selected Customizations, and save the zip in an accessible location.

7. Extract the XML file, and open in an XML editor of your choice.

8. Add the following lines of code in the entities where you want the Add Attachment button to show:

```
<Button
Icon="/_imgs/AttachmentIcon.gif"
  Url="http://<serverURL>/<UploadApplication>"
WinParams=""
WinMode="2"
>  <Titles>
    <Title LCID="1033" Text="Test" />
  </Titles>
  <ToolTips>
```

```
      <ToolTip LCID="1033" Text="Info on Test" />
    </ToolTips>
  </Button>
```

9. Select Customization.

10. Select Import Customization.

To configure SharePoint to accept a URL for filtering data, follow these steps. (Before you can configure the CRM, ensure that the QueryString web part is connected to the document library.)

1. Navigate to the new site.

2. On the top link bar, click Site Actions.

3. Select Edit Page.

4. Drag and drop the QueryString web part.

5. Configure the web part with the name of the URL parameter defined as CRMRecordID.

6. Click OK.

7. Select the drop-down arrow on the top right of the web part, and select Connections.

8. Select Get Filter Values From to connect the document library.

9. Select Exit Edit Mode.

In the following steps, we create an IFrame for each entity with the URL filter, This will show the SharePoint portal application inside Microsoft Dynamics CRM. Follow these steps to achieve this integration:

1. Open the Microsoft Dynamics CRM application.

2. Select Customizations from the left navigation pane.

3. Select Customize Entities.

4. Open the Accounts entity.

5. Select Forms and Views.

6. Open the form.

7. Select Add a Tab from the Common Tasks list located on the right side.

8. Give it a name (for example, Attachments), and then click OK.

9. Navigate to the new tab created.

10. Select Add a Section, and give it a friendly name (for example, SharePointAttachments). Then click OK.

11. Select the new IFrame created.

12. Select Add an IFrame with the following properties:

    Name: `SharePointAttachmentIFrame`

    URL: `about:blank`

13. Select Form Properties from the Common Tasks list located on the right side.

14. Select OnLoad.

15. Click Edit.

16. Enter the following code:

```
crmForm.all.tab4Tab.onclick = function()
{
if(crmForm.all.IFRAME_ SharePointIFrame.url.length < 15)
{
crmForm.all.IFRAME_iBASE.url = "http://<SharePointServer>/SiteCirectory/
➥CRMDocuments? CRMRecordID=" + crmForm.all.accountnumber.value;
    }
```

17. Click OK.

18. Select Save and Close to save the form modifications.

19. Select Save and Close to save the entity modifications.

20. Select the Accounts entity, and then select Publish to deploy the changes.

Licensing for SharePoint

Licensing for Microsoft SharePoint Server 2007 is as follows:

- **Server license (required):** This must be loaded on the server with the selected version (Standard or Enterprise).

- **Standard client access licenses (CALs) (required):** With this license, users can access the server and receive the core capabilities. A CAL is required for every user who needs to access the server.

- **Enterprise CALs (only required for Enterprise functionality):** A separate license that must be purchased on top of the Standard CALs. The Enterprise CAL's enable the enterprise functionality of SharePoint.

> **NOTE**
>
> It is not possible to purchase **just** the Enterprise CAL; instead, you must purchase **both** the Standard and Enterprise CAL if you want to make Enterprise features available to your users.

- **Internet Connector for MOSS:** This is a separate license that is designed for implementations where the services are externally facing and users from the Internet will be using the server. This is considered a full license (including Enterprise functions) and is licensed per server. No additional CALs are required as part of this license.

Although no additional CALs are required as part of the Internet Connector, the license extends only to external users. You still must purchase CALs (both Standard or Enterprise if required) for your internal users.

> **NOTE**
>
> It is important to note that an Internet Connector license is required for **each** public-facing MOSS server. In situations where organizations have multiple servers for a MOSS solution (for example, for load balancing or a server farm), every server that can be accessed externally must have a separate license.

- ▶ **Forms Server:** Although Forms Server is included with the Enterprise edition of MOSS, this can optionally be licensed separately if you have the Standard edition of MOSS.

  As previously described, Forms Server works with Microsoft Office InfoPath client, allowing forms-driven solutions.

- ▶ **Forms CAL:** Similar to the Forms Server license, this licensing can be obtained independently and is licensed based on usage.

- ▶ **Internet Connector for Forms Server:** Licensed per server, it makes the Forms Server accessible to users on the Internet.

- ▶ **MOSS for Search (Standard or Enterprise):** If you're interested in only extended search capabilities for your organization, this separately licensed application can be deployed extending MOSS Search features. The Standard edition limits indexing to 500,000 documents; organizations with requirements greater than that should consider the Enterprise version.

As always, you must consider the appropriate Windows Server CALs as part of your overall solution.

> **NOTE**
>
> Microsoft Dynamics CRM CALs or the Microsoft Dynamics CRM Internet Connector license is required if you want to access the data through the Microsoft SharePoint interface.

Summary

This chapter discussed the different ways to integrate the suite of SharePoint products with Microsoft Dynamics CRM. This chapter specifically showed examples of the following capabilities:

- ▶ Displaying Microsoft Dynamics CRM data inside various SharePoint technologies
- ▶ Enabling the SharePoint Search capabilities on the Microsoft Dynamics CRM database

▶ Creating a CRM dashboard using KPIs and displaying it in SharePoint

▶ Displaying CRM dashboards and other custom dashboards (Cisco phone system, ERP systems, homegrown applications, and so on) in a single view

▶ Displaying a SharePoint dashboard with the Microsoft Dynamics CRM application

▶ Leveraging SharePoint document management capabilities to enhance the Attachment feature in Microsoft Dynamics CRM

It is important to note that this chapter was meant to show you the variety of options available. The examples in this chapter illustrate the high-level feature sets that can be leveraged to optimize internal business processes and used to make more informed data-driven decisions. However, this is by no means an exhaustive list of capabilities, and your specific business needs may exceed what is outlined in this chapter.

CHAPTER 6

Business Intelligence

Customer relationship management (CRM) is an essential profitability and growth vehicle. It provides effective management of marketing initiatives, sales execution, and service portfolios. It also enables cross-departmental collaboration, such as the marketing department handing over campaign leads directly to sales, customer services passing on a customer satisfaction index to sales before the next sales call, or customer services providing feedback to the product managers for the most requested features that they hear about in a support call.

Seeing the Big Picture

Although the CRM system creates and maintains the activity record for sales, marketing, and service departments, and facilitates the collaboration between them through workflows, the secret sauce that brings about the ultimate profit impact is analytics, also known as business intelligence (BI). BI provides an all-around view of customer interaction activities and records as managed or experienced by the marketing, sales, and customer services teams. Architecturally speaking, BI can also be considered an abstraction layer above the deployed CRM system, while also integrating into the CRM system at the grassroots level (see Figure 6.1).

Microsoft Dynamics CRM manages and exposes this interdepartmental information in multiple ways, such as, through standard stock reports from the CRM user interface, and through the Microsoft BI tool stack, which provides online analytical processing (OLAP) capability using SQL Server Analysis Services (SSAS) cubes, dashboard capability using PerformancePoint Server, and ad hoc analytical capability through Excel. This chapter provides a brief overview of the value of using BI tools with the CRM data, along with a click-through example of building a sample BI application.

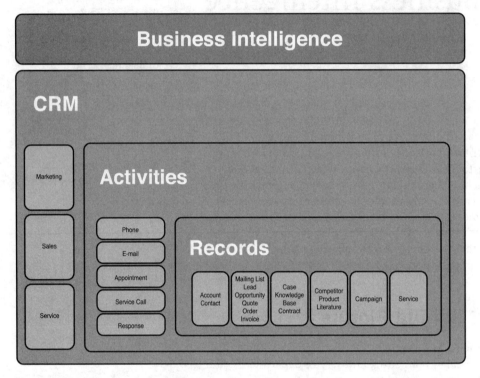

FIGURE 6.1   Microsoft Dynamics CRM and business intelligence.

What Is BI?

BI is a set of technologies used to gain insight into past, present, and future possibilities in business activities, to assist better business decisions. These technologies typically extract useful data from various back-office systems—such as enterprise resource planning (ERP), supply-chain management (SCM), general ledger (GL), and customer relationship management (CRM), and so on—and then transform and load it into a data warehouse or data marts. This data is then aggregated, enriched with business calculations in an OLAP cube, and finally presented to an information worker through a corporate performance dashboard that provides a visual summary of the key indicators or through flexible ad hoc analysis tools for in-depth slicing and dicing of the data.

The Secret Sauce in Your CRM Success

Many standard metrics related to customer trends and demographic information are available in the CRM system out of the box. Here are some examples of the analysis that the standard reports can provide:

- ▶ Opportunities and sales cycle reports

- ▶ Pipeline and sales forecast reports

- ▶ Campaign response reports

- ▶ Customer satisfaction reports

- ▶ Case resolution reports

These stock reports, although useful for viewing basic information, generally do not align well with the corporate goals and key performance metrics unique to individual companies. Every company can have CRM strategies, directions, or initiatives peculiar to its market situation. These reports also do not take the surrounding information into account, which can be critical in understanding the market situations or influencers. This "custom" requirement for every company demands cognizance and requires a tailored response that includes integrating a BI initiative with the CRM strategy according to the atypical needs.

Regardless of the industry, companies that have integrated their CRM and BI strategy have experienced significant competitive advantage. The premise is that analysis of relationships between the surrounding information and the direct customer interaction information can predict customer behaviors more effectively than possible with just the standard reports. To arrive at such results, however, significant time has to be spent in formulating business questions and then aligning the BI implementation with the direction in which the company wants to go or with any particular process that a company wants to improve (see Figure 6.2).

Here are some scenarios for using BI for CRM in cross-departmental settings. BI can enable a salesperson to have an insight into the history of customer issues logged by support staff before proposing a new deal. Similarly, field marketing can use the sales data of lead conversion to better target customers at an industry or product vertical event. Another example is that BI can reduce cost by calculating the efficiency of the case resolution process (for example, to determine whether service staff should be onsite or offsite). In many other cases, standard reports won't suffice, and an integrated BI application will results in insights much closer to corporate goals and strategies.

Implementation Guidelines

Success of a CRM project depends on how well it serves the profitability and growth of a company. As mentioned earlier, the key secret sauce in making this happen is BI. Success of a BI project for a CRM system, in turn, depends on how well the methodology of aligning the business goals and business processes with the implementation efforts is followed. The challenges in implementing a BI application for CRM can vary from company to

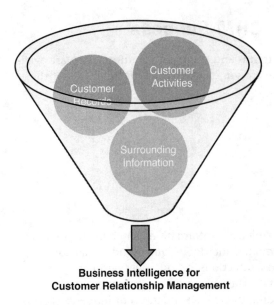

**Business Intelligence for
Customer Relationship Management**

FIGURE 6.2   Business data required for BI.

company. These challenges will depend on various factors, such as the maturity level of IT organizations, the type of industry, and even the selected technologies. But there is still a base guideline that all successful BI projects can follow.

▶ **Consolidated, centralized data warehouse:** It is preferable that a centralized repository is created to store and maintain data from CRM and from all other source systems. This will enable the enterprise to do cross-subject area analysis by correlating data from disparate data sources.

▶ **External data:** Adding as much richness as possible by integrating ancillary and surrounding data will enhance the competitive edge of the enterprise by allowing the discovery of latent influencers of customer behaviors.

▶ **Data cleansing:** There is a chance that the data imported from the CRM systems contains duplicate, incomplete, or wrong entries. Also, the external data imported can contain similar problems and may not merge with the CRM data very well. This data can be cleaned and referenced for better data integrity and stewardship. See Chapter 8, "Master Data Management (MDM)," for a discussion about this related topic.

▶ **Strategy alignment:** Aligning key BI metrics with the corporate goals and strategies puts the BI effort in the desired direction and provides a baseline to measure the progress against. As the company direction changes, the CRM scorecards can be tweaked to reflect the same.

▶ **Business process identification:** Core business processes that can either provide the input for the BI project or that can consume the key metrics need to be identified. Occasionally, some key data elements may not be captured in CRM records. This finding can lead to a separate initiative to generate the missing strategic data.

▶ **Process change management or refinement:** The final guideline in an integrated BI and CRM project is to go through a CRM process change management or refinement, as per the understanding gained from the data, and then to evaluate the effects of the change over time as a feedback mechanism.

Most companies have notably varied business goals, processes, and systems. They can also have very different challenges in terms of their sales, marketing, and service functional groups. When implementing BI systems, remember that there is no "one size fits all" solution. BI systems, by definition, have to be tailored to business needs, even though the products underneath can be the standard BI tools.

Embedded BI

BI provides powerful insights into the customer data, which is typically not possible through standard reports. However, managing the actions taken on those insights is not a traditional aspect of BI. BI, when "embedded" into a transactional system like CRM, with actionable information is called embedded BI. This type of integration is done by placing the BI dashboards or ad hoc capabilities inside the transactional tools that users can use conveniently. Embedded BI can also go as far as suggesting actions to the information workers based on the computed data analysis. Embedded BI is different from an operational report because an operational report would have simply taken the stored data from the local repository, whereas, these embedded BI tools behind the scenes go back into centralized data repositories and provide rich supplementary information.

Caution: BI Is Not CRM

Many companies claim that if they have a BI system they don't need a CRM system because of the powerful insights about customers that their BI provides. Although it might seem obvious that BI by itself is not a complete CRM system, such confusion still prevails. One way to distinguish the two is to note that while a BI system can enable companies to integrate external data and gain insights into the actions taken, it does not have an inherent ability to take actions on them. To take the action in a systematic way, one still has to go back into a system that is meant for taking them, such as a CRM system. Although both BI and CRM systems can benefit each other through integration, they are not meant to replace each other. BI provides the insight into past, present, and even future possibilities of business transactions, and CRM completes the business cycle by integrating actions into the analytics offered by BI.

Microsoft Business Intelligence Roadmap

Microsoft has progressively invested in its BI product offerings since the SQL Server 7.0 days. Its most current offering and the near-future release updates are discussed in this section. Simply speaking, the Microsoft BI tools are covered within the three product suites: Microsoft Office SharePoint Server 2007, Microsoft Office 2007, and Microsoft SQL

Server 2008. All three product suites have more granular-level components and features that when used in permutation and combination enable capabilities ranging from data integration, aggregation, reporting, and all the way up to ad hoc analysis, self-service reporting, dashboards, and collaborative decision making (see Figure 6.3). The tight integration between the three product suites, especially for the purposes of BI, is a unique value proposition Microsoft brings to the table. This enables lower cost of operation and faster development time by leveraging existing investments and skills. The following diagram depicts how the products stack up to provide the mentioned BI capabilities.

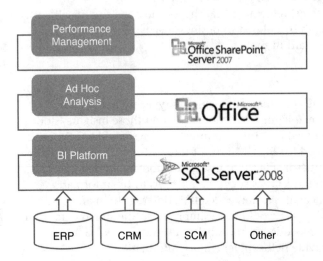

FIGURE 6.3   Interface layers from data to presentation layer.

SQL Server 2008 consists of four essential BI components: the core SQL Server Database engine (SSDB), SQL Server Analysis Services (SSAS), SQL Server Integration Services (SSIS), and SQL Server Reporting Services (SSRS). Consider what you can accomplish with these individual components. For instance, SSDB enables users to create and manage a data warehouse for a CRM system with filtered views as a logical data abstraction layer in a relational database. SSAS enables users to create powerful calculation in a multidimensional data cube. SSIS enables users to process the data from all possible data sources in a powerful ETL (extract, transform, and load) tool. And finally, SSRS enables users to create standard and scheduled reports.

Microsoft Office 2007, with the classic and most common BI tool in the world, Excel, is an indispensable part of the BI tool stack. It enables users to connect to SSAS and to the relational database to perform spreadsheet-type analysis. End users can make use of the Excel functions in an already familiar environment. Excel has also been improved and extended to provide ease of use.

Microsoft Office SharePoint 2007 can be used as a display mechanism for the key performance indicators (KPIs), scorecards, and strategy maps built using the PerformancePoint Server 2007. Together, these enable users to create performance management dashboards. At the time of this writing, SQL Server 2008 R2 (Kilimanjaro) and Microsoft Office SharePoint 2010 (Office 14) have already been announced and are going to contain several important BI updates. The top ones that stand out for this discussion are master data services, self-service reporting, and fast search. Master data services will help in creating a common reference lookup repository for further semantic integration between CRM, BI, and other enterprise resource management systems.

Microsoft BI Tool Stack: In Pictures

Figure 6.4 shows a typical deployment architecture for a BI project (this one involving the Microsoft BI tool stack). Going from left to right, the data moves from the source system and is processed in an SSIS ETL pipeline for cleansing (and other transformations). The data is then loaded and stored in a data warehouse, which becomes the central repository for all analytical needs. Depending on the subject areas and analytical needs, multidimensional cubes are created with all the calculations, attributes, and hierarchies familiar and useful to users. Finally, the well-organized and well-integrated rich data is consumed by users through reports, dashboards, and ad hoc analysis tools.

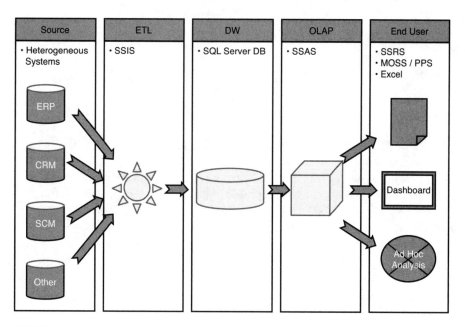

FIGURE 6.4   Microsoft Dynamics data flow process.

Figure 6.5 shows the SSIS package for ETL purposes, as a project type in the familiar inter-face of Visual Studio. SSIS is a powerful data integration engine that can assist in extract-ing data from databases, text files, and from web services. With SQL Server 2008, the SSIS pipeline has been optimized for faster operations, such as reference lookups, sorting, aggregating, and loading data into tables.

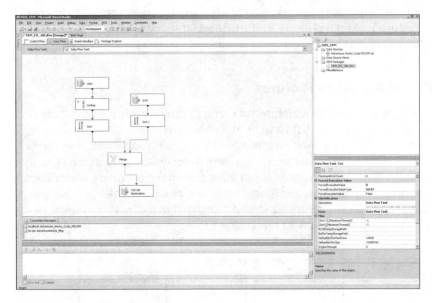

FIGURE 6.5   SSIS showing the data flow.

Figure 6.6 shows the filtered views available for analytical needs, pre-created as part of the Microsoft Dynamics CRM standard installation.

Figure 6.7 shows the analytical capabilities of Excel 2007. Excel not only has nice charting and color-coding capabilities, it also has an easy parameter-selection interface that includes the new pivot table selection pane on the right.

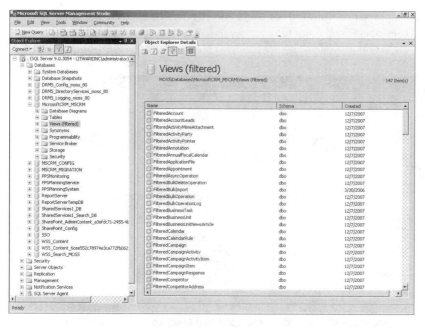

FIGURE 6.6   Microsoft Dynamics CRM filtered views.

FIGURE 6.7   Analyzing Microsoft Dynamics CRM data in Excel.

Figure 6.8 shows a dashboard created using PerformancePoint Server. It has a scorecard on the left and embedded charts and spreadsheets on the right. The best part is that these dashboards can be deployed to hundreds of users and still can be entirely personalized using hidden and user-operable parameters.

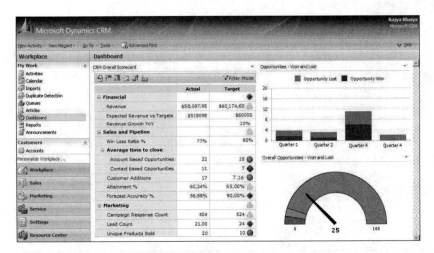

FIGURE 6.8   PerformancePoint dashboards embedded into Microsoft Dynamics CRM.

Going Forward: Predictive Analytics

While multidimensional analysis (or OLAP) can present the data for deep exploration with power slice-and-dice capability, predictive analytics or data mining can provide the futuristic outlook or possibilities using machine-learning algorithms to predict sales, marketing effectiveness, and service efficiency.

Such predictions can help in reprioritizing resource utilization, both human and facilities, help in preparing a better marketing list, and even forecast the sales pipeline. Algorithms can detect the relationships between, say, the products and the sales teams, and determine the likelihood of the success of a sales call. The algorithms can also predict things such as which products are good to sell together, which attributes influence the likelihood of a certain outcome, or can categorize customers into small pockets based on their profiles. Some of these algorithms are even sophisticated enough to predict the next likely event in a sequence of occurrences, or in a series of time.

Microsoft provides the following data mining algorithms out of the box:

- ▶ Microsoft Decision Tree
- ▶ Microsoft Linear Regression
- ▶ Microsoft Naïve Bayes
- ▶ Microsoft Clustering
- ▶ Microsoft Association Rules

▶ Microsoft Sequence Clustering

▶ Microsoft Time Series

▶ Microsoft Neural Networks

Demo Clickthrough

This section contains a short clickthrough demo of a sample BI application that starts with defining a cube and ends with using that cube with a business dashboard. The intent of this clickthrough is not to provide in-depth knowledge of the cube building and dashboard building process but to provide a jump start for BI for CRM based on the pre-created filtered views. The BI application, as mentioned earlier in this chapter, can be enriched by first going through the exercise of defining the corporate goals and then aligning the implementation with the corporate strategies. In this example we will build dashboards for opportunity and support analysis, showing a business flow from selling the opportunity to supporting it over time.

Cube Building

The tool for building OLAP cubes in the Microsoft world is SSAS. In the SQL Server 2005 release, the development tool for the cubes is Visual Studio. A Visual Studio shell ships with SQL Server Business Intelligence Development Studio (BIDS). There is also a special project type for the BI projects, in which SSAS, SSRS, and SSIS projects can be created.

Create an Analysis Services Project

1. In BIDS, select File, New, Project (see Figure 6.9).
2. Select Business Intelligence Projects from Project Types, and then click Analysis Services Project.
3. Name the new project **SSAS_MSCRM**. Leave the location for the project as default.

NOTE

After the new project is created, right-click the SSAS_CRM database icon in Solutions Explorer and select Properties. In the Properties window, click Deployment and make sure the server name is appropriate.

---

4. If an Analysis Services instance is installed on the local computer, then localhost should do the job. If not, select the Analysis Services server available for testing the sample click-through.

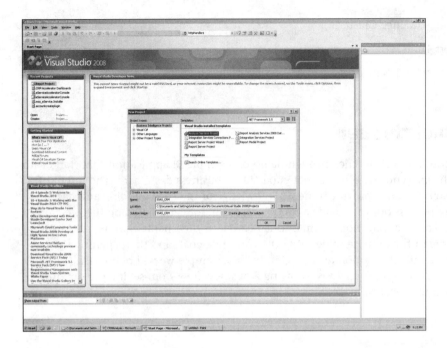

FIGURE 6.9   Create a new project.

Create a Data Source

1. Right-click the Data Sources folder in Solutions Explorer and select New Data Source to open the Data Source Wizard.

2. In the Data Source Wizard, click Next, and then select New to create a new data connection string.

3. In the Connection Manager dialog, to create a new connection string, type in the server name (for example, localhost) and select the Contoso_MSCRM database from the drop-down.

4. Click OK to close the dialog box, and click Next to reach Impersonation Information screen.

5. Select Use the Service Account as the Impersonation Method, especially if the SSAS server is localhost (see Figure 6.11).

6. Click Next and Finish to create the data source with the name Microsoft CRM MSCRM

Create a Data Source View

1. Right-click the Data Source View folder to start creating a data source view using the data source just created.

2. Click Next on the Welcome screen and Next on the Data Source screen.

3. On the Select Tables and Views screen, type **Filtered** in the Filter text box and apply the filter.

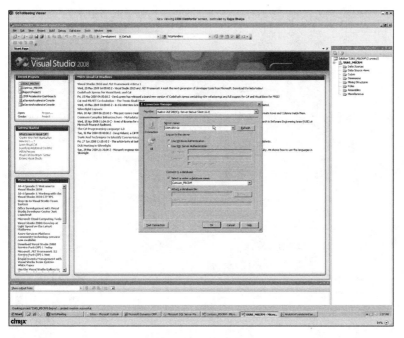

FIGURE 6.10   Connection Manager settings.

4. Select the following views from the Available objects and move them in the Included objects:

dbo.FilteredAccount

dbo.FilteredContact

dbo.FilteredInscident

dbo.FilteredOpportunity

5. Click Next and Finish to create the data source view (see Figure 6.12).

6. In the data source view, right-click anywhere on the background and select **New Relationship**.

7. Create a new relationship as shown in Figure 6.13, relating **accountid** from dbo.FilteredAccount to the **accountid** column in dbo.FilteredOpportunity. Ensure that the accountid column from the Filtered Account table is selected as the **primary key**.

8. Click **OK**. When prompted to **create a logical primary key** on the destination table, click **Yes**.

Repeat steps 6–8 for the following relationships (see Figure 6.14):

▶ **accountid** from dbo.FilteredAccount to **accountid** column in dbo.FilteredIncident

▶ **accountid** from dbo.FilteredAccount to **accountid** column in dbo.FilteredContact

▶ **contactid** from dbo.FilteredContact to **contacttid** column in dbo.FilteredIncident

▶ **contactid** from dbo.FilteredContact to **contactid** column in dbo.FilteredOpportunity

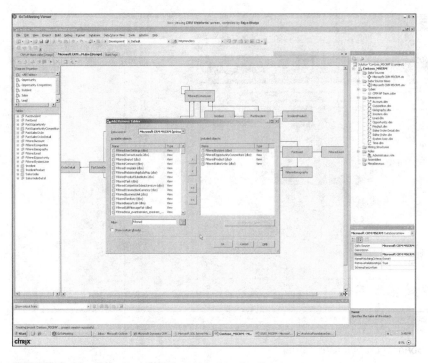

FIGURE 6.11   Data Source Wizard: Authentication.

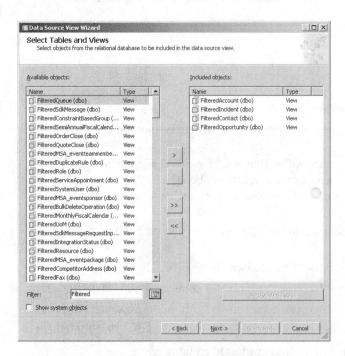

FIGURE 6.12   Data Source Wizard: Select Tables and Views

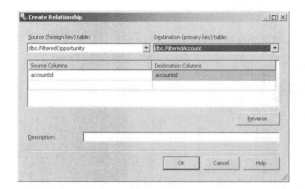

FIGURE 6.13   Create relationships.

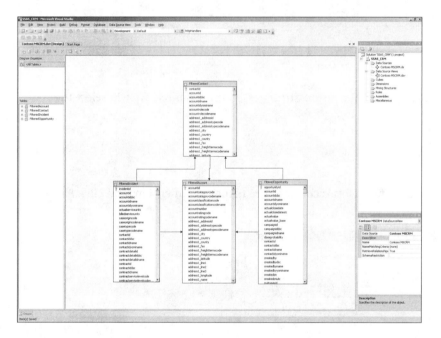

FIGURE 6.14   Data source view.

Create Dimensions: DimAccount

1. Right-click the Dimensions folder in Solution Explorer, and select New Dimension; then click Next on the Welcome screen.

2. On the Select Creation Method screen, choose Use an Existing Table.

3. To specify the source information, select the FilteredAccount as the main table and Name Column as the name (see Figure 6.15). Then click Next.

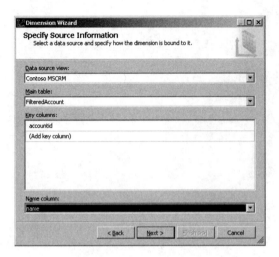

FIGURE 6.15   Specify source information.

4. Select the appropriate dimension attributes. In this example, we will select the following (see Figure 6.16):

AccountId

Address1_Country

Address1_City

5. Then click Next, enter **DimAccount** as the name for dimension, and click Finish.

FIGURE 6.16   Specify dimension attributes.

Create Relationships

1. Right-click DimAccount under Dimensions in Solution Explorer, and click View Design.

2. Click Attribute Relationship, and drag and drop the City over the Country attribute to create the relationships, as shown in Figure 6.17.

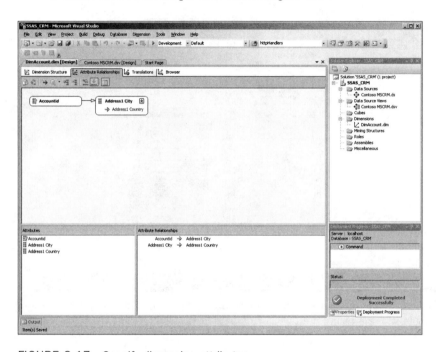

FIGURE 6.17   Specify dimension attributes.

3. Click the relationship between City and Country, and change the relationship to Rigid.

4. On the Dimension Structure tab, drag and drop Country, City, and AccountId in the Hierarchies screen (see Figure 6.18). Also change the name of the hierarchy to **AccountGeography**.

5. Change the hierarchy name in the Properties window as follows:

    Address1_City to **City**

    Address1_Country to **Country**

    AccountId to **Account Name**

6. Change the AttributeHierarchyVisible property to False for the following:

    Address1_City

    Address1_Country

    AccountId

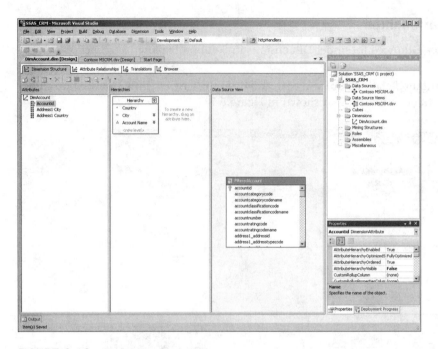

FIGURE 6.18   Dimension hierarchies.

NOTE

To enable Microsoft Office Communications Server (OCS) integration, you can add the telephone attribute with the callto: prefix.

Create Dimensions: DimIncident

1. Right-click the Dimensions folder in Solution Explorer, and select New Dimension; then click Next on the Welcome screen.

2. On the Select Creation Method screen, choose Use an Existing Table.

3. Specify the source information, select the main table as FilteredIncident, and title for the name column. Then click Next.

4. Uncheck all check boxes on Select Related Tables screen.

5. Select the appropriate dimension attributes. In this example, we will select the following:

   IncidentId

   Casetypecode

   Contractservicelevelcode

   CustomerSatisfaction

   Statuscode

   Subjectid

6. Then click Next, enter **DimIncident** as the name for dimension, and click Finish.

7. Right-click DimIncident under Dimensions in Solution Explorer, and click View Design.

8. Click Properties and change the Attribute Name and NameColumn to the following:

IncidentId

Name: **Incident**

NameColumn: **FilteredIncident.Title**

Casetypecode

Name: **Case Type**

NameColumn: **FilteredIncident.Casetypename**

Contractservicelevelcode

Name: **Contract Service Level**

NameColumn: **FilteredIncident.Contractservicelevelname**

CustomerSatisfactioncode

Name: **Customer Satisfaction**

NameColumn: **FilteredIncident.Customersatisfactionname**

Statuscode

Name: **Status**

NameColumn: **FilteredIncident.Statuscodename**

Subjectid

Name: **Subject**

NameColumn: **FilteredIncident.Subjectidname**

Create Dimensions: DimOpportunity

1. Right-click the Dimensions folder in Solution Explorer, and select New Dimension; then click Next on the Welcome screen.

2. On the Select Creation Method screen, choose Use an Existing Table.

3. Specify the source information, select the main table as FilteredOpportunity, and name as the column name. Then click Next.

4. Uncheck all check boxes on the Select Related Tables screen.

5. Select the appropriate dimension attributes. In this example, we will select the following:

OpportunityId

Customeridtype

Opportunityratingcode

Ownerid

Owningbusinessunit

stepname

Statuscode

6. Then click Next, enter **DimOpportunity** as the name for dimension, and click Finish.

Create Relationships

1. Right-click DimOpportunity under Dimensions in Solution Explorer, and click View Design.

2. Click Attribute Relationship, and drag and drop the Ownerid over the owningbusinessunit attribute to create the relationships.

3. On the Dimension Structure tab, drag and drop Owningbusinessunit, OwnerId, and OpportunityId in the Hierarchies screen. Also change the name of the hierarchy to **OpportunityOwner**.

4. Change the hierarchy name in the Properties window as follows:

OpportunityId

Name: **Opportunity**

NameColumn: **FilteredOpportunity.name**

Customeridtype

Name: **Customer Type**

Opportunityratingcode

Name: **Opportunity Rating**

NameColumn: **FilteredOpportunity.Opportunityratingcodename**

Ownerid

Name: **Owner**

NameColumn: **FilteredOpportunity.Owneridname**

Owningbusinessunit

Name: **Owning BU**

stepname

Name: **Sales Stage**

NameColumn: **FilteredOpportunity.Stepname**

Statuscode

Name: **Status**

NameColumn: **FilteredOpportunity.Statuscodename**

5. Change the AttributeHierarchyVisible property to False for the following:

Ownerid

Owningbusinessunit

NOTE

You can also create a time dimension to allow your organization to do time-based analyses.

Create a Cube

1. Right-click Cubes, and then click New Cube.
2. Click Next on the Welcome screen, and select Use Existing Tables on the Select Creation Method screen. Then click Next.
3. Select FilteredAccount, FilteredIncident, and FilteredOpportunity on the Select Measure Groups screen, and then click Next.
4. Select the following for the measures:

   FilteredAccount:

   Creditlimit

   Revenue

   Filtered Account Count

   FilteredOpportunity:

   Actualvalue

   Estimatedvalue

   Filtered Opportunity Count

   FilteredIncident:

   Actualserviceunits

   Billedserviceunits

   Filtered Incident Count

5. Select all the dimensions on the Select Existing Dimensions screen.
6. Uncheck all the values on the Select New Dimensions screen.
7. Then click Next, enter **ContosoMSCRM** for the name for dimension, and click Finish.

Set Data Types

1. Right-click the ContosoMSCRM, and select View Designer.
2. In the Cube Structure tab, Click Show Measures Grid.
3. Change the measures with the appropriate data types (as shown in Figure 6.19).

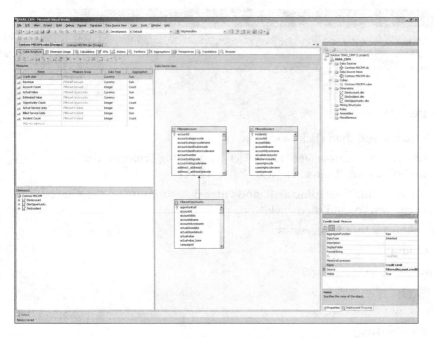

FIGURE 6.19   Cube measures.

Create Calculations

1. Display the Calculations tab.
2. Click New Calculated Member.
3. Enter the following values:

    Name: **[Opportunity Actual vs Estimated]**

    Expressions: **[Measures].[Actual Value] / [Measures].[Estimated Value]**

    Format string: **Percent**
4. Process and deploy the cube. Browse the cube for testing (as shown in Figure 6.20).

Creating a New Mining Structure

1. Right-click Mining Structure, and then click New Mining Structure.
2. On the Select the Definition Method screen, select From Existing Relational Database or Data Warehouse.

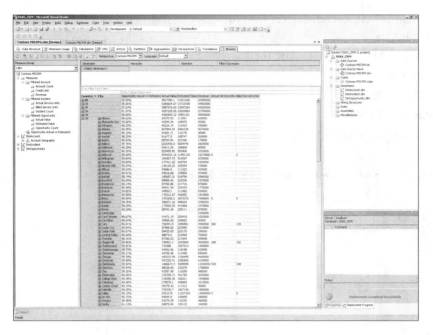

FIGURE 6.20   Browsing a cube.

3. On the Create the Data Mining Structure screen, select Microsoft Association Rules.

4. On the Select Data Source View screen, select contoso_MSCRM.

5. Select FilteredIncident on the Specify Tables Types screen.

6. Select the following on the Specify the Training Data screen (see Figure 6.21):

ticketnumber as Input

productidname as Input and Predictable

subjectidname as Input

7. Click Next, and then enter the name as **Incident and Mining** *model name* **as Product Association**.

8. Opening the mining model, click the mining model viewer, and click Dependency Network to observe the corelationship of the data (see Figure 6.22).

Building a Dashboard

1. From the Start menu, mouse over All Programs, mouse over PerformancePoint Server, and open Dashboard Designer.

2. Right-click Data Sources, and then click New Data Sources.

3. Enter the name as **MSCRM**, and select the check box to grant read permissions to all authenticated users

4. Under the Standard Connections, use the following values:

Server: **localhost**

Database: **SSAS_CRM**

Cube: **Contoso_MSCRM**

5. Save the project file as **MSCRM_Dashboard**.

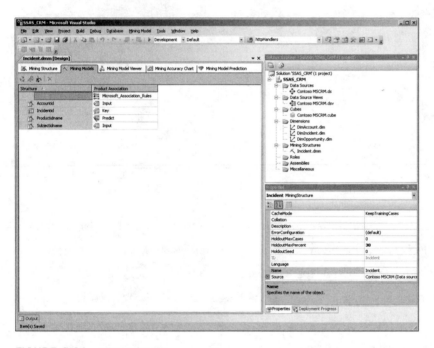

FIGURE 6.21   Mining model.

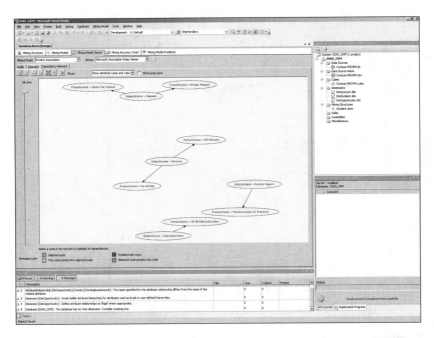

FIGURE 6.22   Mining model viewer.

Create a Scorecard

1. Right-click Scorecard and select New Scorecard Using the Analysis Services Template.
2. Use **Opportunity Target Fulfillment** as the scorecard name, and select the check box to grant read permissions to all authenticated users.
3. On the Data Source screen, select MSCRM, and then click Next.

NOTE

Select the appropriate data type for the various KPI data.

4. On the Select KPIs to Import screen, enter the values shown in Figure 6.23.

NOTE

Repeat the steps above to add more KPIs to your dashboard.

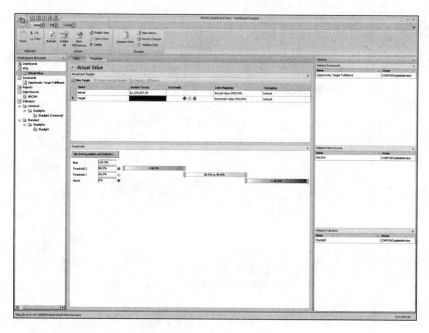

FIGURE 6.23   KPI thresholds.

5. Click Next, and then click Finish.

Create a Report

1. Right-click Reports, and then click New Report.
2. Select Analytic Chart (see Figure 6.24).
3. Enter the following values on the Create an Analytic Chard Report screen:

   Name: Revenue **Geography**

   Data Source: **MSCRM**
4. Click Next, then Finish.
5. On the Reports Designing screen, do the following (as shown in Figure 6.25):

   Add Revenue as Series.

   Add DimAccount Account Geography as the Bottom Axis.

Creating a Dashboard

1. Right-click Dashboards, and then click New Dashboards.
2. Enter **CRMDashboard** as the dashboard name, and select the check box to grant read permissions to all authenticated users.

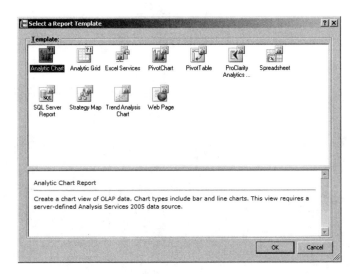

FIGURE 6.24   Report selection screen.

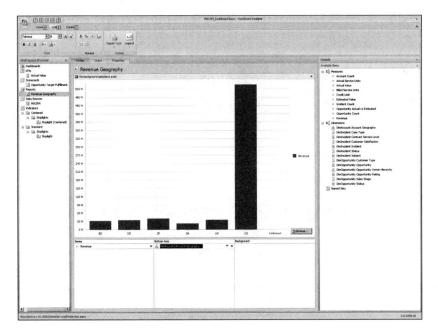

FIGURE 6.25   Sample report.

3. Drag and drop the reports from the Available Items windows into the Dashboard Editor (see Figure 6.26).

4. Save and publish the dashboards.

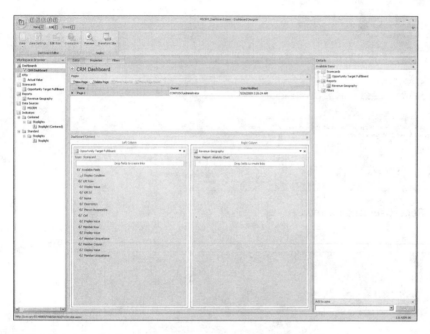

FIGURE 6.26   CRM dashboards, showing multiple reports.

Summary

In this chapter, we showed how to create a Microsoft SQL Server Analysis Services cube and how to build Microsoft SharePoint Server dashboards using the PerformancePoint Services engine.

CHAPTER 7

Digital Phone Integration

Integration of CRM with a phone system ensures consistent data entry and allows phone-based agents to focus on customers and not their case management tools.

Microsoft Dynamics CRM is not Telephony Application Program Interface (TAPI) natively compliant. However, third-party vendors have built solutions that can be leveraged to perform the following:

▶ Place an outbound call from within the system

▶ Recognize an incoming call and open the related information from Microsoft Dynamics CRM automatically

▶ Send and receive faxes

In addition, because of this level of integration, calls can be recorded and then attached directly to the Microsoft Dynamics CRM record for playback later.

> **NOTE**
>
> Recording calls exceeds the scope of this chapter and largely depends on not only the type of system you have, but also how it is set up.
>
> If you're interested in this level of integration, consult with your manufacturer. (Several companies offer this as an add-on solution.)

This chapter outlines the technology and existing tools for telephone integration.

To enable phone integration for incoming and outgoing calls, you need a couple of things:

▶ A phone system that supports computer telephony integration (CTI/SIP/TAPI)

  Usually, Voice over IP (VoIP) and modern phone systems (PBX) support CTI. Some
  legacy phone systems have add-ons/plug-ins to add this functionality. There are two
  types of integration, one where the link software runs on the user's PC, and the
  other, where the software runs on the server. Also, in some cases, suppliers offer
  proprietary interfaces, but increasingly TAPI and Telephony Services API (TSAPI) are
  offered as a standard interface.

  Session Initiation Protocol (SIP) is the new communication protocol that has
  replaced TAPI as the core API set for initiating and receiving calls in a VoIP environment. Microsoft Office Communicator uses SIP for all voice communications.

  Developers and integrators need to understand the appropriate phone system so that
  they can develop against the appropriate APIs. In general, all old phone systems are
  TAPI-based. All the new phone systems are SIP-based. Cisco Call Manager supports
  SIP and TAPI.

▶ A link with your CRM

  This is the software component that links Microsoft Dynamics CRM to the phone
  system. This software implements a variety of user interface features for the user
  (such as dial, transfer, and so on). Usually, the major phone system manufacturers
  provide this software; however, it is possible to build your own if your manufacturer
  doesn't provide it.

TAPI Architecture Defined

From the end-user perceptive, the architecture of a digital telephone integration is simple:
End users have a physical phone and a computer that has the TAPI client that interacts
with the phone system. Figure 7.1 shows the physical layout from an end-user perceptive.

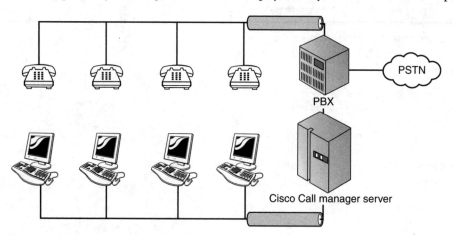

FIGURE 7.1   VoIP physical landscape.

However, the software behind the functions has a lot of complex integration. Several software interface layers allow endless possibilities for integration. Figure 7.2 shows the different interfaces available. For example, you can have an array of different phone systems (VoIP solutions from Avaya and Cisco, and you can have non-VoIP solutions that can interface with TSPI) and services that are potentially connected in the TSPI layer. The TSPI interface unifies all communication for the TAPI to be used for the end-user solution.

A practical use for this applies to this scenario: We have various call centers distributed throughout the world using different phone systems, but the company has a single CRM solution using Microsoft Dynamics CRM. So, when the customer calls any call center in the company, the TAPI client should be able to query the CRM system.

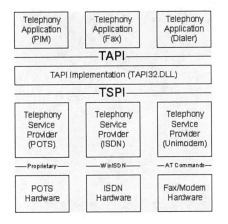

FIGURE 7.2   TAPI interface landscape.

The TAPI layer, as shown in the Figure 7.2, can be connected to several hardware interfaces. Therefore, you can use a spectrum of physical phones and have a mixed environment.

Telephony Manufacturers/Third-Party Solutions (SIP-Based Solutions)

The telephone manufacturers mentioned in this section have partnered with Microsoft to develop their own solutions for their telephone systems, and offer out-of-the-box solutions for integration with Microsoft Dynamics CRM.

Microsoft Office Communication Server (OCS) R2 Agent Communications Panel for Microsoft Dynamics CRM 4.0

The Agent Communications Panel is integrated into the Microsoft Dynamics CRM 4.0 web application. The Agent Communications Panel enables users to telephone others (to make and receive calls), to instant message (IM) co-workers and customers, and to make conference calls. The link between your communication system and the Microsoft Dynamics CRM application enables you to have access to all of your customer information.

Figure 7.3 shows a sample of the Agent Communications Panel interacting with Microsoft Dynamics.

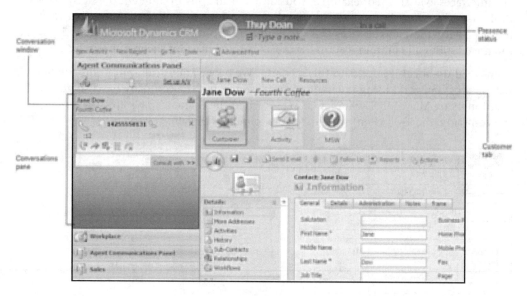

FIGURE 7.3 Sample Agent Communications Panel.

NOTE

This integration was primarily designed for service agents. However, this solution can be used by salespeople, too.

The Agent Communications Panel has the following components:

▶ The Conversations pane displays active conversations.

▶ The Customer tab enables you to access the customer information for the active conversations. You can view and edit the customer contact or account form. You can also add a new activity record to log your conversation.

▶ The New Call tab enables you to contact customers or colleges. You can communicate with the customers or other contacts via telephone or IM.

▶ You can also manage your Contacts list.

▶ Share presence status with others. You can choose to grant more access to certain teams regarding your status.

▶ Switching between voice devices enables you to be able to switch phones without the other person noticing a difference.

NOTE

This is a SIP-based system, designed for the new server-client communication system. Microsoft Office Communicator 2007 R2 is supported.

Server Components
Requirements: Ensure that .NET 3.5 SP1 is installed on both the server and the client machines running Microsoft Dynamics CRM 4.0.

Installing the Agent Communications Panel
1. Log on to the server as a Microsoft Dynamics CRM deployment administrator.
2. Launch the install package.
3. Review and accept the license agreement, and then click Install.
4. Click Finish.

Customizing the Agent Communications Panel
With the Agent Communications Panel, you can customize organization-specific elements on the user interface. The following customizing options are available:

▶ Configure the Response Group Service feature. This enables you to have a communication agent system in your organization. This feature allows you to have specialized groups of people in the call center who can help customers based on the data in certain fields.

▶ Change the default form for the customer information. Allows companies to use the same contact record and have a customized form for different groups of people (Sales, Marketing, or Service).

▶ Create custom buttons. Allows quick-access buttons with customized functions.

Configuring the Response Group Service Integration Feature
The Response Group Service is a new feature in Microsoft Office Communications Server 2007 R2. This is a powerful feature that can help direct the communication and the information directly to the engaged user.

It enables administrators to create and configure workflows to route and queue incoming conversations. For example, if an engineer requires assistance from the product company, the engineer places a call to the service call center for the product. The Communication Server should retrieve the relevant information about the caller from the Microsoft Dynamics CRM system. The Communication Server can initiate a workflow, which can analyze the call time and the caller and refer to a scheduled activity. At that point, the system can transfer the call to the person with the specialized skills to handle it.

To configure the Response Group Service integration feature, follow these steps:

1. In the CRM application, select Settings, Agent Communications Parameters.
2. Open ResponseGroupServiceIntegration. To enable the Response Group Service integration feature, set Parameter Value to True, and then click Save and Close.

3. Open ResponseGroupServiceWebServiceUri. Enter the URL of the Response Group web service (https://<OCS_Server>/rgs/clients/ProxyService.asmx), and then click Save and Close.

Changing the Default Form for the Customer Information

You can specify the form that displays when a user clicks the Customer button under the Customer tab. The customer information can be displayed in either the contact or account form. The contact form is the default view used.

To change the default form, follow these steps:

1. In the CRM application, select Settings, Agent Communications Parameters.
2. Open CustomerFormDisplayed, set Parameter Value to either Contact or Account, and then click Save and Close.

Creating Custom Buttons

You can create custom buttons to add to the Agent Communications Panel user interface. Custom buttons can be added to either the Customer or Resources tab and can be used to support applications such as call scripting and knowledge bases.

> **NOTE**
>
> The maximum number of buttons allowed per tab, including the default buttons, is 10.

To create a custom button, follow these steps:

1. In the CRM application, select Settings, Agent Communications Buttons.
2. Select New. Then enter the appropriate values:

    Name: Enter the display name for the button.

    Target URL: Enter the URL for the resource.

    Tool Tip: Enter the text to display on mouse over.

    Icon URL: Enter the path to the image file of the button icon.

    Button Order: Select the button placement order. The button order in each of the tabs is oriented from left to right.

    Tab Location: Select either Customer or Resources to specify the location of the custom buttons

> **NOTE**
>
> If the custom button is placed on the Customer tab, the customer or account ID is appended to the target URL when the button is launched. This enables you to reference the customer or account ID in your application.

3. Click Save and Close.

Cisco Unified CallConnector for Microsoft Dynamics CRM

Cisco first released a call connector in 2004, and they have been upgrading it ever since. The call connector by Cisco is called the Cisco Unified CallConnector for Microsoft Dynamics CRM, and it enables organizations to integrate the two industry-leading enterprises (Microsoft and Cisco) to aid in better customer-care solutions.

Advanced features of the connector include the following:

- ▶ **Screen pops:** Opens contact records and creates new phone call activity records as calls are placed or received (see Figure 7.4)

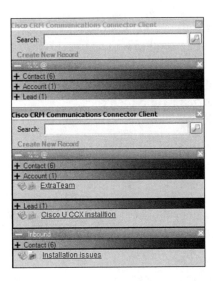

FIGURE 7.4   Cisco CallConnector screen pops.

- ▶ **Click-to-dial:** Supports the Click-to-Dial feature from a Microsoft CRM contact record

- ▶ **Call duration tracking:** Tracks the duration of phone calls and associates them with phone activity records

- ▶ **Call information capture:** Captures incoming and outgoing call information, including calling number, called number, and call start and end times

- ▶ **Customer record creation:** Easily creates a new CRM customer record when a new customer call arrives

As long as you have deployed the Cisco CallManager 4.x or later, there is no cost for this connector. However, certain requirements apply: the server component Cisco CallManager 4.x or later, the client component .NET Framework 2.0 or later, the user account enabled for CTI integration, and TAPI installed on the client (as described later).

> **NOTE**
>
> The client needs to have a thick client installed, which will interface with a server component, which is usually installed on the Microsoft Dynamics CRM server.

To install the Cisco Unified CallConnector, follow these steps:

1. Log in to the CRM web server.
2. Install the server component CUCCServerInstaller.exe. You can download this from http://www.cisco.com/public/sw-center/index.shtml.
3. Click Next on the Welcome screen.
4. At the License Agreement screen, select the I Agree option, and then click Next
5. Choose the destination folder on the Select Installation folder screen, and then click Next.
6. Click Next to begin installation on the Confirm Installation screen.
7. The Configuration Screen will display. Select the defaults, and then click OK.
8. Click Close to complete installation.

To configure the Cisco Unified CallConnector, follow these steps:

1. Launch the configuration options by selecting Start, Programs, Cisco, and then set the following configurations:

   Select Cisco CallConnector Server Configuration. The Configuration window will display, as shown in Figure 7.5

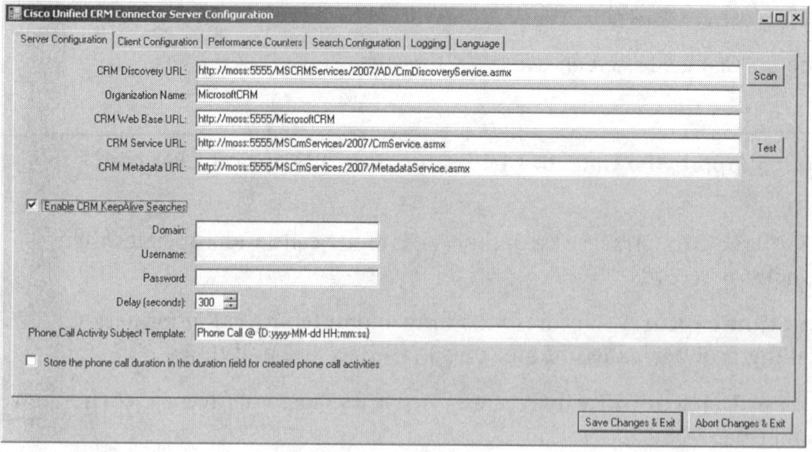

FIGURE 7.5   Cisco CallConnector options, Server Configuration tab.

2. Enter the appropriate URL information for the Microsoft Dynamics CRM server. Using our example in Figure 7.5, you would replace moss:5555 with the name of your server and port. (If you are on the default port [i.e., port 80], you enter only the machine name.)

> **NOTE**
>
> You can verify each of the addresses entered by navigating to a browser and entering them there. Each should load a page.

3. Enter the organization the server will be using.

4. Click Enable CRM KeepAlive Searches. When this is enabled, it allows an active connection to the CRM for faster search results.

5. Click the Edit Phone Number Processor Configuration button on the Client Configuration tab (see Figure 7.6). On this screen, you can configure the dialing rules for various locations, to automate dialing.

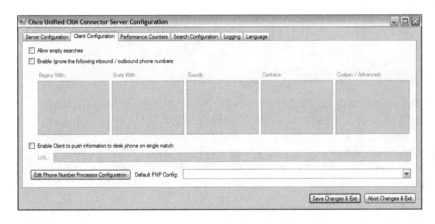

FIGURE 7.6   Cisco CallConnector Client Configuration tab.

Optional settings are for keepalive searches. These allow faster searches for end users. This is useful when you have many users and want to remove the authentication overhead.

Phone number processing is the most important part of the configuration. Every country has a different number processing pattern. It is vital to configure this properly.

Pattern recognizer and search format capabilities combine to find the appropriate record in the CRM.

Figure 7.7 shows a standard configuration. Your configuration might differ depending on your setup. Click the Utilities button to launch a wizard. The wizard walks administrators through standard settings for most locations. However, you can change the dialing rules, and you can change phone number recognition patterns based on the different implementation systems you may be dealing with.

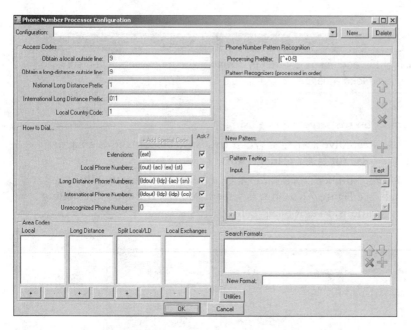

FIGURE 7.7   Cisco CallConnector options, Phone Number Processor Configuration options.

6. On the Dialing Rules Wizard screen, click New and enter a name for the configuration. The name should be something that will be easy for end users to understand, such as San Francisco Call Center.

7. Click OK.

8. Click the Utilities button.

9. Select Wizards / Templates from the menu.

10. Select the wizard that matches your region. If a wizard does not have your region listed, you must configure the phone number pattern (PNP) manually. After configuring the PNP, click OK.

11. Click Save Changes & Exit.

NOTE

The independent software vendor (ISV) integration needs to be configured in Microsoft Dynamics CRM to enable end users to access this function.

To enable ISV configuration, follow these steps:

1. Open the Dynamics CRM website with administrative privileges.
2. Open the Settings section.
3. Select the System Settings option.
4. In the System Settings window, click the Customization link.
5. In the Custom Menus and Toolbars section, click the Selection button.
6. Add Outlook and Web Application.
7. Click the >> button to add them to the selected values.
8. Click OK.

Client Installation

Client installation requires four major steps:

▶ Install the Java Runtime Environment.

▶ Install and configure the Cisco TSP client.

▶ Install the Cisco JTAPI client.

▶ Install and configure the Cisco MSCRM connector client.

1. Install the Java Runtime Environment

1. Download the Java Runtime Environment (JRE) from http://www.java.com/en/ download/manual.jsp.
2. Launch the installer.
3. Accept the license agreement.
4. On the Java Setup – Complete dialog box, click Finish.

2. Install and Configure the Cisco TSP Client

1. Download the Cisco TAPI service provider (TSP) client from the Cisco download center.
2. Launch the installer.
3. On the Language Selection screen, select the appropriate language, and then click Next.
4. On the Welcome screen, click Next.
5. On the Choose Destination Location dialog box, enter the installation folder and click Next.
6. To the question about multiple instances for Cisco Unified CallManager TSP, answer No.

7. Click Next to begin the installation.

8. Click Finish.

NOTE

It is important to reboot the machine before proceeding to the next steps. Otherwise, the next steps will fail.

To configure the TSPs, complete the following steps:

1. Open the Control Panel.

2. Select Phone and Modem Options.

3. Display the Advanced tab.

4. Select CiscoTSP001, as shown in Figure 7.8.

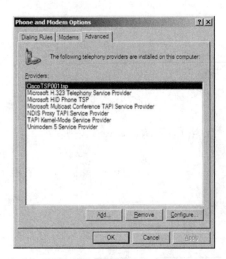

FIGURE 7.8   Advanced tab from Phone and Modem Options.

5. Click Configure.

6. Enter a username and password for the Cisco phone system.

7. The username and password is for logging in to the Cisco phone system, which enables the tie between the Cisco phone line to the computer. To obtain this username and password, contact your Cisco system administrator.

8. Enter the DNS name or the IP address of the local Cisco phone server.

9. Click OK.

10. Click Close.

NOTE

It is important to reboot the machine before proceeding to the next steps. Otherwise, the next steps will fail.

3. Install the Cisco JTAPI Client

1. Navigate to the location with the JTAPI installer and launch the setup for the Cisco JTAPI client.
2. On the Welcome screen, click Next.
3. Click Next on the Choose Installation Folder Location screen.
4. Confirm the settings, and then click Next to begin the installation.
5. Click Finish.

4. Install and Configure the Cisco MSCRM Connector Client

1. Download and launch the setup from the Cisco website (http://www.cisco.com/public/sw-center/index.shtml).
2. Agree to the license agreement.
3. On the Select Installation Destination screen, click Next.
4. Click Next on the Confirm Installation screen.
5. Click Finish to complete the setup.

After the server has been set up and configured, you need to configure the client. After you install and configure the TAPI on the client machine, the CallConnector client allows you to choose the physical/soft phone to which you want to attach this API, as follows:

1. To view the configuration options, right-click the Cisco CallConnector icon in the lower-right corner of the desktop and select Configuration (see Figure 7.9).

FIGURE 7.9   Launch the configuration for the *Cisco* CallConnector client.

2. Select the device that you want to integrate (get the phone number from). This is where you can select a Cisco phone or a regular analog phone. Figure 7.10 shows the Microsoft Dynamics CRM client configuration options.

FIGURE 7.10   Cisco CallConnector client with the CRM client configuration options.

3. On the Client Configuration tab, enter the server name where Cisco CallConnector client is installed (see Figure 7.11).

Then select the behavior required from the integration from among the following user preferences:

▶ **Automatically Create Activity When Only One Match:** This allows service centers to have an automatic log for all matched incoming calls.

▶ **Automatically Display Record When Only One Match:** This allows the screen to pop up automatically when only one match is found.

▶ **Automatically Create Activity on Click-to-Dial:** This allows an activity to be logged into the system when the agent places a call.

Figure 7.11 shows the user preference options.

4. Click OK to accept the changes.

NOTE

You can configure the Cisco CallConnector client for use with an analog telephone. This potential configuration enables remote users who don't have a Cisco phone at home to leverage some of these features.

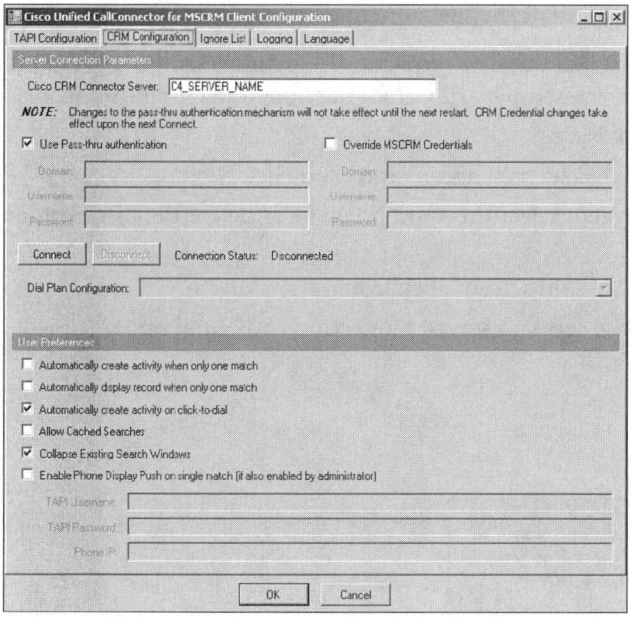

FIGURE 7.11   Cisco CallConnector user preferences.

c360 CTI for Microsoft CRM

c360 CTI (Computer Telephony Integration) is a third-party application that enables integration between telephone systems (via TAPI) and Microsoft Dynamics CRM. Similar to the Cisco and Avaya products, this product also detects incoming phone calls (displays the caller's name and number), automatically produces activities for incoming and outgoing calls, and much more. The CTI provides the following capabilities:

- ▶ Connects telephone systems with Microsoft Dynamics CRM
- ▶ Detects incoming calls and displays caller information
- ▶ Opens a contact or an account upon the lifting of the receiver
- ▶ Creates activities for incoming and outgoing calls
- ▶ Simplifies the process of making outgoing calls

This CTI application has been successfully tested on the following phone systems:

- ▶ Alcatel OmniPCX Office
- ▶ Nortel BCM 50
- ▶ Siemens HiPath 3550 5.0
- ▶ 3com VoIP system SuperStack 3 NBX Networked Telephony
- ▶ TeleVantage 6
- ▶ Avaya S8500 Communication Manager 3.1

To install c360 CTI, you first need to install the server component, as follows:

1. Download the setup from the c360 website. (Typically, the setup is sent in an email to every customer.) Then launch the setup by running Telephone Integration Setup.msi.

2. On the Welcome screen, click Next.

3. Select English on the Language Selection screen, and then click Next.

4. On the Destination Folder screen, select the appropriate location for the installation, and then click Next.

5. On the Ready to Install the Program screen, click Install.

   Once the files are copied to the server, a server connection configuration screen will display, as shown in Figure 7.12.

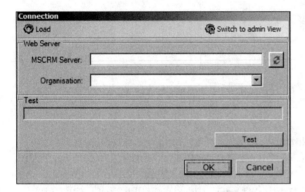

FIGURE 7.12   c360 server connection configuration screen.

6. Enter the appropriate server name and organization, and then click OK.

7. During the installation, configure ISV.config. Select the appropriate entities that require CTI within your organization (see Figure 7.13).

8. By default, Accounts and Contacts is selected. You can make any changes if needed.

9. Click Finish to complete the installation.

After the server component has been installed, you will see the Call Number button shown in the Figure 7.14

System administrators may change the configuration if desired at a later stage. To configure additional settings for c360, follow these steps:

1. Click Start.

2. Click All Programs.

3. Click c360.

4. Click Telephone Integration for MSCRM 4.

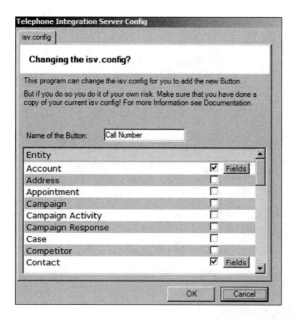

FIGURE 7.13   c360 server ISV configuration screen.

FIGURE 7.14   Account screen with the Call Number button.

5. Click Telephone Integration Setup to launch the same configuration as shown during setup (refer back to Figure 7.13).

NOTE

Click the Fields button to view the more advanced functions (to select the fields to search) that are available.

To install the client component, follow these steps:

1. Locate the installer and launch setup.
2. On the Welcome screen, click Next.
3. Agree to the license agreement, and then click Next.
4. Select English on the Language screen.
5. Select the following in the Startup Options screen:

   Automatically Start TI When Windows Starts.

   Start TI After Setup.

   Then click Next.

6. Choose the installation folder, and then click Next.

7. Click Install to begin installation

8. Enter the following server connection options (see Figure 7.15):

    MSCRM Server.

    Organization.

    Then click OK.

9. Select the appropriate TAPI device. Figure 7.16 shows all the TAPI devices available from the Windows system.

10. Click Finish.

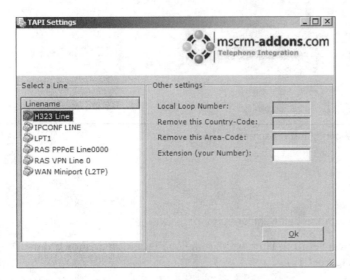

FIGURE 7.16   Client TAPI selection screen from c360.

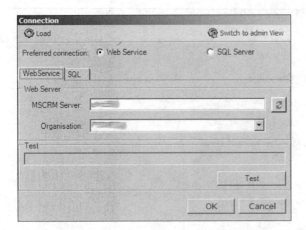

FIGURE 7.15   Client connection configuration.

Logging Call Actions

With CTI, the incoming and outgoing calls are automatically logged in the Microsoft Dynamics CRM system. Figure 7.17 shows the log of the phone calls in the CRM database. The creation of the activities happens automatically; this action is performed with the security context of the person placing or receiving the phone call.

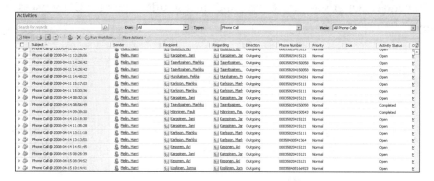

FIGURE 7.17   Sample calls logged for a specific entity.

The following attributes about the call are automatically logged in Microsoft Dynamics CRM:

▶ Start time

▶ Duration

▶ Call direction (incoming/outgoing)

▶ Call priority (set to Normal by default)

▶ Activity status (set to Open by default)

▶ Sender (CRM user placing or receiving the call)

▶ Owner (CRM user placing or receiving the call)

▶ Regarding (customer record participating in the call)

Summary

This chapter examined how to automatically look up customers when incoming/outgoing calls are initiated. To enable this capability, we recommend that you use one of the products mentioned in this chapter. However, you can build a custom solution that uses the technology described in this chapter. SIP and TAPI are standards used by various vendors to unify the end-user solution.

Using CTI automation can allow organizations to provide a better customer experience. This also reduces the chance of human error, which is one of the most common requests organizations with large customer bases make. This integration also prefilters result sets to help the customer service representative accurately identify the customer.

Various solutions are available for CTI. If you have a Cisco CallManager, it is recommended to use the Cisco proprietary CTI Integration application. Otherwise, you can choose your solution from among other VoIP vendors (for example, c360). Genesys Labs is a market leader in contact center software as well, and their solutions provide CTI services for legacy telephony hardware.

CHAPTER 8

Master Data Management (MDM)

Master data management (MDM) is a critical part of every organization. To ensure optimum business processes, every organization must establish policies and procedures to create and maintain a singular dataset in the organization. This dataset usually contains customer details (for example, name, phone number, address, and any other supplemental information about the customer). Organizations can maintain data integrity by implementing the appropriate policies. Healthy data usually wins the trust of internal users and increases adoption of any CRM system, which can help companies make more informed decisions. Unhealthy data usually results from not having appropriate business processes to maintain the data, and so data silos are created and these prevent the integration of systems. This chapter discusses the importance of MDM and how it and emerging best practices are vital to your organization.

What Is MDM?

Master data management (MDM) refers to the policies and procedures that are implemented within the CRM system. The objective of MDM is to provide a process for data collection, consolidation, and integration between multiple systems. MDM also enables an organization to monitor and generate automated reports based on required business processes. This is usually a recursive process that evolves over time with growing company needs.

To understand MDM, you must first understand the various data structures:

- **Unstructured:** Any form of available data (in emails, articles, or any other documents).

- **Transactional:** An aggregation of any data captured during the course of the transaction.

- **Reference data:** All the related data that describes the core recordset. This usually contains any supplemental information that can be used for analysis (for example, list of countries, products, industries).

- **Metadata:** A formal data structure in a formal database combined with documents and definitions on the data.

- **Hierarchical:** A data structure that has layers and steps, a rudimentary structure that is defined in a tree structure (essential to create an MDM).

- **Master:** Subject areas, domain areas, and entity type.

Why MDM Is Important

MDM enables companies to increase internal efficiencies and drastically reduce operational cost and complexity. Thus, MDM reduces manual data entry and analyses and so improves the quality of the data. Healthy data allows organizations to make better decisions, giving the company a competitive edge over others.

The MDM process is broken down into the following key components (see Figure 8.1):

- **Understanding the current data:** This phase consists of profiling a segment of data, evaluating the attributes, and researching the datasets. For example, if the company directive is to ensure that the CRM data has the appropriate industry

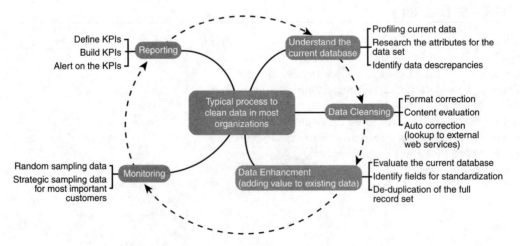

FIGURE 8.1   Master data life cycle.

selected for the customer, the master data team evaluates the pick-list values for the industry and identifies any discrepancies in the data.

▶ **Data cleansing:** A series of sequential procedures will be followed during this phase. Data cleansing usually comprises four different parts:

  ▶ Correcting the format of the data (usually for phone numbers, ZIP codes)

  ▶ Content evaluation, which surfaces the inconsistent datasets

  ▶ Autocorrection phase, which can retrieve data from various external sources (SIC code, Hoover's reports, LinkedIn, and more) and update the CRM system

  ▶ Manual correction

▶ **Data enhancement:** Adding any supplemental information that may prove useful in the future.

▶ **Monitoring:** Random sampling of data and ensuring the health of such.

▶ **Reporting:** Building key performance indicators (KPIs) and monitoring the general health of the data.

MDM is often used to ensure that an organization does not duplicate master data in different operations, a common occurrence in a complex and large organization. In CRM, it is important to maintain one recordset for one customer to avoid multiple copies and to have a consolidated view of the information across various systems. For example, you don't want an existing customer to be contacted by a salesperson soliciting the same service or product. (Such a mistake might occur if, for example, the sales department and the customer relationship department information are not synced).

This problem may be amplified by mergers and acquisitions. Consider the example of World Savings being taken over by Wachovia being taken over by Wells Fargo. This entire takeover process would have created three (World Savings, Wachovia, and Wells Fargo) sets of customer data. When the three companies merge, the integrators need to ensure that the customer records are merged as the organization is merging. Another potential problem that may happen during this merger is the redundancies of products and services offered by the organization; typically, this is put on a backburner and addressed at a later stage. A consolidated view of customer contact information, along with the products and services used, can enable the business analyst to provide better options for the management to choose from. MDM can help reduce serious operational problems and increase operational efficiency, which will then lead to smarter business decisions.

MDM tools provide a suitable file system structure and an adaptive data warehouse system, an operational database enabled with data mining and analysis capabilities, and they allow for automated reporting and exception-based reporting. Document all of this, and diagram it for easier understanding. You can use any available modeling methodology acceptable to the organization.

MDM Tools

SQL Server 2008 R2 Master Data Services (see Figure 8.2) enables organizations to define business processes and the data processes for the SQL server. Thus, organizations can implement human-to-human, human-to-system, system-to-human, and system-to-system workflows.

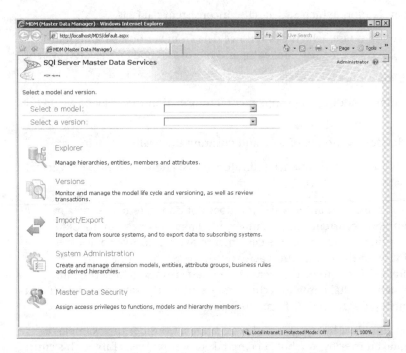

FIGURE 8.2   Master Data Services home page for SQL Server.

Summary

MDM enables an organization to integrate various information systems into one consolidated and coherent system. A healthy CRM system results in high user adoption. Salespeople are attracted to a single system with a healthy dataset. If the dataset is poor, you might be caught in a downward spiral that may lead to internal users losing trust in the quality of the data. In most organizations, MDM is a recursive process. The salespeople are usually the best source of the information and are the biggest consumers of the information.

It is important to implement a process to extract the information and to then store it in a centralized location. A good MDM strategy allows for communication with different functional business roles in an organization and keeps them informed of the effort of the other roles in the organization. It also implements best practices that enforce corporate standards. Implementing MDM in an organization will empower the company to develop and deploy an automated information management solution.

CHAPTER 9

Social Network Integration

Microsoft wanted to build a horizontal platform that developers could use to create their own systems. By providing a solid, fully featured platform that was easy to develop on, organizations could create powerful CRM systems tailored to their own needs, and third-party companies could create deep, vertical-market CRM applications that they could host or sell. A typical approach for companies that build CRM products is a closed or black-box approach in which the product is self-contained. In today's world, people are managing the contact information in social networks. Therefore, organizations can leverage this opportunity to ensure that the internal systems are up-to-date.

In addition to centralization, standardization, simplification, and integration of data, web service integration into Microsoft Dynamics CRM provides additional layers of content that proves useful in relating to handling an entity's customer relationship database. There are many benefits to reap in terms of integrating many tools put out by Microsoft and others. CRM 4.0 enables you to integrate and leverage web services and other service-oriented architectures.

In MS Dynamics CRM, the SDK used is the exact same web services SDK used internally by Microsoft developers. The product is infinitely modifiable and extensible at nearly any layer. Web services such as Facebook and LinkedIn create innovative services that previously would have been impossible or prohibitively expensive to deploy. With data and code effortlessly connected, businesses can rapidly adapt and take advantage of new opportunities. For example

- ▶ A sales team can try to establish a 360-degree view of customer interactions, behaviors, buying patterns, and sales opportunities to cultivate more profitable relationships.

- ▶ The marketing team can plan ahead, observe trends, and track real-time results.

- ▶ You can deliver high-value customer service with integrated interaction and knowledge management and thus enable your service professionals to share answers and insight with customers with ease.

In today's competitive business landscape, relationships have never mattered more. Whether you are in sales, business development, or some other role, you can gain an instant edge with information gained through these added CRM initiatives. In addition, you can support the development of marketing strategy by developing the organization's knowledge in areas such as identifying customer segments, improving customer retention, and improving product offerings.

LinkedIn

LinkedIn is a massive professional networking website, with more than 35 million registered members and growing rapidly. It enables members to share contact information, knowledge, experiences, and new ideas. Specific contacts can be added on contact lists, and searching for contacts has never been easier. Members can control their profile and showcase their achievements, knowledge, and experience based on how they want to market themselves. This enables them to find the best possible opportunities in their professional careers. In short, LinkedIn is a networking website for professionals.

Entities with Microsoft Dynamic CRM architecture can seek to increase their productivity by leveraging LinkedIn's influential network of professionals. At present, LinkedIn is slowly releasing application programming interfaces (APIs) to enable developers to integrate their popular business-networking site with external applications.

To integrate LinkedIn with your Microsoft Dynamic CRM environment, just follow these steps:

1. Create the iFrame.
2. Navigate to the Settings tab.
3. Click Customizations.
4. Select Customize Entities.
5. Click the Account record.
6. Click Forms and Views under the Details section.
7. Click the form record.
8. Add a Tab and name it **LinkedIn**.
9. Add a section and name it **LinkedIn**.
10. Add an IFrame and name it **IFRAME_LinkedIn**.
11. Uncheck the Restrict Cross-Frame Scripting box.

12. Select the Automatically Expand to Use Available Space box under the Row Layout section of the Formatting tab.

13. Click OK to save the IFrame changes.

14. Click the form properties under the Common Tasks section of the Account form.

15. Select OnLoad from the Event list.

16. Click Edit.

17. Enter the following code:

```
var CRM_FORM_TYPE_CREATE = 1;
var CRM_FORM_TYPE_UPDATE = 2;
switch (crmForm.FormType)
{
case CRM_FORM_TYPE_UPDATE:
crmForm.all.IFRAME_LinkedIn.src="http://www.linkedin.com/search?search=&company
➥=" + crmForm.all.name.DataValue+ "
➥&searchLocationType=I&countryCode=us&postalCode=" +
➥crmForm.all.address1_postalcode.DataValue+ "&distance=50&sortCriteria=3";
break;

}
```

18. Click OK to close the Event Detail Properties window.

19. Click OK to close the Form Properties window.

20. Click the Save and Close button on the Account form.

21. Click Publish from the Action menu on the Account Entity form. The change is now available to your application.

Facebook

To build a collaborative business environment, you integrate web services and thus leverage the complexity of an existing IT enterprise infrastructure. Web service integration enables you to overcome internal barriers, exploit external prospective opportunities, and create new applications to add a competitive edge.

Facebook is a popular social networking website in which users connect and communicate with each other. Facebook features include the ability to send messages; update personal information and status; and notify friends, relatives, acquaintances, and so on. Initially, the website consisted of members of U.S. colleges, universities, and schools. Today, however, it has an open membership that consists of more than 100 million members worldwide.

Facebook detractors consider it merely a distraction that just connects people and enables them to kill time online. However, this web service represents amazing potential. If you leverage it appropriately, Facebook is an effective tool to reach new markets; to link up with customers, colleagues, and business relationships; and to generate opportunities. At present, Facebook has gone from the stage of being just another social networking tool and is now a prevailing medium of communication for individuals, groups, and large businesses.

Figure 9.1 shows how CRM fits within social networking. And although CRM isn't necessarily the only mechanism that people have to communicate with each other, you can use it to capture information about peer-to-peer interactions between constituents.

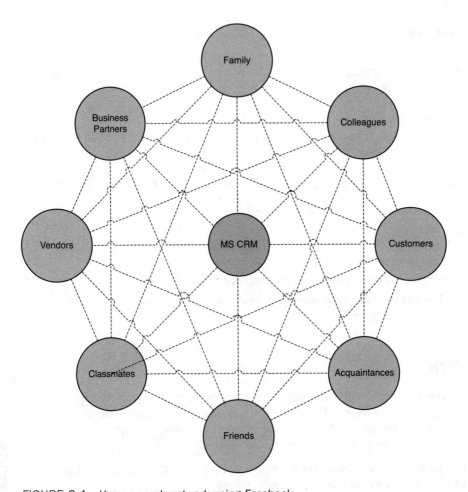

FIGURE 9.1   Human mesh network using Facebook.

Integrating web services such as Facebook into Microsoft Dynamics CRM provides the management and the sales force with rich data pertaining to existing and prospective customer and other important business relationships.

This kind of integration provides several benefits, including the following:

▶ Better assessment of opportunity management

▶ Tracking customer preferences, trends, and responses

- Generation of ideas for targeted marketing campaigns

- Analyzing customer behavior to make decisions about products and services

- Assessing brand loyalty

- Target groups formed from client base according to selected criteria

Seeing the potential of growth, Facebook, Inc., created Facebook Connect, a platform that enables users to integrate Facebook into their own website, product, or service. Microsoft CRM can be integrated with Facebook Connector to utilize social media and CRM capabilities for the purpose of tracking, understanding, and contacting current and prospective customers and other key business relationships.

The main benefits derived from using Facebook Connect are as follows:

- Access to contact information of customers/contacts/business relationships/others

- Leverage users' personal interests to show more relevant information and surface personalized content from friends such as reviews or comments

- Sharing content between profiles through personal messages, newsfeeds, blogs, or social group channels on Facebook

- Use of the Facebook API to develop applications for users

This section now reviews a basic example of the integration process. The example illustrates the quick integration of the Contoso website with Facebook Connect. We set up the Connect application and add a small code section to the Contoso website. Upon completion of the following steps, Contoso administrators can log in to Facebook and connect with other Facebook users whose information may be on the Contoso website:

1. Create an application with the Facebook Developer application.

   You must first create a new application. To do so, navigate to http://www.facebook.com/developers/createapp.php.

   Enter a name for your application in the Application Name field.

   Accept the Developer Terms of Service, and then click the Save Changes button.

   On the Basic tab, enter a callback URL. (Make no changes to the defaults.) This URL points to the top-level directory of the site that will be implementing Facebook Connect. (This is usually your domain—for example, http://www.contoso.com—but could also be a subdirectory.)

   Carefully note the API key; it will be required.

   Display the Connect tab, and then click Change Your Facebook Connect Logo and browse to an image file (maximum of 99 pixels wide by 22 pixels tall and in JPG, GIF, or PNG format).

   If your site is going to implement Facebook Connect across a number of subdomains of your site (for example, foo.contoso.com and bar.contoso.com), you need to enter a base domain (contoso.com in this case). Specifying a base domain enables you to make calls using the PHP and JavaScript client libraries and to get and store session information for any subdomain of the base domain. For more information about subdomains, refer to "Supporting Subdomains in Facebook Connect" at http://developers.facebook.com.

2. Create a cross-domain communication channel file called **xd_receiver.htm** and place it in a directory relative to the callback URL that you entered in the previous step. For instance, suppose you're using http://www.contoso.com as your callback URL, but you want to store your Facebook Connect files in their own subdirectory (perhaps http://www.contoso.com/connect). You should create the xd_receiver.htm file in the directory in which you'll be serving your Connect web pages (http://www.contoso.com/connect in our example). Copy the following content into the file:

```
<!DOCTYPE html PUBLIC "-//W3C//DTD XHTML 1.0 Strict//EN"
    "http://www.w3.org/TR/xhtml1/DTD/xhtml1-strict.dtd">
<html xmlns="http://www.w3.org/1999/xhtml" >
<body>
    <script
src="http://static.ak.connect.facebook.com/js/api_lib/v0.4/XdCommReceiver.
➥js" type="text/javascript"></script>
</body>
</html>
```

> **NOTE**
>
> This file allows your application and Facebook to send data back and forth.

3. Create another HTML file in the same directory as the one you created in the preceding step (for instance, http://www.contoso.com/connect/test.html). Within the <html> tag for test.html, add xmlns:fb="http://www.facebook.com/2008/fbml", as in the following:

```
<html xmlns="http://www.w3.org/1999/xhtml"

xmlns:fb="http://www.facebook.com/2008/fbml">
```

4. Next, in your newly created test.html file, you need to refer to the Facebook JavaScript Feature Loader file. This allows your site access to all the features of Facebook Connect in JavaScript, such as XFBML, JavaScript API calls, and so forth. This script should be referenced in the body of your file, not in the head:

```
<script
src="http://static.ak.connect.facebook.com/js/api_lib/v0.4/

FeatureLoader.js.php" type="text/javascript"></script>
```

5. You can render a Facebook Connect login button using XFBML on your page, right alongside of your normal HTML. For instance, after the two lines that you just added, you could use a line of markup like this:

```
<fb:login-button></fb:login-button>
```

This renders the Facebook Connect login button, so that you can connect your Facebook account to your site. Optionally, you can add a JavaScript handler to the callback button to be called when the user has logged in, as follows:

```
<fb:login-button onlogin="facebook_onlogin();"></fb:login-button>
```

6. Finally, you need to include the following script after the login button:

```
<script type="text/javascript">
    FB.init("<YOUR_API_KEY_HERE>", "<path from web root>/xd_receiver.htm");
</script>
```

7. Try loading the test.html page you just created and try connecting to Facebook. You just implemented the first step of Facebook Connect!

Here are the entire contents of test.html:

```
<html xmlns="http://www.w3.org/1999/xhtml"
xmlns:fb="http://www.facebook.com/2008/fbml">
<head></head>
<body>
<script src="http://static.ak.connect.facebook.com/js/api_lib/v0.4/
➥FeatureLoader.js.php" type="text/javascript"></script>
<fb:login-button></fb:login-button>

<script type="text/javascript">
    FB.init("<YOUR_API_KEY_HERE>", "xd_receiver.htm");
</script>
</body>
</html>
```

1. Open the Microsoft Dynamics CRM application.
2. Select Customizations from the left navigation.
3. Select Customize Entities.
4. Open the Accounts entity.
5. Select Forms and Views.
6. Open the form.
7. Select Add a Tab from the Common Tasks area.
8. Give it a name (for example, SharePoint Account Dashboard); then click OK.
9. Navigate to the new tab created.
10. Select Add a Section, and give it a friendly name (for example, SharePointSection). Then click OK.
11. Select the new IFrame created.

12. Select Add an IFrame with the following properties:

   Name: `SharePointIFrame`

   URL: `http://<SiteURL>/`

13. Select Pass Record Object-Type Code and Unique Identifier as Parameters.

14. Click OK.

15. Click Save and Close to save the form modifications.

16. Click Save and Close to save the entity modifications.

17. To deploy the changes, click the Accounts entity and then select Publish.

Facebook integration opens a whole new world as far as connecting with and understanding key stakeholders of the business is concerned. CRM integration into this website generates a massive contact management structure. Because people are on the run and keep switching locations, jobs, or contacts, it can become quite tedious to regularly update such information. Facebook lessens this difficulty by showing regular updates to CRM users. Moreover, the blogs, discussion forums, and group activities contribute toward enhancing existing CRM information.

There are already several success stories of businesses building applications specifically aimed at the Facebook platform and market. One of the more popular applications is SplashCast, which has features similar to YouTube but is aimed at video content for private audiences and sharing among friends. Other applications help users to discover new music recommended by friends.

> **NOTE**
>
> Using the Connector, customers can submit tickets, suggestions, inquiries, and complaints directly through Facebook. They can follow up on them and their progress. Customers can also access their profiles and view a history of their submitted cases and interactions with the company. Companies can define their target clients through profile segmentation in Microsoft Dynamics CRM and then directly target them with their marketing campaigns through Facebook in the form of notification newsfeeds.

Twitter

While Microsoft has developed an Accelerator specifically for social media that works with Twitter, it hasn't been made available to the public at the time of publication. A simple way to achieve integration between Microsoft Dynamics CRM and Twitter without the Accelerator is to embed an iFrame with an automatic lookup of the Account record on Twitter.

There are other ways to use web service calls to retrieve the data and store the response in the Microsoft Dynamics CRM directly. Here is one alternative:

1. Open the Microsoft Dynamics CRM application.
2. Select Customizations from the left navigation.
3. Select Customize Entities.
4. Open the Accounts entity.
5. Select Forms and Views.
6. Open the form.
7. Select Add a Tab from the Common Tasks area.
8. Give it a name (for example, Twitter conversations), and then click OK.
9. Navigate to the new tab created.
10. Select Add a Section, and give it a friendly name (for example, TwitterSection). Then click OK.
11. Select the new IFrame created.
12. Select Add an IFrame with the following properties:

    Name: `TwitterIFrame`

    URL: `https://twitter.com/search/users?q=<AccountName>`
13. Click OK.
14. Click Save and Close to save the form modifications.
15. Click Save and Close to save the entity modifications.
16. To deploy the changes, click the Accounts entity and then select Publish.

Summary

Because users update their own private contact information on various websites such as LinkedIn and Facebook, integrating with the social networks enables companies to retrieve updated information directly from the end users. This rich source of data can help companies minimize the effort required to maintain personal information about users.

Before the release of this book, but too late to be reviewed, Microsoft released its Social Networking Accelerator. This accelerator takes the integration concepts explored in this chapter to the next level and provides rich reporting interfaces and easy management of the applications. Be sure to check for this accelerator at http://www.codeplex.com/crmaccelerators.

As we've discussed throughout this book, one of the most powerful features of Microsoft Dynamics CRM is its extendibility. Because it is so flexible, we have a number of options when adding features/enhancements. Mapping integration is one of the most popular requests for integration.

We focus on two Microsoft technologies in this chapter (Live Search Maps and Microsoft MapPoint), but have also included Google integration (Google Maps). This list is by no means exhaustive and can be extended to your favorite mapping application if you like.

While we have an entire chapter on this subject, this is a relatively easy integration to perform and provides great value to users. As is explained further in this chapter, we have seen both sales and service individuals use these features for planning visits, locating accounts by radius, and mapping distances.

These solutions make use of inline frames (IFrame) integration, which enables you to restrict cross-frame scripting for security purposes and configure formatting and scrolling options. Because the proposed IFrame solutions in this chapter are all custom created, you can have a lot of say in the final look and feel of the solution.

NOTE

When working with IFrames, it is important to note that they load asynchronously and may not be completely loaded before the CRM form is loaded. In addition, IFrames typically require an external connection (either to the intranet server or the Internet) and can present challenges when a user is in an offline mode.

When working with integrated IFrames, there are two ways to pass information to the IFrame: either with the `HttpRequest.QueryString` property if using ASPX, or with the `window.location.search` property in JavaScript if using an HTML page. Either can be used to contextually display information based on what is passed to it from Microsoft Dynamics CRM.

Microsoft Live Search Maps

Also known as MSN Maps or Bing Maps, Microsoft Live Search Maps is part of Microsoft's Virtual Earth framework and provides mapping technology. Another way to think of Live Search Maps is as a website that offers extensibility options while utilizing Microsoft's Virtual Earth as the underlying platform.

> **NOTE**
>
> Microsoft Virtual Earth can be licensed separately and offers a greater set of capabilities than the Microsoft Live Search Maps application. Therefore, developers seeking to do more than simple address lookup mapping should look at the Microsoft Virtual Earth product.

Figure 10.1 shows the Microsoft account in Microsoft Dynamics CRM with a new tab called Live Map that has the Live Search Maps integrated.

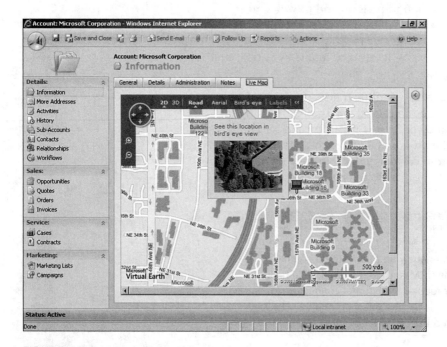

FIGURE 10.1   Microsoft Live Map integration.

We can easily scroll or change the orientation on the map once it is loaded, and we can change the view options available across the top. Figure 10.2 has the same location, but Bird's Eye is selected.

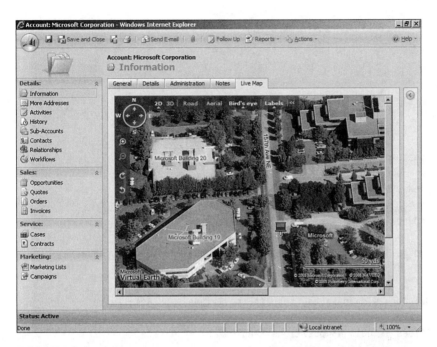

FIGURE 10.2   Microsoft Live Maps integration with Bird's Eye selected.

To create a Live Search integration, complete the following steps:

1. Use the following code to create a new web page with an .htm extension:

```
<!DOCTYPE html PUBLIC "-//W3C//DTD XHTML 1.0 Transitional//EN"
"http://www.w3.org/TR/xhtml1/DTD/xhtml1-transitional.dtd">
<html xmlns="http://www.w3.org/1999/xhtml">
<head>
    <title>MSN Map</title>
    <meta http-equiv="Content-Type" content="text/html; charset=utf-8" />

    <script type="text/jscript"
➥src="http://dev.virtualearth.net/mapcontrol/mapcontrol.ashx?v=5"

mce_src="http://dev.virtualearth.net/mapcontrol/mapcontrol.ashx?v=5"></script>

    <script type="text/javascript">

var vMap = null;
```

10

```
function initialize()
{
   var crmAddress = GetCRMAddress();
   if(crmAddress != '')
   {
                LocateAddress(crmAddress);
   }
   else
   {
                DisplayMessage();
   }
}

function LocateAddress(address)
{
   vMap = new VEMap('MapHolder');

   vMap.LoadMap();

   vMap.Find(null,address,null,null,0,10,true,true,true,true,MapAddress);
}

function MapAddress(shapeLayer, results, positions, moreResults, e)
{
   if(positions != null && positions.length > 0)
   {
           addressLatLong = new VELatLong(positions[0].LatLong.Latitude,
➥positions[0].LatLong.Longitude);

           addressPushPin = new VEShape(VEShapeType.Pushpin,addressLatLong);

           vMap.AddShape(addressPushPin);

           vMap.SetCenterAndZoom(addressLatLong,15);
   }
   else
   {
           DisplayMessage();
   }
}
function GetCRMAddress()
{
   var address = '';

   var addressLine1 = parent.document.forms[0].all.address1_line1.DataValue;
```

```
    var postalCode =
parent.document.forms[0].all.address1_postalcode.DataValue;

    var city = parent.document.forms[0].all.address1_city.DataValue;

    var stateOrProvince =
parent.document.forms[0].all.address1_stateorprovince.DataValue;

    var country = parent.document.forms[0].all.address1_country.DataValue;

    if(addressLine1 == null && postalCode == null && city == null &&
stateOrProvince == null && country == null)
    {
            address = '';
    }
    else
{
            address = addressLine1+", "+postalCode+" "+city+"
("+stateOrProvince+"), "+country;
    }
    return address;
}

function DisplayMessage()
{
    var lbl = document.getElementById('lblMessage');
    lbl.style.display = "inline";

    var div = document.getElementById('MapHolder');
    div.style.display = "none";
}
</script>

</head>
<body onload="initialize()">
    <form>
            <div id="MapHolder" style="width: 700px; height: 350px">
            </div>
            <label id="lblMessage" style="display: none; font-family: @Arial
Unicode MS; font-size: small; font-weight: bold; color: #15428b;">
                    Unable to locate the selected address in Live Map - Add
required Street, City and State information and then save the record.</label>
    </form>
</body>
</html>
```

2. Save the HTM into a new folder where the CRMWeb is served (normally in
C:\Program Files\Microsoft Dynamics CRM Server\CRMWeb or in
C:\InetPub\wwwroot). In this example, we've created a new directory called Maps,
as shown in Figure 10.3. (Be sure the directory is configured in Internet Information
Services [IIS] as a virtual directory.)

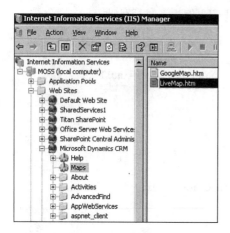

FIGURE 10.3   New IIS virtual directory for MSN Maps.

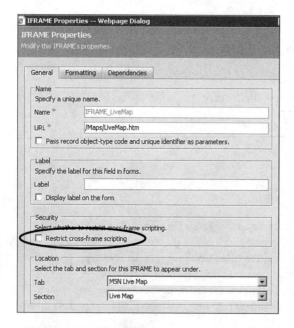

FIGURE 10.4   IFrame Properties page for Live Search integration.

3. Navigate to the customization screen for accounts in Microsoft Dynamics CRM, and add a new tab, section, and IFrame.

   Be sure to configure the IFrame, as shown in Figure 10.4, by adding a name and the URL to the page you just created. In addition, be sure to unselect Restrict Cross-Frame Scripting in the Security section.

4. Display the Formatting tab and select Automatically Expand to Use Available Space.

5. Save and publish the account.

This example will work with as many or as few of the parameters supplied. For example, if you have only a city, it will show the city. If there is no data entered on the saved form, the error message Unable to Locate the Selected Address in Live Map - Add Required Street, City and State Information and then Save the Record will display. (You can easily customize this on the HTML page by modifying the label tag with the ID of `lblMessage`.)

MapPoint Integration

MapPoint is an extendable product and technology that enables users to create complex mapping and data scenarios. It is significantly more sophisticated than the other mapping technologies in that it has geographic information system (GIS) integration with latitude and longitude options. We have included it within its own section because the application, MapPoint 2009, can be used without an Internet connection, which is a common scenario where users don't have access to call the MapPoint web services.

We will review two different options:

▶ Windows-based usage of MapPoint 2009 (without Internet connection)

▶ MapPoint web service integration (Internet connection required)

MapPoint 2009

With this option, we can leverage the MapPoint 2009 software development kit (SDK) to display Microsoft Dynamics CRM data within the application.

> **NOTE**
>
> It is important to note that MapPoint is a compiled .NET application and not a web application.

10

In the example, we modify a MapPoint user interface control and create a text box that shows the Microsoft Dynamics CRM accounts based on the account name, add a Search button, and a data grid to show the resulting/matching accounts and finally include a Locate button that locates the selected address on the MapPoint map.

The Search button includes the business logic to fetch the Microsoft Dynamics CRM accounts using a fetch query based on the user input to retrieve all the accounts in Microsoft Dynamics CRM that match the account name entered in the text box. Figure 10.5 shows the final custom application.

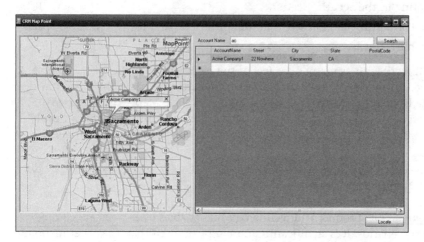

FIGURE 10.5   MapPoint 2009 with custom CRM integration for accounts.

To deploy the Windows-based usage of MapPoint 2009, complete the following steps:

1. On a computer that has MapPoint 2009 installed, create a new Windows application and reference the MapPoint assemblies.

2. Create two class files: one for Business Logic and one for Data Access.

   For the Business Logic page, use this code:

```
using System;
using System.Collections.Generic;
using System.Collections.Specialized;
using System.IO;
using System.Data;
using System.Configuration;
using System.Text;
using System.Xml;

namespace MapPointApp
{
    class BusinessLogic
    {
        #region Global Declaration
        DataAccessLayer mscrmAccess = null;
        #endregion
```

```
public BusinessLogic()
{
    mscrmAccess = new DataAccessLayer();
}

public DataTable GetAccountDetails(string accName)
{
    StringBuilder fetchXML = new StringBuilder();
    fetchXML.Append(@"<fetch mapping=""logical""><entity
    name=""account"">");
    fetchXML.Append(@"<attribute name=""name"" />");
    fetchXML.Append(@"<attribute name=""address1_line1"" />");
    fetchXML.Append(@"<attribute name=""address1_city"" />");
    fetchXML.Append(@"<attribute name=""address1_stateorprovince""
    />");
    fetchXML.Append(@"<attribute name=""address1_postalcode"" />");
    fetchXML.Append(@"<filter><condition attribute=""name""
    operator=""like"" value=""");
    fetchXML.Append(accName);
    fetchXML.Append(@"%""/></filter></entity></fetch>");

    string resultSet =
    mscrmAccess.ExecuteCRMQuery(fetchXML.ToString());
    XmlDocument xmlDocument = new XmlDocument();

    xmlDocument.LoadXml(resultSet);
    string xPath = @"/resultset/result";
    XmlNodeList xmlNodeList = xmlDocument.SelectNodes(xPath);

    DataTable caseDataTable = new DataTable();

    DataColumn dColumn;

    dColumn = new DataColumn();
    dColumn.DataType = Type.GetType("System.String");
    dColumn.ColumnName = "AccountName";
    caseDataTable.Columns.Add(dColumn);

    dColumn = new DataColumn();
    dColumn.DataType = Type.GetType("System.String");
    dColumn.ColumnName = "Street";
    caseDataTable.Columns.Add(dColumn);

    dColumn = new DataColumn();
    dColumn.DataType = Type.GetType("System.String");
```

```
            dColumn.ColumnName = "City";
            caseDataTable.Columns.Add(dColumn);

            dColumn = new DataColumn();
            dColumn.DataType = Type.GetType("System.String");
            dColumn.ColumnName = "State";
            caseDataTable.Columns.Add(dColumn);

            dColumn = new DataColumn();
            dColumn.DataType = Type.GetType("System.String");
            dColumn.ColumnName = "PostalCode";
            caseDataTable.Columns.Add(dColumn);

            foreach (XmlNode node in xmlNodeList)
            {
                DataRow dRow = caseDataTable.NewRow();
                if (node.SelectSingleNode("name") != null)
                {
                    dRow["AccountName"] =
➥node.SelectSingleNode("name").InnerText;
                }
                if (node.SelectSingleNode("address1_line1") !=.null)
                {
                    dRow["Street"] =
➥node.SelectSingleNode("address1_line1").InnerText;
                }
                if (node.SelectSingleNode("address1_city") != null)
                {
                    dRow["City"] =
➥node.SelectSingleNode("address1_city").InnerText;
                }
                if (node.SelectSingleNode("address1_stateorprovince") != null)
                {
                    dRow["State"] =
➥node.SelectSingleNode("address1_stateorprovince").InnerText;
                }
                if (node.SelectSingleNode("address1_postalcode") != null)
                {
                    dRow["PostalCode"] =
➥node.SelectSingleNode("address1_postalcode").InnerText;
                }
                caseDataTable.Rows.Add(dRow);
            }

            return caseDataTable;
```

```
        }

    }
}
```

For the Data Access layer, use this code:

```
using System;
using System.Collections.Generic;
using System.Text;
using System.Web.Services.Protocols;
using MapPointApp.CRMSDK;

namespace MapPointApp
{
    class DataAccessLayer
    {
        #region global Declaration
        protected string crmServer = null;
        protected CrmService crmService = null;
        protected string crmWebServicesUrl = null;
        #endregion

        public DataAccessLayer()
        {
            crmServer = "http://192.168.0.1:5555/mscrmservices";
            string userName = "administrator";
            string userPwd = "password";
            string userDomain = "crmdev";
            string crmOrgName = "Webfortis";

            if (crmServer.Length == 0 || (!crmServer.StartsWith("http://") &&
➥!crmServer.StartsWith("https://")))
            {
                throw new ApplicationException("CRM server url is wrong, please
➥contact your system administrator.");
            }

            if (!crmServer.EndsWith("/"))
            {
                crmServer += "/2007/";
            }
            else
            {
```

```
                crmServer += "2007/";
            }

            crmWebServicesUrl = string.Concat(crmServer, "CrmService.asmx");


            crmService = new CrmService();
            crmService.Url = crmWebServicesUrl;
            crmService.Credentials = new System.Net.NetworkCredential(userName,
    ↪userPwd, userDomain);

            crmService.PreAuthenticate = true;
            CrmAuthenticationToken token = new CrmAuthenticationToken();
            token.OrganizationName = crmOrgName;
            token.AuthenticationType = 0;
            crmService.CrmAuthenticationTokenValue = token;
        }

        public string ExecuteCRMQuery(string fetchXML)
        {
            try
            {
                //Fetch XML Execution
                return crmService.Fetch(fetchXML);
            }
            catch (SoapException Ex)
            {
                throw new ApplicationException("Unable to retrieve CRM records.
    ↪Please contact your system administrator", Ex);
            }
            catch (Exception Ex)
            {
                throw new ApplicationException("Unable to retrieve CRM records.
    ↪Please contact your system administrator", Ex);
            }
        }
    }
}
```

Be sure to change the section in the Data Access layer with your server, username,
user password, domain, and organization, as shown in Figure 10.6.

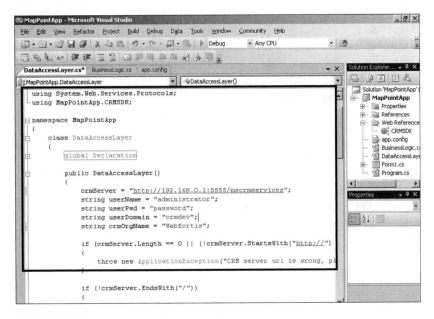

FIGURE 10.6   Server-specific credentials.

3. Create a new form within the solution with the following code:

```csharp
using System;
using System.Collections.Generic;
using System.ComponentModel;
using System.Data;
using System.Drawing;
using System.Text;
using System.Windows.Forms;

namespace MapPointApp
{
    public partial class Form1 : Form
    {

        #region Global Declaration
            BusinessLogic bLogic = null;
            MapPoint.Map objMap = null;
            MapPoint.Location objLoc = null;
            MapPoint.FindResults objResults = null;
            MapPoint.Pushpin objPushpin = null;
            MapPoint.Symbol objSymbol = null;
            object key = 1;
        #endregion

        public Form1()
```

```
        {
            InitializeComponent();

            bLogic = new BusinessLogic();

            objMap = MPC.NewMap(MapPoint.GeoMapRegion.geoMapNorthAmerica);

        }

        public void GetAccountDetails()
        {
            DataTable accountTable =
➥bLogic.GetAccountDetails(txtAccName.Text);
            dataGridView1.DataSource = accountTable;
        }

        private void btnLocate_Click(object sender, EventArgs e)
        {
            DataGridViewRow selectedRow = dataGridView1.SelectedRows[0];

            string accName = selectedRow.Cells[0].Value.ToString();
            string street = selectedRow.Cells[1].Value.ToString();
            string city = selectedRow.Cells[2].Value.ToString();
            string state = selectedRow.Cells[3].Value.ToString();
            string postalCode = selectedRow.Cells[4].Value.ToString();

            objResults = objMap.FindAddressResults(street, city, "", state,
➥postalCode, MapPoint.GeoCountry.geoCountryUnitedStates);

            objLoc = (MapPoint.Location)objResults.get_Item(ref key);

            objMap.AddPushpin(objLoc, accName).Highlight = true;

            objPushpin = objMap.FindPushpin(accName);
            objPushpin.BalloonState = MapPoint.GeoBalloonState.
➥geoDisplayBalloon;
            //objSymbol = objMap.Symbols.Add("C:/WINDOWS/Prairie Wind.bmp");
            //objPushpin.Symbol = objSymbol;
            //objPushpin.BalloonState = MapPoint.GeoBalloonState
➥.geoDisplayBalloon;
            objLoc.GoTo();
        }

        private void btnSearch_Click(object sender, EventArgs e)
        {
```

```
        GetAccountDetails();
    }
}
}
```

4. The resulting solution will look similar to Figure 10.7 and will allow you to enter CRM account information and search for matches.

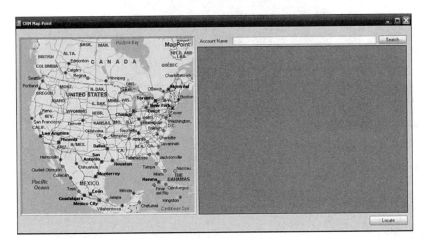

FIGURE 10.7   Custom MapPoint form.

To use the form, enter all or part of a CRM account and click Search. The grid will display the resulting matches from CRM (as shown in Figure 10.8), and when you select a row and click Locate, the location will display (see Figure 10.9).

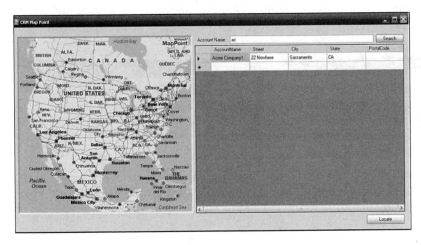

FIGURE 10.8   Searching for accounts in CRM through MapPoint.

10

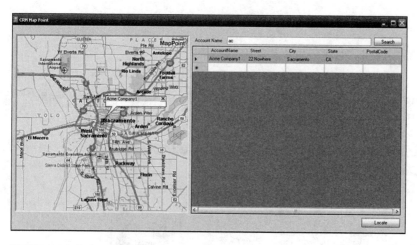

FIGURE 10.9   Mapped CRM account.

MapPoint Web Services

MapPoint web services integration makes use of the MapPoint web service application programming interfaces (APIs).

When working with Microsoft Dynamics CRM accounts, there are already longitude and latitude parameters for addresses. (Most organizations don't use these attributes, however). When working with MapPoint web services, we can pass an address from Microsoft Dynamics CRM to MapPoint web services via the FindAddress service and receive back the longitude and latitude parameters. (Locations and thumbtacks in MapPoint require longitude and latitude values for address.)

Unlike Microsoft Live Search, MapPoint web services is not a free service; however, you can get a free developer account, which will allow you start to create some integrations. To sign up for an account, navigate to https://mappoint-css.partners.extranet.microsoft.com/MwsSignup/Eval.aspx.

> **NOTE**
>
> With the developer account for MapPoint web services, you will get full access to the MapPoint web services APIs and a staging environment that you can use to build applications for proof-of-concept purposes.

For our example, we're going to create a custom web application that we'll integrate into the Microsoft Dynamics CRM account form via an IFrame to show the map, and we'll pass the address values from Microsoft Dynamics CRM to MapPoint web services.

To deploy a MapPoint web services application, complete the following steps:

1. Using Visual Studio, create an ASPX page with the following code:

```
<%@ Page Language="C#" AutoEventWireup="true" CodeFile="Default2.aspx.cs"
Inherits="Default2" %>

<!DOCTYPE html PUBLIC "-//W3C//DTD XHTML 1.0 Transitional//EN"
"http://www.w3.org/TR/xhtml1/DTD/xhtml1-transitional.dtd">

<html xmlns="http://www.w3.org/1999/xhtml" >
<head runat="server">
    <title>Untitled Page</title>
     <script type="text/javascript">
            function GetCRMAddress()
           {
                    var address = '';

                    var addressLine1 =
➥parent.document.forms[0].all.address1_line1.DataValue;

                    var postalCode =
➥parent.document.forms[0].all.address1_postalcode.DataValue;

                    var city =
➥parent.document.forms[0].all.address1_city.DataValue;

                    var stateOrProvince =
➥parent.document.forms[0].all.address1_stateorprovince.DataValue;

                    var country =
➥parent.document.forms[0].all.address1_country.DataValue;

                    var address = '';
                    if(addressLine1 == null && postalCode == null && city ==
➥null && stateOrProvince == null && country == null)
                    {
                            address = '';
                    }
                    else
                    {
                            address = addressLine1 + '!' + postalCode + '!' +
➥city + '!' + stateOrProvince + '!' + country;
                            document.getElementById('hdnaddress').value =
➥address;

                            alert(address);
```

10

```
alert(document.getElementById('hdnaddress').value);
                    }
                    return address;
            }
    </script>
    </head>
<body>
    <form id="form1" runat="server">
    <div>
            <asp:ImageMap ID="ImageMap1" runat="server" Width="505px">
            </asp:ImageMap> 
            <asp:HiddenField ID="hdnaddress" runat="server" />
            </div>
    </form>
</body>
</html>
```

And the following code-behind:

```
using System;
using System.Data;
using System.Configuration;
using System.Collections;
using System.Web;
using System.Web.Security;
using System.Web.UI;
using System.Web.UI.WebControls;
using System.Web.UI.WebControls.WebParts;
using System.Web.UI.HtmlControls;

public partial class Default2 : System.Web.UI.Page
{
    protected void Page_Load(object sender, EventArgs e)
    {
            string crmAddress = Request.QueryString["Address"].ToString();
            ImageMap1.ImageUrl = "Default.aspx?address =" + crmAddress;

    }
}
```

2. Create another ASPX page with no code on it, but with the following code in the code-behind (CS) page:

```
using System;
using System.Data;
using System.Configuration;
using System.Web;
```

```csharp
using System.Web.Security;
using System.Web.UI;
using System.Web.UI.WebControls;
using System.Web.UI.WebControls.WebParts;
using System.Web.UI.HtmlControls;
using System.Net;
using System.IO;
using net.mappoint.staging;

public partial class _Default : System.Web.UI.Page
{
    protected void Page_Load(object sender, EventArgs e)
    {
        FindServiceSoap FindService = new FindServiceSoap();
        FindService.Credentials = new NetworkCredential("Account ID",
➥"Password");
        FindService.PreAuthenticate = true;

        string crmAddress = Request.QueryString["address"].ToString();

        string[] arAddress = new string[4];

        // define which character is separating fields
        char[] splitter = { '!' };

        arAddress = crmAddress.Split(splitter);

        // mAddress = (Address)addresses[i];
        FindAddressSpecification spec = new FindAddressSpecification();
        spec.InputAddress = new Address();
        spec.InputAddress.AddressLine = arAddress[0];
        spec.InputAddress.PostalCode = arAddress[1];
        spec.InputAddress.PrimaryCity = arAddress[2];
        spec.InputAddress.CountryRegion = arAddress[3];
        spec.InputAddress.Subdivision = "Seattle";

        //spec.InputAddress = new Address();
        //spec.InputAddress.AddressLine = "2360 Mendocino Ave.";
        //spec.InputAddress.PostalCode = "95403";
        //spec.InputAddress.PrimaryCity = "Santa Rosa";
        //spec.InputAddress.CountryRegion = "United States";


        spec.DataSourceName = "MapPoint.NA";

        FindResults results = FindService.FindAddress(spec);
```

10

```
        Location[] myLocation = new Location[1];
        myLocation[0] = new Location();
        myLocation[0].LatLong = new LatLong();
        myLocation[0].LatLong = results.Results[0].FoundLocation.LatLong;
        Pushpin[] pushpins = new Pushpin[1];
        pushpins[0] = new Pushpin();
        pushpins[0].PinID = "Pin1";
        pushpins[0].IconName = "0";
        pushpins[0].Label = "CustomerAddress";
        pushpins[0].IconDataSource = "MapPoint.Icons";
        pushpins[0].LatLong = results.Results[0].FoundLocation.LatLong;


        //Call MapPoint Render Web Service
        RenderServiceSoap RenderService = new RenderServiceSoap();
        RenderService.Credentials = new NetworkCredential("Account ID",
➥"Password");


        MapViewRepresentations mvRep =
➥RenderService.GetBestMapView(myLocation, "MapPoint.NA");
        ViewByBoundingRectangle[] mviews = new ViewByBoundingRectangle[1];
        mviews[0] = mvRep.ByBoundingRectangle;

        MapSpecification mspec = new MapSpecification();
        //mspec.Options = moptions;
        mspec.Views = mviews;
        mspec.Pushpins = pushpins;
        mspec.DataSourceName = "MapPoint.NA";
        MapImage[] image = RenderService.GetMap(mspec);

        //Display the resulting map in the picture box.
        System.IO.Stream streamImage;
        streamImage = new System.IO.MemoryStream(image[0].MimeData.Bits);

        Response.Clear();
        Response.ContentType = image[0].MimeData.MimeType;
        //myImage.MimeData.MimeType;
        Response.BinaryWrite(image[0].MimeData.Bits);
        Response.End();
    }

}
```

NOTE

Be sure to change the account ID and the password in the previous code, as shown here:

```
FindServiceSoap FindService = new FindServiceSoap();FindService.Credentials =
➥new NetworkCredential
  ("Account ID", "Password");

FindService.PreAuthenticate = true;
```

Use the account ID and password that you created when signing in to the developer access portal at https://mappoint-css.partners.extranet.microsoft.com/MwsSignup/Eval.aspx.

This aspect of the code is important in that it initializes the application to make use of the methods and classes in the web service.

NOTE

The FindAddress service mentioned previously is contained within this code via the following snippet:

```
FindAddressSpecification spec = new FindAddressSpecification();

spec.InputAddress = new Address();

spec.InputAddress.AddressLine = arAddress[0];

spec.InputAddress.PostalCode = arAddress[1];

spec.InputAddress.PrimaryCity = arAddress[2];

spec.InputAddress.CountryRegion = arAddress[3];

spec.InputAddress.Subdivision = "Seattle";

spec.DataSourceName = "MapPoint.NA";

FindResults results = FindService.FindAddress(spec);
```

This is where the address information retrieved from Microsoft Dynamics CRM is used to return the longitude and latitude parameters with reference to the selected Microsoft Dynamics CRM account.

NOTE

The MapPoint web service provides a Render Server API to automatically zoom based on the geography covered by address and location via the following snippet:

```
//Call MapPoint Render Web Service
        RenderServiceSoap RenderService = new RenderServiceSoap();

        RenderService.Credentials = new NetworkCredential("Account ID",
➥"Password");
```

10

```
        MapViewRepresentations mvRep =
➥RenderService.GetBestMapView(myLocation, "MapPoint.NA");
        ViewByBoundingRectangle[] mviews = new ViewByBoundingRectangle[1];
        mviews[0] = mvRep.ByBoundingRectangle;
        MapSpecification mspec = new MapSpecification();
                //mspec.Options = moptions;
        mspec.Views = mviews;
        mspec.Pushpins = pushpins
        mspec.DataSourceName = "MapPoint.NA";
        MapImage[] image = RenderService.GetMap(mspec);
```

Use the account ID and password that you created when signing into the developer access portal at https://mappoint-css.partners.extranet.microsoft.com/MwsSignup/Eval.aspx.

NOTE

The image map control is what's used to show the map with the selected address and location, as shown here:

```
System.IO.Stream streamImage;

streamImage = new System.IO.MemoryStream(image[0].MimeData.Bits);

Response.Clear();

Response.ContentType = image[0].MimeData.MimeType;

Response.BinaryWrite(image[0].MimeData.Bits);

Response.End();
```

---

3. Save the solution into a new folder where the CRMWeb is served (normally in C:\Program Files\Microsoft Dynamics CRM Server\CRMWeb or in C:\InetPub\wwwroot). In this example, we've created a new directory called Maps, as shown in Figure 10.10. (Be sure the directory is configured in IIS as a virtual directory.)

4. Navigate to the customization screen for accounts in Microsoft Dynamics CRM, and add a new tab, section, and IFrame.

   Be sure to configure the IFrame, as shown in Figure 10.11, by adding a name and the URL to the page you just created. In addition, be sure to unselect Restrict Cross-Frame Scripting in the Security section.

5. For the Account form, add the following code to the OnLoad event:

```
var address = '';
var schemaNames =
'address1_line1,address1_postalcode,address1_city,address1_country';
```

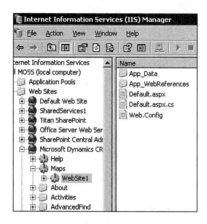

FIGURE 10.10   New IIS virtual directory for MapPoint web services integration.

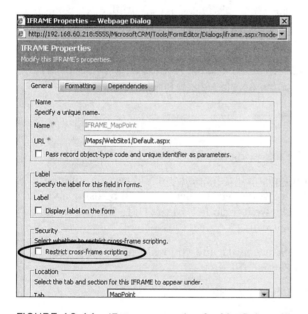

FIGURE 10.11   IFrame properties for MapPoint web services integration.

```
var schemaNameArray = schemaNames.split(",");

for(count = 0; count < schemaNameArray.length; count++)
{
   var o = document.getElementById(schemaNameArray[count]);
 if(o != null)
 {
  if(o.value != '')
   {
```

```
    address = address + '!' + o.value ;
    }
  }
}

var URL = '/Maps/WebSite1/Default2.aspx?Address=' + address;

crmForm.all.IFRAME_MapPoint.src = URL;
```

Google Maps Integration

Similar to how Microsoft Live Search maps are created, Google uses an integrated HTML page to show its mapping technology. One main difference, however, is the requirement for a Google API key. This is a required step and is dependent on the URL of your site. The key can be obtained from http://code.google.com/apis/maps/signup.html, after agreeing to various terms and conditions.

To obtain a Google API key, complete the following steps:

1. Navigate to http://code.google.com/apis/maps/signup.html and agree to the terms and conditions, and enter the URL for your website. Because we'll be using a virtual directory called Maps in this example, we'll include it in the URL. Select Generate API Key to continue, as shown in Figure 10.12.

2. You will be asked to sign in to Google accounts, and you will then receive your Google Maps API key, as shown in Figure 10.13.

3. Create a new HTML page with the following code:

```
<!DOCTYPE html PUBLIC "-//W3C//DTD XHTML 1.0 Transitional//EN"
"http://www.w3.org/TR/xhtml1/DTD/xhtml1-transitional.dtd">
<html xmlns="http://www.w3.org/1999/xhtml">
<head runat="server">
    <meta http-equiv="content-type" content="text/html; charset=UTF-8" />
    <title>MSCRM Google Map</title>

    <script src="http://maps.google.com/maps?file=api&amp;v=2.x&amp;key=<< Enter
➥Key Here>>"
            type="text/javascript"></script>
```

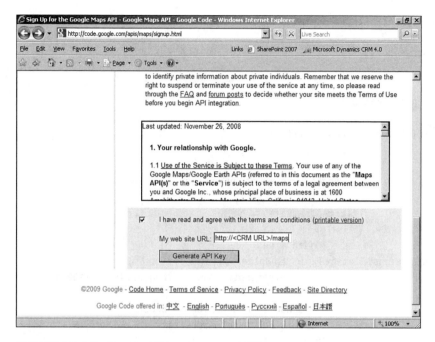

FIGURE 10.12   Google API key terms and URL.

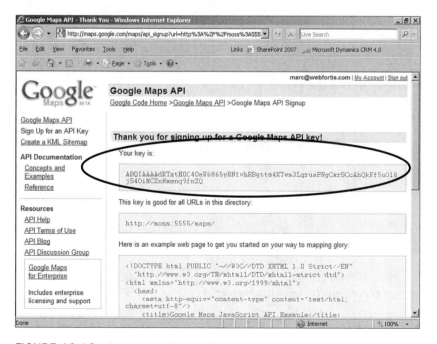

FIGURE 10.13   Generate a Google Maps API key.

```
<script type="text/javascript">

var gMap = null;
var geocoder = null;

function initialize()
{
    if (GBrowserIsCompatible())
    {

                var crmAddress = GetCRMAddress();

                if(crmAddress != ',')
                {
                        gMap = new
➥GMap2(document.getElementById("MapHolder"));
                        //gMap.setCenter(new GLatLng(37.4419, -122.1419),
➥13);

                        geocoder = new GClientGeocoder();
                        LocateAddress(crmAddress);
                }
                else
                {
                        DisplayMessage();
                }
    }
}
    function LocateAddress(address)
{
    if (geocoder)
    {
      geocoder.getLatLng(address,function(point)
      {
          if (!point)
          {DisplayMessage();}
          else
          {
            gMap.setCenter(point, 13);
            var marker = new GMarker(point);
            gMap.addOverlay(marker);
            marker.openInfoWindowHtml(address);
          }
      }
    );
    }
}
```

```
function GetCRMAddress()
{
   var schemaNames =
➥'address1_line1,address1_line2,address1_line3,address1_city,
➥address1_stateorprovince,address1_country,address1_postalcode';
   var schemaNameArray = schemaNames.split(",");
   var address = '';

   for(count = 0; count < schemaNameArray.length; count++)
   {
           var o = parent.document.getElementById(schemaNameArray[count]);

           if(o != null)
           {
                   if(o.value != '')
                   {
                           address = address + ',' + o.value ;
                   }
           }
   }

   return address;
}

function DisplayMessage()
{
   var lbl = document.getElementById('lblMessage');
   lbl.style.display = "inline";

   var div = document.getElementById('MapHolder');
   div.style.display = "none";
}
</script>

</head>
<body>
   <body onload="initialize()" onunload="GUnload()">
           <form>
                   <div id="MapHolder" style="width: 700px; height: 350px">
                   </div>
                   <label id="lblMessage" style="display:none;
➥font-family:@Arial Unicode MS; font-size:small; font-weight:bold;
➥color:#15428b;">Unable to locate the given address in Google Maps - Please
➥update the address information and save the record then try
➥again.</label>
```

10

```
        </form>
    </body>
  </body>
  </html>
```

Figure 10.14 shows Microsoft Dynamics CRM with Google Maps integration.

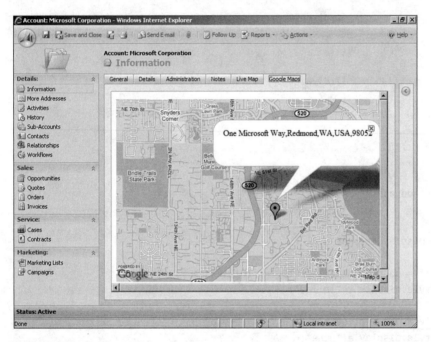

FIGURE 10.14   Google Maps integration.

Summary

In this chapter, you learned how to integrate several mapping technologies with Microsoft Dynamics CRM 4.0.

Although a majority of the functionality shown in this chapter relies on an Internet connection, utilizing MapPoint 2009 does not depend on an Internet connection.

It is important to note that what we have illustrated barely skims the surface of what can you can do with mapping technologies. The following is just a partial list of other possibilities:

▶ Select a list of accounts from Microsoft Dynamics CRM and use mapping technology to map the most efficient path to visit them.

▶ Using the preceding example and enhanced services from MapPoint web services, include traffic conditions.

▶ Capture mapping information for all site visits with notes reflecting who, what, and why.

▶ Show drive times to capture miles driven from the office to the account (for expense reporting).

▶ Show mapping information that includes GIS metric information, such as densities, crime rates, and related metric data.

10

Microsoft Dynamics CRM 4.0 Accelerators*

A client recently inquired, "What are the CRM accelerators, and do they make CRM faster?"

Well, in a way they do. Not necessarily with the speed of the program but with the speed of adoption, development, time to market, and sales cycle.

Because a CRM system can be difficult to adopt within certain organizations, the "glitz" of these accelerators can provide an added benefit and visibility that's needed to get salespeople and managers to more readily adopt CRM. In addition, the CRM accelerators such as the Event Manager or the eService accelerator speed development of CRM integration to the Web.

If you're a Microsoft Dynamics CRM solution provider, one of the goals of your business is to sell or provide either licensing or service for CRM. The accelerators speed the sales and development cycles by offering rich out-of-the-box functionality for vertical and horizontal markets, and in fact Reuben Krippner, a senior product manager for CRM, refers to the CRM accelerators as a "diagonal market" solution, meaning they can appeal to and be used by nearly any organization.

If you're an IT manager or CRM administrator, you can leverage your investment in CRM by implementing function-rich solutions at a fraction of the cost. For example, if your company has the need to manage customers through your

---

* This chapter was researched and prepared largely by Patrick Austin of Webfortis. Patrick Austin is both Microsoft CRM certified and Scribe certified and has extensive experience working on integration projects and custom vertical solutions.

website with one common repository of data, or the need to mine data through social networking, implementation of the eService and Social Networking accelerators, respectively, will replace costly development or third-party products that might orphan data in disparate databases. In addition, other CRM accelerators can provide enhanced insight into sales forecasting and analytics, provide enterprise search capabilities, provide CRM users with a better overall picture of accounts and contacts, and help management staff monitor CRM usage and auditing.

They extend the already powerful CRM 4.0 functionality by providing "prebuilt" solutions from Microsoft, and as CRM gains a wider audience, it's become obvious that CRM is not just any old customer relationship management software; it's a platform for rapid application development and can help any organization go to market faster without the hassle of building something from the ground up.

Our goal within this chapter is to highlight the following aspects of a select group of CRM accelerators:

▶ The purpose of each CRM accelerator

▶ The level of effort required to install and maintain the accelerator

▶ The effect each accelerator has on CRM once installed

▶ Additional applications for each accelerator

We've hand picked the CRM Accelerators we feel bring the most value to the majority of CRM systems; however, we strongly recommend you check for new updates and releases from the accelerators download site, as Microsoft frequently updates and releases new Accelerators.

NOTE

You can download the accelerators from the Codeplex website at http://crmaccelerators. codeplex.com.

The accelerators are unique to Microsoft in that they are open source and allow for alternate configuration, including complete rewrite if desired.

In short, think of the accelerators as "templates" that are provided by Microsoft that can be modified for your particular requirements.

In addition, it is important to realize that although the accelerators' customizations use officially "supported" CRM methods, you will have a difficult time getting support from Microsoft with them. In other words, adding an accelerator solution to your implementation will still qualify you for support (unlike other modifications that might place your implementation in an unsupportable state), but Microsoft support will refer you to an implementation partner for advanced configuration and troubleshooting issues.

CRM Accelerators

At the time of this writing, the CRM accelerators listed in Table 11.1 have either been released or are planned for release.

TABLE 11.1   CRM Accelerators

Accelerator	Description
Analytics	Business intelligence, dashboards, graphing, and OLAP cubes.
Business Data Auditing	Provides basic audit capabilities, which can be enhanced using workflow.
Business Productivity Newsfeed	Provides insight into CRM user activity.
Business Productivity Workflow Tools	Extend CRM's workflow capabilities.
Enterprise Search	View, edit, and search for CRM data directly from SharePoint.
eService	Web portal for providing non-CRM users access to CRM entities, such as cases.
Event Management	Manage the planning, execution, and metrics surrounding events.
Extended Sales Forecasting	Enhance CRM's sales forecasting with tools for users and managers.
Notifications	CRM users monitor changes to CRM entities through RSS.
Partner Relationship Management	Distribute leads and opportunities across channel partners.
Portal Integration	Rapidly extend business processes using point-and-click configuration.
Sales Performance International (SPI) Sales Methodology	Integration and customization based on sales methodologies.
Social Networking	Analyze customers' conversations on social networking sites.

Microsoft Dynamics CRM Online and the Accelerators

The accelerators have been designed to work primarily within a CRM On-Premise environment; however, there are certain aspects of the accelerators that provide value, albeit not the fully intended functionality, for CRM Online.

What this means is that although you can use some of the accelerators for CRM Online (as shown in Table 11.2), because of the limitations of working with CRM Online (for example, the inability to run custom code and the required use of Windows Live authentication), full use of the accelerators is limited.

TABLE 11.2   The Differences Between CRM On-Premise and CRM Online for the Accelerators

Accelerator	Works with CRM Online?	Additional Required Components
Analytics	No	▶ SQL Analysis Services ▶ MOSS if PerformancePoint dashboards are needed
Business Data Auditing	No	–
Business Productivity Newsfeed	No	–
Business Productivity Workflow Tools	No	–
Enterprise Search	No	MOSS
eService	▶ Customizations only ▶ Core portal value is not available	–
Event Management	▶ No extranet event management registration ▶ No custom reports	–
Extended Sales Forecasting	▶ No custom reports	–
Notifications	No	–
Partner Relationship Management	TBD	–
Portal Integration	TBD	–
Sales Methodologies	No	–
Social Networking	TBD	–

The eService accelerator contains some customizations that can prove valuable, such as the ability to track audits to the CRM case, CRM contact, and CRM account entities; however, the core value of the eService accelerator is the capability to enable customers to create and modify CRM cases, modify CRM account and contact data, and schedule CRM services through a custom portal, and this is not available with CRM Online. (It is available, however, if you create a custom portal on your own servers and then integrate with your CRM Online implementation.)

Analytics Accelerator

The Analytics accelerator is designed to leverage an existing investment in SQL Server, using SQL Analysis Services, and it provides the following functionality:

▶ Dashboards, graphing, business intelligence (BI) elements.

▶ SQL Analysis Services, predictive analytics, online analytical processing (OLAP) cubes.

▶ Utilizes PerformancePoint Server with scorecards.

▶ Report deployment needs to occur (very simple) and can be leveraged with new reports (requires SQL Server Reporting Services [SSRS] skills).

▶ SQL Server 2008 dashboards, which provide a framework to deliver more robust dashboards than SQL Server 2005.

Figure 11.1 shows the Analytics Accelerator: CRM Sales dashboard.

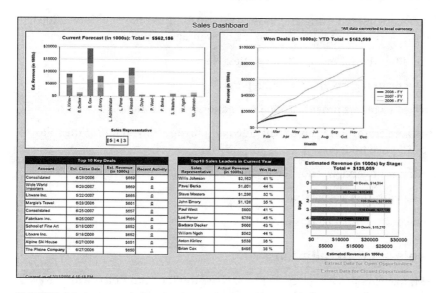

FIGURE 11.1   Analytics Accelerator: CRM Sales Usage dashboard.

▶ **Basic:** For organizations that need basic reporting. If you're looking for a quick win to your sales reporting team, these reports can be deployed quickly and easily.

▶ **Rationalized:** For organizations that need more than the basic reports provide; trending using a SQL Server Analysis Services (SSAS) cube.

▶ **Dynamic:** For organizations familiar with reporting and analysis services who can utilize Performance Point Server dashboards.

This accelerator intends to help sales managers in the following ways:

▶ **Account Executive dashboard:** Provides insight into sales representative's performance to date with open opportunities, probability, estimated close date, competitors, total estimated revenue, and a weighted value

▶ **Sales Manager dashboard:** Provides insight into the top 10 key deals and top 10 sales leaders for the year

▶ **Service dashboard:** Provides insight into the top 10 high-priority cases and associated details such as customer satisfaction level and elapsed time

▶ **CRM Sales Usage dashboard:** Provides insight into the value employees have in different areas of the business such as how many contacts and activities a sales representative has created, and the number of neglected leads and opportunities

Prerequisites and Modifications

This accelerator is composed of multiple releases, with Release 1 (R1) providing simple cube definition; Release 2 (R2) providing SSRS 2008 reports, dashboards, and SSAS cube development); and Release 3 (R3) providing more advanced SSAS capabilities and Microsoft Office PerformancePoint Server scorecards.

SQL Server 2008 offers richer reporting and dashboard capabilities than SQL Server 2005, and in the future this accelerator will be able to take advantage of these new features.

This accelerator modifies the following CRM entities:

▶ Adds four new main reports and five subreports.

▶ The rationalized elements provide a SSAS cube and sales trending data extract.

After the Analytics accelerator has been downloaded and unzipped, you'll find the following materials in the Source folder:

▶ Documentation for overview, cube deployment, and report installation

▶ Reports for use with this accelerator

▶ Visual Studio code to enhance this accelerator

Analytics Accelerator Installation

1. Within CRM, navigate to Workplace, Reports, New. You'll be prompted with a New Report screen. Configure each field as follows:

   ▶ **Report Type:** Existing File

   ▶ **File Location:** \Installation\1-Basic\SQL Server 2005\Account Executive\ Account Executive Dashboard.rdl (making sure the full path to your extracted files exists)

   ▶ **Name:** Account Executive Dashboard

   ▶ **Description:** Analytics Accelerator - Account Executive Dashboard

   ▶ **Categories:** Sales Reports

   ▶ **Related Record Types:** Blank

> ▸ **Display In:** Reports Area

> ▸ **Administration Tab, Viewable By:** Organization

After you've completed the configurations, your New Report screen should match Figure 11.2.

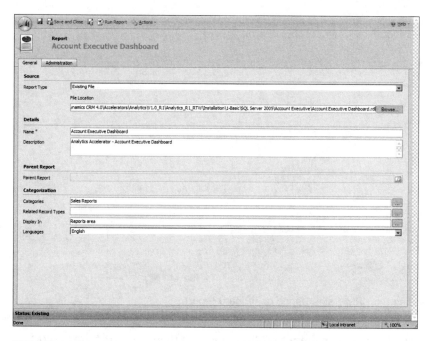

FIGURE 11.2   Adding the Account Executive dashboard report.

2. Click Save and New to create the new CRM report and then create the next report.

3. Add the CRM Sales Usage dashboard report and configure each field as follows:

> ▸ **Report Type:** Existing File

> ▸ **File Location:** \Installation\1-Basic\SQL Server 2005\CRM Usage\ CRM Sales Usage Dashboard.rdl (making sure the full path to your extracted files exists)

> ▸ **Name:** CRM Sales Usage Dashboard

> ▸ **Description:** Analytics Accelerator - CRM Sales Usage Dashboard

> ▸ **Categories:** Administrative

> ▸ **Related Record Types:** Blank

> ▸ **Display In:** Reports Area

> ▸ **Administration Tab, Viewable By:** Organization

After you've completed the configurations, your New Report screen should match Figure 11.3.

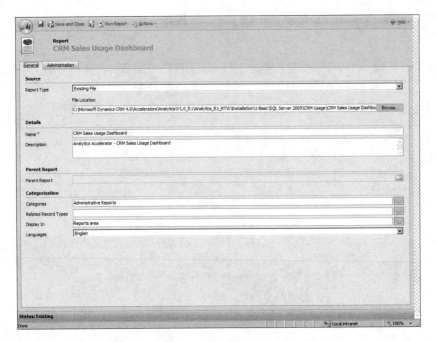

FIGURE 11.3   Adding the CRM Sales Usage dashboard report.

4. Click Save and New to create the new CRM report and then create the next report.

5. Add the CRM Sales Usage Dashboard Details subreport and configure each field as follows:

- ▶ **Report Type:** Existing File
- ▶ **File Location:** \Installation\1-Basic\SQL Server 2005\CRM Usage\ CRM Sales Usage Dashboard Details.rdl (making sure the full path to your extracted files exists)
- ▶ **Name:** CRM Sales Usage Dashboard Details
- ▶ **Description:** Analytics Accelerator - CRM Sales Usage Dashboard Details
- ▶ **Parent Report:** CRM Sales Usage Dashboard
- ▶ **Categories:** Blank
- ▶ **Related Record Types:** Blank
- ▶ **Display In:** Blank
- ▶ **Administration Tab, Viewable By:** Organization

After you've completed the configurations, your New Report screen should match Figure 11.4.

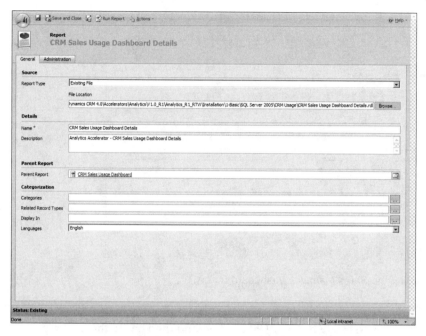

FIGURE 11.4   Adding the CRM Sales Usage Dashboard Details report.

8. Click Save and New to create the new CRM Report and then create the next report.

9. Add the Sales Manager Dashboard report and configure each field as follows:

   ▶ **Report Type:** Existing File

   ▶ **File Location:** \Installation\1-Basic\SQL Server 2005\Sales Manager\ Sales Manager Dashboard.rdl (making sure the full path to your extracted files exists)

   ▶ **Name:** Sales Manager Dashboard

   ▶ **Description:** Analytics Accelerator - Sales Manager Dashboard

   ▶ **Categories:** Sales Reports

   ▶ **Related Record Types:** Blank

   ▶ **Display In:** Reports Area

   ▶ **Administration Tab, Viewable By:** Organization

After you've completed the configurations, your New Report screen should match Figure 11.5.

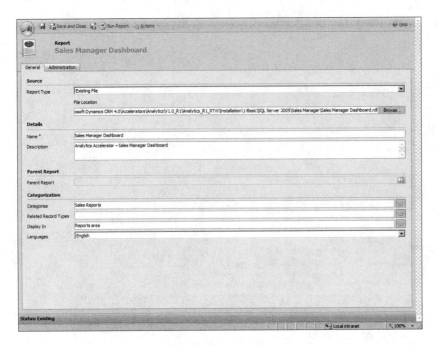

FIGURE 11.5   Adding the Sales Manager Dashboard report.

10. Click Save and New to create the new CRM Report and then create the next report.

11. Add the Sales Manager Dashboard Closed Details report and configure each field as follows:

- ▶ **Report Type:** Existing File

- ▶ **File Location:** \Installation\1-Basic\SQL Server 2005\Sales Manager\ Sales Manager Dashboard Closed Details.rdl (making sure the full path to your extracted files exists)

- ▶ **Name:** Sales Manager Dashboard

- ▶ **Description:** Analytics Accelerator - Sales Manager Dashboard Closed Details

- ▶ **Parent Report:** Sales Manager Dashboard Closed Details

- ▶ **Categories:** Blank

- ▶ **Related Record Types:** Blank

- ▶ **Display In:** Blank

- ▶ **Administration Tab, Viewable By:** Organization

After you've completed the configurations, your New Report screen should match Figure 11.6.

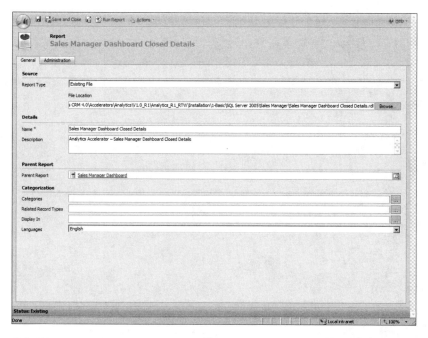

FIGURE 11.6   Adding the Sales Manager Dashboard Closed Details report.

12. Click Save and New to create the new CRM Report, and then create the next report.

13. Add the Sales Manager Dashboard Open Details report and configure each field as follows:

- ► **Report Type:** Existing File
- ► **File Location:** \Installation\1-Basic\SQL Server 2005\Sales Manager\ Sales Manager Dashboard Open Details.rdl (making sure the full path to your extracted files exists)
- ► **Name:** Sales Manager Dashboard Open Details
- ► **Description:** Analytics Accelerator - Sales Manager Dashboard Open Details
- ► **Parent Report:** Sales Manager Dashboard
- ► **Categories:** Blank
- ► **Related Record Types:** Blank
- ► **Display In:** Blank
- ► **Administration Tab, Viewable By:** Organization

After you've completed the configurations, your New Report screen should match Figure 11.7.

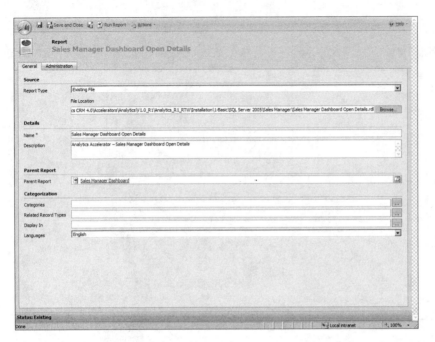

FIGURE 11.7   Adding the Sales Manager Dashboard Open Details report.

14. Click Save and New to create the new CRM Report and then create the next report.

15. Add the Sales Manager Dashboard Recent Activity Details report and configure each field as follows:

> ▶ **Report Type:** Existing File
>
> ▶ **File Location:** \Installation\1-Basic\SQL Server 2005\Sales Manager\ Sales Manager Dashboard Recent Activity Details.rdl (making sure the full path to your extracted files exists)
>
> ▶ **Name:** Sales Manager Dashboard Recent Activity Details
>
> ▶ **Description:** Analytics Accelerator - Sales Manager Dashboard Recent Activity Details
>
> ▶ **Parent Report:** Sales Manager Dashboard
>
> ▶ **Categories:** Blank
>
> ▶ **Related Record Types:** Blank
>
> ▶ **Display In:** Blank
>
> ▶ **Administration Tab, Viewable By:** Organization

After you've completed the configurations, your New Report screen should match Figure 11.8.

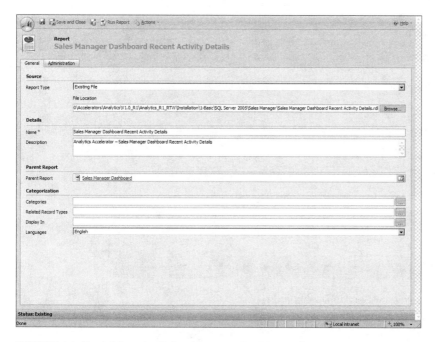

FIGURE 11.8   Adding the Sales Manager Dashboard Recent Activities Details report.

16. Click Save and New to create the new CRM Report and then create the next report.

17. Add the Service Dashboard report and configure each field as follows:

▶ **Report Type:** Existing File

▶ **File Location:** \Installation\1-Basic\SQL Server 2005\Support\Service Dashboard.rdl (making sure the full path to your extracted files exists)

▶ **Name:** Service Dashboard

▶ **Description:** Analytics Accelerator - Service Dashboard

▶ **Categories:** Service Reports

▶ **Related Record Types:** Blank

▶ **Display In:** Reports Area

▶ **Administration Tab, Viewable By:** Organization

After you've completed the configurations your New Report screen should match Figure 11.9.

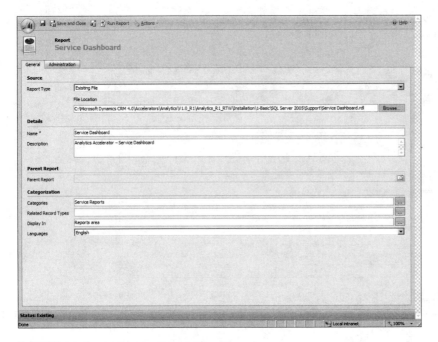

FIGURE 11.9   Adding the Service Dashboard report.

18. Click Save and New to create the new CRM Report and then create the next report.

19. Add the Service Dashboard Details report and configure each field as follows:

- ▶ **Report Type:** Existing File
- ▶ **File Location:** \Installation\1-Basic\SQL Server 2005\Support\Service Dashboard Details.rdl (making sure the full path to your extracted files exists)
- ▶ **Name:** Service Dashboard Details
- ▶ **Description:** Analytics Accelerator - Service Dashboard Details
- ▶ **Parent Report:** Service Dashboard
- ▶ **Categories:** Blank
- ▶ **Related Record Types:** Blank
- ▶ **Display In:** Blank
- ▶ **Administration Tab, Viewable By:** Organization

After you've completed the configurations, your New Report screen should match Figure 11.10.

20. Click Save and Close to create the new CRM report and then close.

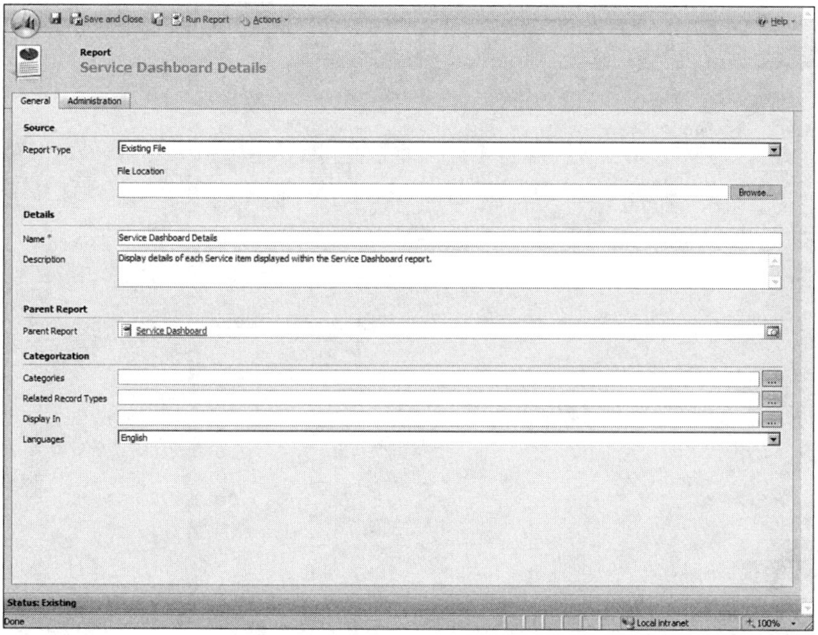

FIGURE 11.10   Adding the Service Dashboard report.

At the time of this writing, the first release of the Analytics Accelerator was available, with release 2 promising a number of enhancements to the first release and support for SQL Server 2008 dashboards. Release 3 will deliver more advanced SQL Server Analysis Services (SSAS) capabilities, as well as Microsoft Office PerformancePoint Server scorecards.

eService Accelerator

The eService accelerator is all about extending Microsoft Dynamics CRM customer service functionality and making it available to the Internet. However, this functionality can also be applied to almost any CRM entity within CRM with only a small number of configuration changes by adjusting the ASP.NET user control to point to a different entity. In addition, this accelerator allows for attachments of files to CRM cases and handles all login processes by utilizing the ASP.NET membership provider.

Figure 11.11 is an example of the eService accelerator's portal.

Prerequisites and Modifications

The following prerequisites exist for the eService accelerator:

▶ A website running the .NET Framework. If you are running CRM On-Premise, you can use your existing CRM web server for this website.

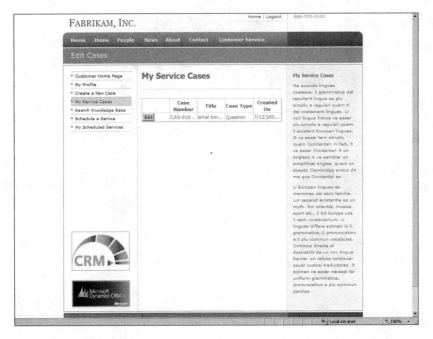

FIGURE 11.11   Portal profile example.

▶ The standard implementation is designed to work with Active Directory authentication; however, because source code is provided, an Internet-facing deployment (IFD) implementation is possible.

▶ This accelerator has not been road-tested within 64-bit environments.

▶ Secure Sockets Layer (SSL) is highly recommended because this accelerator allows users to access potentially sensitive customer data.

NOTE

The Microsoft Dynamics CRM External Connector license is required if the portal is exposed on the Internet.

This accelerator modifies the following CRM entities:

▶ Adds new CRM case attributes

▶ Case form changes

▶ New case relationship

▶ Contact form changes

▶ Contact relationships

▶ Account relationships

▶ eService audit configuration

▶ eService audits for account, case, and contact

▶ eService workflows for account, case, and contact

For a detailed breakdown of the changes made, review the "Microsoft Dynamics CRM eService Installation Guide.doc" that's included in the \Documentation folder included with the download files.

> **NOTE**
>
> The eService accelerator installation merges new customizations with existing customizations; however, be sure to back up your customizations before performing an implementation.

Once the eService accelerator is downloaded and unzipped, you'll find the following materials in the Source folder:

- ▶ Documentation for installation, configuration, administration, and end-user training
- ▶ All required customization files
- ▶ Sample HTML, CSS, and images for a sample website
- ▶ Visual Studio source code for all examples

eService Accelerator Installation

There are four main components to the installation:

- ▶ CRM entity customizations
- ▶ ASP.NET user controls
- ▶ Custom CRM workflow assembly
- ▶ Interface for configuring the eService user controls

The steps for performing a standard installation are listed in the following subsections.

Create an eService Accelerator User

1. You will need to assign a user that the eService accelerator will use for authentication. This user can be used for other accelerators or other CRM purposes if desired, although it's recommended that you don't use a person's existing login; explicitly create this user for the purpose of handling CRM requests.
2. Within Active Directory, create a user whose logon name is **crmwebuser** or similar. This can be done by right-clicking an administrative user and selecting Copy (to inherit all the administrator's permissions).

3. If your user does not exist within CRM, add it. Within CRM, create the crmwebuser and assign the appropriate email address if necessary.

4. Assign the appropriate role to this user (for example, System Administrator). Alternatively, a new role could be created that allows only this user to modify entities relating to the accelerator (for example, case and note).

Prepare the Installation

1. Run the installation executable that was downloaded from Codeplex. At the time of this writing, this is eService_v1.0_RTW.exe.

2. Once you've extracted the files, the wizard can be used to configure most of the necessary components (see Figure 11.12).

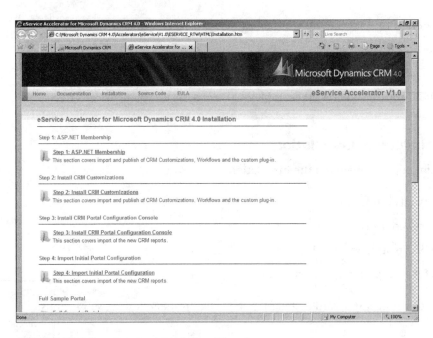

FIGURE 11.12   eService Installation Wizard.

Configuring ASP.NET Membership

1. Within the Installation Wizard, click Step 1: ASP.NET Membership. This is the same as navigating to the \Installation\Step 1 - ASP.NET Membership\ folder and then running the aspnet_regsql.exe application. This will guide you through configuring ASP.NET membership for the eService accelerator. Figure 11.13 is an example of the ASP.NET SQL Server Setup Wizard.

2. Click Next to begin and Figure 11.14 will display.

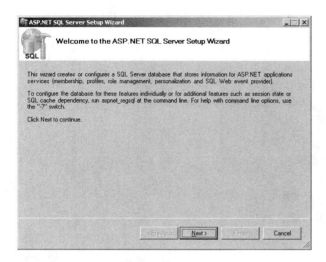

FIGURE 11.13   ASP.NET SQL Server Setup Wizard.

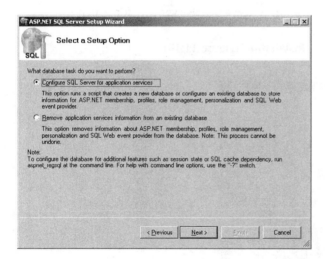

FIGURE 11.14   ASP.NET SQL Server Setup Wizard - Configuration.

3. Select Configure SQL Server for Application Services, and then click Next.

4. Select the server and database to use with this configuration (see Figure 11.15).

   ▶ Select Windows Authentication to utilize an Active Directory account to authenticate to the SQL Server. You'll need to ensure that the user that this website's application pool runs as (normally NT AUTHORITY\NETWORK SERVICE) also has privileges to write and read to the database that gets created.

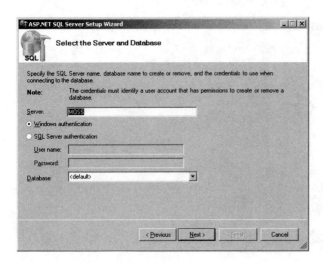

FIGURE 11.15   ASP.NET SQL Server Setup Wizard — Server and Database.

▶ Select SQL Server Authentication to use a SQL Server user for which to authenticate.

5. Click Next to continue with the installation (Figure 11.16).

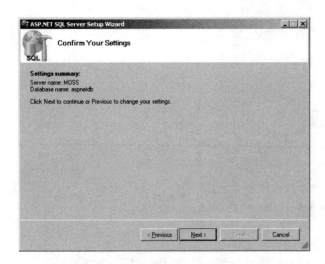

FIGURE 11.16   ASP.NET SQL Server Setup Wizard — Settings Overview.

6. You'll be prompted to review your settings. Click Next to continue.

7. Once the installation has completed, you'll be prompted to finish (see Figure 11.17). This completes the step 1 part of installation.

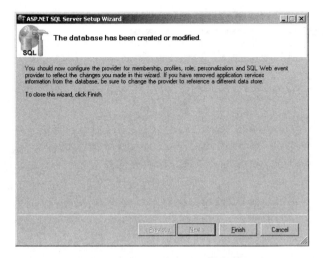

FIGURE 11.17   ASP.NET SQL Server Setup Wizard — Finish.

Run msa_eService.Install.exe

The msa_eService.Intall.exe will not overwrite existing forms, onLoad events, or onSave events. Instead, all new customizations will be merged with these existing customizations. In addition, *before* running this EXE, you'll be provided with specific instructions for configuring this command-line utility.

1. Within the \Installation\Step 2 - CRM Customizations folder, open the register.xml file (see Figure 11.18).

   ▶ Set Server to the CRM web service URL (the URL you use to access the front page of CRM; for example, http://<servername>:<port>).

   ▶ Set Org to the name of the organization. Remember not to use spaces in the name. (For example, MicrosoftCRM is used if the Org name is Microsoft CRM.)

   ▶ Set Domain accordingly.

   ▶ Set UserName to your logged-in username or a CRM user with a high level of privileges, such as a user with a System Administrator role.

   ▶ Save your changes.

2. Before running the msa_eService.Install.exe, make sure you're logged in to Windows as a user that exists within CRM, and you have appropriate permissions to make the customizations, such as System Administrator. If this is not possible, this EXE is– flexible enough to impersonate a specific user account. See the "\Documentation\ Technical Architecture and Extensibility Guide" for additional information.

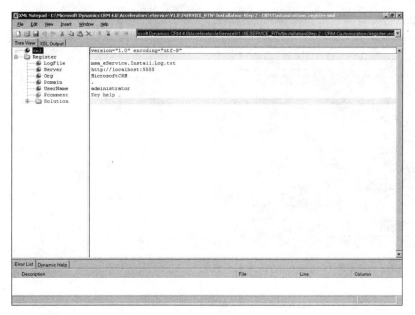

FIGURE 11.18   Editing the register.xml file.

3. Open a command prompt and navigate to the folder that contains the msa_eService.Install.exe, or double-click the EXE for the same results (see Figure 11.19).

FIGURE 11.19   Running the msa_eService.Install.exe from a command prompt.

4. You'll be prompted to enter the password of the user you assigned within the Register.xml file. Type it and then press Enter. After authenticating, the program will create a CRM connection, import custom workflow assemblies, import contact customizations, import case customizations, import custom entities, import workflows, import a site map, and then publish all customizations. This process takes a few minutes, so be patient.

5. When the program has completed successfully, you'll be prompted to press Enter to continue (see Figure 11.20).

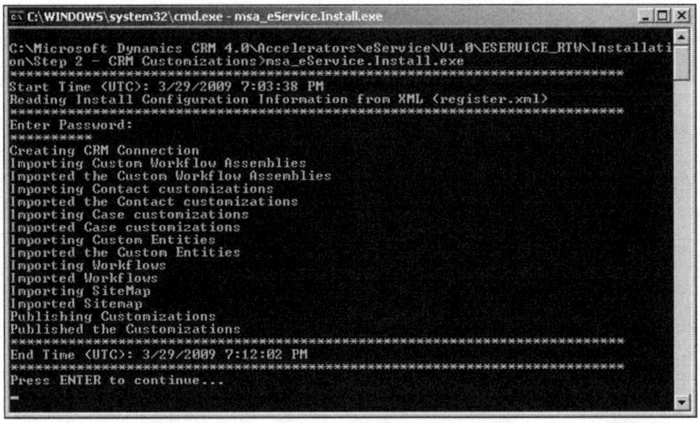

FIGURE 11.20   Successful Installation of msa_eService.Install.exe at the command prompt.

6. If you encounter any problems during the installation, additional information may be available within the msa_eService.Install.Log.txt file located within the same directory as the EXE.

Prepare the Console Files

1. Within the Installation Wizard, click Step 3: Install CRM Portal Configuration Console. This is the same as navigating to the Installation\Step 3 - Accelerator Console Files folder within the extracted files for this accelerator.

2. Open the Accelerator Console Web Files folder and then copy the eService folder. Navigate to the C:\Program Files\Microsoft Dynamics CRM Server\CRMWeb\ISV folder, and then paste the eService folder (see Figure 11.21).

3. Open the Accelerator Console Assembly folder and then copy the eServiceAccelerator.Web.Configuration.dll file. Navigate to the C:\Program Files\Microsoft Dynamics CRM Server\CRMWeb\bin folder, and then paste the DLL file (see Figure 11.22).

Import the eService Customizations

1. Open CRM and on the CRM toolbar, click the Tools option, and then select Import Data.

2. When the Import window appears, navigate to the Installation\Step 4 - Data Import folder within the extracted files for this accelerator and select eservice_portal_config.csv. Then click Next.

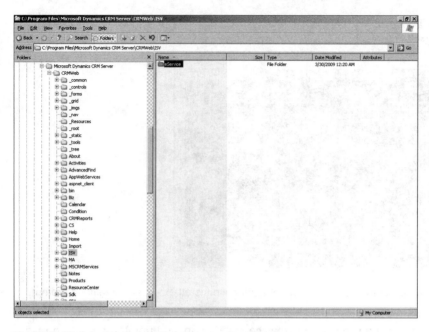

FIGURE 11.21 Copy the eService console web files.

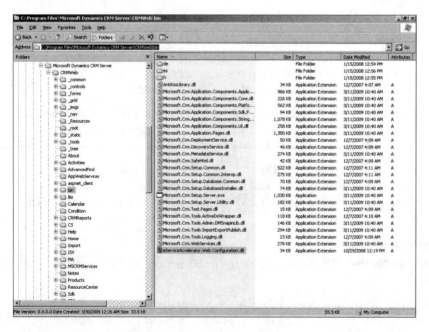

FIGURE 11.22 Copy the eService console assembly DLL.

3. Within the Record Type drop-down list, select eService Configuration. The Data Map field should display Automatic. Then click Next through the remaining screens and click Import once displayed. This will begin the import process, which will take a few minutes.

Modify the New Workflows

1. Now you need to make edits to the new workflows (see Figure 11.23). Six of the workflows will need to reference the crmwebuser we previously created. You can assign a user within your organization that has been designated as the primary portal user, or you can choose to use crmwebuser. In addition, one of the workflows will require you to update the URL that directs a customer to the website.

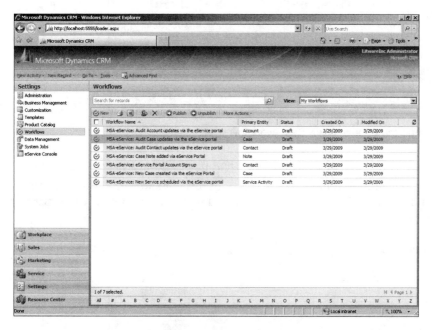

FIGURE 11.23   Workflows added during the msa_eService.Install.exe installation.

NOTE

The accelerator ships with a Microsoft Dynamics CRM web user assigned. We need to remove this user and add an appropriate user, such as the crmwebuser we created.

---

2. Edit the workflow labeled MSA-eService: New Case created via the eService Portal. Figure 11.24 shows this workflow.

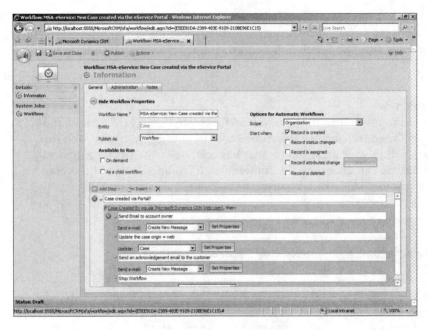

FIGURE 11.24   Edit the eService New Case workflow.

3. Edit the Case:Created By Equals field to the appropriate CRM user.

4. Edit the Send Email to Account Owner portion of this workflow by clicking the Set Properties button, and then update the From field with the appropriate CRM user (see Figure 11.25).

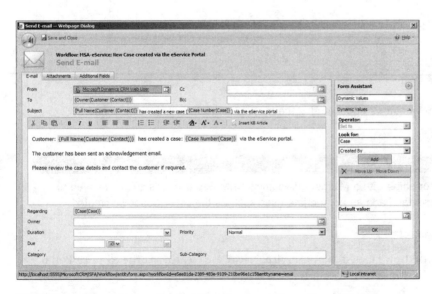

FIGURE 11.25   Edit the eService New Case workflow with a new user.

5. Click Save and Close to close the email template window. Then click Save and Close to save the changes to this workflow.

6. Edit the MSA-eService: Case Note added via the eService Portal workflow (see Figure 11.26).

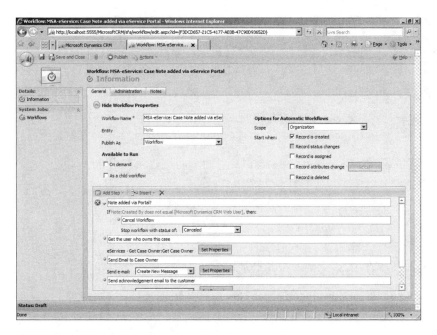

FIGURE 11.26   Edit the eService New Case workflow.

7. Update the Note: Created by Does Not Equal field with the appropriate user, making sure to remove reference to Microsoft Dynamics CRM Web User user.

8. Edit the MSA-eService: Audit *Account* Updates via the eService Portal workflow and update the Modified by (User) Does Not Equal field with the appropriate user, making sure to remove reference to Microsoft Dynamics CRM Web User user.

9. Edit the MSA-eService: Audit *Case* Updates via the eService Portal workflow and update the Case: Modified by Does Not Equal field with the appropriate user, making sure to remove reference to Microsoft Dynamics CRM Web User user.

10. Edit the MSA-eService: Audit *Contact* Updates via the eService Portal workflow and update the Modified by (User): User Does Not Equal field with the appropriate user, making sure to remove reference to Microsoft Dynamics CRM Web User user.

11. Edit the MSA-eService: New Service Scheduled via the eService Portal workflow and update the Service Activity: Created by Equals field with the appropriate user, making sure to remove reference to Microsoft Dynamics CRM Web User user.

12. Edit the MSA-eService: eService Portal Account Sign-Up workflow and edit both URLs within the Send an Email with Instructions on How to Create an eService Portal

Account (Set Properties) window (see Figure 11.27). The first page will allow users to create a new account. (By default, this is the CreateUserAccount.aspx page in the Sample Portal site.) The second URL is the default page that existing users will see when they visit the site.

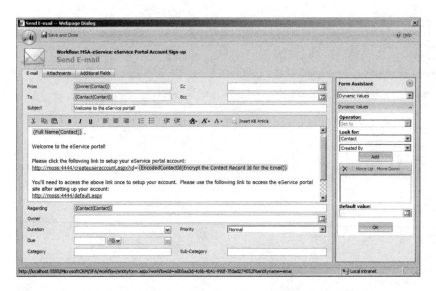

FIGURE 11.27   Edit the URLs within the eService New Case workflow.

13. Within the CRM Workflows window, select all workflows that begin with MSA-eService, and then publish them. You should be prompted to publish seven workflows. If for any reason the workflows do not publish, review the previous steps and make sure the CRM user you've assigned has the appropriate CRM security role.

eService Configuration

1. Within Settings, Customization, eService Configuration, verify that the eService Configuration entity is displayed within the Settings area of CRM. If it is not, check the Settings check box and then Save and Close. (You don't have to publish the eService Configuration entity again.) Restart your browser.

2. Configure the settings for the eService Configuration entity via Settings, eService Configuration. Select and then edit the eService Config V1 eService configuration listed (see Figure 11.28).

NOTE

If you do not see the eService Config area or the eService Config V1, make sure you've followed the Console instructions discussed previously. In addition, you can close your browser and try again. Don't try to add a new eService configuration at this point.

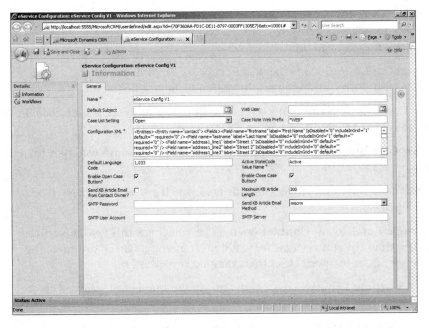

FIGURE 11.28   Settings for the eService configuration.

The fields within the eService Configuration screen are as follows:

▶ **Default Subject:** When a case is created via the web portal, it will be assigned the default subject that you select here.

▶ **Web User:** Select the appropriate CRM user (for example, crmwebuser) to use as the portal user who has the following privileges:

  ▶ Create, Read, and Update CRM cases, notes, and document attachments

  ▶ Create and Read CRM service activities

  ▶ Send and Read emails

  ▶ Create, Read, and Update the custom entities associated with this accelerator

▶ **Case List Setting:** This field contains two options:

  ▶ **Open:** Only open cases display when the customer logs in to the portal.

  ▶ **All:** All cases (both open and closed) display when the customer logs in to the portal.

▶ **Case Note Web Prefix:** Use this prefix within a CRM note or keyword within a Knowledge Base (KB) article to make it public to a web user. This provides a layer of flexibility so that internal notes can be added without a customer seeing them. It also means that a KB article using this keyword can be searched via the web portal. By default, nothing is public unless the prefix is typed.

▶ **Configuration XML:** Do not make edits to this field, because this XML should be configured only through the eService Console. To keep users from accidentally editing this field, make it read-only.

▶ **Default Language Code:** 1033 is the default code for English. For a full list of country codes, visit: http://msdn.microsoft.com/en-us/library/0h88fahh.aspx.

▶ **Active StateCode Value Name:** This is the default names of the case state code. In the English edition of Microsoft Dynamics CRM, this is Active.

▶ **Enable Open Case Button:** By checking this field, you're allowing customers to reopen cases.

▶ **Enable Close Case Button:** By checking this field, you'll enable customers to be able to close open cases.

▶ **Send KB Article Email from Contact Owner?:** If you check this field, KB articles will be emailed from the contact's owner (CRM user). If you uncheck this field, the email will be sent from the portal user (for example, crmwebuser).

▶ **Maximum KB Article Length:** This sets the maximum number of returned characters for KB articles.

▶ **Send KB Article Email Method:** This drop-down list contains two items:

   ▶ **SMTP:** Set to SMTP if KB articles are emailed to customers through an SMTP account.

   ▶ **MSCRM:** Set to MSCRM if KB articles are emailed via Microsoft Dynamics CRM. This is the recommended item if the CRM Email Router component is installed.

NOTE

It is recommended that the following fields be completed even if using the MSCRM drop-down list item. Failure to do so may result in email errors from the web portal.

▶ **SMTP Server:** Your SMTP server.

▶ **SMTP User Account:** The user account used to authenticate access to the SMTP account.

▶ **SMTP Password:** The user account password used to authenticate access to the SMTP account.

Full Sample Portal

1. Within the Installation Wizard, click Full Sample Portal. This is the same as navigating to the \Installation\Sample Portal folder.

2. Select all files within this folder and copy.

3. Within C:\Program Files, create a new folder called **Microsoft Dynamics CRM Customer Portal**, and then paste all files from the Sample Portal folder.

4. Within this new folder, edit the web.config file and edit the following entities (see Figure 11.29).

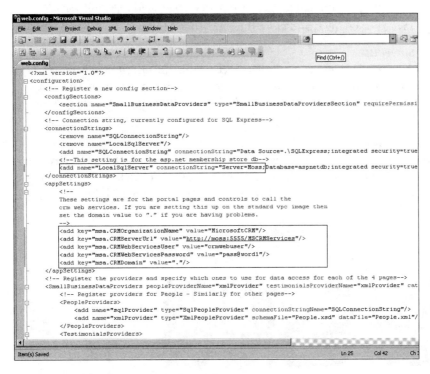

FIGURE 11.29   Edit the Web Config file.

▶ LocalSqlServer

▶ msa.CRMOrganizationName so that it matches your organization name.

▶ msa.CRMServerURL

▶ msa.CRMWebServicesUser

▶ msa.CRMWebServicesPassword

▶ msa.CRMDomain

5. Open Internet Information Services Manager (inetmgr).

6. Create a new website named **Microsoft Dynamics CRM Customer Portal**.

7. Select Port 4444 as the default TCP port this website should use.

8. Select C:\Program Files\Microsoft Dynamics CRM Customer Portal as the website home directory, making sure to Allow Anonymous Access to This Web Site.

9. Allow the following permissions:

Read

Run scripts (such as ASP)

10. Once created, navigate to the Properties window of the new website, click the ASP.NET tab, and select ASP.NET version 2.0.50727.

11. Within the Properties window, click the Documents tab and add Default.aspx.

12. Click OK to save your changes and close the Properties window.

Configure the SQL Server User

For the NT Authority\Network Service to properly access the ASPNETDB database, you must create a new NT Authority\Network Service user within SQL Server Management Studio, and grant db_owner access to schemas owned by the user, and db_owner to the Database role membership.

Testing the eService Accelerator

1. We're now ready to view the site. Open a web browser and navigate to the server at the port specified (for example, http://localhost:4444/). Then click the Customer Service link to view the customer's access to the portal (see Figure 11.30).

FIGURE 11.30   Sample portal.

2. We can test the system by returning to CRM and adding a new contact, making sure to select Web Portal Contact-Level Customer to the new eServices Access Level field.

3. Once added, CRM will fire workflow to send the contact an email. Check to see your workflows fired (see Figure 11.31).

4. The contact's History should contain the notification email. Open it to see the email details, including links to log in. The link within the email can then be used within the sample portal to create a new user and to log in (see Figure 11.32).

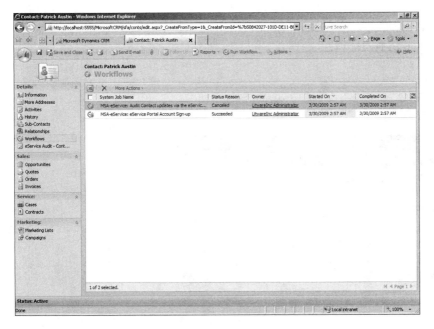

FIGURE 11.31   View eService workflow.

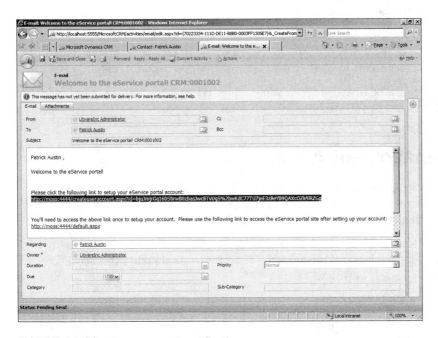

FIGURE 11.32   Contact email notification.

5. Copy the link from the notification email and paste it into your browser. You should then see the default new user login page. Complete the fields to create a new portal user, as shown in Figure 11.33.

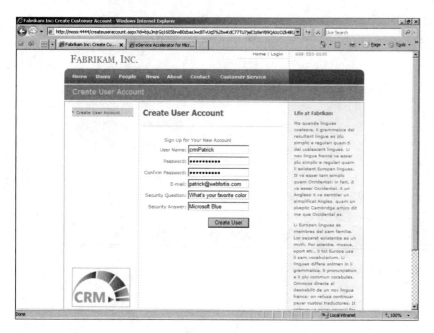

FIGURE 11.33   Portal login example.

6. Once you've created a new user and logged in to the site using your new credentials, you'll have direct access to contact data within CRM (see Figure 11.34).

Your portal should now be installed. With some minor HTML/CSS changes, you can match the look and feel of your website.

Event Management Accelerator

The CRM Event Management accelerator provides functionality for event management within CRM. Out of the box, CRM offers rich campaign management, and this accelerator takes your marketing campaigns to the next level.

One of the main features of this accelerator is extending CRM campaign functionality to a web portal, although a web portal is not required, and the functionality this accelerator provides can be used solely within CRM.

This accelerator, shown in Figure 11.35, provides the following functionality:

▶ Event planning, such as booking a venue, managing presenters, managing catering, and managing presentations and content preparation

FIGURE 11.34   Portal profile example.

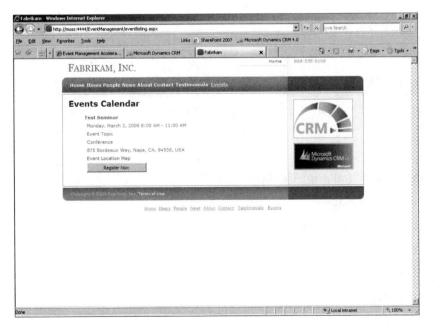

FIGURE 11.35   Events calendar within the sample portal.

- Event attendee management features, including inviting the target audience via phone, fax, letter, and email, and the Web

- Allow CRM users to manage registrations via phone, letter, fax, email, and web

- Track all customers who attend the event

- Event Review - Microsoft Dynamics CRM reports that measure the effectiveness and return on investment (ROI) of the event

Prerequisites and Modifications

The following prerequisites exist for the Event Management accelerator:

- A website running the .NET Framework.

- The standard implementation is designed to work with AD authentication; however, because source code is provided, an IFD implementation is possible.

- This accelerator has not been road-tested within 64-bit environments.

- SSL is highly recommended because this accelerator allows users to access potentially sensitive customer data.

- If you've implemented IFD or service provider licensing agreement (SPLA) deployments, you must modify the authentication code within the portal.

- This portal is single-tenant, and so it will point to only one organization within a CRM deployment. If you're running multitenancy, you need to deploy a web portal for each organization.

> **NOTE**
>
> The Microsoft Dynamics CRM External Connector license is required if the portal is exposed on the Internet.

This accelerator modifies the following CRM entities:

- Adds new campaign attributes

- Adds new campaign response attributes

- Adds many new CRM entities for events

- Adds new CRM views

- Adds new CRM plug-in

- Modify campaign forms

- Adds new JavaScript functions

▶ Adds ASP.NET user controls

For a detailed breakdown of modifications, review the Microsoft Dynamics CRM Event Management Accelerator Installation Guide.doc that's included in the \Documentation folder included with the download files. All files can be downloaded from the Codeplex website at http://crmaccelerators.codeplex.com.

Once the eService accelerator is downloaded and unzipped, you'll find the following in the Source folder:

▶ Documentation for installation and extensibility

▶ All required customization files

▶ Sample HTML, CSS, and images for a sample website portal

▶ Visual Studio source code for all examples

Event Management Installation

There are four main components to the installation:

▶ CRM entity customizations

▶ ASP.NET user controls

▶ Custom CRM workflow assembly

▶ Interface for configuring the eService user controls

The following subsections outline the steps for a standard installation.

Create an Event Management Accelerator User

1. You will need to assign a user for which the Event Management accelerator will use for authentication. You can either configure your own user, or you can create a user specifically for use with the accelerator. Within Active Directory, create a user whose logon name is **crmwebuser** or similar. This can be done by right-clicking an administrator user and selecting Copy (to inherit all the administrator permissions).

2. If your user does not exist within CRM, add it. Within CRM, create the crmwebuser and assign the appropriate email address if necessary.

3. Assign the appropriate role to this user (for example, System Administrator).

Prepare the Installation

1. Run the installation executable that you downloaded from Codeplex. At the time of this writing, this is EventManagement_V1.0_RTW.exe.

2. Once you've extracted the files, you can use the wizard to configure most of the necessary components (see Figure 11.36).

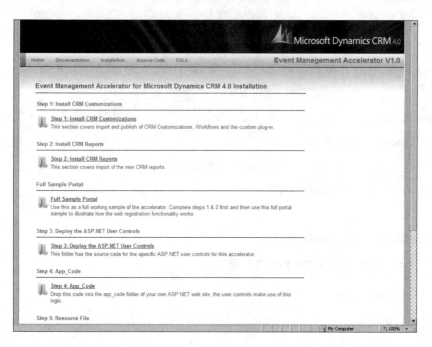

FIGURE 11.36   Event Management accelerator Installation Wizard.

Wizard Step 1: Install CRM Customizations

1. Within the Event Management accelerator Installation Wizard, click Step 1: Install CRM Customizations. The \Installation\Step 1 - CRM Customizations\ folder is displayed. Copy the EventManagement-Customizations.xml file to your desktop.

2. Open CRM and navigate to Settings, Customization, Import Customizations.

3. Click Browse and open EventManagement-Customizations.xml on your desktop. Then click Upload, and the Event Management customizations will display (see Figure 11.37).

> **NOTE**
>
> When installing the Event Management accelerator, you will lose any changes you have made to the entities previously described (limited to form changes and not schema changes). Be sure to back up your customizations before performing an implementation.

4. Select all displayed customizations, and then click Import Selected Customizations. All customizations should import successfully.

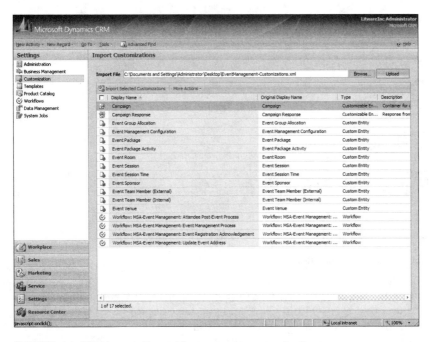

FIGURE 11.37   Import Event Management customizations.

5. Navigate to Settings, Customization, Customize Entities. Ensure that the new event customizations are present within the list of CRM entities, and then click More Actions, Publish All Customizations.

6. Run msa_eventmanagement.Install.exe.

NOTE

The msa_eventmanagement.Intall.exe will not overwrite existing forms, onLoad events, or onSave events. Instead, all new customizations will be merged with these existing customizations. In addition, *before* running this EXE, you'll receive specific instructions about configuring this command-line utility.

---

7. Within the \Installation\Step 1 - CRM Customizations\ folder, open the register.xml file (see Figure 11.38).

  ▶ Set Server to the CRM web service URL, which is the URL you use to access the front page of CRM; for example, http://localhost:5555.

  ▶ Set Org to the name of the organization. Remember not to use spaces in the name. (For example, MicrosoftCRM is used if the org name is Microsoft CRM.)

  ▶ Set Domain accordingly. Within the standard virtual PC image for CRM, use a period (.).

▶ Set UserName to your logged-in username or a CRM user with a high level of privileges, such as a user with a System Administrator role.

▶ Save your changes.

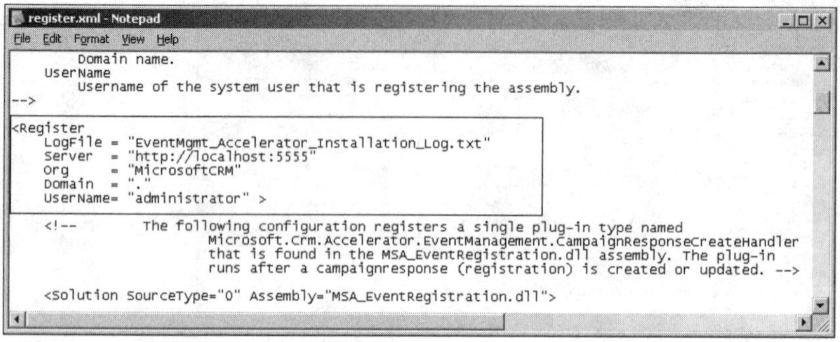

FIGURE 11.38   Editing the register.xml file.

8. Before running the msa_eventmanagement.Install.exe, make sure you're logged in to Windows as a user that exists within CRM, and you have appropriate permissions to make the customizations, such as System Administrator.

9. Navigate to the \Installation\Step 1 - CRM Customizations\ folder and run the msa_eventmanagement.Install.exe.

10. You'll be prompted to enter your password. Type it and then press Enter. After authenticating, the program will create a CRM connection, delete duplicate solutions if detected, and then register the MSA_EventRegistration.

11. When the program has completed successfully, you are prompted to press Enter to continue (see Figure 11.39).

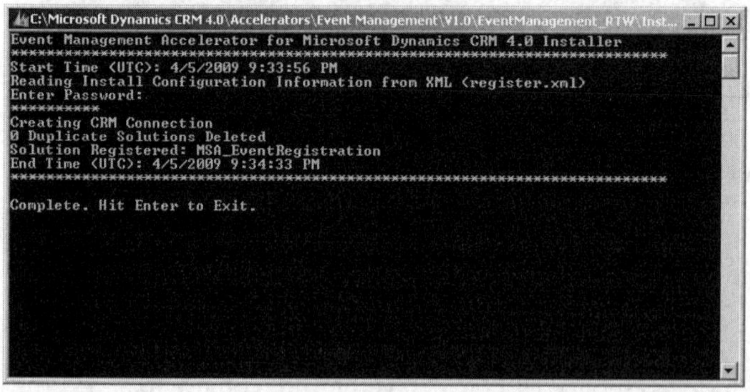

FIGURE 11.39   Successful Installation of msa_eventmanagement.Install.exe at the command prompt.

12. If you encounter any problems during the installation, additional information may be available within the msa_eventmanagement.Install.Log.txt file located within the same directory as the EXE.

Wizard Step 2: Install CRM Reports

1. Within the Event Management accelerator Installation Wizard, click Step 2: Install CRM Reports. This displays the location of the CRM reports you'll be importing next.

2. Within CRM, navigate to Workplace, Reports, New. You'll be prompted with a New Report screen. Configure each field as follows:

   ▶ **Report Type:** Existing File

   ▶ **File Location:** \Installation\Step 2 – Reports\Event Attendee List.rdl (making sure the full path to your extracted files exists)

   ▶ **Name:** Event Attendee List

   ▶ **Description:** Optional text describing the report

   ▶ **Categories:** Marketing Reports

   ▶ **Related Record Types:** Campaigns and Campaign Responses

   ▶ **Display In:** Reports Area, Forms for related record types, Lists for related record types

   ▶ **Administration Tab, Viewable By:** Organization

   After you've completed the configurations, your New Report screen should match Figure 11.40.

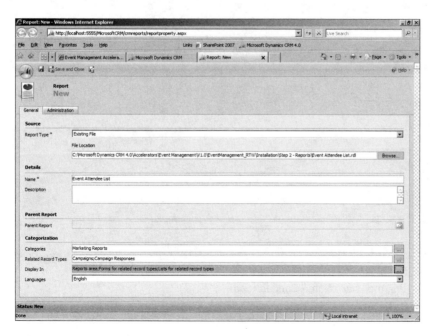

FIGURE 11.40   Adding the Event Attendee List report.

3. Click Save and Close to create the new CRM report.

4. Within CRM, navigate to Workplace, Reports, New. You'll be prompted with a New Report screen. Configure each field as follows:

▸ **Report Type:** Existing File

▸ **File Location:** \Installation\Step 2 – Reports\Event Name Badges.rdl (making sure the full path to your extracted files exists)

▸ **Name:** Event Name Badges

▸ **Description:** Optional text describing the report

▸ **Categories:** Marketing Reports

▸ **Related Record Types:** Campaigns and Campaign Responses

▸ **Display In:** Reports Area, Forms for related record types, Lists for related record types

▸ **Administration Tab, Viewable By:** Organization

After you've completed the configurations, your New Report screen should match Figure 11.41.

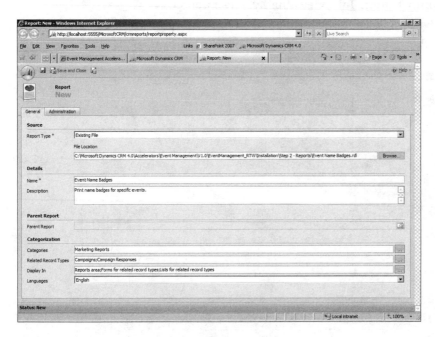

FIGURE 11.41   Adding the Event Name Badges report.

5. Click Save and Close to create the new CRM report.

Wizard Step 3: Full Sample Portal

1. Create a new folder for the sample portal (for example, C:\Program Files\Microsoft Dynamics CRM Customer Portal\EventMgr).

2. Within the Event Management accelerator Installation Wizard, click Full Sample Portal. This displays the location of the full sample portal files. Copy all files within this folder, and then paste them to the \Microsoft Dynamics CRM Customer Portal\EventMgr folder you just created.

3. Within the \Microsoft Dynamics CRM Customer Portal\EventMgr folder, edit the web.config file and modify the following entities (see Figure 11.42).

   ▶ msa.CRMOrganizationName so that it matches your organization name

   ▶ msa.CRMServerURL

   ▶ msa.CRMWebServicesUser

   ▶ msa.CRMWebServicesPassword

   ▶ msa.CRMDomain

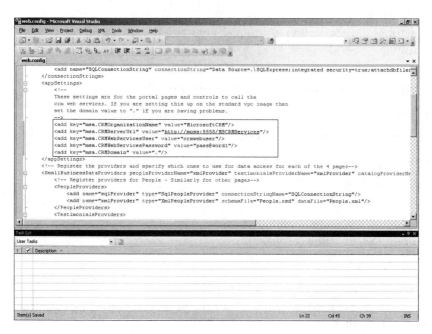

FIGURE 11.42   Edit the Web Config file.

4. Save your changes to the web.config file and then close it.

5. Open Internet Information Services Manager (inetmgr).

6. Create a new website named **Microsoft Dynamics CRM Event Manager**.

7. Select port 4444 as the default TCP port this website should use.

8. Select the folder (for example, C:\Program Files\Microsoft Dynamics CRM Customer Portal\EventMgr) as the website home directory, making sure to Allow Anonymous Access to This Web Site.

9. Allow the following permissions:

    ▸ Read

    ▸ Run scripts (such as ASP)

10. Once created, navigate to the Properties window of the new website, click the ASP.NET tab, and select ASP.NET version 2.0.50727.

11. Within the Properties window, click the Documents tab and add Default.aspx.

12. Click OK to save your changes and close the Properties window.

CRM Customizations

1. Within CRM, we need to ensure that the Event Management Configuration entity is displayed within CRM Settings. Navigate to Settings, Customization, Customize Entities; open the Event Management Configuration window, and place a check mark within the Settings check box.

2. Close your browser and reopen it and then open CRM.

3. Navigate to Settings, Customization, Customize Entities, Campaign, and open the Campaign entity.

4. Navigate to Attributes and open the statuscode attribute.

5. Within the Type section, edit the following types and note their list value:

    ▸ **Launched:** Default value is 2.

    ▸ **Waitlisting:** Default value is 200,000.

    ▸ **Sold Out:** Default value is 200,001.

6. Close the Campaign entity windows.

7. Navigate to the Campaign Response entity and note the following list values for the responsecode attribute:

    ▸ **Registered:** Default value is 200,000.

    ▸ **Waitlist:** Default value is 200,002.

    ▸ **Registration Canceled:** Default value is 200,001.

8. Navigate to the Campaign Response entity and note the following list values for the channeltypecode attribute:

    ▸ **Web:** Default value is 200,000.

9. Close all open entity windows; navigate to Settings and then to the Event Management Configuration entity (see Figure 11.43).

10. Click New, and the New Event Management Configuration window will display. We'll now apply the settings we've just recorded within previous steps. Configure the window with the following settings (see Figure 11.44):

    ▸ **Name:** Event Management Config V1

    ▸ **Event Is Open Status Code:** Launched

    ▸ **Event Is Waitlisting Status Code:** Waitlisting

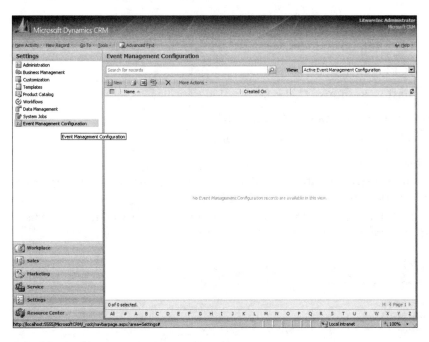

FIGURE 11.43   Event Management configuration.

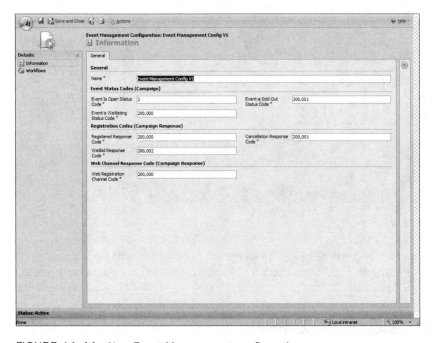

FIGURE 11.44   New Event Management configuration.

- **Event Is Sold Out Status Code:** Sold Out

- **Registered Response Code:** Registered

- **Waitlist Response Code:** Waitlist

- **Cancellation Response Code:** Registration Canceled

- **Web Registration Channel Code:** Web

11. Click Save and Close to save your configurations.

Publish the CRM Workflow

1. Open CRM and navigate to Settings, Workflows. There are four new workflows listed that begin with MSA and should be in a Draft status.

2. Open the MSA-Event Management. Attendee Post-Event Process workflow and edit the Campaign Response: Attended Event equals [Yes] step (see Figure 11.45).

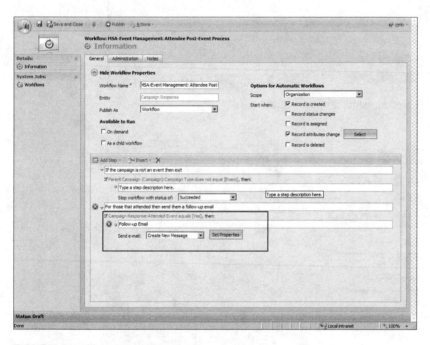

FIGURE 11.45   Edit workflow.

3. Click Set Properties and edit the From field so that the email is sent from a valid CRM user (for example, CRM Web User). The click Publish to save your changes and publish the workflow.

NOTE

The accelerator ships with a Microsoft Dynamics CRM web user assigned. You need to remove this user and add an appropriate user, such as the crmwebuser we created.

---

4. Open the MSA-Event Management: Event Management Process workflow and scroll down to Stage 2: Invitations and Registration Management, and then change the Create: Marketing List drop-down list item to Task. Then click Set Properties. The Create Task for This Workflow screen then displays. Type the following within the Subject field: **Create segmented marketing list for prospective attendees.** While you're in the screen, scroll around to note all portions of this comprehensive workflow. Then click Publish to save your changes and publish the workflow.

5. Open the MSA-Event Management: Event Registration and Acknowledgement workflow (see Figure 11.46). You'll be editing each of the four Set Properties buttons to assign the proper CRM user within the From fields.

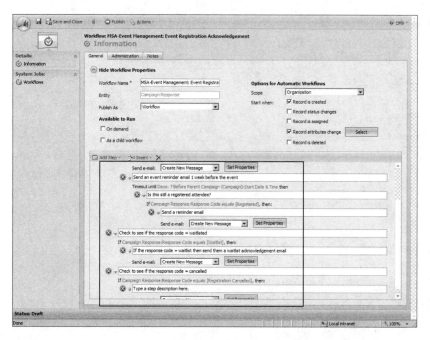

FIGURE 11.46   Edit Event Registration Acknowledgement workflow.

6. Scroll down to the Set Properties button of the Campaign Response: Response Code Equals [Registered] step. Click Set Properties and assign an appropriate CRM user within the From field (for example, CRM Web User), making sure to remove Microsoft Dynamics CRM Web User user.

7. Scroll down and edit the From fields within each of the remaining Set Properties buttons. After you've made the four edits, click Publish to save your changes and then publish the workflow.

8. Publish the MSA-Event Management: Update Event Address workflow.

Testing the Portal

1. Within CRM, navigate to Marketing, Campaigns and click New to create a new campaign.

2. Configure the following fields:

   ▸ **Name:** Test Seminar

   ▸ **Status Reason:** Launched

   ▸ **Campaign Type:** Event (Note that when you select Event, the Event Details tab is enabled, as shown in Figure 11.47.)

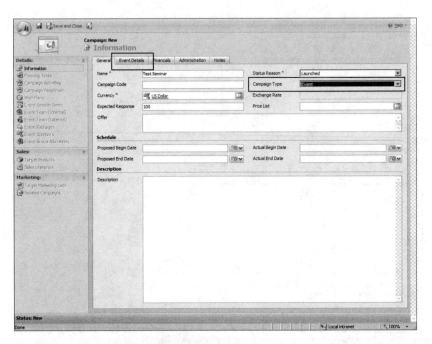

FIGURE 11.47   Create a new campaign.

3. Once the Event Details tab is enabled, you can configure your event (see Figure 11.48).

4. Save and close the campaign.

5. You're now ready to test the portal. Open your browser and navigate to the portal (for example, http://moss:4444/). Once open, click Events within the top navigation bar. This will display your events, as shown in Figure 11.49.

6. Click Register Now to register to the event. Note the required fields, and then register for the event (see Figure 11.50).

7. Once registered, you should receive a successful confirmation screen.

FIGURE 11.48   Create a new campaign.

FIGURE 11.49   Events calendar within the sample portal.

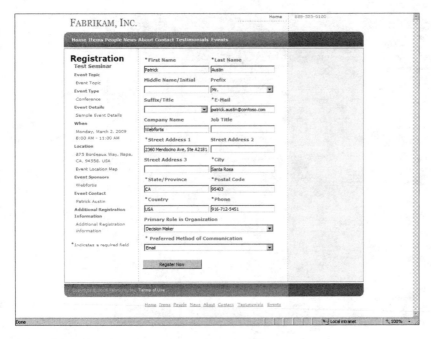

FIGURE 11.50   Register for an event.

8. Within CRM, we can review the Campaign to see the new attendee details (see Figure 11.51).

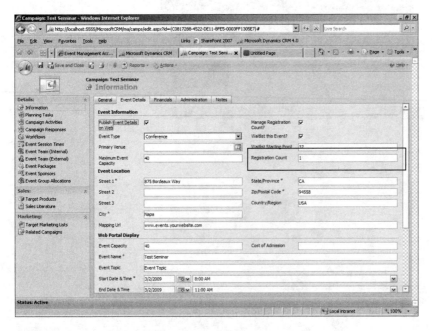

FIGURE 11.51   Event details with new attendee

9. Within the campaign or event, the campaign responses will also display event attendees and their details (see Figure 11.52).

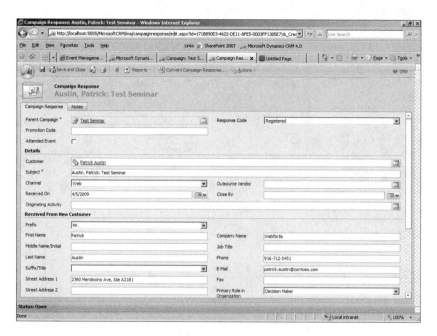

FIGURE 11.52   Campaign response with new attendee.

Extended Sales Forecasting Accelerator

The Extended Sales Forecasting accelerator is composed of the following components:

▶ Custom goal and goal audit entities

▶ A script function to retrieve Fiscal Period Reporting settings

▶ A set of reports for viewing goal and attainment information

▶ A new role to support the new goal entity

▶ The addition of the Goal Lookup field on the opportunity form

▶ Four workflow definitions to handle notifications and approvals of goals

▶ Documentation of the goal-creation process, reports, and custom entity and installation instructions

The Extended Sales Forecasting accelerator (shown in Figure 11.53) provides an easy-to-use
process to monitor revenue goals and track sales performance against the goals, using a
hierarchical approach if desired (VP Sales, then Sales Managers, and then Salespeople).
This approach is frequently referred to as *goal-based forecasting*.

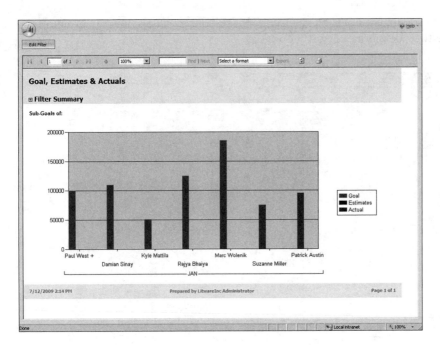

FIGURE 11.53   Sales Forecasting accelerator.

Prerequisites and Modifications

The following prerequisites exist for the Extended Sales Forecasting accelerator:

▶ Fiscal settings must be configured within CRM. If not configured, they will not be used by the script, and the goal period will have to be set manually.

This accelerator modifies the following CRM entities:

▶ Adds new goal entity

▶ Adds new goal audit entity

▶ Adds script to retrieve Fiscal Period Reporting settings

▶ Adds new reports

▶ Adds new role

▶ Modifies opportunities

▶ Adds new workflows

For a detailed breakdown of modifications, review the documents within the \Documentation folder included with the download files. All files can be downloaded from the Codeplex website at http://crmaccelerators.codeplex.com.

Once the eService accelerator is downloaded and unzipped, you'll find the following materials in the Source folder:

▸ Documentation for licensing, solutions, and installation (and a user guide)

▸ All required customization files

▸ Custom reports

Extended Sales Forecasting Accelerator Installation

1. Run the installation executable that you downloaded from Codeplex. At the time of this writing, this is ExtendedSalesForecasting_V1.0_RTW.exe.

2. After you've extracted the files, a wizard is displayed that you can use to configure the accelerator, as shown in Figure 11.54.

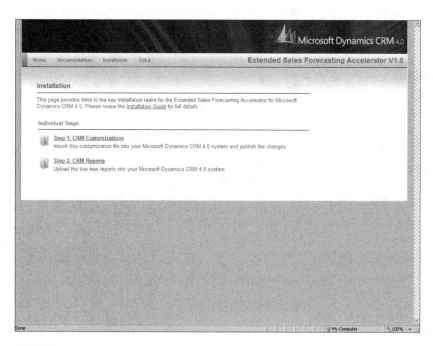

FIGURE 11.54   Extended Sales Forecasting Accelerator Installation Wizard.

Wizard Step 1: CRM Customizations

1. Before you can use this accelerator, you must configure your organization's fiscal year settings within CRM, Settings, Business Management, Fiscal Year Settings. Be sure to review the \Documentation\ Microsoft Dynamics CRM Extended Sales Forecasting Installation_Guide.doc before attempting to configure the fiscal year settings.

> **NOTE**
>
> Once the fiscal year settings are set within CRM, they cannot be changed unless a support ticket is opened with Microsoft. You may want to perform testing within a test environment (such as the CRM 4 virtual PC image from Microsoft or test server) before implementing fiscal year settings within a production environment.

2. Within the Extended Sales Forecasting accelerator Installation Wizard, click Step 1: CRM Customizations. The \Installation\Step 1 - CRM Customizations\ folder displays. Copy the extended_sales_forecasting.xml file to your desktop. You'll perform this step because the default installation directory of the accelerators contains too many characters for the CRM Import Customizations entity.

3. Within CRM, navigate to Settings, Customization, Import Customizations and browse to the extended_sales_forecasting.xml file on your desktop. Upload the customizations, and then import (see Figure 11.55). You may receive an alert about localization while importing; it's safe to ignore.

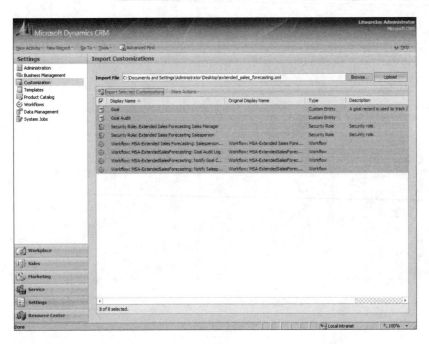

FIGURE 11.55   Import customizations.

4. Within CRM, update the Goal entity so that it is displayed in CRM's navigation panes. Navigate to Settings, Customization, Customize Entities, Goal and add check boxes to Areas That Display This Entity (for example, Sales or Workplace).

5. Edit the Opportunity entity so that the new Goal field is displayed. Edit the main Opportunity entity form and add the Goal field (msa_goalid), as shown in Figure 11.56.

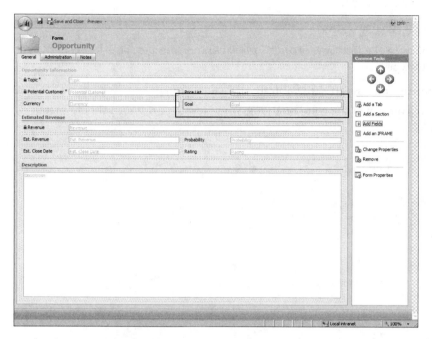

FIGURE 11.56   Opportunity customization.

6. Within the Customize Entities window, select More Actions and then Publish All Entities to publish the new Goal entities and opportunity modification.

7. Within Settings, Workflow, publish the four newly imported workflows beginning with MSA-Extended Sales Forecasting.

8. After adding the Goal entity, only the system administrator has access to the entity. Grant access to the security roles of users who need to view the Goal entity. A detailed explanation of how to administer the proper security roles is provided within the \Documentation\ Microsoft Dynamics CRM Extended Sales Forecasting Installation_Guide.doc file.

Wizard Step 2: CRM Reports

1. Before adding these two reports to CRM, make sure you do not modify the original filenames.

2. Within CRM, navigate to Workplace, Reports, New. You'll be prompted with a New Report screen. Configure each field as follows:

  ▶ **Report Type:** Existing File

  ▶ **File Location:** \Installation\Step 2 – CRM Reports\MSA Goals – Graph.rdl (making sure the full path to your extracted files exists)

▶ **Name:** Sales Forecasting Graph

▶ **Description:** Optional text describing the report

▶ **Categories:** Sales Reports

▶ **Related Record Types:** Goals

▶ **Display In:** Reports Area, Forms for related record types, Lists for related record types

▶ **Administration Tab, Viewable By:** Organization

After you've completed the configurations, your New Report screen should match Figure 11.57.

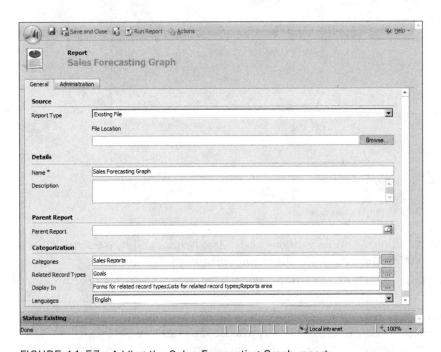

FIGURE 11.57   Adding the Sales Forecasting Graph report.

3. Click Save and Close to create the new CRM report.

4. Within CRM, navigate to Workplace, Reports, New. You'll be prompted with a New Report screen. Configure each field as follows:

▶ **Report Type:** Existing File

▶ **File Location:** \Installation\Step 2 - CRM Reports\MSA Goals - Matrix.rdl (making sure the full path to your extracted files exists)

▶ **Name:** Sales Goals Matrix

▶ **Description:** Optional text describing the report

▶ **Categories:** Sales Reports

▶ **Related Record Types:** Goals

▶ **Display In:** Reports Area, Forms for related record types, Lists for related record types

▶ **Administration Tab, Viewable By:** Organization

After you've completed the configurations, your New Report screen should match Figure 11.58

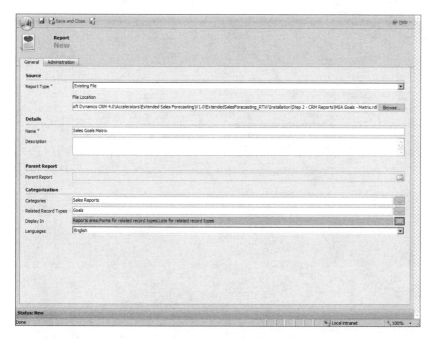

FIGURE 11.58   Adding the Sales Forecasting Graph report.

5. Click Save and Close to create the new CRM report.

6. Optionally, you can configure the default filters for these reports. Highlight either report within the Reports window and select More Actions, Edit Default Filter. This can prove helpful if you're reporting against time periods or other criteria that requires filtering.

Testing the Extended Sales Forecasting Accelerator

NOTE

An extensive explanation of hierarchical goals exists within the \Documentation\ Microsoft Dynamics CRM Extended Sales Forecasting Accelerator User_Guide.doc of this accelerator's folder.

1. Within CRM, we will create a new parent goal. Navigate to Sales, Goals and click the New button.

NOTE

Note that the Name field is autopopulated once you select the Owner and the Start Date.

2. Select the Owner, Start Date, and Meet fields, and then click Save (see Figure 11.59).

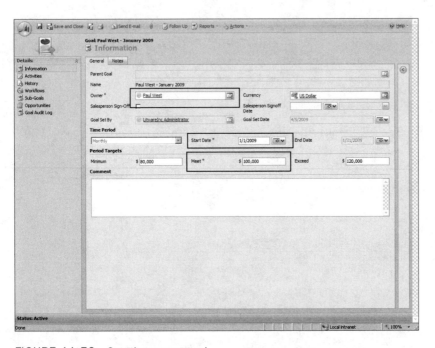

FIGURE 11.59   Creating a new goal.

3. Now create a subgoal using the following settings:

   ▶ **Owner:** Select an appropriate owner, making sure that their security role allows that owner to access the Goal entity.

   ▶ **Start Date:** Set an appropriate start date.

   ▶ **Meet:** Set a sales goal.

   Creating a subgoal allows for sales managers to compare their sales goals against the salespeople they manage. It also provides drill-down capabilities within the Goal reports.

4. Within Workplace, Reports, run the Sales Forecasting Graph report. Once you run the report, the parent goal is displayed (for example, the Sales Manager). Then click the Goal section of the report to open the subgoals; the salesperson's goals will display (see Figure 11.60).

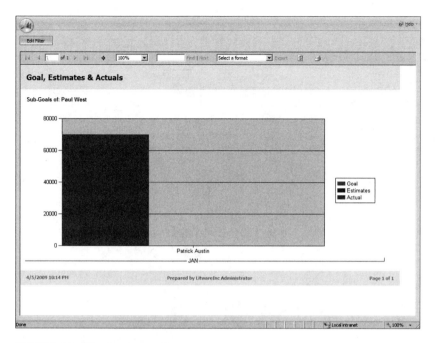

FIGURE 11.60   Goal reporting.

5. To view metrics against sales goals, we can assign a goal within an opportunity. Create a new opportunity, and then set a goal with a goal you've previously created (see Figure 11.61).

▶ Workflow. When a new sales goal is created, a task is assigned to the owner, and the owner can review the goal.

▶ If you mark the task as Completed, a workflow will send an email to the user who assigned the goal. The goal will be marked as Signed Off.

▶ If you mark the task as Canceled, the user who assigned the goal will be notified that the goal has been rejected.

Newsfeed Business Productivity Accelerator

The Newsfeed Business Productivity accelerator for Microsoft Dynamics CRM 4 could possibly be the answer to organizations whose users have not successfully adopted CRM 4. This accelerator has an appealing and easy-to-understand interface that provides insight into business data, for any level of user.

The Newsfeed Business Productivity accelerator provides the following solutions:

▶ Newsfeed report showing current CRM user activity

▶ Sample workflows used to add items to the newsfeed

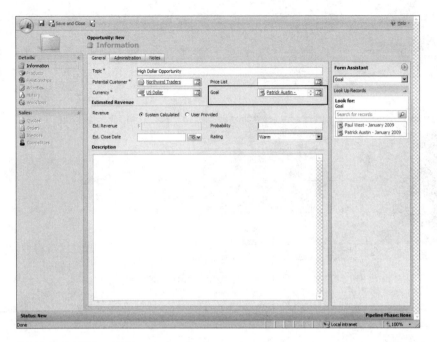

FIGURE 11.61   Create an opportunity and assign goal.

For a detailed breakdown of modifications, review the documents within the
\Documentation folder included with the download files. All files can be downloaded
from the Codeplex website at http://crmaccelerators.codeplex.com.

Once the newsfeed accelerator is downloaded and unzipped, you'll find the following
materials in the Source folder:

▶ Documentation for installation

▶ Source code

▶ Custom report

▶ Workflow

Installing the Newsfeed Business Productivity Accelerator

1. Open CRM and select Settings, Customization, Import Customizations. Import the
   \SourceCode\Workflows\newsfeed_oob_workflows.xml file into CRM. You'll be
   importing four workflows, as shown in Figure 11.62.

2. If using the Extended Sales Forecasting accelerator, import the \SourceCode\SF
   Workflows\newsfeed_esf_workflows.xml to also display Sales Forecasting results.

3. Publish the workflows.

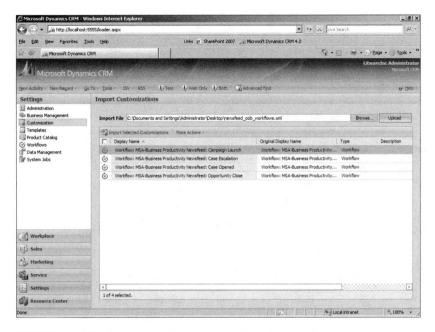

FIGURE 11.62   Import the Newsfeed workflows.

4. Import the custom report using the following configuration (see Figure 11.63):

   ▶ Existing File, which is found within C:\Microsoft Dynamics CRM
     4.0\Accelerators\BusProd\Newsfeed\V1.0\BusProd_Newsfeed_RTW\SourceCo
     de\SSRS\CRM Newsfeed.rdl.

   ▶ Update Categories to include Sales Reports. You could use all categories or none.

   ▶ Set the Related Record Types to Activities.

   ▶ Set the Display In to Reports Area and Lists for Related Record Types.

   ▶ Click the Administration tab and set the report to be available to the organiza-
     tion. CRM user permissions will still apply so that users will see only records
     for which they have permission to view.

5. Optionally, you can modify the list of activities that appear in the Newsfeed dashboard by adding the string newsfeed: to any note within a record.

This accelerator can be extended easily by building workflow to enhance the data
displayed within the custom report, or by updating the CRM site map, you can set the
newsfeed report as the "home page' for all CRM users.

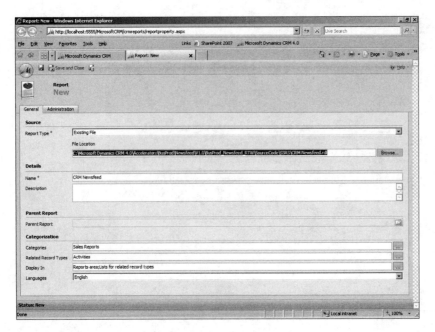

FIGURE 11.63   Import the Newsfeed report.

Notifications Accelerator

The purpose of this accelerator is to allow the publisher (CRM) to post timely CRM-centric updates to the reader's RSS reader of choice. For example, if a new lead is assigned to a salesperson, rather than send an email or expect the salesperson to check his leads within CRM, the lead is published, and the salesperson sees it the next time he opens his RSS reader. RSS publications can apply to any entity within CRM if users desire.

The Notifications accelerator uses RSS to drive information via any RSS reader client. RSS stands for Really Simple Syndication and enables content publishers to syndicate or post information automatically. RSS provides readers a way to aggregate their favorite feeds with timely updates within Outlook or many other types of RSS readers, including readers that can live within cell phones or PDAs.

In other words, rather than create a CRM workflow that pushes email to CRM users when a new CRM lead is assigned to them, add an RSS feed to CRM users' Outlook, Windows Vista gadgets, or RSS applications on their cell phones so that they may consume this data on demand.

The Notifications accelerator is composed of the following components:

- Salespeople see when a new lead has been assigned to them.

- Customer service can see when new cases have been assigned to them.

- Keeps up-to-date on events happening across the organization.

- ▶ Custom RSS pages can be managed via a custom dynamic link library (DLL) within the ISV folder (fully automated installation, including source code).

- ▶ Eliminates email; now users choose what they receive.

- ▶ Embedded within toolbar is an RSS menu. Subscribe or choose subscription.

- ▶ Select almost any entity within CRM and then any subset of the entity: My Active Accounts, My Active Contacts, My Open Leads, My Campaigns, My Active Cases, and so forth.

- ▶ Use any RSS reader, including mobile phones, or Outlook 2007 or Vista gadgets.

- ▶ Within Outlook 2007, you can configure New Item Alerts that pop up and show that you have a new RSS feed item.

Figure 11.64 shows the Notifications accelerator.

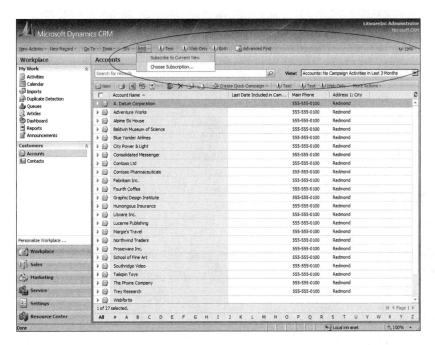

FIGURE 11.64   The Notifications accelerator.

For a detailed breakdown of modifications, review the documents within the \Documentation folder included with the download files. All files can be downloaded from the Codeplex website at http://crmaccelerators.codeplex.com.

Once the notifications accelerator is downloaded and unzipped, you'll find the following materials in the Source folder:

▶ Documentation for installation, data flow, and licensing

▶ Source code (Visual Studio 2008 is required to work with the solution files.)

Installing the Notifications Accelerator

The following steps walk you through the installation of this accelerator:

1. Download and run the executable, CRMNotifications_V1.0_RTW.exe. This contains detailed instructions and an overview of the accelerator, and all files required to install the accelerator.

2. Within the Installation Wizard, click Fully Automated Installation.

> **NOTE**
>
> The Fully Automated Installation option provides the same functionality as navigating to the \Installation\Full Install folder and then running Setup.exe.

3. Run the Setup.exe.

4. When prompted for the organization, place a check mark next to your organization, and then click Install, as shown in Figure 11.65.

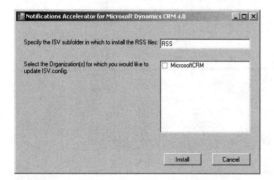

FIGURE 11.65   Notifications installation, organization selection.

5. You must enable ISV.Config customizations for the RSS drop-down to appear within CRM. Within Microsoft Dynamics CRM, select Settings, Administration, System Settings, Customization and set the Custom Menus and Toolbars section to reflect which clients you want the RSS menu to appear within (Web/Outlook/Outlook Offline), as shown in Figure 11.66.

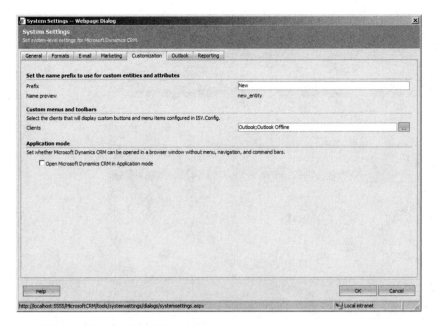

FIGURE 11.66 Enable ISV customizations.

NOTE

For more information about ISV configurations, visit http://msdn.microsoft.com/en-us/library/cc150842.aspx.

Using the Notifications Accelerator

The Notifications accelerator can be applied to many scenarios. For example, you could enable Windows Vista gadgets on your desktop and then display all your active cases, or you could use the Outlook RSS reader and view them in Outlook.

Figure 11.67 shows how to configure the Notifications accelerator to subscribe to My Active CRM Cases, and Figure 11.68 shows how they will appear in Outlook if Customer Issue is selected.

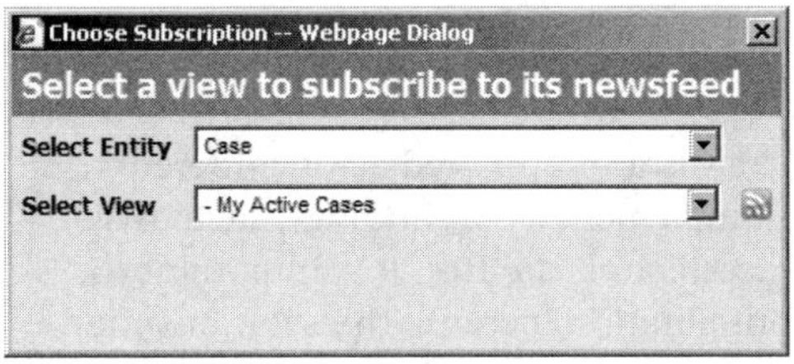

FIGURE 11.67 Subscribe to My Active Cases.

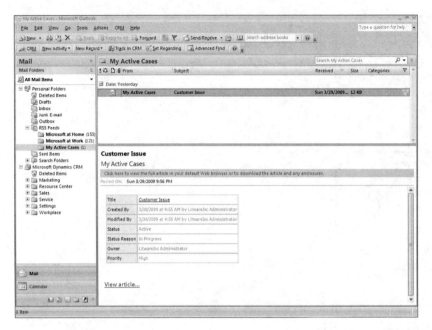

FIGURE 11.68   View active cases within Outlook.

NOTE

Outlook is used as an example for displaying this RSS feed, although the RSS feed can be viewed in any RSS reader, including Internet Explorer.

You can easily see the power of this accelerator as it quickly and effortlessly pushes information out with little configuration necessary from the end user. Organizations have used this accelerator to publish information to their internal intranet sites and to external websites.

Summary

In this chapter, we covered the CRM accelerators and the wide array of applications and features they provide.

It is important to remember that although accelerators are supported across different deployment scenarios, they frequently leverage complementary technology, such as SQL Server, MOSS, and so on. In addition, while the accelerators are free, it is important to plan on spending time and resources on their configuration, because the solutions they bring are generic in nature and will require customization of the solution to your particular needs and environment.

The goal of this chapter was to provide insight into the power of CRM's integration capabilities and into the feature-rich functionality of the CRM accelerators. If you've ever been exposed to the complexities of extending CRM, you'll certainly appreciate the enormous amount of effort that's gone into these accelerators and the enormous amount of time and energy you'll save by implementing them instead of building a solution from the ground up.

CHAPTER 12

Monitoring Dynamics CRM Using System Center Operations Manager

System Center Operations Manager (SCOM) is a crucial component in a Microsoft Dynamics CRM deployment. SCOM helps in optimizing and maintaining the Microsoft Dynamics CRM implementation. Microsoft Dynamics CRM consists of three tiers, and failure to maintain them (a common occurrence) can result in a poor end-user - experience.

This chapter shows you how to manage all the tiers using SCOM, and explains how to use Microsoft Operations Manager 2005 (MOM) or SCOM to maintain and optimize Microsoft Dynamics CRM performance.

SCOM Overview

SCOM enables system administrators to manage the network and servers end to end. This product integrates with Windows seamlessly, helping increase efficiency and stability in a Microsoft Dynamics CRM environment. Figure 12.1 shows the SCOM home screen.

Microsoft System Center Operations Manager 2007 (SCOM) is the successor to Microsoft Operations Manager 2005 (MOM). The "MOM Versus SCOM" section of this chapter describes the differences between them in detail.

Because SCOM supports high-availability features such as clustering and failover, you can use this application to manage IT environments. SCOM can also collect Simple Network Management Protocol (SNMP) and other partner-solution data within the application. SCOM provides a unified monitoring solution, enabling administrators to view the health of all dependent and nondependent systems in a single application.

Built-in role-based security allows administrators responsible for different areas to manage their own applications and infrastructure.

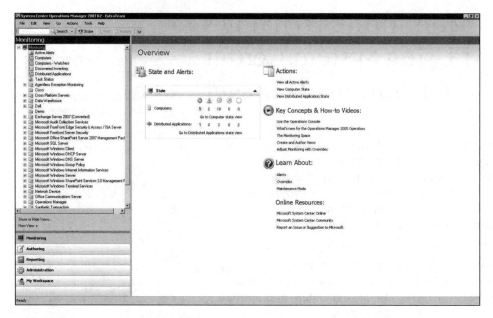

FIGURE 12.1   SCOM home screen.

SCOM 2007 can also run routine tasks, and it provides aggregated reporting to help decrease analysis and troubleshooting time. In addition, it includes management packs for more than 50 different applications that can contribute toward a systemwide solution.

Management Packs

Management-pack predefined monitoring settings enable agents to monitor specific services or applications in SCOM 2007. The Microsoft Dynamics CRM Management Pack provides administrators with basic performance counters (as shown in Figure 12.2). To learn more about this management pack, see the "Installing the Microsoft Dynamics CRM 4.0 Management Pack" section later in this chapter. SCOM also allows other applications to be integrated into the unified monitoring system. You can download the installation files from Microsoft.com.

MOM Versus SCOM

SCOM is the new version of MOM. The initial version of MOM provided administrators with a consolidated view of server health. The new version of SCOM enables administrators to view the different layers of the solution being provided to the end user (client

FIGURE 12.2   SCOM Management Pack screen.

computer health, server health, and data-tier health). SCOM provides both service-oriented monitoring and self-tuning thresholds. Table 12.1 contrasts MOM and SCOM.

TABLE 12.1   MOM Versus SCOM

	Microsoft Operations Manager 2005	System Center Operations Manager 2007
Service-Oriented Monitoring	–	**X**
Model-based architecture	–	X
Monitoring templates	–	X
SNMPv2 support	X	X
Server roles	X	X
High availability	X	X
Monitoring engine	X	X
Notifications	X	X
Consolidated console	–	X
XML management packs	–	X
Reporting	X	X
Self-Tuning Thresholds	–	**X**
Active Directory integration	–	X

TABLE 12.1   MOM Versus SCOM

	Microsoft Operations Manager 2005	System Center Operations Manager 2007
Windows PowerShell command console	–	X
Client Monitoring	**–**	**X**
XML management packs	–	X
Reporting	X	X
Role-based security	–	X

Service-Oriented Monitoring

To increase the value of the monitoring systems, service-oriented monitoring is vital. Until now, IT could manage only the conventional computer components (for example CPU, memory use, disk use, and network use). With the new service-oriented monitoring options, IT can provide true "application uptime." Service-oriented monitoring enables IT to manage all the individual dependencies of the CRM system (Windows, Internet Information Services [IIS], Microsoft CRM services, SQL Server, and reporting services) to preserve true end-user experience.

Self-Tuning Thresholds

All systems need to be tuned depending on the task that is being performed at that moment. For example, when a backup task is initiated, more CPU and memory are typically required. Therefore, the thresholds need to vary to allow faster backups. Self-tuning can provide additional memory and CPU during the time that service is running, to maintain the user experience. The self-tuning threshold monitors a set of predefined performance counters and sets an upper and lower threshold based on system usage. The system generates alerts automatically if system performance exceeds normal thresholds.

Client Monitoring

Client monitoring is a new feature in SCOM 2007. This allows organizations to manage client computers without installing a monitoring agent on the individual computers. The Agentless Exception Monitoring (AEM) feature gathers and stores the Dr. Watson application crash logs so that they can be reviewed and analyzed by operators or developers for debugging purposes.

Microsoft Dynamics CRM Architecture

Before we begin managing the infrastructure, we need to understand the different tiers of the Microsoft Dynamics CRM landscape (see Figure 12.3). The three crucial tiers that comprise the CRM environment are the client, application, and data tiers. It is important that each individual tier be healthy and that the communications between the tiers be stable.

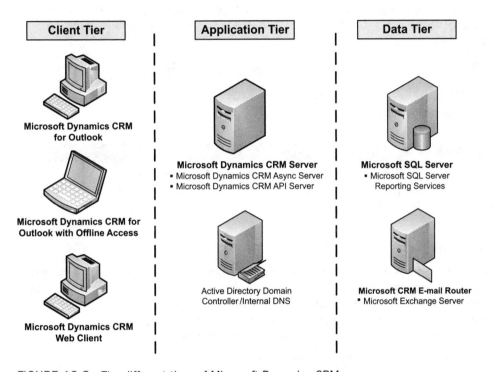

FIGURE 12.3   The different tiers of Microsoft Dynamics CRM.

> **NOTE**
>
> The tiers in Figure 12.3 represent a standard deployment. For organizations that use clustering or load balancing, the same tiers would exist, but across multiple servers.
>
> In addition, the application tier can be deployed across multiple servers if application server roles are used.

Client Tier

The client tier is used by the end users accessing the Microsoft CRM system. If the company doesn't have a standard for client machines, this can be a little challenging. Typically, users have a poor Microsoft Dynamics CRM experience when the following components are not performing at or above acceptable thresholds in this tier:

- ▶ Ping time to Microsoft Dynamics CRM (latency)
- ▶ Cache expiration times
- ▶ Compression technology

In addition to these possible causes of a poor client experience, offline access might create problems, too (for example, if you use the Microsoft Dynamics CRM client for Outlook). If your organization is using this feature, make sure to add additional health-monitoring performance counters for the Microsoft SQL 2005 Express. Common counters for SQL Express include the following:

- ▶ Processor
- ▶ Memory
- ▶ Offline database size

NOTE

System Center Configuration Manager provides a way to deploy and maintain the client configuration settings. Medium to large organizations can deploy a standard configuration and policy for all clients.

Application Tier

The application tier is responsible for retrieving the data from the data tier, processing the necessary business logic (workflows), and serving web pages to the client tier. If your organization has several users using Microsoft Dynamics CRM, you may want to consider load balancing the application or using the application role servers. (See Chapter 2, "Infrastructure Design Considerations," for more information.)

Performance problems generally occur in the following areas:

- ▶ System resource bottlenecks
    - ▶ Processor
    - ▶ Memory
- ▶ Plug-ins
- ▶ SDK code
- ▶ ASPX customization
- ▶ Asynchronous server process

Data Tier

The data tier stores the data and returns any results for the query made by the application tier. The database tier of Microsoft Dynamics CRM 4.0 includes both Microsoft SQL Server and the physical databases that contain the data related to the organization.

The data tier usually has only a few limitations:

- System resource bottlenecks
    - Processor
    - Memory
    - Disk layout
    - Disk RAID
- SQL indexes

To optimize SQL Server, SQL administrators must analyze and perform various tasks to optimize Microsoft Dynamics CRM. The most common cause of performance bottlenecks is sparsely populated columns. SQL administrators need to weigh the pros and cons for the environment. Here is a list of different optimizations that can be performed on SQL Server, with some recommendations:

- **Use SQL Server 2008 compression.**
    - **Analysis:** Most columns in Dynamics CRM tables are sparsely populated (except for system columns and required columns such as Account ID, Name, Phone Number, and Email Address). SQL Server 2008 has new compression features that improve the performance of a Microsoft Dynamics CRM 4.0 implementation.
    - **Recommendation:** Identify the largest tables in the Dynamics CRM database (usually the activity tables). Estimate savings for each table by using the sp_estimate_data_compression_savings stored procedure. When the estimates are returned, enable page compression on tables with mostly static data, and enable row compression on entity tables.
- **Use SQL Server 2008 filtered indexes.**
    - **Analysis:** Filtered views are used to generate the grids within the Microsoft Dynamics CRM application. This action usually loads anywhere from 25 to 200 records (based on the user's setting). The Dynamics CRM application automatically creates some indexes on the SQL Server tables to optimize the user experience. However, filtered indexes allow Dynamics CRM administrators to map these indexes better to the views.
    - **Recommendation:** Only create filtered indexes on most frequently executed queries or longest running queries.
- **Use SQL Server 2008 sparse columns.**
    - **Analysis:** The sparse columns feature in SQL 2008 is a great feature enhancement, which reduces the space required to store data in user-specified columns.

Also, by setting these columns as sparse, Dynamics CRM administrators optimize the access to columns that contain mostly null values.

▶ **Recommendations:** Designating a column as sparse is useful only when the column contains mostly null values. Consider using sparse columns when the space saved is at least 20 percent to 40 percent, to strike a balance between saving disk space and any CPU overhead.

▶ **Use filtered indexes and sparse columns.**

▶ **Recommendation:** Use only this combination of filtered indexes and sparse columns if the table has a large number of sparse columns and contains a lot of data.

▶ **Use filtered indexes and row compression.**

▶ **Recommendation:** Using filtered indexes in conjunction with row compression yields both performance improvements and space savings.

▶ **Perform and maintain backups more efficiently by Using SQL Server 2008 backup compression.**

▶ **Recommendation:** Enable backup compression to increase the efficiency of performing and maintaining backups.

Installing the Microsoft Dynamics CRM 4.0 Management Pack

The Microsoft Dynamics CRM 4.0 Management Pack has built-in metrics for a healthy CRM environment. The management pack collects performance-analysis and capacity-planning data by tracking various system metrics. This management pack has predefined thresholds for the monitoring and alerting engine to warn administrators of potential problems.

By managing these Microsoft Dynamics CRM components in SCOM, administrators can quickly and accurately react to critical events or key performance bottlenecks, and take appropriate action to prevent Microsoft Dynamics CRM system outages.

The SCOM Management Pack monitors the following components:

▶ Microsoft Dynamics CRM asynchronous processing service

▶ Microsoft Dynamics CRM deletion service

▶ Operability of ISV plug-ins

▶ IIS - World Wide Web Publishing

▶ Web application requests processing

- Simple Object Access Protocol (SOAP) exceptions, and unexpected failures
- Detects brute-force attacks and denial-of-service attacks
- Microsoft Dynamics CRM database indexes
- Database query processing

Installation of the Management Pack

In this section, we install the appropriate management packs for the Microsoft Dynamics CRM platform:

1. Search for and download the Microsoft Dynamics CRM Management Pack from http://www.microsoft.com/downloads/.
2. Launch Setup.
3. Read and agree to the license agreement, and then click Next
4. Select Everyone to ensure that the management packs are available for everyone who is allowed to administer the SCOM system (see Figure 12.4).

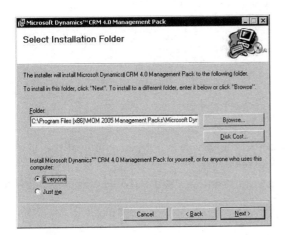

FIGURE 12.4   Setup location for the management pack.

5. Click Next and then Finish to complete setup.

NOTE

The Microsoft Dynamics CRM Management Pack works with both MOM and SCOM 2007.

SCOM is a great tool for monitoring the system as a whole and can produce a consolidated view of the health of the system.

SCOM stores all the historical data, but aggregating and viewing the data in a single view can be time-consuming. Figure 12.5 shows a consolidated view with the uptime of the servers. The figure shows a hierarchical view of servers, grouped by the various services running on different servers.

Availability Details

Measures: **State % of Total**, Filter empty rows

Entity Monitors	Uptime							Downtime		
	White	Green	Yellow	Planned Main..	Health Servi..	Disabled		Red	Unplanned Ma..
⊟ IIS Web Server	100.00%	16.67%	83.22%	0.00%	0.00%	0.11%	0.00%	0.00%	0.00%	0.00%
⊟ IIS 2003 Application..	100.00%	16.67%	83.22%	0.00%	0.00%	0.11%	0.00%	0.00%	0.00%	0.00%
⊞ ConnectWise.extratea..	100.00%	16.67%	83.22%	0.00%	0.00%	0.12%	0.00%	0.00%	0.00%	0.00%
⊟ hongkong.extrateam.c..	100.00%	16.67%	83.22%	0.00%	0.00%	0.12%	0.00%	0.00%	0.00%	0.00%
⊞ DefaultAppPool	100.00%	16.67%	83.22%	0.00%	0.00%	0.12%	0.00%	0.00%	0.00%	0.00%
⊞ jerez.extrateam.com	100.00%	16.67%	83.24%	0.00%	0.00%	0.09%	0.00%	0.00%	0.00%	0.00%
⊞ OCS-GCF.extrateam.com	100.00%	16.67%	83.23%	0.00%	0.00%	0.10%	0.00%	0.00%	0.00%	0.00%
⊞ shanghai.extrateam.c..	100.00%	16.67%	83.22%	0.00%	0.00%	0.12%	0.00%	0.00%	0.00%	0.00%
⊞ spa.extrateam.com	100.00%	16.67%	83.23%	0.00%	0.00%	0.10%	0.00%	0.00%	0.00%	0.00%
⊞ IIS 2003 Web Site	100.00%	16.67%	83.22%	0.00%	0.00%	0.11%	0.00%	0.00%	0.00%	0.00%
⊟ MSSQLSERVER	100.00%	16.67%	83.24%	0.00%	0.00%	0.10%	0.00%	0.00%	0.00%	0.00%
⊞ SQL 2000 Agent	100.00%	16.67%	83.24%	0.00%	0.00%	0.09%	0.00%	0.00%	0.00%	0.00%
⊞ SQL 2005 Agent	100.00%	16.67%	83.23%	0.00%	0.00%	0.10%	0.00%	0.00%	0.00%	0.00%
⊟ SQL Database	100.00%	16.67%	83.24%	0.00%	0.00%	0.10%	0.00%	0.00%	0.00%	0.00%
⊞ ConnectWise.extratea..	100.00%	16.67%	83.22%	0.00%	0.00%	0.12%	0.00%	0.00%	0.00%	0.00%
⊞ SQL 1.extrateam.com;M..	100.00%	16.67%	83.24%	0.00%	0.00%	0.09%	0.00%	0.00%	0.00%	0.00%
⊞ SQL 2005 Computers	99.50%	16.67%	82.73%	0.00%	0.00%	0.10%	0.00%	0.50%	0.50%	0.00%
⊞ SQL Instances	100.00%	16.67%	83.23%	0.00%	0.00%	0.10%	0.00%	0.00%	0.00%	0.00%

FIGURE 12.5   SCOM data in a pivot table.

Figure 12.6 shows server uptime. In this example, the service is not performing at the optimal level because of server (one server) unavailability.

FIGURE 12.6   SCOM data in a graphical format.

You can use Microsoft toolkits to build some of the dashboards and thus leverage the following systems:

- ▶ **SCOM 2007 R2:** Monitor server health (via performance counters, event logs, and service status).

- ▶ **Microsoft SQL Server Database Server:** Store data collected by SCOM.

- ▶ **Microsoft SQL Server Integration Services:** Transform transactional databases into data warehouses.

- ▶ **Microsoft SQL Server Analysis Services:** Organize SCOM data in an analytical format (dimensions, fact table, measures, and key performance indicators).

- ▶ **Microsoft Office SharePoint Server 2007:** Provide the foundation layer to view aggregated data from many sources.

- ▶ **Microsoft Performance Point Services 2007:** Create a presentation layer for a high-level view of the entire system.

Summary

This chapter explained the monitoring system for the Microsoft Dynamics CRM system from end to end (data tier, application tier, client tier). SCOM has management packs specifically designed for Microsoft Dynamics CRM and provides a service-oriented monitoring solution for organizations. Using this feature, organizations can identify and maintain the appropriate dependencies and can provide higher uptime for end users.

SCOM provides a complete solution in a unified view for all dependent applications and systems. SCOM can be extended, and system integrators can deploy a system-health dashboard.

CHAPTER 13

Integrating with Visual Studio Team System (VSTS)

Throughout this book, we explain integration with multiple applications that can result in substantial benefit for end users and administrators. In this chapter, we discuss how to drive value to organizations that develop, maintain, and create software or that want to use Microsoft technologies for product management.

This chapter focuses on using CRM to better enable organizations to respond to customer requests by integrating CRM with Team Foundation System (TFS). There is no reason, however, why you can't take the ideas from this chapter and use TFS to manage CRM projects just as easily.

Visual Studio Team System (VSTS) is a development suite that enables users to create work items that are essentially development tasks (and is explained in more detail throughout this chapter). Suppose, for example, that we are a company that develops software. We would use work items to set development tasks during development, after release (with discovered issues), and for ongoing product enhancement. If customers that use our software complain about a feature or a bug, they could notify our offices. We could log their complaints and act on them by logging the complaints, evaluating them, sending them to the development team for review, checking development status, periodically notifying the customer, and finally resolving the issue and issuing a new release of the software. Alternatively, we could create a customer portal that customers could access, log their issues, and have the issues automatically be received by Microsoft Dynamics CRM as a case. Microsoft Dynamics CRM would then send the issue to the development team, all the while notifying the customer of the progress of the issue. Because TFS isn't natively externally facing, it falls short as to working with it and the customer.

NOTE

While not natively externally facing, there is a solution that can be downloaded from Microsoft to make TFS externally facing. The solution is called "Visual Studio Team System Web Access 2008 Power Tool" and can be downloaded from http://www. microsoft.com/downloads/details.aspx?FamilyId=C568FBA9-3A62-4781-83C6-FDFE79750207&displaylang=en.

For our example in this chapter, we have decided to notify Team Foundation Server (TFS) upon the follow-up activity for any open case in CRM. We modified the service activity and instead display it as a development task. However, there is no reason that you couldn't easily create a custom entity called development tasks, and upon creating/saving the new development tasks associated with an open case have the workflow outlined in this chapter.

We show the functionality using the service activity because it allows us to leverage the built-in reminder functions of Microsoft Dynamics CRM (open/closed status) and have them show up in our activities view for easier management.

To create a working integration with VSTS and Microsoft Dynamics CRM, we need to leverage the web services from TFS for the following:

▶ The creation of a Work Item in TFS

▶ An event handler for the TFS Work Item change event that closed the related CRM incident (case) when a Work Item is closed/resolved in TFS

In addition, we'll create a plug-in for the following functions:

▶ To retrieve the Microsoft Dynamics CRM case with the related CRM development task activity ID (in this case, the service activity ID)

▶ To create the work item in TFS with the case and the development task activity content by calling the web service for work item creation (as explained earlier)

▶ To update the service activity with the newly created work item ID

Figure 13.1 illustrates the process graphically.

Although the chapter is oriented toward companies that want to use a combination of technology for this management, the options explained here are by no means exhaustive. If the examples in this chapter don't fit your needs exactly, they should provide a good base from which to build on.

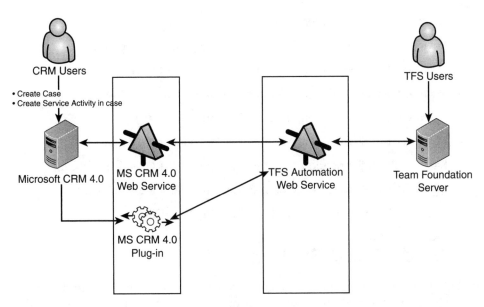

FIGURE 13.1   Graphic representation of the example solution.

The technology that we leverage in this chapter includes the following:

▶ Microsoft Dynamics CRM

▶ Microsoft Visual Studio Team System

▶ ASP.NET web development

▶ Plug-in development for Microsoft Dynamics CRM

Required Environment

The following environment/architecture is minimally required to set up a TFS automation project:

▶ Microsoft Dynamics CRM 4.0 with the latest service packs and rollup updates

▶ Microsoft TFS 2005 with Visual Studio Team Explore 2005 and the latest service packs, and the following DLLs added to the .NET Framework global assembly cache (GAC):

　　▶ Microsoft.TeamFoundation.Client.dll

　　▶ Microsoft.TeamFoundation.Common.dll

　　▶ Microsoft.TeamFoundation.Common.Library.dll

　　▶ Microsoft.TeamFoundation.dll

　　▶ Microsoft.TeamFoundation.VersionControl.Client.dll

▶ Microsoft.TeamFoundation.VersionControl.Common.dll

▶ Microsoft.TeamFoundation.VersionControl.Common.Integration.dll

▶ Microsoft.TeamFoundation.WorkItemTracking.Client.Cache.dll

▶ Microsoft.TeamFoundation.WorkItemTracking.Client.DataStore.dll

▶ Microsoft.TeamFoundation.WorkItemTracking.Client.dll

▶ Microsoft.TeamFoundation.WorkItemTracking.Client.Provision.dll

▶ Microsoft.TeamFoundation.WorkItemTracking.Client.QueryLanguage.dll

▶ Microsoft.TeamFoundation.WorkItemTracking.Client.RuleEngine.dll

▶ Microsoft.TeamFoundation.WorkItemTracking.Proxy.dll

Visual Studio Team System

VSTS uses TFS as the backend platform for source control and reporting (specifically for project tracking), and it is used primarily for software projects where multiple users need to share access.

TFS primary units of work are called work items. Work items are individual units of work that need to be completed and can consist of the following types:

▶ Bug

▶ Task

▶ Quality of service requirement

▶ Scenario

When VSTS is integrated with TFS, Team Explorer allows for project management, including all the features of TFS (version control, shelving, builds, and so on).

You can find more information about VSTS and TFS at http://msdn.microsoft.com/en-us/teamsystem/default.aspx.

VSTS and Microsoft Dynamics CRM Integration

In this chapter, our solution allows the TFS event service to expose a set of events that when fired can perform actions such as sending email or making Simple Object Access Protocol (SOAP)-based web service calls.

Whenever a work item is closed in the TFS server, we'll pass the change via a notification service that will include the work item ID to the TFS automation web service. The subscribing WorkItemChangedEvent in TFS will integrate with Microsoft Dynamics CRM and change the case status to Resolved by Development when the respective work item in TFS is closed/resolved.

NOTE

We're setting the status, but we could easily update any other field/workflow based on the TFS work item change event by modifying the supplied code.

Microsoft Dynamics CRM Customizations

The following customizations are required in our example.

Service Activity

The service activity entity in Microsoft Dynamics CRM has been customized to include custom attributes to track the work items created in TFS 2005. In addition, the service activity entity has been renamed to development task.

NOTE

As noted previously, we are using the service activity to push data to VSTS to leverage the built-in features of Microsoft Dynamics CRM and Outlook integration. With the same functionality described in this chapter, it would be relatively straightforward to use a custom entity instead. However, if you use a custom entity, you can't use the follow-up feature we describe.

Table 13.1 shows the required minimal changes necessary to the service activity entity.

TABLE 13.1   Required Attribute Changes to the Service Activity Entity

Name	Schema Name	Type	Required Level
Work Item Id	new_workitemid	Nvarchar(100)	No Constraint
Work Item Type	new_workitemtype	Picklist ▶ Bug ▶ Quality of Service Requirement ▶ Risk ▶ Scenario ▶ Task	Business Required

Case Entity

We'll use the Follow Up option in the Form Assistant pane to create the follow-up development task activity when a case requires development support to resolve it. The follow-up form activity type picklist shows all CRM activities, and based on the user's selection, the respective activities' "required" fields are displayed.

Luckily, the Follow Up option in the Form Assistant pane can be customized by setting the necessary attributes as Business Required, and Microsoft CRM will display the fields in the follow-up portion inside the Form Assistant.

In addition, the case entity's Status Reason attribute is customized by adding a new pick-list value called Resolved by Development. The new picklist value is added to track the closing of the related work item (from TFS).

Table 13.2 shows the required minimal changes necessary to the Case entity.

TABLE 13.2   Required Attribute Changes to Case Entity (Resolved by Development Is a New Option to the Existing Status Reason Field.)

Name	Schema Name	Type	Required Level
Do Not Send E-mail Update	new_donotsend emailupdate	Bit	Business Required
Status Reason	statuscode	Status ▶ In Progress ▶ On Hold ▶ Waiting for Details ▶ Researching ▶ Resolved by Development	Business Required

Integration Code

Our solution uses two main Visual Studio 2005 solutions and three Visual Studio 2005 projects, as follows:

- ▶ TFSAutomation solution
- ▶ TFSAutomation project
- ▶ WorkItemsWebService project
- ▶ TFSAutomationConsumer solution
- ▶ DevelopmentTaskWorkItemCreation project

TFS Automation Solution

Within the TFSAutomation solution, there are two projects: TFSAutomation and WorkItemsWebService.

The TFSAutomation project is designed as a class library with the methods to create the work items in the TFS server. It has the WorkItemsAutomation class and the AddWorkItem method to execute the work item creation process in TFS based on the values passed to it from the WorkItemsWebServices project as input parameters.

Figure 13.2 shows the class.

The WorkItemsWebServiceProject project is designed with three classes to provide the work item creation and work item status change notification features as web services methods. The project uses the WorkItemsAutomation project assembly for TFS work item creation.

Figure 13.3 shows the classes.

FIGURE 13.2   WorkItemsAutomation class.

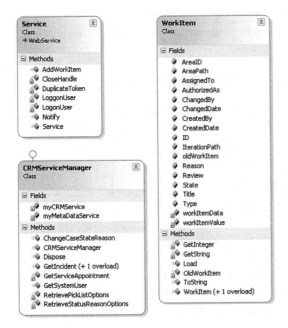

FIGURE 13.3   WorkItemsWebServiceProject classes.

The classes are described as follows:

- Service class: Two web methods are exposed:

  - **AddWorkItem web method:** Creates a new work item in the TFS server based on the values passed to it as input parameters.

  - **Notify web method:** Acts as the event handler for the WorkItemsChangeEvent notification event of the TFS server. It updates the related case in CRM when the TFS's work item is set to Resolved/Closed.

- CRMServiceManager class: Helper class designed to provide the CRM-related methods to support the service class. It helps in retrieving the following information from CRM:

  - Case based on the work item ID

  - Case record based on case record ID (GUID)

- ▶ CRM user record based on user record ID (GUID)

- ▶ Update the case status to Resolved by Development

- ▶ WorkItem class: It is designed to act as the structure to hold the TFS work item information as a .NET object for manipulation.

To set up the TFSAutomation solution, follow these steps:

1. Create a new Visual Studio 2005 solution called **TFSAutomation**.

2. Create a new class library project called **TFSAutomation** under the TFSAutomation solution (see Figure 13.4).

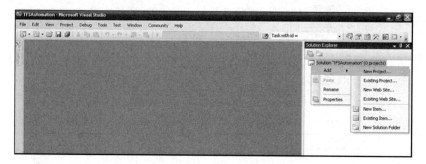

FIGURE 13.4   Creating a new project called TFSAutomation.

3. Rename the default Class1.cs to **WorkItemsAutomation.cs**.

4. Add the following TFS client-related DLL references, as shown in Figure 13.5, by right-clicking the References node and selecting Add Reference:

Microsoft.TeamFoundation.Client

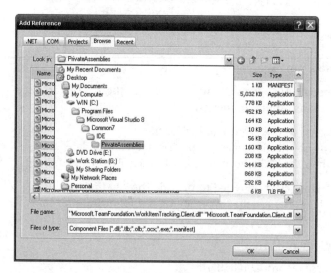

FIGURE 13.5   Adding the necessary TFS DLLs.

Microsoft.TeamFoundation.WorkItemTracking.Client

> **NOTE**
>
> Visual Studio Team Explorer 2005 must be installed to have the DLLs in the development machine's Program Files folder.

After the DLLs have been added, the project should look similar to Figure 13.6.

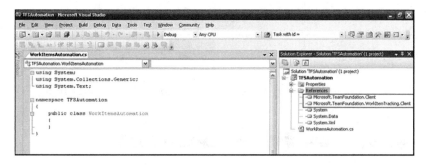

FIGURE 13.6   Project with the TFS DLLs added.

5. Add the TFS work item namespace references to the WorkItemAutomation class, as shown in Figure 13.7.

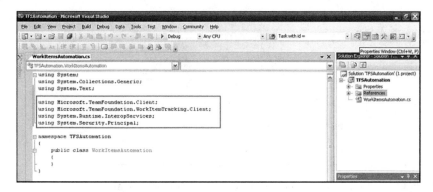

FIGURE 13.7   Namespace references included.

6. Create a new class diagram called **classdiagram1.cd** by right-clicking the TFSAutomation project and selecting View Class Diagram, as shown in Figure 13.8.

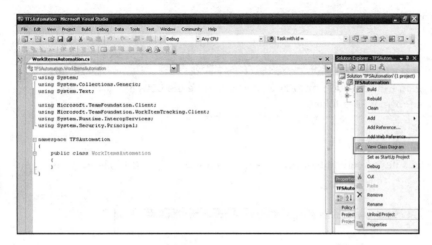

FIGURE 13.8   New class diagram.

7. Add the AddWorkItem method to the WorkItemsAutomation class, as shown in Figure 13.9.

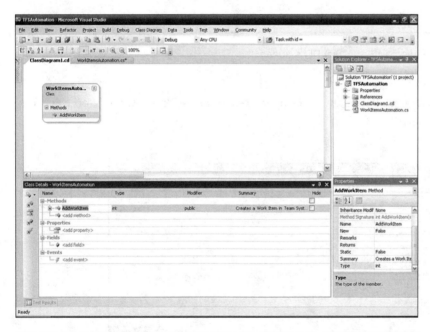

FIGURE 13.9   AddWorkItem Method added to the WorkItemsAutomation class.

8. Add the following input parameters with their summaries, as shown in Figure 13.10:

   ▶ `string teamURL`

   ▶ `string title`

▶ string description   ▶ string projectName

▶ string assignedTo   ▶ string workItemType

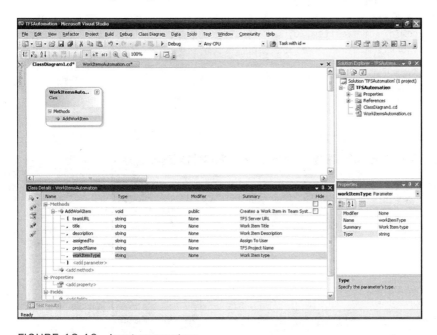

FIGURE 13.10   Input parameters.

9. Add code to the AddWorkItem Method by selecting the AddWorkItem and selecting View Code, as shown in Figure 13.11.

10. When the code appears, replace the highlighted throw line (as shown in Figure 13.12), with the following code:

```
try
{
WorkItemStore myWorkItemStore;
//Connect to Team Server
TeamFoundationServer tfs = new TeamFoundationServer(teamURL);

//Get work item store
myWorkItemStore = (WorkItemStore)tfs.GetService(typeof(WorkItemStore));

//Set new work item infos
Project proj = myWorkItemStore.Projects[projectName];
WorkItemType type = proj.WorkItemTypes[workItemType];

WorkItem myWorkItem = new WorkItem(type);
myWorkItem.Title = title;
myWorkItem.Description = description;
```

```
myWorkItem.Fields["Assigned To"].Value = assignedTo;

//Save new work item in TFS Server
myWorkItem.Save();
int myWorkItemId = myWorkItem.Id;
    return myWorkItemId;
}
catch (Exception ex)
{
throw (ex);
}
```

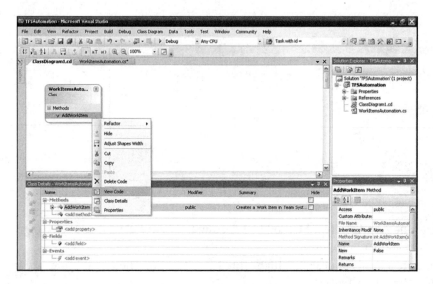

FIGURE 13.11   Adding code to the AddWorkItem Method.

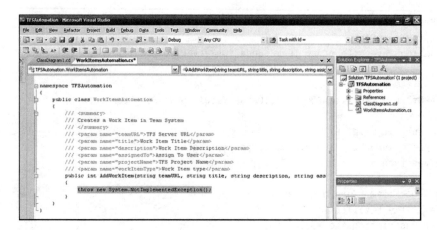

FIGURE 13.12   Where to add the code to the AddWorkItem Method.

Compile the project, as we'll need to reference the resultant DLL (found in the bin directory) in the next steps.

To set up the WorkItemsWebService project, follow these steps:

1. Create a new .NET web service website called **WorkItemsWebService** under the TFSAutomation solution.

2. Add the MSCRM service and Metadata Services web references by selecting Add Web Reference, as shown in Figure 13.13.

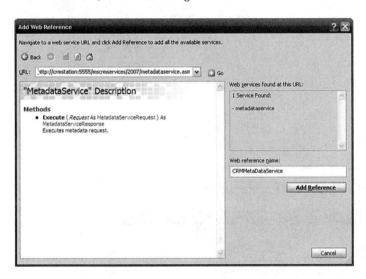

FIGURE 13.13   Adding the MSCRM Metadata service.

Be sure to select the MSCRM Metadata service URL and the MSCRM service URL (http://<<crm server name>>/mscrmservices/2007/CrmServiceWsdl.aspx?unique-name=<<organization name>>), where <<crm server name>> is the name of your server that is running Microsoft Dynamics CRM and <<organization name>> is the name of your organization.

Once added, they should appear as shown in Figure 13.14.

3. Add the TFSAutomation project output DLL as a reference to the WorkItemsWebService project. Once added, the project references should appear, as shown in Figure 13.15.

4. Modify the web.config, and add the other GAC references by replacing `<compilation debug="false" />` with the following assembly list:

```
<compilation debug="true">
<assemblies>
        <add assembly="Microsoft.TeamFoundation.Client, Version=8.0.0.0,
➡Culture=neutral, PublicKeyToken=B03F5F7F11D50A3A" />
```

FIGURE 13.14   The MSCRM service and Metadata service.

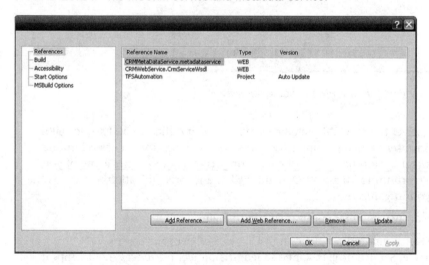

FIGURE 13.15   Project references.

```
        <add assembly="Microsoft.TeamFoundation.WorkItemTracking.Client,
➥Version=8.0.0.0, Culture=neutral, PublicKeyToken=B03F5F7F11D50A3A"/>
        <add assembly="System.Security, Version=2.0.0.0, Culture=neutral,
➥PublicKeyToken=B03F5F7F11D50A3A"/>
        <add assembly="Microsoft.TeamFoundation, Version=8.0.0.0,
➥Culture=neutral, PublicKeyToken=B03F5F7F11D50A3A"/>
        <add assembly="Microsoft.TeamFoundation.Common, Version=8.0.0.0,
```

```
              Culture=neutral, PublicKeyToken=B03F5F7F11D50A3A"/>
                      <add
➥assembly="Microsoft.TeamFoundation.WorkItemTracking.Client.RuleEngine,
➥Version=8.0.0.0, Culture=neutral, PublicKeyToken=B03F5F7F11D50A3A"/>
                      <add
➥assembly="Microsoft.TeamFoundation.VersionControl.Common.Integration,
➥Version=8.0.0.0, Culture=neutral, PublicKeyToken=B03F5F7F11D50A3A"/>
                      <add
➥assembly="Microsoft.TeamFoundation.WorkItemTracking.Client.QueryLanguage,
➥Version=8.0.0.0, Culture=neutral, PublicKeyToken=B03F5F7F11D50A3A"/>
                          <add assembly="Microsoft.TeamFoundation.VersionControl.Client,
➥Version=8.0.0.0, Culture=neutral, PublicKeyToken=B03F5F7F11D50A3A"/>
                          <add assembly="Microsoft.TeamFoundation.WorkItemTracking.Proxy,
➥Version=8.0.0.0, Culture=neutral, PublicKeyToken=B03F5F7F11D50A3A"/>
                      <add
➥assembly="Microsoft.TeamFoundation.WorkItemTracking.Client.Cache,
➥Version=8.0.0.0, Culture=neutral, PublicKeyToken=B03F5F7F11D50A3A"/>
                          <add assembly="Microsoft.VisualC, Version=8.0.0.0, Culture=neutral,
➥PublicKeyToken=B03F5F7F11D50A3A"/>
                      <add
➥assembly="Microsoft.TeamFoundation.WorkItemTracking.Client.DataStore,
➥Version=8.0.0.0, Culture=neutral, PublicKeyToken=B03F5F7F11D50A3A"/>
                      <add
➥assembly="Microsoft.TeamFoundation.WorkItemTracking.Client.Provision,
➥Version=8.0.0.0, Culture=neutral, PublicKeyToken=B03F5F7F11D50A3A"/>
                          <add assembly="Microsoft.TeamFoundation.VersionControl.Common,
➥Version=8.0.0.0, Culture=neutral, PublicKeyToken=B03F5F7F11D50A3A"/>
                          <add assembly="System.Windows.Forms, Version=2.0.0.0,
➥Culture=neutral, PublicKeyToken=B77A5C561934E089"/>
                          <add assembly="Microsoft.TeamFoundation.Common.Library,
➥Version=8.0.0.0, Culture=neutral, PublicKeyToken=B03F5F7F11D50A3A"/>
                  </assemblies>
              </compilation>
```

Figure 13.16 shows the references from the GAC.

5. Modify the <appSettings> entry to include the following values/keys:

```
<add key="TFS_URL_Address" value=""/>
<add key="Domain" value=""/>
<add key="UserName" value=""/>
<add key="Password" value=""/>
<add key="Code" value=""/>
<add key="CRMUser" value=""/>
<add key="CRMUserPassword" value=""/>
<add key="CRMUserDomain" value=""/>
<add key="CRMOrganizationName" value=""/>
```

```
<add key="CaseStatusReasonValue" value=""/>
<add key="WorkItemTrackingCacheRoot" value=""/>
```

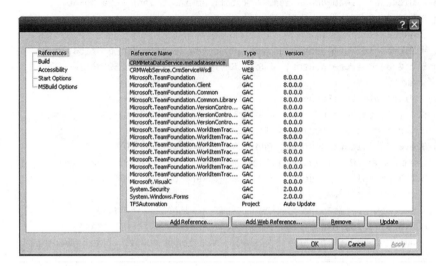

FIGURE 13.16   Project references with GAC references.

The key values need to be populated with the following values:

▶ TFS_URL_Address: The URL address of the TFS server. For example: <add
key="TFS_URL_Address" value="http://TFSServer:8080/"/>.

▶ Domain: Domain name where the TFS server is installed.

▶ UserName: Domain username having read/write access to the projects in the
TFS server.

NOTE

The username is impersonated to access the TFS and, as such, it is important that
this user has a profile created within the TFS workspace and that they have run the VS
Team Explorer at least once on that machine with that username.

▶ Password: TFS server user password.

▶ Code: Project code used for integration purposes.

▶ CRMUser: CRM admin or CRM user with organization-level read/write permission for Case and service activity records.

▶ CRMUserPassword: CRM user password.

▶ CRMUserDomain: MSCRM user's domain name.

▶ CRMOrganizationName: MSCRM user's organization name.

▶ CaseStatusReasonValue: MSCRM case status reason set when a work item is closed in TFS server. An example might be <add key="CaseStatusReasonValue" value="Resolved by Development"/>.

NOTE

The MSCRM Case – Status Reason field should be customized to include the custom status reason value added during the case configuration of Microsoft Dynamics CRM earlier in this chapter.

▶ WorkItemTrackingCacheRoot: Work item tracking cache root folder. The folder should have read/write privilege for the user (IIS_WG) group or create a subfolder under the TFS automation website's physical path. An example of this might be <add key="WorkItemTrackingCacheRoot" value="C:\TFSTestWebsite\TFSCache "/>.

To create this folder, create a new folder **TFSCache** under the WorkItemsWebService project and update the WorkItemTrackingCacheRoot appSetting key with the new folder's physical path.

6. Add the following namespace references to the App_Code\Service.cs:

```
using TFSAutomation;
using System.Web.Configuration;
using System.Xml;
using System.Security.Principal;
using System.Runtime.InteropServices;
using CRMWebService;
using System.Net;
using System.Configuration;
```

7. Add the following .dll's used for impersonation above the constructor method in the Service class, as shown in Figure 13.17:

```
#region DllImports

[DllImport("advapi32.dll")]
private extern static bool LogonUser(string lpsznombreDeUsuario, string
lpszDomain, string lpszPassword, int dwLogonType, int dwLogonProvider, ref
IntPtr phToken);

[DllImport("kernel32.dll")]
 private extern static bool CloseHandle(IntPtr handle);

[DllImport("advapi32.dll")]
 private extern static bool DuplicateToken(IntPtr ExistingTokenHandle, int
SECURITY_IMPERSONATION_LEVEL, ref IntPtr DuplicateTokenHandle);

#endregion
```

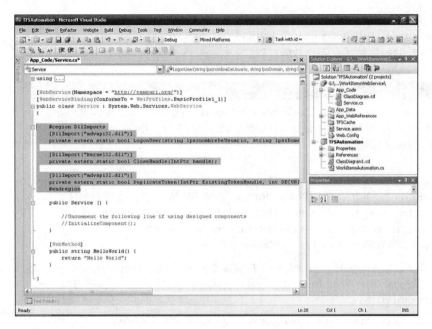

FIGURE 13.17   DLL imports.

8. Replace the HelloWorld web method with the following code:

```
#region AddWorkItem
/// <summary>
/// Add Work Item to TFS
/// </summary>
/// <param name="code">TFS Automation Project Code</param>
/// <param name="title">Work Item Title</param>
/// <param name="caseId">Related CRM Case Id</param>
/// <param name="assignedToUserId">Assigned to CRM User Id</param>
/// <param name="projectName">Work Item Project Name</param>
/// <param name="workItemType">Work Item Type</param>
/// <returns>Work Item ID Number</returns>
 [WebMethod]
public int AddWorkItem(string code, string title, string caseId, string
➥assignedToUserId, string projectName, string workItemType)
{
  //Check for project code
        if (code != WebConfigurationManager.AppSettings["Code"])
        {
            return -1;
        }
        WorkItemsAutomation workItemsAutomation = new WorkItemsAutomation();
```

```
//Impersonate current logged on user
WindowsImpersonationContext impersonatedUser = LogonUser();

//Initialize MSCRM Manager
CRMServiceManager myCRMServiceManager = new CRMServiceManager();

// Get CRM incident based on the case id parameter
CRMWebService.incident myIncident =
➥myCRMServiceManager.GetIncident(caseId);

//Get CRM system user based on the assignedTo parameter
CRMWebService.systemuser userInfo =
➥myCRMServiceManager.GetSystemUser(assignedToUserId);

//Read incident description
string description = string.Empty;
if (myIncident.description != null)
{
    description = myIncident.description;
}

//Read CRM Sytem User's full name
string userFullName = string.Empty;
if(userInfo.fullname != null)
{
    userFullName = userInfo.fullname;
}
int WorkItemID = -1;
try
{
    //Add work item to TFS
    WorkItemID = workItemsAutomation.AddWorkItem(
        WebConfigurationManager.AppSettings["TFS_URL_Address"],
        title, description, userFullName, projectName, workItemType);
    return WorkItemID;
}
catch (Exception ex)
{
    throw (ex);
}
finally
{
    if (impersonatedUser != null)
    {
        impersonatedUser.Undo();
```

13

```
        }
    }
}
#endregion
```

9. By adding the following code, create a new Notify web method to process the WorkItemsChangeEvent event of the TFS server:

```
#region Notify


/// <summary>
/// TFS WorkItemsChangeEvent Handler
/// </summary>
/// <param name="eventXml">Event XML</param>
/// <param name="tfsIdentityXml">TFS Identiy XML</param>


 [SoapDocumentMethod(Action =
➥"http://schemas.microsoft.com/TeamFoundation/2005/06/Services/
➥Notification/03/Notify", RequestNamespace =
➥"http://schemas.microsoft.com/TeamFoundation/2005/06/Services/
➥Notification/03")]
 [WebMethod]
public void Notify(string eventXml, string tfsIdentityXml)
{
        //Load Work Item
        WorkItem myWorkItem = new WorkItem(eventXml);
        try
        {
            CRMServiceManager myCRMServiceManager = new CRMServiceManager();
            // Get Case by work item id
            CRMWebService.incident myIncident =
➥myCRMServiceManager.GetIncident(myWorkItem.ID);
            if (myIncident != null)
            {
                if (myWorkItem.State == "Closed" ¦¦
                    myWorkItem.State == "Resolved")
                {
                    //Change CRM Case Status Reason
                    myCRMServiceManager.ChangeCaseStateReason(myIncident,
➥ConfigurationSettings.AppSettings["CaseStatusReasonValue"]);
                }
            }
        }
        catch (SoapException soapExp)
        {
            throw new ApplicationException(soapExp.Detail.InnerText, soapExp);
```

```
        }
        catch (Exception ex)
        {
            throw ex;
        }
    }
    #endregion
```

10. Use the following code to add a private method LogonUser to impersonate the current user for creating work items in the TFS server:

```
#region LogonUser
/// <summary>
/// Impersonate Current User
/// </summary>
/// <returns>Windows Impersonation Context</returns>
private WindowsImpersonationContext LogonUser()
{
        if (WebConfigurationManager.AppSettings["UserName"] == null ||
            WebConfigurationManager.AppSettings["UserName"] == "")
        {
            return null;
        }
        const int LOGON32_PROVIDER_DEFAULT = 0;
        // This parameter causes LogonUser to create a primary token.
        const int LOGON32_LOGON_INTERACTIVE = 2;
        const int SecurityImpersonation = 2;
        IntPtr _tokenHandle = IntPtr.Zero;
        IntPtr _dupeTokenHandle = IntPtr.Zero;
        bool returnValue = false;
        try
        {
            returnValue =
➥LogonUser(WebConfigurationManager.AppSettings["UserName"],
                WebConfigurationManager.AppSettings["Domain"],
                WebConfigurationManager.AppSettings["Password"],
                LOGON32_LOGON_INTERACTIVE, LOGON32_PROVIDER_DEFAULT, ref
➥_tokenHandle);
        }
        catch (NullReferenceException ex)
        {
            throw new Exception("Missing Parameter.", ex);
        }
        if (false == returnValue)
        {
            throw new Exception("Authentication Failure.");
```

```
        }
        else
        {
            bool retVal = DuplicateToken(_tokenHandle, SecurityImpersonation,
➥ref _dupeTokenHandle);
            WindowsIdentity newId = new WindowsIdentity(_dupeTokenHandle);
            WindowsImpersonationContext impersonatedUser = newId.Impersonate();
            return impersonatedUser;
        }
    }
    #endregion
```

11. Add a new class called WorkItem.cs for handling the TFS work item information as a .NET object, and replace the default contents of the WorkItem class with the following code:

```
using System;
using System.Data;
using System.Configuration;
using System.Web;
using System.Web.Security;
using System.Web.UI;
using System.Web.UI.WebControls;
using System.Web.UI.WebControls.WebParts;
using System.Web.UI.HtmlControls;
using System.Xml.Xsl;
using System.Xml.XPath;
using System.Xml;
using System.Text;
using System.Reflection;
using System.IO;
/// <summary>
/// Summary description for WorkItem
/// </summary>
public class WorkItem
{
    public string Type;
    public int ID;
    public int Review;
    public int AreaID;
    public string Title;
    public string AreaPath;
    public string State;
    public string Reason;
    public string AssignedTo;
    public string ChangedBy;
    public string CreatedBy;
```

```
    public DateTime ChangedDate;
    public DateTime CreatedDate;
    public string AuthorizedAs;
    public string IterationPath;
    public WorkItem oldWorkItem = null;
    private string workItemValue = "NewValue";
    private XmlElement workItemData;
    #region WorkItem
    public WorkItem() { }
    public WorkItem(string eventXml)
    {
        XmlDocument xd = new XmlDocument();
        xd.LoadXml(eventXml);
        XmlElement eventData = xd.DocumentElement;
        Load(eventData);
        oldWorkItem = OldWorkItem(eventData);
    }
    #endregion
    #region OldWorkItem
    private static WorkItem OldWorkItem(XmlElement eventData)
    {
        WorkItem workItem = new WorkItem();
        workItem.workItemValue = "OldValue";
        workItem.Load(eventData);
        return workItem;
    }
    #endregion
    #region Load
    public void Load(XmlElement eventData)
    {
        this.workItemData = eventData;
        this.Type = GetString("System.WorkItemType");
        this.Title = GetString("System.Title");
        int.TryParse(GetInteger("System.Id"), out this.ID);
        int.TryParse(GetInteger("System.Rev"), out this.Review);
        int.TryParse(GetInteger("System.AreaId"), out this.AreaID);
        this.AreaPath = GetString("System.AreaPath");
        this.State = GetString("System.State");
        this.Reason = GetString("System.Reason");
        this.AssignedTo = GetString("System.AssignedTo");
        this.ChangedBy = GetString("System.ChangedBy");
        this.CreatedBy = GetString("System.CreatedBy");
        DateTime.TryParse(GetString("System.ChangedDate"), out this.Changed-
Date);
        DateTime.TryParse(GetString("System.CreatedDate"), out this.Created-
Date);
```

```
            this.AuthorizedAs = GetString("System.AuthorizedAs");
            this.IterationPath = GetString("System.IterationPath");
        }

        #endregion
        #region GetString
        private string GetString(string TagName)
        {
            try
            {
                return workItemData.SelectSingleNode
("CoreFields/StringFields/Field[ReferenceName='" +
➥TagName + "']/" + workItemValue).InnerText;
            }
            catch (Exception ex)
            {
                return "";
            }
        }
        #endregion
        #region GetInteger
        private string GetInteger(string TagName)
        {
            try
            {
                return
➥workItemData.SelectSingleNode
➥("CoreFields/IntegerFields/Field[ReferenceName='"
➥ + TagName + "']/" + workItemValue).InnerText;
            }
            catch (Exception ex)
            {
                return "";
            }
        }
        #endregion
        #region ToString
        public override string ToString()
        {
            StringBuilder sb;
            if (workItemValue == "NewValue")
            {
                sb = new StringBuilder("WorkItem New Values<br>");
            }
            else
            {
```

```
              sb = new StringBuilder("WorkItem Old Values<br>");
          }
          FieldInfo[] fields = this.GetType().GetFields();
          foreach (FieldInfo field in fields)
          {
              sb.Append(field.Name);
              sb.Append(":");
              if (field.GetValue(this) != null)
              {
                  sb.Append(field.GetValue(this));
              }
              sb.Append("<br>");
          }
          return sb.ToString();
      }

      #endregion
  }
```

12. Add another class called CRMServiceManager under the WorkItemsWebService project to handle the MSCRM-related calls. Replace the default contents with the following code:

```
using System;
using System.Data;
using System.Configuration;
using System.Collections.Specialized;
using System.Web;
using System.Web.Security;
using System.Web.UI;
using System.Web.UI.WebControls;
using System.Web.UI.WebControls.WebParts;
using System.Web.UI.HtmlControls;
using System.Web.Configuration;
using System.Net;
using CRMWebService;
using CRMMetaDataService;
/// <summary>
/// Summary description for CRMServiceManager
/// </summary>
public class CRMServiceManager : IDisposable
{
    //CRM Services
    private CRMWebService.CrmService myCRMService = null;
    private CRMMetaDataService.MetadataService myMetaDataService = null;
    #region Constructor
    public CRMServiceManager()
```

```
    {
        string CRMUser = "";
        string CRMUserPassword = "";
        string CRMUserDomain = "";
        //Read CRM User info from web config
        CRMUser = ConfigurationSettings.AppSettings["CRMUser"];
        CRMUserPassword = ConfigurationSettings.AppSettings["CRMUserPassword"];
        CRMUserDomain = ConfigurationSettings.AppSettings["CRMUserDomain"];
        //CRM Web Service
        myCRMService = new CRMWebService.CrmService();
        myCRMService.Url =
➥ConfigurationSettings.AppSettings["CRMWebService.CrmServiceWsdl"];
        myCRMService.Credentials = new NetworkCredential(CRMUser,
➥CRMUserPassword, CRMUserDomain);
        // Set up the CRM Service.
        CRMWebService.CrmAuthenticationToken token = new
➥CRMWebService.CrmAuthenticationToken();
        token.AuthenticationType = 0;
        token.OrganizationName =
➥ConfigurationSettings.AppSettings["CRMOrganizationName"];
        myCRMService.CrmAuthenticationTokenValue = token;
        myCRMService.PreAuthenticate = true;
        //CRM Metadata Web Service
        myMetaDataService = new CRMMetaDataService.MetadataService();
        myMetaDataService.Url =
➥ConfigurationSettings.AppSettings["CRMMetaDataService.metadataservice"];
        myMetaDataService.Credentials = new
➥System.Net.NetworkCredential(CRMUser, CRMUserPassword, CRMUserDomain);
        // Set up the CRM Metadata Service.
        CRMMetaDataService.CrmAuthenticationToken metaDataToken = new
➥CRMMetaDataService.CrmAuthenticationToken();
        metaDataToken.AuthenticationType = 0;
        metaDataToken.OrganizationName =
➥ConfigurationManager.AppSettings["CRMOrganizationName"];
        myMetaDataService.CrmAuthenticationTokenValue = metaDataToken;
        myMetaDataService.PreAuthenticate = true;
    }
    #endregion
    #region Destructor
    public void Dispose()
    {
        myCRMService.Dispose();
    }
    #endregion
    #region TFS Add Work Item Relate CRM Calls
    /// <summary>
```

```
/// Get CRM Incident based on CRM Incident id
/// </summary>
/// <param name="caseId">CRM Incident ID</param>
/// <returns>CRM Incident</returns>
public CRMWebService.incident GetIncident(string caseId)
{
    try

    {
        Guid regardingobjectid = new Guid(caseId);
        if (regardingobjectid == null)
        {
            return null;
        }
        // Creates a column set holding the names of the columns to be
➥retrieved
        ColumnSet colsPrincipal = new ColumnSet();
        //// Sets the Column Set's Properties
        colsPrincipal.Attributes = new string[] { "description" };
        // Create a ConditionExpression
        ConditionExpression conditionPrincipal = new ConditionExpression();
        // Sets the ConditionExpressions Properties so that the condition
➥is true when the
        // ownerid of the account Equals the principalId
        conditionPrincipal.AttributeName = "incidentid";
        conditionPrincipal.Operator = ConditionOperator.Equal;
        conditionPrincipal.Values = new object[1];
        conditionPrincipal.Values[0] = regardingobjectid;
        // Create the FilterExpression
        FilterExpression filterPrincipal = new FilterExpression();
        // Set the FilterExpression's Properties
        filterPrincipal.FilterOperator = LogicalOperator.And;
        filterPrincipal.Conditions = new ConditionExpression[] {
➥conditionPrincipal };
        // Create the Query Expression
        QueryExpression queryPrincipal = new QueryExpression();
        // Set the QueryExpression's Properties
        queryPrincipal.EntityName = EntityName.incident.ToString();
        queryPrincipal.ColumnSet = colsPrincipal;
        queryPrincipal.Criteria = filterPrincipal;
        // Create the Request Object
        RetrieveMultipleRequest retrievePrincipal = new
➥RetrieveMultipleRequest();
        // Set the Request Object's Properties
        retrievePrincipal.Query = queryPrincipal;
        // Execute the Request
```

13

```
            RetrieveMultipleResponse principalResponse =
   (RetrieveMultipleResponse)myCRMService.Execute(retrievePrincipal);
            if
(principalResponse.BusinessEntityCollection.BusinessEntities.Length == 0)
            {
                return null;
            }
            else
            {
                CRMWebService.incident myIncident;
                myIncident =
➥((CRMWebService.incident)(principalResponse.BusinessEntityCollection.
BusinessEntities[0]));
                return myIncident;
            }
        }
        catch (Exception ex)
        {
            throw (ex);
        }
    }
    /// <summary>
    /// Get CRM System User
    /// </summary>
    /// <param name="userId">User id</param>
    /// <returns>CRM System user</returns>
    public CRMWebService.systemuser GetSystemUser(string userId)
    {
        try
        {
            Guid userobjectid = new Guid(userId);
            if (userobjectid == null)
            {
                return null;
            }
            // Creates a column set holding the names of the columns to be
➥retreived
            ColumnSet colsPrincipal = new ColumnSet();
            //// Sets the Column Set's Properties
            colsPrincipal.Attributes = new string[] { "fullname" };
            // Create a ConditionExpression
            ConditionExpression conditionPrincipal = new ConditionExpression();
            // Sets the ConditionExpressions Properties so that the condition
            // is true when the ownerid of the account Equals the principalId
            conditionPrincipal.AttributeName = "systemuserid";
```

```
                conditionPrincipal.Operator = ConditionOperator.Equal;
                conditionPrincipal.Values = new object[1];
                conditionPrincipal.Values[0] = userobjectid;
                // Create the FilterExpression
                FilterExpression filterPrincipal = new FilterExpression();
                // Set the FilterExpression's Properties
                filterPrincipal.FilterOperator = LogicalOperator.And;
                filterPrincipal.Conditions = new ConditionExpression[] {
➥conditionPrincipal };
                // Create the Query Expression
                QueryExpression queryPrincipal = new QueryExpression();
                // Set the QueryExpression's Properties
                queryPrincipal.EntityName = EntityName.systemuser.ToString();
                queryPrincipal.ColumnSet = colsPrincipal;
                queryPrincipal.Criteria = filterPrincipal;
                // Create the Request Object
                RetrieveMultipleRequest retrievePrincipal = new
➥RetrieveMultipleRequest();
                // Set the Request Object's Properties
                retrievePrincipal.Query = queryPrincipal;
                // Execute the Request
                RetrieveMultipleResponse principalResponse =
  (RetrieveMultipleResponse)myCRMService.Execute(retrievePrincipal);
                if
(principalResponse.BusinessEntityCollection.BusinessEntities.Length == 0)

                {
                    return null;
                }
                else
                {
                    CRMWebService.systemuser mySystemUser;
                    mySystemUser =
➥((CRMWebService.systemuser)(principalResponse.BusinessEntityCollection.
➥Business
Entities[0]));
                    return mySystemUser;
                }
            }
        catch (Exception ex)
        {
            throw (ex);
        }
    }
    #endregion
    #region TFS Event Notification Related CRM Calls
    /// <summary>
```

13

```
/// Get CRM Incident based on work item id
/// </summary>
/// <param name="workItemID">TFS work item id</param>
/// <returns>CRM Incident</returns>
public CRMWebService.incident GetIncident(int workItemID)
{
    try
    {
        CRMWebService.serviceappointment myServiceappointment;
        myServiceappointment = GetServiceAppointment(workItemID);
        if (myServiceappointment == null)
        {
            return null;
        }
        Lookup regardingobjectid = myServiceappointment.regardingobjectid;
        // Creates a column set holding the names of the columns to be
➥retreived
        ColumnSet colsPrincipal = new ColumnSet();
        // Sets the Column Set's Properties
        colsPrincipal.Attributes = new string[] { "incidentid" ,
➥"statecode" , "statuscode" };
        // Create a ConditionExpression
        ConditionExpression conditionPrincipal = new ConditionExpression();
        // Sets the ConditionExpressions Properties so that the condition
        // is true when the ownerid of the account Equals the principalId
        conditionPrincipal.AttributeName = "incidentid";
        conditionPrincipal.Operator = ConditionOperator.Equal;
        conditionPrincipal.Values = new object[1];
        conditionPrincipal.Values[0] = regardingobjectid.Value;
        // Create the FilterExpression
        FilterExpression filterPrincipal = new FilterExpression();
        // Set the FilterExpression's Properties
        filterPrincipal.FilterOperator = LogicalOperator.And;
        filterPrincipal.Conditions = new ConditionExpression[] {
➥conditionPrincipal };
        // Create the Query Expression
        QueryExpression queryPrincipal = new QueryExpression();
        // Set the QueryExpression's Properties
        queryPrincipal.EntityName = EntityName.incident.ToString();
        queryPrincipal.ColumnSet = colsPrincipal;
        queryPrincipal.Criteria = filterPrincipal;
        // Create the Request Object
        RetrieveMultipleRequest retrievePrincipal = new
➥RetrieveMultipleRequest();
        // Set the Request Object's Properties
```

```
                    retrievePrincipal.Query = queryPrincipal;
                    // Execute the Request
                    RetrieveMultipleResponse principalResponse =
➥(RetrieveMultipleResponse)myCRMService.Execute(retrievePrincipal);
                    if
➥(principalResponse.BusinessEntityCollection.BusinessEntities.Length == 0)
                    {
                        return null;
                    }
                    else
                    {
                        CRMWebService.incident myIncident;
                        myIncident =
➥((CRMWebService.incident)(principalResponse.BusinessEntityCollection.
BusinessEntities[0]));
                        return myIncident;
                    }
            }
            catch (Exception ex)
            {
                throw (ex);
            }
        }
        /// <summary>
        /// Get CRM Service Appointment based on work item id
        /// </summary>
        /// <param name="workItemID">TFS Work Item Id</param>
        /// <returns>CRM Service Appointment</returns>
        private CRMWebService.serviceappointment GetServiceAppointment(int
➥workItemID)
        {
            // Creates a column set holding the names of the columns to be
➥retreived
            ColumnSet colsPrincipal = new ColumnSet();
            // Sets the Column Set's Properties

            colsPrincipal.Attributes = new string[] { "regardingobjectid" };

            // Create a ConditionExpression
            ConditionExpression conditionPrincipal = new ConditionExpression();
            // Sets the ConditionExpressions Properties so that the condition is
            // true when the ownerid of the account Equals the principalId
            conditionPrincipal.AttributeName = "new_workitemid";
            conditionPrincipal.Operator = ConditionOperator.Equal;
            conditionPrincipal.Values = new object[1];
```

```
        conditionPrincipal.Values[0] = workItemID;
        // Create the FilterExpression
        FilterExpression filterPrincipal = new FilterExpression();
        // Set the FilterExpression's Properties
        filterPrincipal.FilterOperator = LogicalOperator.And;
        filterPrincipal.Conditions = new ConditionExpression[] {
➥conditionPrincipal };
        // Create the Query Expression
        QueryExpression queryPrincipal = new QueryExpression();
        // Set the QueryExpression's Properties
        queryPrincipal.EntityName = EntityName.serviceappointment.ToString();
        queryPrincipal.ColumnSet = colsPrincipal;
        queryPrincipal.Criteria = filterPrincipal;
        // Create the Request Object
        RetrieveMultipleRequest retrievePrincipal = new
➥RetrieveMultipleRequest();
        // Set the Request Object's Properties
        retrievePrincipal.Query = queryPrincipal;
        // Execute the Request
        RetrieveMultipleResponse principalResponse =
➥(RetrieveMultipleResponse)myCRMService.Execute(retrievePrincipal);
        if (principalResponse.BusinessEntityCollection.BusinessEntities.Length
== 0)
        {
            return null;
        }
        else
        {
            CRMWebService.serviceappointment myServiceappointment;
            myServiceappointment =
➥((CRMWebService.serviceappointment)
(principalResponse.BusinessEntityCollection.BusinessEntities[0]));

            return myServiceappointment;
        }
    }
    /// <summary>
    /// Change Case State Reason
    /// </summary>
    /// <param name="myIncident">CRM Incident</param>
    /// <param name="statusReasonStr">Status Reason string value</param>
    public void ChangeCaseStateReason(CRMWebService.incident myIncident, string
➥statusReasonStr)
    {
        if (CRMWebService.IncidentState.Active != myIncident.statecode.Value)
        {
```

```
            return;
        }
        NameValueCollection statusReasonOptions =
RetrieveStatusReasonOptions(EntityName.incident.ToString());

        myIncident.statuscode.Value =
➥int.Parse(statusReasonOptions[statusReasonStr]);
        myCRMService.Update(myIncident);
    }
    #region Close Case
    //public void CloseIncident(CRMWebService.incident incident)
    //{
    //    try
    //    {
    //        if (CRMWebService.IncidentState.Active !=
➥incident.statecode.Value)
    //        {
    //            return;
    //        }
    //        CRMWebService.incidentresolution muIncidentResolution = new
➥incidentresolution();

    //        muIncidentResolution.incidentid = new Lookup();
    //        muIncidentResolution.incidentid.type =
➥EntityName.incident.ToString();
    //        muIncidentResolution.incidentid.Value =
➥incident.incidentid.Value;
    //        /*
    //        muIncidentResolution.ownerid = new Owner();
    //        muIncidentResolution.ownerid.type =
➥EntityName.systemuser.ToString();
    //        muIncidentResolution.ownerid.Value = <Guid of the user>;
    //        */
    //        CloseIncidentRequest closeIncidentRequest = new
➥CloseIncidentRequest();
    //        closeIncidentRequest.IncidentResolution = muIncidentResolution;
    //        closeIncidentRequest.Status = -1;
    //        myCRMService.Execute(closeIncidentRequest);
    //    }
    //    catch (Exception ex)
    //    {
    //        throw (ex);
    //    }
    //}
    #endregion
    #endregion
```

```
#region Helper Methods
/// <summary>
/// Retrieve Status Reason picklist Options
/// </summary>
/// <param name="entityName">CRM entity name</param>
/// <returns>Status Reason Options in Name value collection</returns>
private NameValueCollection RetrieveStatusReasonOptions(string entityName)
{
    RetrieveAttributeRequest request = new RetrieveAttributeRequest();
    request.EntityLogicalName = entityName;
    request.LogicalName = "statuscode";
    RetrieveAttributeResponse response =
➥(RetrieveAttributeResponse)myMetaDataService.Execute(request);
    //Picklist Options Collection
    NameValueCollection statusOptionsCollection =
➥new NameValueCollection();
    AttributeMetadata currentAttribute = response.AttributeMetadata;
    if (currentAttribute.SchemaName.Length > 0)
    {
        Type attributeType = currentAttribute.GetType();
        statusOptionsCollection.Clear();
        if (attributeType == typeof(StatusAttributeMetadata))
        {
            //The PicklistAttributeMetadata describes the options available
➥in a picklist.
            StatusAttributeMetadata statusMetadata =
➥(StatusAttributeMetadata)currentAttribute;
            foreach (StatusOption option in statusMetadata.Options)
            {
                //The Options array contains all available options. The
➥OptionValue is stored in the database,
                //while the Description is displayed to the user.
                statusOptionsCollection.Add
(option.Label.UserLocLabel.Label,
option.Value.Value.ToString());
            }
        }
    }
    return statusOptionsCollection;
}
/// <summary>
/// Retrieve Pick List Options
/// </summary>
```

```
/// <param name="entityName">CRM Entity Name</param>
/// <param name="picklistAttributeName">Picklist attribute Name</param>
/// <returns>Picklist Options in Name value collection</returns>
private NameValueCollection RetrievePickListOptions(string entityName,
➥string picklistAttributeName)
{
    RetrieveAttributeRequest request = new RetrieveAttributeRequest();
    request.EntityLogicalName = entityName;
    request.LogicalName = picklistAttributeName;
    RetrieveAttributeResponse response =
➥(RetrieveAttributeResponse)myMetaDataService.Execute(request);
    //Picklist Options Collection
    NameValueCollection picklistOptionsCollection = new
➥NameValueCollection();
    AttributeMetadata currentAttribute = response.AttributeMetadata;
    if (currentAttribute.SchemaName.Length > 0)
    {
        Type attributeType = currentAttribute.GetType();
        picklistOptionsCollection.Clear();
        if (attributeType == typeof(PicklistAttributeMetadata))
        {
            //The PicklistAttributeMetadata describes the options available
➥in a picklist.
            PicklistAttributeMetadata picklistMetadata =
➥(PicklistAttributeMetadata)currentAttribute;
            foreach (Option option in picklistMetadata.Options)
            {
                //The Options array contains all available options. The
➥OptionValue is stored in the database,
                //while the Description is displayed to the user.
                picklistOptionsCollection.
Add(option.Label.UserLocLabel.Label,
option.Value.Value.ToString());
            }
        }
    }
    return picklistOptionsCollection;
}
#endregion
}
```

13. Build the entire TFSAutomation solution.

TFSAutomationConsumer Solution

The project contained within the TFSAutomationConsumer solution is called the DevelopmentTaskWorkItemCreation project. It is a Microsoft Dynamics CRM plug-in designed to provide an interface between Microsoft Dynamics CRM and the TFS Automation web service. The plug-in is developed to be executed when a new Development Activity record is created in Microsoft Dynamics CRM, and it will read the necessary information for work item creation in TFS from the currently created development task and its regarding case record of Microsoft Dynamics CRM.

Figure 13.18 shows the classes.

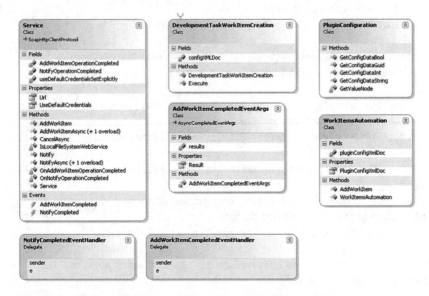

FIGURE 13.18   DevelopmentTaskWorkItemCreation classes.

The classes are described as follows:

▶ **DevelopmentTaskWorkItemCreation class:** Microsoft Dynamics CRM service activity plug-in used to create a work item in TFS when a new service activity is created in CRM. The service activity is updated with the newly created work item ID. The plug-in is designed to host on the prestage execution of the service activity creation.

▶ **PluginConfiguration class:** A helper class designed to provide methods to manipulate and access the unsecure configuration string of the plug-in. The configuration information will be provided when the plug-in is registered with MSCRM.

▶ **WorkItemsAutomation class:** A helper class designed to provide methods to interact with WorkItemsWebService web services for work item creation in TFS.

To set up the TFSAutomationConsumer solution, follow these steps:

1. Create a new Visual Studio 2005 solution called **TFSAutomationConsumer**.

2. Create a new class library project called **DevelopmentTaskWorkItemCreation**.

3. Rename the default Class1.cs to **DevelopmentTaskWorkItemCreation.cs**.

4. Add the following Microsoft Dynamics CRM SDK DLL references to the DevelopmentTaskWorkItemCreation class:

   ▸ Microsoft.crm.sdk.dll

   ▸ Microsoft.crm.sdktypeproxy.dll

> **NOTE**
>
> The DLLs come with the Microsoft Dynamics CRM SDK package, which can be downloaded from Microsoft.com/downloads.

5. Add the TFS automation work item web service WorkItemsWebService; its proxy class will be used to call the web service to create work items in TFS for when a new development activity is created in Microsoft Dynamics CRM, as shown in Figure 13.19.

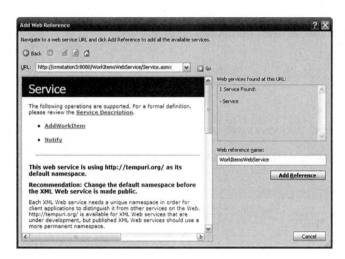

FIGURE 13.19   WorkItemsWebService web service.

The URL is in the format of http://<<server name>>/WorkItemsWebService/Service. asmx, where <server name> is the name of your server that is has the TFS automation web service installed.

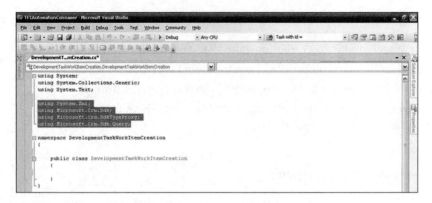

FIGURE 13.20   Namespace references added.

6. Add the following Microsoft Dynamics CRM SDK namespace references to the
   DevelopmentTaskWorkItemCreation class, as shown in Figure 13.20:

   ▶ System.Xml

   ▶ Microsoft.Crm.Sdk

   ▶ Microsoft.Crm.SdkTypeProxy

   ▶ Microsoft.Crm.Sdk.Query

7. Implement the IPlugin interface, as shown in Figure 13.21.

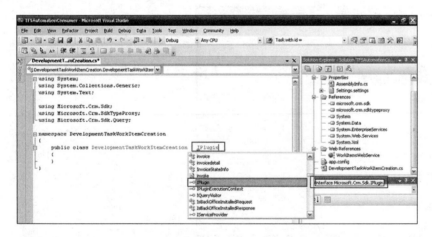

FIGURE 13.21   Set inheritance.

8. Add a new private variable `configXMLDoc` of type `XmlDocument` to hold the plug-in
   configuration information, as follows:

```
//Plug-in config xml
private XmlDocument configXMLDoc = null;
```

9. Create a new constructor method of **DevelopmentTaskWorkItemCreation** class to read the unsecure plug-in configuration information (provided during the plug-in registration) and load it into a new XML document object for manipulation, as follows:

```
public DevelopmentTaskWorkItemsCreation (string unsecure, string secure)
{
    configXMLDoc = new XmlDocument();
    configXMLDoc.LoadXml(unsecure);
}
```

10. Create a new `Execute` method with `IPluginExecutionContext` object as an input parameter, as follows:

```
public void Execute(IPluginExecutionContext context)
{
}
```

11. Add the following code to the `Execute` method body:

```
Try
{
    if (context.InputParameters.Properties.Contains("Target") &&
        context.InputParameters.Properties["Target"] is DynamicEntity)
    {
        // Get information regarding the service activity creation
        DynamicEntity newServiceActivityRecord =
➥context.InputParameters.Properties["Target"] as DynamicEntity;
        // Verify this is a service activity entity
    if (newServiceActivityRecord.Name =
➥EntityName.serviceappointment.ToString())
        {
            //Verify this is executing in offline mode on Outlook client
            if (!context.IsExecutingInOfflineMode)
            {
                if
➥(newServiceActivityRecord.Properties.Contains("new_workitemtype") &&
                    newServiceActivityRecord.Properties.Contains("ownerid") &&
                    newServiceActivityRecord.Properties.Contains("subject") &&
➥newServiceActivityRecord.Properties.Contains("regardingobjectid"))
                {
                    string title =
➥newServiceActivityRecord.Properties["subject"].ToString();
                    //Retrive owner
                    Owner  assignedToUser =  (Owner)
➥newServiceActivityRecord.Properties["ownerid"];
```

```
                        string assignedToUserId = assignedToUser.Value.ToString();
                        //Retrive regarding case id
                        Lookup regardingCase =
➥(Lookup)newServiceActivityRecord.Properties["regardingobjectid"];
                        string caseId = regardingCase.Value.ToString();
                        //Retrive selected work item type
                        Picklist workItemType = (Picklist)
➥newServiceActivityRecord.Properties["new_workitemtype"];
                        int selectedWorkItemType = workItemType.Value;
                        //Project code from plug-in config
                        string projectCode =
➥PluginConfiguration.GetConfigDataString(configXMLDoc, "Code");
                        //TFS Project name from plug-in config
                        string tfsProjectName =
➥PluginConfiguration.GetConfigDataString(configXMLDoc,"TFSProjectName");
                        //Create work item in TFS
                        WorkItemsAutomation wIAutomation = new
➥WorkItemsAutomation();
                        wIAutomation.PluginConfigXmlDoc = configXMLDoc;
                        CrmNumber workItemId = new
➥CrmNumber(wIAutomation.AddWorkItem(projectCode, title, caseId,
➥assignedToUserId, tfsProjectName, selectedWork
                        CrmNumberProperty workItemIdProperty = new
➥CrmNumberProperty("new_workitemid",workItemId);
                        //Update follow-up activity with newly created work item id
                        if(newServiceActivityRecord.Properties.
➥Contains("new_workitemid"))
                        {
                            newServiceActivityRecord.Properties["new_workitemid"] =
➥workItemIdProperty;
                        }
                        else
                        {
                            newServiceActivityRecord.Properties.
➥Add(workItemIdProperty);
                        }
                    }
                }
            }
        }
    }
}
catch (InvalidPluginExecutionException plugInEx)
{
    throw new ApplicationException("Error occurred during TFS Work Item
➥creation. Please contact your system administrator. " + plugInEx.Message,
➥plugInEx);
```

```
}
catch (TypeInitializationException TypeEx)
{
    throw new ApplicationException(TypeEx.Message, TypeEx);
}
catch (ApplicationException AppEx)
{
    throw AppEx;
}
catch (Exception ex)
{
    throw new ApplicationException(ex.Message, ex);
}
```

This code is designed to retrieve the current Development Activity record, and it reads the required work item information from the current Development Activity record and the regarding Case record.

The following properties/field values are retrieved (the retrieved information is passed to the `AddWorkItem` method of the `WorkItemAutomation` class for work item creation in TFS):

- ▶ Development Activity
    - ▶ Subject
    - ▶ Owner (GUID)
    - ▶ Work Item Type
- ▶ Case (regarding object)
    - ▶ Description
- ▶ Plug-in configuration
    - ▶ Project Code
    - ▶ TFS Project Name

12. Add a new helper class PluginConfiguration.cs in the DevelopmentTaskWorkItemCreation project to handle all the plug-in configuration-related manipulations.

The following code should be added to the newly created `PluginConfiguration` class:

```
using System;
using System.Collections.Generic;
using System.Text;
using System.Xml;
namespace DevelopmentTaskWorkItemCreation
{
    /// <summary>
    /// Helper class for reading plug-in config infos
```

```
    /// </summary>
    class PluginConfiguration
    {
        /// <summary>
        /// Get Value Node
        /// </summary>
        /// <param name="doc">Config XML data</param>
        /// <param name="key">settings key</param>
        /// <returns>String value</returns>
        private static string GetValueNode(XmlDocument doc, string key)
        {
            XmlNode node = doc.SelectSingleNode(String.Format("Settings/
➥setting[@name='{0}']", key));
            if (node != null)
            {
                return node.SelectSingleNode("value").InnerText;
            }
            return string.Empty;
        }
        /// <summary>
        /// Get Config Data Guid
        /// </summary>
        /// <param name="doc">Config XML Doc</param>
        /// <param name="label">settings label</param>
        /// <returns>Guid object</returns>
        public static Guid GetConfigDataGuid(XmlDocument doc, string label)
        {
            string tempString = GetValueNode(doc, label);
            if (tempString != string.Empty)
            {
                return new Guid(tempString);
            }
            return Guid.Empty;
        }
        /// <summary>
        /// Get Config Data Bool
        /// </summary>
        /// <param name="doc">Config XML Doc</param>
        /// <param name="label">settings lable</param>
        /// <returns>bool value</returns>
        public static bool GetConfigDataBool(XmlDocument doc, string label)
        {
            bool retVar;
            if (bool.TryParse(GetValueNode(doc, label), out retVar))
            {
                return retVar;
```

```
        }
        else
        {
            return false;
        }
    }
    /// <summary>
    /// Get Config Data Int
    /// </summary>
    /// <param name="doc">Config XML Doc</param>
    /// <param name="label">settings lable</param>
    /// <returns>integer value</returns>
    public static int GetConfigDataInt(XmlDocument doc, string label)
    {
        int retVar;
        if (int.TryParse(GetValueNode(doc, label), out retVar))
        {
            return retVar;
        }
        else
        {
            return -1;
        }
    }
    /// <summary>
    /// Get Config Data String
    /// </summary>
    /// <param name="doc">Config XML Doc</param>
    /// <param name="label">settings lable</param>
    /// <returns>string value</returns>
    public static string GetConfigDataString(XmlDocument doc, string label)
    {
        return GetValueNode(doc, label);
    }
    }
}
```

13. With the following code, add another helper class called WorkItemsAutomation.cs in
    the DevelopmentTaskWorkItemCreation project to handle all the work item
    creation/access related calls:

```
using System;
using System.Collections.Generic;
using System.Text;
using System.Security.Principal;
using System.Net;
using System.Xml;
```

```
namespace DevelopmentTaskWorkItemCreation
{
    /// <summary>
    /// Work Item Creation Helper Class
    /// </summary>
    class WorkItemsAutomation
    {
        private XmlDocument pluginConfigXmlDoc = null;
        /// <summary>
        /// Plug-in Configuration Xml Document
        /// </summary>
        public XmlDocument PluginConfigXmlDoc
        {
            set
            {
                pluginConfigXmlDoc = value;
            }
        }
        public WorkItemsAutomation()
        {
            pluginConfigXmlDoc = new XmlDocument();
        }
        #region AddWorkItem
        public int AddWorkItem(string Code, string title, string caseId, string
➥assignedTo, string projectName, int workItemType)
        {
            //Read TFS user credential info from plug-in config xml
            string TFSUserName = PluginConfiguration.
➥GetConfigDataString(pluginConfigXmlDoc, "TFSUserName");
            string TFSUserPassword =
PluginConfiguration.GetConfigDataString(pluginConfigXmlDoc,
➥"TFSUserPassword");
            string TFSUserDomain =
PluginConfiguration.GetConfigDataString(pluginConfigXmlDoc,
➥"TFSUserDomain");
            //Initialize TFS automation - work items web service
            WorkItemsWebService.Service workItemsWebService = new
➥WorkItemsWebService.Service();
            workItemsWebService.Credentials = new
➥NetworkCredential(TFSUserName, TFSUserPassword, TFSUserDomain);
            workItemsWebService.Url =
PluginConfiguration.GetConfigDataString(pluginConfigXmlDoc,
➥"TFSAutomationWebService");
            int WorkItemID = 0;
            try
            {
```

```
                string workItemTypeDesc = "";
                switch (workItemType)
                {
                    case 1:
                        {
                            workItemTypeDesc = "Bug";
                            break;
                        }
                    case 2:
                        {
                            workItemTypeDesc = "Quality of Service
➥Requirement";
                            break;
                        }
                    case 3:
                        {
                            workItemTypeDesc = "Risk";
                            break;
                        }
                    case 4:
                        {
                            workItemTypeDesc = "Scenario";
                            break;
                        }
                    case 5:
                        {
                            workItemTypeDesc = "Task";
                            break;
                        }
                }
                //Add work item in TFS
                WorkItemID = workItemsWebService.AddWorkItem(Code, title,
➥caseId, assignedTo, projectName, workItemTypeDesc);
            }
            catch (Exception ex)
            {
                throw new ApplicationException(ex.Message, ex);
            }
            workItemsWebService.Dispose();
            return WorkItemID;
        }
        #endregion
    }
}
```

13

14. The DevelopmentTaskWorkItemCreation assembly must be signed before deploying to the Microsoft Dynamics CRM server. To sign the assembly with a strong name, open the property pages of the project. Under the Signing tab, select the Sign the Assembly check box, and then in the Choose a Strong Name Key File drop-down box, select New, as shown in Figure 13.22.

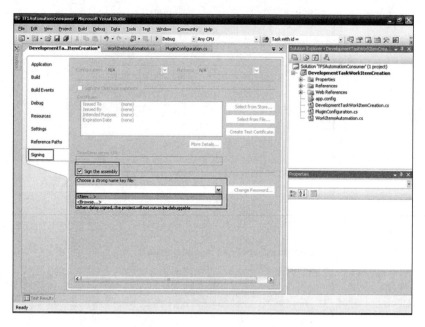

FIGURE 13.22   Signing the assembly.

Provide the key filename, unselect the Protect My Key File with a Password option, and then click OK to continue.

15. Add a class diagram DevelopmentTaskWorkItemCreation project by right-clicking the project and selecting View Class Diagram.

The class diagram should look like Figure 13.23.

16. Build the solution by right-clicking the solution and selecting Build Solution.

Deployment

The configuration procedure to set up the web services and plug-in is described in this section.

TFS Automation Web Services Deployment

Although the TFS Automation web services could be deployed on the server in which TFS 2005 is running (if a separate computer), the steps outlined here are for a single-server installation.

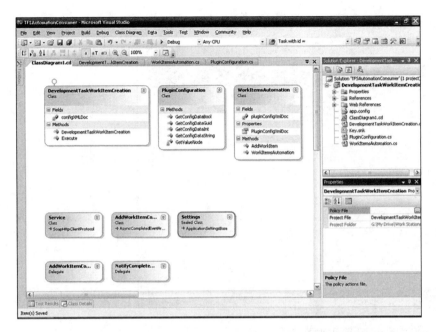

FIGURE 13.23   Class diagram for the DevelopmentTaskWorkItemCreation project.

To deploy the TFS Automation web services project, complete the following steps:

1. Create a new website within IIS, being sure to uncheck the Allow Anonymous Access to This Web Site check box.

2. Point to the sources from the TFSAutomationConsumer application.

3. Test the web service by browsing to the service.asmx page in Internet Explorer. The result should look similar to that shown in Figure 13.24.

TFS Automation Event Subscription

To subscribe to the TFS event, we need to use the open source application Team Foundation Server Event Subscription Tool. The tool is a GUI tool for subscribing to events on a TFS server and replaces the command tool bissubscribe.exe. Figure 13.25 shows the tool.

You can download it from Codeplex at http://tfseventsubscription.codeplex.com.

To use the Team Foundation Server Event Subscription Tool, just complete the following steps:

1. Download the tool. Once downloaded, extract it to the TFS server where the TFS Automation web service is installed.

2. Click the Connect button to connect to the TFS server and enter the TFS server name, as shown in Figure 13.26 (where your TFS server is entered).

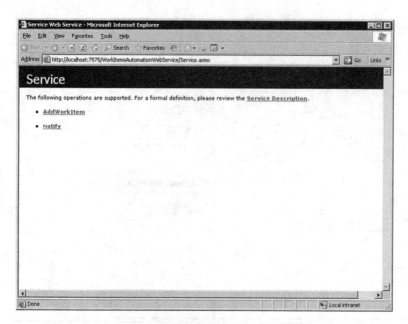

FIGURE 13.24   Service.asmx web service.

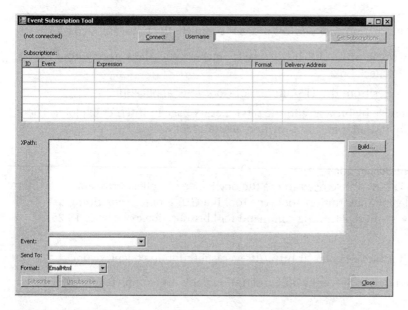

FIGURE 13.25   Team Foundation Server Event Subscription Tool.

16. Complete the following information for subscribing to the WorkItemChangedEvent, as shown in Figure 13.27, and click Subscribe:

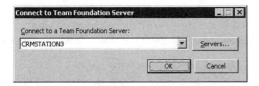

FIGURE 13.26   Connect to a TFS server.

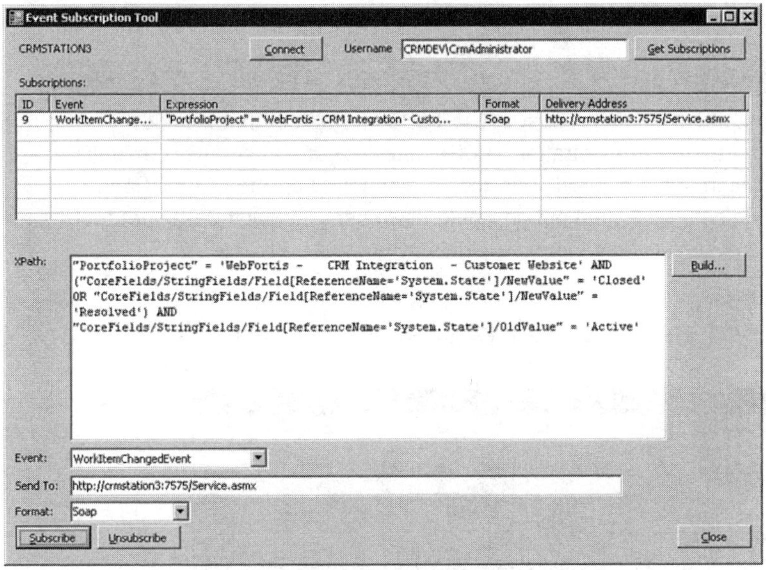

FIGURE 13.27   WorkItemChangedEvent subscription.

- ▶ **Event:** WorkItemChangedEvent

- ▶ **Send To:** http://<<server>>/service.asmx

- ▶ **Format:** SOAP

- ▶ **XPath:** "PortfolioProject" = '<<TFS Project Name>>' AND
  ("CoreFields/StringFields/Field[ReferenceName='System.State']/NewValue" =
  'Closed' OR
  "CoreFields/StringFields/Field[ReferenceName='System.State']/NewValue" =
  'Resolved') AND
  "CoreFields/StringFields/Field[ReferenceName='System.State']/OldValue" =
  'Active'

NOTE

The <<TFS Project Name>> is the name of the project in the TFS server that the new
work items will be created in.

4. Close the application.

TFS Automation Consumer Plug-In Registration

The TFS Automation Consumer plug-in is designed to create a new work item in TFS for each Development Activity created in Microsoft Dynamics CRM.

To deploy the TFS Automation Consumer plug-in, complete the following steps:

1. Download the CRM Plugin Registration Tool from Codeplex at http://code.msdn. microsoft.com/crmplugin and launch the PluginRegistration.exe from the unzipped Plug-In Registration Tool folder.

> **NOTE**
>
> The CRM Plugin Registration Tool is an easy-to-use but powerful tool that includes samples and allows for the easy registration of CRM plug-ins. Of course, they can still be deployed via command line if desired. This tool is also found on the CRI SDK and come with source code as well. A final option would be to use the PluginDeveloper tool, which can automate the steps of registering a plugin by giving an XML file.

Figure 13.28 shows the launched CRMP Plugin Registration Tool.

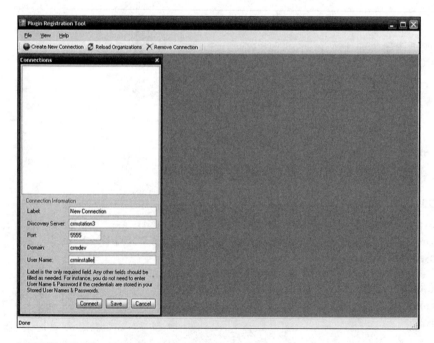

FIGURE 13.28   CRM Plugin Registration Tool.

2. Select Create New Connection to create a connection to the Microsoft Dynamics discovery service server, and enter the label, discovery server, port, domain, and username to the Microsoft Dynamics CRM server.

NOTE

Do not prefix the name with http://.

3. Select Connect and enter the password to continue, as shown in Figure 13.29.

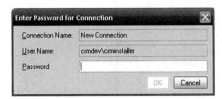

FIGURE 13.29   CRM Plugin Registration Tool connection.

4. Once connected, you'll see a list of the organizations retrieved from the Microsoft Dynamics CRM 4.0 server, as shown in Figure 13.30.

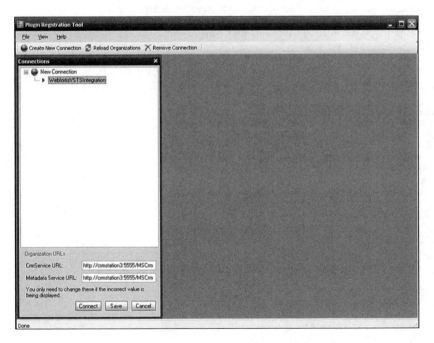

FIGURE 13.30   CRM Plugin Registration Tool organizations.

Select the organization from the list to which you want to deploy the plug-in, and then click the Connect button.

5. Select Register and Register New Assembly, as shown in Figure 13.31.

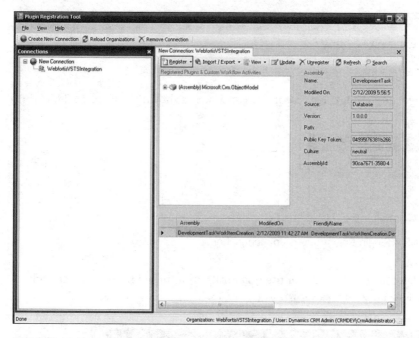

FIGURE 13.31   CRM Plugin Registration Tool Register New Assembly.

6. The Register New Plugin dialog will appear (as shown in Figure 13.32).

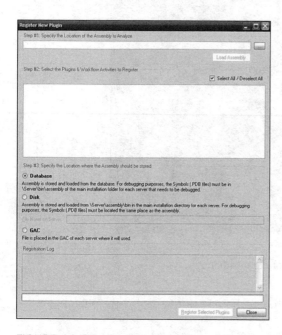

FIGURE 13.32   Register New Plugin dialog.

Browse to the TFS Automation DLL that was created during compilation (named DevelopmentTaskWorkItemCreation.dll); set Database as the location for the assembly, and then click the Register Selected Plugin button.

Upon registration, the alert displays, as shown in Figure 13.33.

FIGURE 13.33   New registration alert.

7. Select the registered [Assembly] DevelopmentTaskWorkItemCreation in the assembly list, and then click the Register New Step subitem from the Register item in the toolbar or in the context menu, as shown in Figure 13.34.

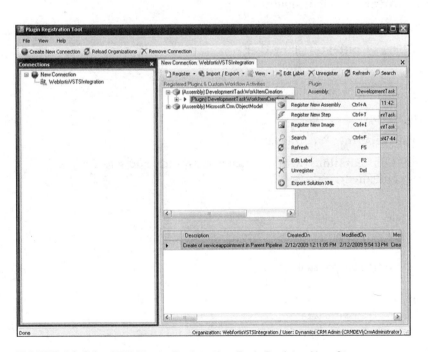

FIGURE 13.34   CRM Plugin Registration Tool: Register New Step.

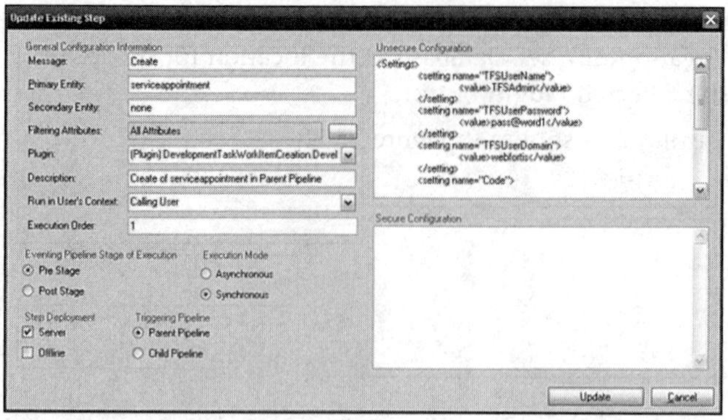

FIGURE 13.35 Update step.

8. The Register New Step screen will display (as shown in Figure 13.35) and set the parameters as follows:

▶ **Message:** Create

▶ **Primary Entity:** serviceappointment

▶ **Secondary Entity:** none

▶ **Filtering Attribute:** All Attributes

▶ **Plugin:** Default Value

▶ **Run in User's Context:** Calling User

▶ **Eventing Pipeline Stage of Execution:** Pre stage

▶ **Execution Mode:** Synchronous

▶ **Step Deployment:** Server

▶ **Triggering Pipeline:** Parent Pipeline

▶ **Unsecure Configuration:** (with user name, passwords, and server names properly configured)

```
<Settings>
    <setting name="TFSUserName">
            <value><<TFS project admin user>></value>
    </setting>
    <setting name="TFSUserPassword">
            <value><<TFS project admin password>></value>
    </setting>
    <setting name="TFSUserDomain">
            <value><<Domain name of TFS admin user>></value>
    </setting>
    <setting name="Code">
            <value><<TFS Automation project code>></value>
```

```
        </setting>
        <setting name="TFSProjectName">
                <value><<TFS project name>></value>
        </setting>
        <setting name="TFSAutomationWebService">
                <value><<http://<<Server>>/Service.asmx>></value>

        </setting>
    </Settings>
```

Once updated, the main Plugin Registration Tool will show the registered plug-in information (see Figure 13.36), and your plug-in is successfully registered with the Microsoft Dynamics CRM server.

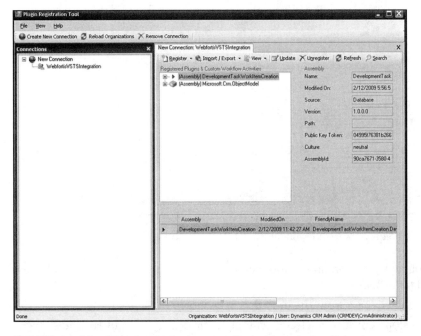

FIGURE 13.36   CRM Plugin Registration Tool with registered plug-in.

Walkthrough

Once deployed, we can confirm that the following events can happen:

1. Microsoft Dynamics CRM users can create cases for their customers. (Or their customers can create/enter their cases automatically through a self-portal website.)

2. The case can be reviewed, a Microsoft Dynamics CRM user can use the follow-up feature to set the case as a development task, and the item will go directly to TFS as a work item.

3. Users on TFS will review the work items and fix the issues.

4. After completing the work item, the users on TFS will update the work item's status as Resolved/Closed, and the respective Microsoft Dynamics CRM case status reason will be updated as Resolved by Development.

These events are illustrated in the following steps:

1. Log in to Microsoft Dynamics CRM and select Cases, being sure to select My Active Cases.

2. Select a case and review it, as shown in Figure 13.37.

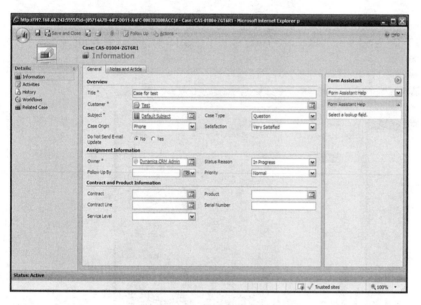

FIGURE 13.37   Closing a work item in Visual Studio 2005 Team Explorer.

3. Click the Follow Up button on the top menu, and the Form Assistant will display, as shown in Figure 13.38.

4. Select Development Task from the drop-down, as shown in Figure 13.39.

5. Once the development task is selected, complete the displayed required fields. The user assigned must be a valid Team System user, as shown in Figure 13.40.

6. Once Save is selected, the form is updated, and the user is alerted by the information displayed on the form, as shown in Figure 13.41.

7. The work item will be created in TFS, and the TFS user can view the work items by expanding the Work Items folder, Team Queries, and double-clicking Active Bugs, as shown in Figure 13.42.

8. The TFS user will work on the work item, eventually resolving it. When they do, they will navigate to the work item, select either Closed or Resolved (as shown in Figure 13.43), and then select Save.

9. The status reason in Microsoft Dynamics CRM will be updated to Resolved by Development, as shown in Figure 13.44.

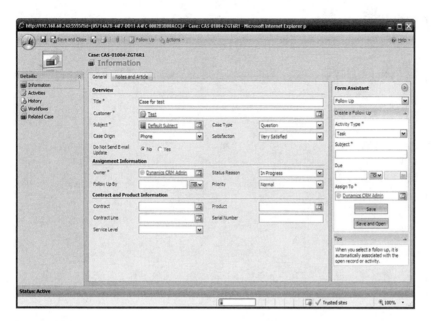

FIGURE 13.38   Case Form Assistant, Follow Up selected.

FIGURE 13.39   Activity drop-down with Development Task selected.

FIGURE 13.40   Activity drop-down with development task required fields.

FIGURE 13.41   Information saved.

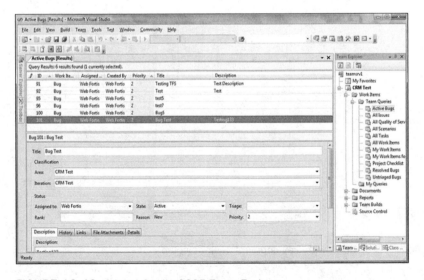

FIGURE 13.42   Visual Studio 2005 Team Explorer.

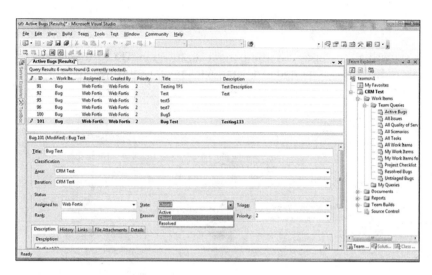

FIGURE 13.43   Closing a work item in TFS.

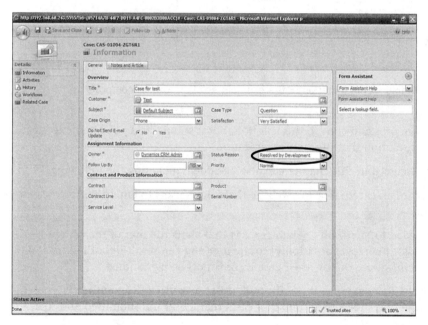

FIGURE 13.44   Microsoft Dynamics CRM status reason updated.

Summary

In this chapter, we showed all the necessary components to integrate TFS with Microsoft Dynamics CRM. Figure 13.45 shows an updated data/logic flow for this integration.

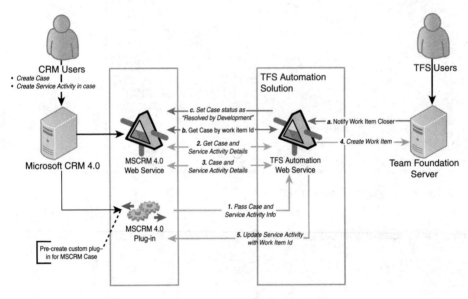

FIGURE 13.45   Graphic representation of the example solution with all components.

Obviously, there are pros and cons to this solution, but it should be a good guide to creating an integration solution that fits your organization.

Some items not discussed in this chapter can also be added, including the following:

▶ The creation of an external-facing website that allows users to enter their own cases for development.

▶ Workflow added to Microsoft Dynamics CRM that alerts the user of the case processing. This adds a high level of visibility to the user and can result in both users and customers being aware of how their case is (or is not) being handled.

▶ Leveraging the first example, the audit trail of the submitted case on the external-facing website that shows the number of cases that a user has submitted and their current resolved status.

CHAPTER 14

BizTalk Server Integration

When considering integration with other systems, remember that Microsoft has long recommended their own stack: BizTalk Server.

BizTalk Server is a middleware application designed to facilitate the communication with systems that generally don't have integration options/adapters out of the box.

What this means is that you can use BizTalk Server to communicate with another system, with BizTalk acting as the conduit between the two applications.

In simpler terms, if we consider that the Atlantic Ocean is one system (CRM) and the Pacific Ocean is another system (ERP) and the Panama Canal is the mechanism for interacting with each (via a series of rules [locks, measured capacity, days/times of operation, and so on]), then the Panama Canal is closely analogous to BizTalk Server.

In this chapter, we review how BizTalk Server can be used to perform an integration with CRM and an ERP system. It should be stressed that the examples in this chapter are specific for an integration with Microsoft Dynamics GP. However, they can be applied to other systems following similar steps.

NOTE

In early Q1 2009, Microsoft announced the release of a non-BizTalk Server integration component for CRM to GP.

This component features "point-to-point" integration (allowing users to easily set which values from each system they want to be integrated) but lacks many of the advanced and custom features that exist with a full-blown middleware product such as BizTalk Server.

This component is expected to be made available in Q3 (or later) of 2009.

In summary, BizTalk can be used for such things as the following:

▶ **Messaging:** Adapters can be used to handle proprietary protocols and can support business data processes/conversions.

▶ **Radio frequency identification (RFID):** Supporting a variety of hardware devices, it provides device abstraction, management, and simulation, which can be used to integrate into existing business processes or backend systems.

▶ **Business rules:** Support for authoritative business rules via the Rules Framework using .NET components or defined XML documents or database tables.

▶ **Business activity monitoring (BAM):** The BAM infrastructure monitors events inside the BizTalk application and publishes those events for metrics and reporting. The reporting can be achieved via the use of KPIs (key performance indicators), automatic alerts, or by Microsoft Office BI tools. BAM includes a set of tools that allows for the management, aggregation, and modification (via APIs) by customer code development.

▶ **Management/operations tools:** These include support for scaling, fault tolerance, load balancing, and the ability to configure and monitor the databases, hosts, and services that are within the scope of the implementation.

Basically, BizTalk can be used to allow Microsoft Dynamics CRM to communicate back and forth with Microsoft Dynamics AX, Microsoft Dynamics GP, Microsoft Dynamics NAV, and other databases such as Oracle, Siebel, PeopleSoft, and SAP.

In this chapter, we look at two such applications: Microsoft Dynamics CRM and Microsoft GP (Great Plains).

NOTE

This chapter explores the use of the application BizTalk Server. This should not be confused with BizTalk.net or the newly renamed Azure BizTalk service Internet service bus (ISB) technology, which is currently in beta.

BizTalk Versions, Licensing, and Requirements

Microsoft BizTalk server is available in four different versions:

▶ Enterprise

▶ Standard

▶ Branch

▶ Developer

All versions are licensed on a per-processor basis, with the exception of the Developer version, which is licensed on a per-user basis.

Typically, organizations with high volume requirements use the Enterprise version, whereas organizations with relatively moderate volume and deployment scenarios use the Standard version. The Branch version is a unique version designed for hub-and-spoke deployment (including RFID), and the Developer edition is available for development and testing purposes.

Originally introduced for use with Windows Server 2000, BizTalk Server has had several iterations, leveraging .NET code since .NET 1.0, and its latest version, BizTalk Server 2006 R2, which leverages Windows Communication Foundation (WCF), and Visual Studio 2005 for designing, mapping, and manipulation.

The following is necessary for a deployment of BizTalk Server 2006 R2, but additional components might be necessary depending on the defined requirements:

▶ Windows Server 2003/Vista/XP

▶ Internet Information Services (IIS) 6.0

▶ Microsoft Office Excel 2003 with Service Pack 2 or Microsoft Office Excel 2007

▶ Visual Studio 2005

▶ SQL Server 2005 with Service Pack 2

▶ SQL Server 2005 Analysis Services with Service Pack 2

▶ SQL Server 2005 Notification Services with Service Pack 2

Architecture

BizTalk is based on a "pub/sub" (publish/subscribe) model. Events in one system are defined, and the data from the event is made available by publication. Other applications are considered subscribers, and if the published data is something they're interested in, they can consume it.

The idea behind this is to provide a level of abstraction whereby the two systems don't have to be connected by any direct mechanism, thereby providing a level of fault tolerance and ease of change/modification.

Figure 14.1 describes this scenario.

The model outlined is not dependent on systems running on your network and may be extended to external systems, too.

BizTalk services have recently been extended to the Internet because there is no reason why the pub/sub can't be extended to the cloud. Although still in beta, we have included

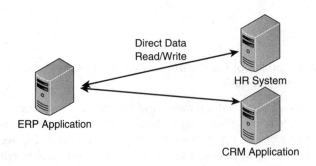

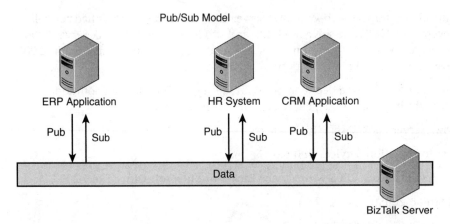

FIGURE 14.1   Direct application connections versus pub/sub connections.

information about using this cloud service in Chapter 15, "Azure Web Services Integration."

BizTalk Server uses connectors and adapters as its means of establishing links to the underlying systems.

Adapters

An adapter is specific to a single product, such as Microsoft Dynamics CRM 4.0. With the adapter, you can integrate Microsoft Dynamics CRM with other applications easily using the BizTalk Server mapping capabilities.

NOTE

You can download the Microsoft BizTalk Server 2006 Adapter for Microsoft Dynamics CRM (available in 32-bit only) from http://www.microsoft.com/downloads/details.aspx?FamilyID=4628fca6-388d-45bc-a154-453b920dbcb8&displaylang=en.

It is important to understand that adapters can be used to push data into the target system, but they cannot be used to pull data from the system. The reason for this is that the events that cause data to be sent from the target system vary depending on the integrated solution, and without a separate adapter, there is no way to know whether the event data is valid/necessary.

An example of this is when an order is created in Microsoft Dynamics CRM. This can be done either in Microsoft Dynamics CRM or it can be done in a corresponding enterprise resource planning (ERP) system. However, consider the ERP system: When the order creation occurs in Microsoft Dynamics CRM, the effects of re-creating the order in the ERP system (without an adapter/connector) can be far-reaching.

Connectors

A connector is a device that has been predefined and is specific for two (or more) applications.

Connectors are preestablished "templates" that use adapters for the underlying applications and include a series of business rules that allow for the quick deployment of an integration solution with minimal development.

They provide ongoing synchronization of data between the applications that the connector is defined for.

A common connector is the Microsoft Dynamics CRM Connector that was released for Microsoft CRM 3.0. This connector uses the Microsoft CRM 3.0 adapter and the adapter for Microsoft Dynamics GP.

14

> **NOTE**
>
> The Microsoft Dynamics CRM Connector enables integration between Microsoft CRM 3.0 and Microsoft Business Solutions Great Plains 8.0 or Microsoft Dynamics GP 9.0, but there is no connector currently available for Microsoft Dynamics CRM 4.0 to Microsoft Dynamics GP.

Message Queuing

Message queuing is a huge component of the reliability, redundancy, and auditing of a system. Without it, data messages that need to be consumed by a system can fail for a variety of reasons (such as network/database failure, permissions, and so forth) and then never be read and written.

Microsoft Message Queuing is included in the latest version of BizTalk Server.

> **NOTE**
>
> For earlier versions of BizTalk Server, you can download the MSMQ adapter from http://www.microsoft.com/downloads/details.aspx?FamilyID=cba87d07-7f50-4d7b-a888-388d123f736e&DisplayLang=en.

Integration with Microsoft Dynamics CRM and GP 10 Example

Because of the lack of a connector for Microsoft Dynamics CRM and GP 10, integration using BizTalk Server can be performed in a number of different ways.

The typical implementation involves the use of the Microsoft Dynamics CRM adapter to push data into CRM, and the creation of custom business rules to push data out when necessary. These custom business rules can be defined as either workflow or plug-ins that monitor an entity or attribute in Microsoft Dynamics CRM. As necessary, the data is pushed from Microsoft Dynamics CRM and made available for consumption by other applications through BizTalk in XML format.

Figure 14.2 describes this scenario.

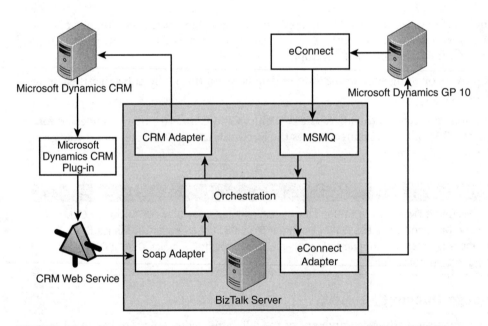

FIGURE 14.2   Recommended integration with Microsoft Dynamics CRM to GP 10.

For less complex integrations, or where it may be acceptable to only update GP (and not push data back to CRM from GP), Figure 14.3 illustrates a one-way integration option. Of course, this kind of integration is less sophisticated, and it could be argued that if you do not need to integrate other data or perform complex data manipulation you could just bypass BizTalk Server and create the integration using .NET components.

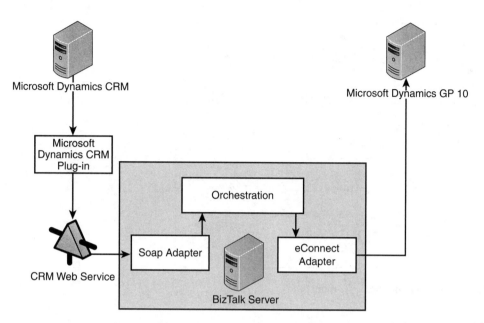

FIGURE 14.3   Recommended integration with Microsoft Dynamics CRM to GP 10, one way.

The concepts of Microsoft Dynamics CRM plug-ins and web services are adequately documented in this book, but we need to explain some of the components to GP:

- ▶ eConnect allows applications to programmatically interact with Microsoft Dynamics GP using .NET, message queuing (MSMQ), and the Microsoft BizTalk Application Integration Component (AIC).

- ▶ eConnect simplifies development effort, because it has a number of integration points for Microsoft Dynamics GP.

  - ▶ As part of BizTalk Server, Orchestration Designer is a Microsoft Visio-based design tool that enables you to create business process drawings that can be compiled and run. (See, for example, Figure 14.4.)

To install the Microsoft BizTalk Adapter for Microsoft Dynamics CRM 4.0, follow the steps as outlined in the Microsoft BizTalk Adapter for Microsoft Dynamics CRM 4.0 – Installation and Usage Guide.doc, which you can download from http://www.microsoft.com/downloads/details.aspx?FamilyID=4628fca6-388d-45bc-a154-453b920dbcb8&displaylang=en.

Once installed, Microsoft Dynamics CRM 4.0 appears in the Administration Console as an available adapter, as shown in Figure 14.5.

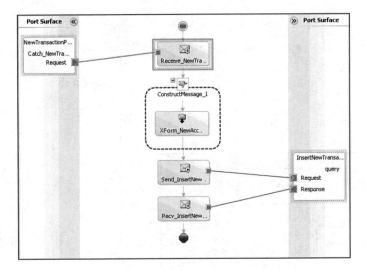

FIGURE 14.4 Sample orchestration.

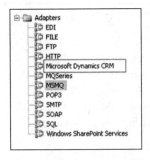

FIGURE 14.5 Adapters in the BizTalk console.

> **NOTE**
>
> The Microsoft BizTalk Adapter for Microsoft Dynamics CRM 4.0 – Installation and Usage Guide.doc explains the techniques for both an On Premise and a hosted (IFD) deployment of Microsoft Dynamics CRM 4.0.

The Connector for Microsoft Dynamics CRM 3.0 enforced a number of business rules that are recommended as best practices when considering deploying an integrated solution consisting of quotes, orders, and invoices. These business rules include the following:

▶ In general, invoices should *not* be created in Microsoft Dynamics CRM, but rather created in the ERP system and then pushed as read-only entities into Microsoft Dynamics CRM. Therefore, the ability to create invoices in Microsoft Dynamics CRM should be removed.

▶ Orders can be optionally created, updated, or deleted in either system depending on your organizational business rules. Generally, it is acceptable to allow full functionality in either system, with updated data moving from one system to the other.

In addition, it is common to enforce business rules associated with inventory when orders are submitted, but this is discretionary and is dependent on the desires of the organization and level of integration required for inventory management.

> **NOTE**
>
> Microsoft Dynamics CRM can be used for inventory management because it contains attributes for on-hand, but it is recommended to use the ERP system as the system of record and update Microsoft Dynamics CRM from the ERP system (and not vice versa).

▶ In an integrated environment, pricing options for quotes, orders, and invoices should be given careful thought, because updating these entities from the back office ERP is highly recommended. (Tax calculations alone warrant this.)

In the following example, we perform a simple integration between GP 10 and Microsoft Dynamics CRM 4.0 whereby an order can be created in Microsoft Dynamics CRM and pushed to GP.

> **NOTE**
>
> Because of the extensibility of BizTalk and publication limitations, we're only showing integration of data from CRM to GP. Many organizations consider this sufficient, but it is not uncommon to have a fully integrated solution between CRM and GP (whereby GP data goes to CRM).

For this example, we are assuming the following environment:

▶ BizTalk Server 2006

▶ GP 10

▶ CRM Adapter

▶ eConnect 10 (with latest service packs and eConnect SDK)

▶ Visual Studio 2005

In addition, we need to identify the CRM schema and GP schema that will be mapped. In our scenario, we're going to map CRM order information and GP order information.

Schema Mappings Between CRM and GP

1. Download and install the CRM Adapter in BizTalk Server.
2. Open Visual Studio and select a new project, as shown in Figure 14.6.

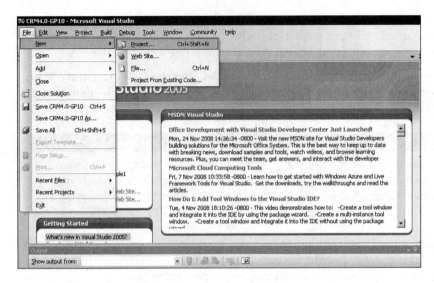

FIGURE 14.6   Selecting a new project in Visual Studio.

3. Select Empty BizTalk Server Project from the available templates under the Project Types for BizTalk Projects, as shown in Figure 14.7.

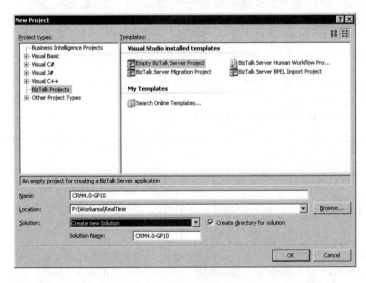

FIGURE 14.7   Select Empty BizTalk Server Project Solution.

4. You now have an empty solution file. Right-click the solution and select Add Generated Items, as shown in Figure 14.8.

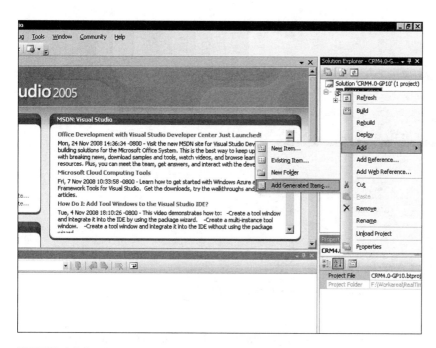

FIGURE 14.8   Add generated items to the solution.

5. Select Add Adapter Metadata from the available options, as shown in Figure 14.9. It is at this step that the connector is utilized.

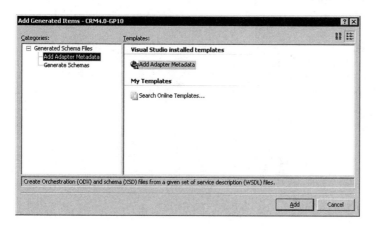

FIGURE 14.9   Add adapter metadata to the project.

6. Select the Microsoft Dynamics CRM 4.0 adapter, as shown in Figure 14.10.

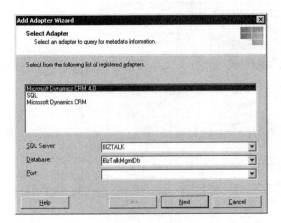

FIGURE 14.10   Add the Microsoft Dynamics CRM 4.0 adapter.

7. Enter the credential information for your Microsoft Dynamics CRM deployment. The CRM server URL is in the format of http://<<server name>>:<<port>>). Figure 14.11 illustrates the required credential information.

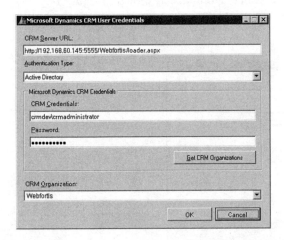

FIGURE 14.11   Microsoft Dynamics CRM 4.0 credential information.

8. Select the actions or the entities that you want to publish in the schema (as shown in Figure 14.12).

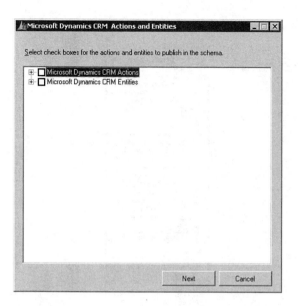

FIGURE 14.12   Select Microsoft Dynamics CRM actions or entities to publish.

9. In our example, we want to fetch the Microsoft Dynamics CRM schema information for the Create action (see Figure 14.13).

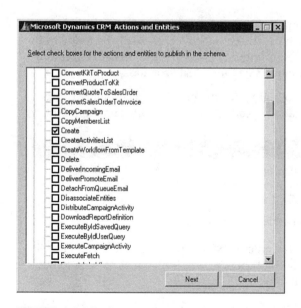

FIGURE 14.13   Select the Microsoft Dynamics CRM actions or entities Create action.

10. We can now navigate the CRM schema file. Figure 14.14 shows the Order schema file.

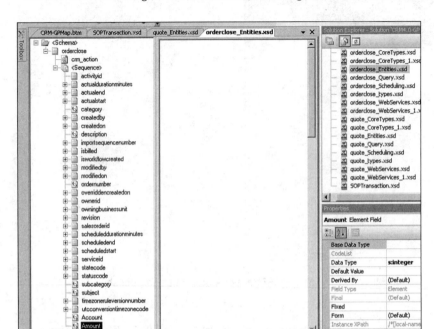

FIGURE 14.14   Microsoft Dynamics CRM Order schema file.

11. Now we need to find the GP schema. Assuming that eConnect 10 and the eConnect SDK are installed on the same machine, the GP schema can usually be found in the following location: C:\Program Files\Common Files\Microsoft Shared\eConnect 10\XML Sample Documents\Incoming XSD Individual Schemas.

To add the schemas to Visual Studio, right-click the project, select Add, Existing Item, and then navigate to the location specified, selecting SOPTransaction.xsd.

NOTE

The schema used by GP is SOPTransaction.xsd

Figure 14.15 shows the GP schema added to Visual Studio.

12. We now have both the Microsoft Dynamics CRM and the Microsoft Dynamics GP schemas. The next step is to map both of the schemas, which may require some functoids depending on the integration.

To create the map file, right-click the project and select Add, New Item, Map. Name it appropriately for your project, and then select Add. Once added, you can select the source schema on the left side, and the right side will be the destination schema.

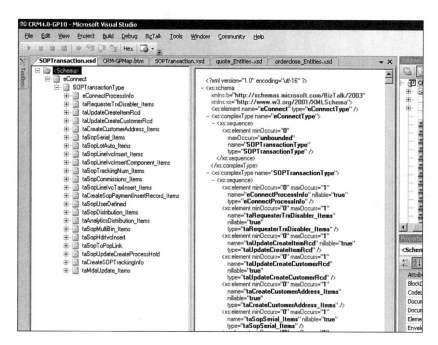

FIGURE 14.15   Microsoft Dynamics GP schema file.

Selecting either Open Source Schema or Open Destination Schema opens the schemas we have available. After we select both schemas, they are ready for mapping. If it is a direct mapping between the two fields, you can just drag and link between the two fields. In cases where we want to apply logic to the mapping, we would reference a functoid.

Figure 14.16 shows the two schemas mapped, with three functoids.

NOTE

A functoid is an object in a mapping and is similar to a function, and generally it is used to concatenate two elements from source messages and assign them to a destination message. (BizTalk includes an array of functoids that are available from the toolbox within BizTalk.)

13. Deploy the application.
14. After the application has been deployed, it is available within the BizTalk Administration Console, as shown in Figure 14.17.

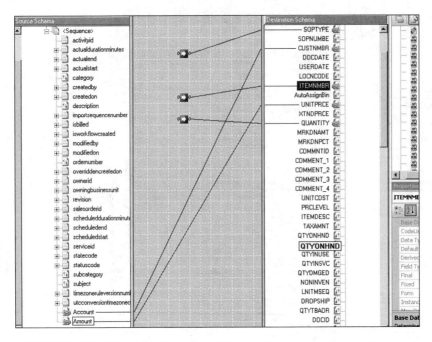

FIGURE 14.16   Microsoft Dynamics CRM and GP schemas mapped.

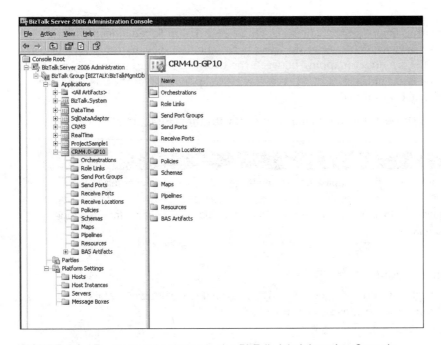

FIGURE 14.17   Deployed solution in the BizTalk Administration Console.

Web Service Creation and SOAP Adapter Configuration

The next step is to create a web service and configure it using a SOAP adapter. This is necessary to receive data from CRM and pass it into BizTalk Server. Because the schemas are already identified for CRM, we need to expose them as web services so that we can pass the values using the plug-in on the CRM side (as discussed later in this chapter).

To create the web service, follow these steps:

1. Deploy the application that we created in the previous steps.

2. Open the same solution and go to Tools, and select BizTalk Web Services Publishing Wizard (see Figure 14.18).

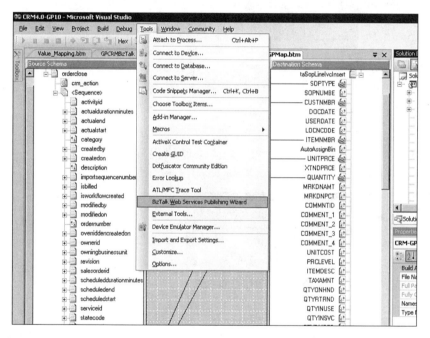

FIGURE 14.18   Selecting the BizTalk Web Services Publishing Wizard in BizTalk.

The BizTalk Web Services Publishing Wizard starts and guides you through the process of deploying a web service.

Select Publish Schemas as Web Services when prompted for the method of creating the web service, and when asked to describe the web service, right-click the WebMethod and select Select Schema Type. Browse for the DLL files of the previously deployed project, specifying the target namespace and location of the project.

3. After the web service has been created, it needs to be configured using a SOAP adapter. Figure 14.19 shows the General tab information for the adapter that is configured using the BizTalk Server Administration Console and selecting the Receive Ports.

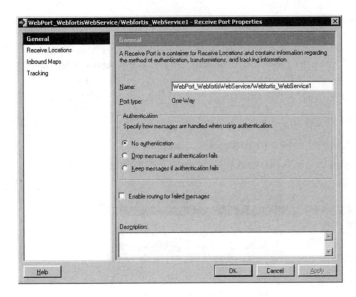

FIGURE 14.19   SOAP adapter General configurations.

4. Set the receive location, as shown in Figures 14.20 and 14.21.

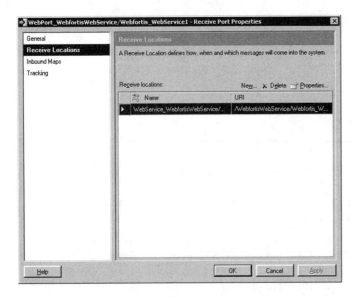

FIGURE 14.20   SOAP adapter receive location configurations.

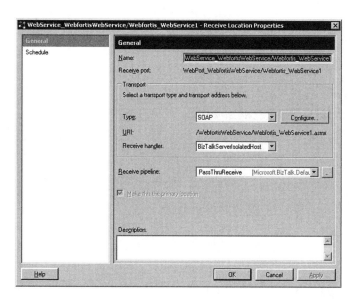

FIGURE 14.21   SOAP adapter receive location General configurations.

5. Click Configure to specify the web service virtual directory that you created in the first step (see Figure 14.22).

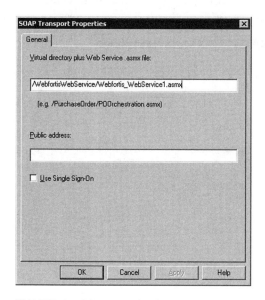

FIGURE 14.22   Specify the virtual directory for the web service .asmx file.

6. The mapping file we created earlier will automatically populate the column for the Inbound Maps tab (see Figure 14.23).

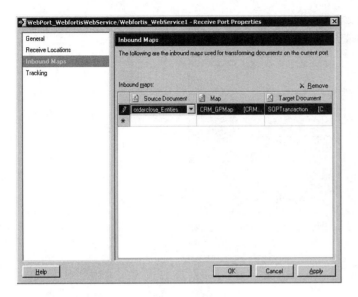

FIGURE 14.23 SOAP adapter inbound maps.

eConnect Configuration

Our next step is to configure the send adapter using eConnect so that we can integrate values into GP from the source. Figure 14.24 shows the configuration for eConnect.

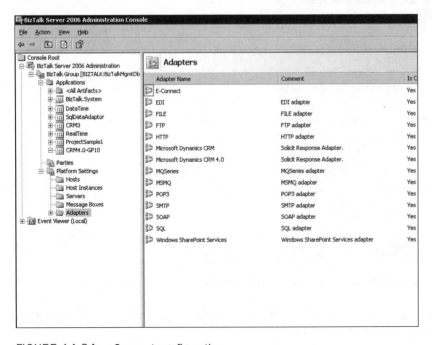

FIGURE 14.24 eConnect configuration.

1. Right-click the eConnect adapter and select Properties.
2. Select Properties (see Figure 14.25) and set the Transport Properties Connection string (see Figure 14.26).

   Because eConnect can be installed anywhere, we can select the database we want to use that is on our network. In our example, we're connected locally (the same computer is running GP), but we can point it to any connected computer using a standard connection string.

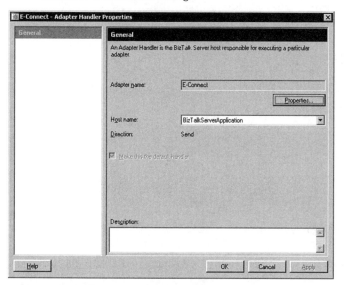

FIGURE 14.25   eConnect properties.

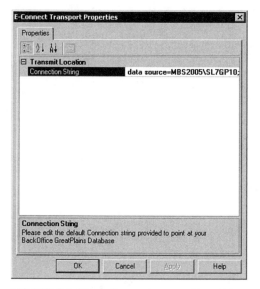

FIGURE 14.26   eConnect connection string.

Configuring the Send Adapter

1. Figure 14.27 shows the send adapter configuration options.

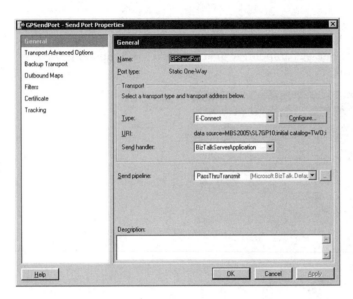

FIGURE 14.27   Send adapter configuration options.

2. The transport connection string can be configured after you click Configure (see Figure 14.28).

FIGURE 14.28   Configure the connection string.

3. Select Outbound Maps (see Figure 14.29).

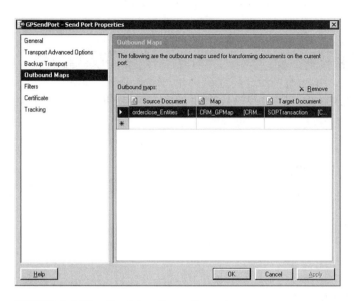

FIGURE 14.29   Configure the outbound maps.

4. Set the filter options. In this example, we set the BTS.ReceivePortName = the web service we created previously. Figure 14.30 illustrates how to set this.

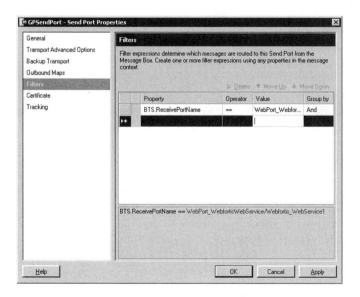

FIGURE 14.30   Filter options.

CRM Plug-In Creation

The CRM plug-in will call the web service and pass the expected values during our selected event (in this case, the Create event).

NOTE

In our example, we're creating a plug-in against the Order entity Create event, but you can modify the example to fire against other events (Save, Delete, and so on) as necessary for your solution.

Use the following code to create the plug-in:

```
using System;
using System.Collections.Generic;
using System.Text;
using Microsoft.Win32;

using Microsoft.Crm.Sdk;
using Microsoft.Crm.SdkTypeProxy;
using CRMGPIntegrationPlugIn.CRMGPBizService;
using CRMGPIntegrationPlugIn.CRMSDK;

namespace CRMGPIntegrationPlugIn
{
    public class CRMOrderProcessing:IPlugin
    {
        private string crmWebServiceUrl = string.Empty;
        private CRMGPIntegrationPlugIn.CRMSDK.CrmService crmService = null;

        public void Execute(IPluginExecutionContext context)
        {
            if (context.InputParameters.Properties.Contains("Target") &&
➥context.InputParameters.Properties["Target"] is Microsoft.Crm.Sdk.DynamicEntity)

            {
                Microsoft.Crm.Sdk.DynamicEntity crmOrder = null;
                crmOrder = (Microsoft.Crm.Sdk.DynamicEntity)context.
➥InputParameters.Properties["Target"];
                if (crmOrder.Name != CRMGPIntegrationPlugIn.
➥CRMSDK.EntityName.salesorder.ToString()) { return; }

                CRMGPBizService.orderclose bizOrder = new
➥CRMGPIntegrationPlugIn.CRMGPBizService.orderclose();
```

```
            //We're not passing the order number as part of this example
            //but if we want to, simply uncomment the code below
                //if (crmOrder.Properties["ordernumber"] != null)
                //{
                //    if (crmOrder.Properties["ordernumber"].ToString() != "")
                //    {
                            //Set the variable to the CRM order number
                //            //bizOrder.ordernumber = crmOrder.Properties
➥["ordernumber"].ToString();
                //    }
                //}

                if (crmOrder.Properties["freightamount"] != null)
                {
                    if (crmOrder.Properties["freightamount"].ToString() != "")
                    {
                        Microsoft.Crm.Sdk.CrmMoney frieghtMoney = new
➥Microsoft.Crm.Sdk.CrmMoney();
                        freightMoney = (Microsoft.Crm.Sdk.CrmMoney)
➥crmOrder.Properties["freightamount"];
                        bizOrder.Amount = freightMoney.Value.ToString();
                    }
                }

                if (crmOrder.Properties["customerid"].ToString()!= "")
                {
                    Microsoft.Crm.Sdk.Customer customer = new
➥Microsoft.Crm.Sdk.Customer();
                    customer = (Microsoft.Crm.Sdk.Customer)
➥crmOrder.Properties["customerid"];

                    string cusname =
➥GetCustomerName(customer.Value.ToString());
                    bizOrder.Account = cusname;
                }

                Webfortis_WebService1 bizService = new Webfortis_WebService1();
                bizService.Webfortis_WebMethod1(bizOrder);

            }

        }

        private string GetCustomerName(string customerId)
        {
         InitializeCRMService();
```

14

```
                    return FetchCRMCustomerName(customerId);
                }

            private void InitializeCRMService()
            {
                string crmServer = GetCRMServiceURL();

                if (crmServer.Length == 0 || (!crmServer.StartsWith("http://") &&
➡!crmServer.StartsWith("https://")))
                {
                    throw new ApplicationException("CRM server url is wrong, please
➡contact your system administrator.");
                }
                if (!crmServer.EndsWith("/"))
                {
                    crmServer += "/2007/";
                }
                else
                {
                    crmServer += "2007/";
                }

                crmWebServiceUrl = string.Concat(crmServer, "CrmService.asmx");

                CRMGPIntegrationPlugIn.CRMSDK.CrmAuthenticationToken token =
➡new CRMGPIntegrationPlugIn.CRMSDK.CrmAuthenticationToken();
                token.AuthenticationType = 0;
                token.OrganizationName = "webfortis";

                crmService = new CRMGPIntegrationPlugIn.CRMSDK.CrmService();
                crmService.Url = crmWebServiceUrl;

                crmService.CrmAuthenticationTokenValue = token;
                crmService.Credentials = System.Net.CredentialCache.
➡DefaultCredentials;
            }

            private string FetchCRMCustomerName(string customerId)
            {

                CRMGPIntegrationPlugIn.CRMSDK.QueryExpression query = new
➡CRMGPIntegrationPlugIn.CRMSDK.QueryExpression();

                query.EntityName = "account";
```

```
            CRMGPIntegrationPlugIn.CRMSDK.ColumnSet columns = new
➥CRMGPIntegrationPlugIn.CRMSDK.ColumnSet();
            columns.Attributes = new string[] { "name" };

            query.ColumnSet = columns;

            query.Criteria = new CRMGPIntegrationPlugIn.CRMSDK.
➥FilterExpression();
            query.Criteria.FilterOperator = CRMGPIntegrationPlugIn.
➥CRMSDK.LogicalOperator.And;

            CRMGPIntegrationPlugIn.CRMSDK.ConditionExpression condition1 = new
➥CRMGPIntegrationPlugIn.CRMSDK.ConditionExpression();
            condition1.AttributeName = "accountid";
            condition1.Operator = CRMGPIntegrationPlugIn.
➥CRMSDK.ConditionOperator.Equal;
            condition1.Values = new object[] { customerId };

            query.Criteria.Conditions = new CRMGPIntegrationPlugIn.
➥CRMSDK.ConditionExpression[] { condition1 };

            CRMGPIntegrationPlugIn.CRMSDK.RetrieveMultipleRequest request = new
➥CRMGPIntegrationPlugIn.CRMSDK.RetrieveMultipleRequest();
            request.Query = query;

            CRMGPIntegrationPlugIn.CRMSDK.RetrieveMultipleResponse response =
➥(CRMGPIntegrationPlugIn.CRMSDK.RetrieveMultipleResponse)crmService.Execute
➥(request);


            CRMGPIntegrationPlugIn.CRMSDK.account Customer = (CRMGPIntegration
➥PlugIn.CRMSDK.account)response.BusinessEntityCollection.BusinessEntities[0];
            string name = "Default";
            if (Customer.name != null)
            {
                name = Customer.name;
            }

            return name;
        }

    private string GetCRMServiceURL()
    {
        string crmURL = String.Empty;
        try
        {
```

```
            // Read the Registry Key
            RegistryKey key = Registry.LocalMachine.OpenSubKey
➥("Software\\Microsoft\\MSCRM", false);

            //Get Server URL from the Registry Key.
            crmURL = (string)key.GetValue("ServerUrl");
        }
        catch (Exception Ex)
        {
            //OnError(Ex);
            throw new ApplicationException();
        }
        return crmURL;
    }
}
```

Results

When we create a new order in Microsoft Dynamics CRM, either directly as an order or when we convert a quote, the information is reflected in GP.

Figure 14.31 shows a new order in Microsoft Dynamics CRM, and Figure 14.32 shows the corresponding information in GP.

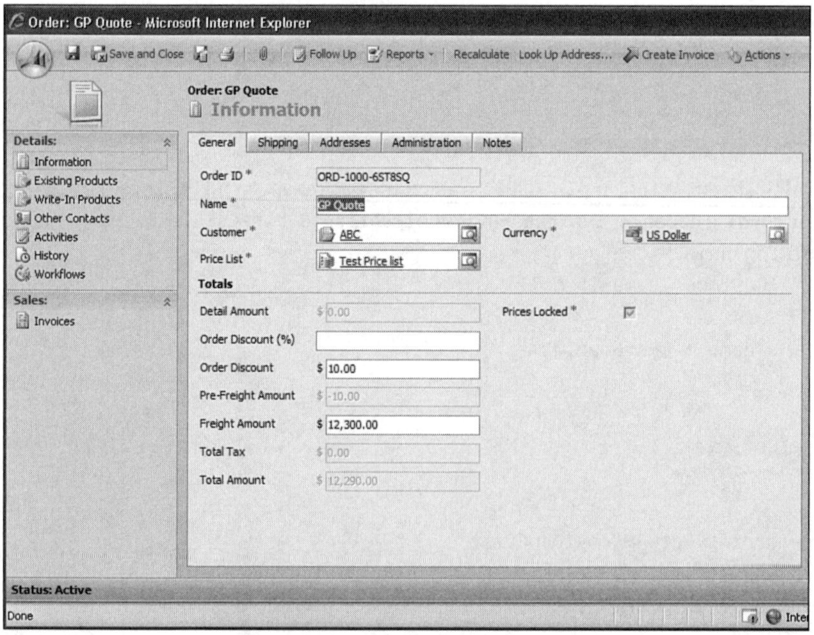

FIGURE 14.31   New order in Microsoft Dynamics CRM.

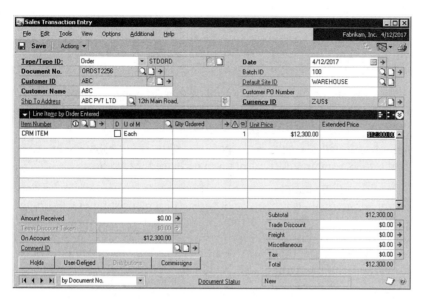

FIGURE 14.32   Microsoft Dynamics GP.

Notice that the customer name and the amount flow from Microsoft Dynamics CRM to GP. In this example, we've kept the unique order number created in each application, but you can integrate that if necessary based on your requirements.

> **NOTE**
>
> If you would like to send the order number, remove the commented lines in the code sample.

When developing a solution similar to this, you need to consider a number of things. Because the options are extensive and our goal is to provide an overview template on how to create an integration using BizTalk, we don't list them all here. However, consideration should be given to the following:

▶ Validation of account credit limits/holds

▶ Account creation permissions on the ERP side

▶ Transport of data from the ERP to the CRM

We highly recommend a serious study of your particular business rules before attempting this kind of integration.

Summary

This chapter covered the options associated with using BizTalk Server as an integration application between CRM and GP.

BizTalk Server is certainly not limited to these two applications, and many organizations have successfully used BizTalk Server to integrate more than two disparate applications successfully.

It is important to note that BizTalk Server is an application with considerable complexity and options and, therefore, is recommended only for experienced integrators.

Of the concepts that you should be familiar with after reading this chapter, the main one is creating the necessary components for this type of integration, consisting of CRM plug-in development and eConnect configuration. Although BizTalk Server configuration options are covered in this chapter, it is an enterprise product that enables you to perform a number of additional functions. Therefore, further independent review is recommended should you require these types of configurations.

Finally, although BizTalk Server has been the integration recommendation by Microsoft for its Dynamics products, it is not the only solution available. We have included information about how to perform other integrations in Chapter 3, "Extending Microsoft Dynamics CRM." In addition, be sure to check our chapters on Scribe before selecting a solution that is right for your organization.

CHAPTER 15

Azure Web Service Integration

When Microsoft first announced to the public in late 2008 the concept that it had been working on for years called Azure, the paradigms associated with integrated solutions changed yet again. Azure presents new possibilities that are only now starting to be realized, and in our opinion, Azure represents the beginning of a fundamental shift in how users and organizations interact with applications and data.

What Is Azure?

Internet-scale cloud computing platforms such as Azure provide a full range of functionality to build a plethora of applications: from consumer web- to enterprise-based, all hosted on Microsoft data centers. Supported by (REpresentational State Transfer [REST] and Simple Object Access Protocol [SOAP]), Azure presents a new open standard–based and interoperable environment enabling new application development to run the cloud or enhance existing applications. Because Azure is an open platform–based computing service, developers will find it particularly useful to build and operate web applications and hybrid solutions and to offer cloud computing support for enterprise-based solutions. Azure follows a traditional building block platform format, with several blocks to build upon. Automated and on-demand response for infrastructure management and application troubleshooting makes it a rather handy tool for future web-based computing architecture.

Now applications can be conveniently operated and maintained through provisions of on-demand compute and storage to host, scale, and manage web and connected applications.

Infrastructure management is automated with a platform that is designed for high availability and dynamic scaling to match usage needs with the option of a pay-as-you-go pricing model.

Developers can create their own personal customer offerings by offering the foundational components of compute, storage, and building block services to author and compose applications in the cloud (see Figure 15.1).

FIGURE 15.1　The Azure services platform.

Windows Azure

Windows created a cloud services operating system, Windows Azure, which facilitates the development, service hosting, and service management environment for the Azure Services Platform. Through the operating system, developers and enterprises are powered with on-demand processing power and storage space to host, scale, and manage web applications online within Windows data centers.

Because it is an open platform, Windows Azure intends to support both Microsoft and non-Microsoft languages and environments. This open platform of Azure ensures that developers can quickly and easily create applications running in the cloud through their knowledge of the Microsoft Visual Studio development environment and the .NET Framework. This benefit greatly reduces the need for up-front technology purchases such as servers and switches.

Microsoft SQL Azure Database

Microsoft SQL Azure Database offers highly scalable, on-demand data storage and query processing utility services. SQL Azure Database is constructed on robust SQL Server technologies and Windows Server and therefore provides highly available, secure, standards-based web services.

Users can store unstructured, semistructured, and structured data through SSD capabilities (web-based services). A rich set of integrated services will enable users to perform relational queries, search, reporting, analytics, integration, and to synchronize data with mobile users, remote offices, and business partners.

Microsoft .NET Services

Microsoft .NET Services provide key building blocks needed by many cloud-based and cloud-aware applications. These services represent a collection of Microsoft-hosted, highly scalable, developer-oriented services. Similar to its .NET Framework, the services provide higher-level class libraries that enable developers to focus more on application logic rather than building and deploying their own cloud-based infrastructure services.

At present, Microsoft .NET Services consist of three central components:

▶ Access control service

▶ Service bus

▶ Workflow service

Through the use of industry-standard protocols, .NET services are also accessible to other development technologies for the purpose of interoperability.

Live Services

As shown in the Figure 15.2, Live Services represents various mechanisms to handle user data and application resources within the Azure Services Platform. Developers can develop rich social applications that can connect with more than 450 million Windows Live users. This ability is facilitated by Live Mesh technologies, which actually synchronize user data and web applications, which in turn can be extended to multiple devices.

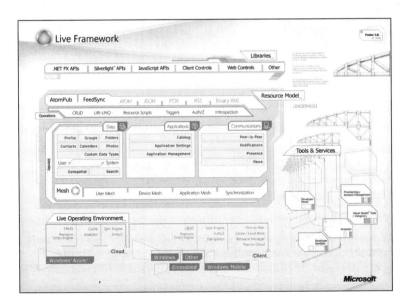

FIGURE 15.2   Live Framework.

Live Services consists of the following services:

- Identity Services

- Directory Services

- Communication Services

- Presence Services

- Geospatial Services

- Search Services

- Mesh Services

Microsoft SharePoint Services and Dynamics CRM Services

The integration of Microsoft SharePoint and CRM services will aid users in developing stronger customer relationships. Developers using Visual Studio can quickly build applications that make the most of SharePoint and CRM capabilities. A broad range of capabilities encompass the spectrum of On-Premises, Online, and the Azure Services Platform.

Architecting Services for Windows Azure

Windows Azure is an operating system for the cloud; layers and layers of software enable you to run applications across multiple server farms. It can handle many dynamic systems, and the layers and layers of software collectively make an operating system for the cloud.

Windows Azure manages services, not just servers. Tell it what you want, and it will help automate the details and will provide you with what you want exactly as you want it.

Windows Azure frees developers from many platform issues. Developers can concentrate more on business and application logic rather than platform issues.

The service life cycle can be automated by Azure, through its model-driven automation, by which the system manages the allocation and deployment of all services included in the platform.

In addition, the system turns the resources into a shared pool. Users pay only for what they use, and the platform ensures complete service isolation.

To consider your system for cloud services capability, each node needs to be viewed as a cache, and the state has to have the ability to be rebuilt from a predefined configuration. Second, every part of the application needs to have the capability to reinitialize to restart, and there must be no presumptions that the previous local state is available. Third, dynamic configuration changes must be dealt with, and your software must be able to handle these changes.

Fourth, after the services have been installed, they are always running; both upgrades or downgrades and schema changes must be handled by services. Do not assume that the services can be reinstalled. Furthermore, services are built using multiple nodes/roles.

Therefore, your service architecture and the communication paths of elements must be immaculately documented. Lastly, upon successful acquisition of Azure, the service will become very large, and state needs to be carefully managed at a larger scale.

The Azure service life cycle comprises four stages. The goal is to automate the life cycle to reduce the cost and increase the availability of the systems as much as possible.

You, the developer/deployer, do the coding/modeling step, in which new services functionality or upgrades are integrated. In the next step, the desired configuration is implemented, and resources are binded. Then, in a test phase, or run phase, resources are incorporated by the developer/deployer. From there onward, everything else is automated; the Windows Azure platform takes the logical model and maps and deploys it to the actual hardware. In the last step, the service life cycle begins to maintain the goal state by monitoring and reacting to events such as hardware/software failures. Throughout these steps, the developer/deployer is always in control and can stop the process wherever desired. There is always a feedback loop for improvement or upgrade purposes. The goal of this life cycle is to minimize costs as much as possible.

The Azure service model guides the automation services, which are described as distributed entities that are authored and configured by the service developer. The mapping to actual hardware is done at deployment. It is basically a hardware abstraction layer for service developers.

Possibilities with Azure and CRM

Here are some ways to leverage Azure to gather data from various locations (Microsoft Dynamics CRM, Dynamics GP, and other data sources) and better optimize the business process for companies whose assets are distributed.

Example for Companies with Distributed Machinery

Companies that have machinery distributed in various locations are perfect candidates for cloud computing integration with CRM. This technology can enable enterprises to better understand the status of the machines. A piece of machinery owned by your company can have an embedded computer capable of monitoring the status, health, and functionality of the machinery in use and update the SQL Azure services with this data. Your company's IT service deployers and developers can modify their system requirements to an extent where information such as location, current status updates, life of machinery, wear and tear, and functionality is automatically sent to their Azure .NET services. In case of breakdowns or machinery nearing breakdown or an unhealthy state, the computer embedded in those machines can invoke a business process in the Azure .NET service and, in turn, open a service ticket inside their CRM system. The CRM database can be modified to follow a logical business process in terms of trouble-shooting and fixing unhealthy or broken-down machinery.

Automation is the key to success here.

Real Estate Industry Uses

The real estate industry provides a similar example. When visitors arrive at a place of interest (one/two-bedroom apartment), a small computer unit is present at the entrance. Visitors type in their personal details. This information can be modified accordingly to rendezvous with the real estate agency's CRM system. The CRM system can be controlled and specifically instructed to automate B2B processes that are invoked to produce such data. Transfer of high-quality data with the lead's details can be sent back to the real estate agent on-site. Based on this information, the enterprises can concentrate their selling on prospective customers or even give recommendations.

Sample Application

In this demo, we develop a web service, test and debug locally on the development fabric (a configuration of the settings needed for the application, irrespective of the underlying hardware), and deploy it to a cloud.

This is an integration to show the data from cloud computing inside the CRM application. Other asynchronous services can be used to integrate with the CRM system.

Developing the Application

In this section, we create a sample Azure .NET application and deploy it to the cloud services. For demonstration purposes, we will create a notes entity, so that you can offload the notes functions to the remote users:

1. Start Visual Studio 2008.
2. Click File.
3. Click New Project.
4. Select Cloud Services.
5. Select Web and Worker and Cloud Services, and then click OK (see Figure 15.3).
6. In the ServiceConfiguration.cscfg file, enter the following code:

```xml
<?xml version="1.0"?>
<ServiceConfiguration serviceName="Notes"
xmlns="http://schemas.microsoft.com/ServiceHosting/2008/10/
➡ServiceConfiguration">
  <Role name="Web">
    <Instances count="5" />
    <ConfigurationSettings>
      <Setting name="AccountName" value="madaladin" />
      <Setting name="AccountSharedKey" value="7iZDzDBmrQo3NOo+4gDC/
➡XFW8ZLLNFYBhP9yFsId/pSPVSO0FFlrmzZ8KBYDBx0MDphcDAE7
➡mItYPxOAqWMInQ==" />
      <Setting name="BlobStorageEndpoint"
➡value="http://madaladin.blob.core.windows.net" />
```

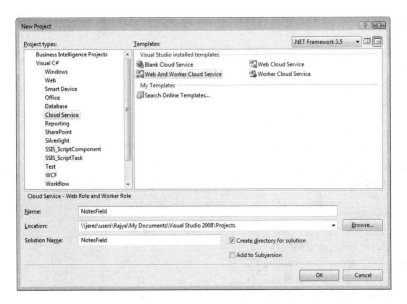

FIGURE 15.3   Creating a new cloud services project.

```
      <Setting name="TableStorageEndpoint"
➥value="http://madaladin.table.core.windows.net" />
      <Setting name="QueueStorageEndpoint"
➥value="http://madaladin.queue.core.windows.net" />
    </ConfigurationSettings>
  </Role>
  <Role name="Worker">
    <Instances count="5" />
    <ConfigurationSettings>
      <Setting name="AccountName" value="madaladin" />
      <Setting name="AccountSharedKey" value="<<Account Key>
      <Setting name="BlobStorageEndpoint"
➥value="http://madaladin.blob.core.windows.net" />
      <Setting name="TableStorageEndpoint"
➥value="http://madaladin.table.core.windows.net" />
      <Setting name="QueueStorageEndpoint"
➥value="http://madaladin.queue.core.windows.net" />
    </ConfigurationSettings>
  </Role>
</ServiceConfiguration>
```

7. In the ServiceDefinition.csdef file, enter the following code:

```
<?xml version="1.0" encoding="utf-8"?>
<ServiceDefinition name="Notes"
➥xmlns="http://schemas.microsoft.com/ServiceHosting/2008/10/ServiceDefinition">
```

15

```
<WebRole name="Web">
  <InputEndpoints>
    <InputEndpoint name="HttpIn" protocol="http" port="80" />
  </InputEndpoints>
  <ConfigurationSettings>
    <Setting name="AccountName" />
    <Setting name="AccountSharedKey" />
    <Setting name="BlobStorageEndpoint" />
    <Setting name="TableStorageEndpoint" />
    <Setting name="QueueStorageEndpoint" />
  </ConfigurationSettings>
</WebRole>
<WorkerRole name="Worker">
  <ConfigurationSettings>
    <Setting name="AccountName" />
    <Setting name="AccountSharedKey" />
    <Setting name="BlobStorageEndpoint" />
    <Setting name="TableStorageEndpoint" />
    <Setting name="QueueStorageEndpoint" />
  </ConfigurationSettings>
</WorkerRole>
</ServiceDefinition>
```

8. In the Default.aspx.cs file, add the following piece of code:

```
using System.Web;
using System.Web.Mvc;
using System.Web.UI;
namespace Notes_WebRole
{
    public partial class _Default : Page
    {
        public void Page_Load(object sender, System.EventArgs e)
        {
            HttpContext.Current.RewritePath(Request.ApplicationPath);
            IHttpHandler httpHandler = new MvcHttpHandler();
            httpHandler.ProcessRequest(HttpContext.Current);
        }
    }
}
```

9. Create a new control and add the following piece of code:

```
using System;
using System.Collections.Generic;
using System.Linq;
using System.Web;
```

```
using System.Web.Mvc;
using System.Web.Mvc.Ajax;
using Microsoft.Samples.ServiceHosting.StorageClient;
namespace Notes_WebRole.Controllers
{
    public class PostsController : Controller
    {
        public ActionResult Index()
        {
            return View(new Models.NotesContext().NotesEntryTable);
        }
        public ActionResult New()
        {
            return View();
        }
        public ActionResult Create([Bind(Prefix="")] Models.NotesEntry entry)
        {
            var svc = new Models.NotesContext();
            svc.AddObject("NotesEntryTable", entry);
            svc.SaveChanges();
            var queue = QueueStorage.Create
➥(StorageAccountInfo.GetDefaultQueueStorageAccountFromConfiguration())
➥.GetQueue("entryqueue");
            queue.PutMessage(new Message(entry.RowKey));
            return RedirectToAction("index");
        }
    }
}
```

10. Create a new model and add the following piece of code:

```
using System;
using System.Collections.Generic;
using System.Linq;
using System.Web;
using Microsoft.Samples.ServiceHosting.StorageClient;
using System.Data.Services.Client;
namespace Notes_WebRole.Models
{
    public class NotesEntry : TableStorageEntity
    {
        public string Title { get; set; }
        public string Body { get; set; }
        public DateTime Posted { get; set; }
        public NotesEntry()
        {
```

```
            Posted = DateTime.UtcNow;
            PartitionKey = "smarx";
            RowKey = string.Format("{0:d10}", DateTime.MaxValue.Ticks -
➥Posted.Ticks);
        }
        public NotesEntry(string title, string body)
            : this()
        {
            Title = title;
            Body = body;
        }
    }
    public class NotesContext : TableStorageDataServiceContext
    {
        public DataServiceQuery<NotesEntry> NotesEntryTable
        {
            get { return CreateQuery<NotesEntry>("NotesEntryTable"); }
        }
    }
}
```

11. Create an ASPX file to upload new notes with the following piece of code:

```
<%@ Page Language="C#" AutoEventWireup="true" CodeBehind="Index.aspx.cs"
Inherits="Notes_WebRole.Views.Posts.Index" %>
<!DOCTYPE html PUBLIC "-//W3C//DTD XHTML 1.0 Transitional//EN"
➥"http://www.w3.org/TR/xhtml1/DTD/xhtml1-transitional.dtd">
<html xmlns="http://www.w3.org/1999/xhtml" >
<head runat="server">
    <title>Notes Index</title>
</head>
<body>
    <% foreach (var entry in ViewData.Model) { %>
        <div>
            <h1><%= entry.Title %></h1>
            <p>Posted at <%= entry.Posted.ToString("yyyy/MM/dd HH:mm") %></p>
            <p><%= entry.Body %></p>
        </div>
    <% } %>
</body>
</html>
```

12. Create an ASPX file to upload new notes with the following piece of code:

```
<%@ Page Language="C#" AutoEventWireup="true" CodeBehind="New.aspx.cs"
➥Inherits="Notes_WebRole.Views.Posts.New" %>
```

```
<!DOCTYPE html PUBLIC "-//W3C//DTD XHTML 1.0 Transitional//EN"
➥"http://www.w3.org/TR/xhtml1/DTD/xhtml1-transitional.dtd">
<html xmlns="http://www.w3.org/1999/xhtml" >
<head runat="server">
    <title>New Notes Post</title>
</head>
<body>
    <form method="post" action='<%= Url.Action("create") %>'>
        <table>
            <tr>
                <th>Title:</th>
                <td><%= Html.TextBox("Title", null, new { size = 100}) %></td>
            </tr>
            <tr>
                <th>Body:</th>
                <td><%= Html.TextArea("Body", null, 40, 80, null) %></td>
            </tr>
            <tr>
                <th />
                <td><input type="submit" value="Submit" /></td>
            </tr>
        </table>
    </form>
</body>
</html>
```

NOTE

Azure SDK is required to view the cloud services project templates.

Testing the Application

This section demonstrates how to use the local cloud emulator to test and debug the Azure services:

1. In Visual Studio, click Debug.
2. Click Start Debugging to launch a website running on your local machine, with the web application.
3. Click the development to view the console status of the application (see Figure 15.4).

FIGURE 15.4   Development fabric with the console running.

Deploying the Application

Once we are satisfied with the functions, we need to deploy to the Azure cloud fabric. In this section, we deploy the application from directly within the Visual Studio environment:

1. In the Solution Explorer, right-click the project name and select Publish (see Figure 15.5).

FIGURE 15.5   Solution Explorer in Visual Studio.

2. It will automatically launch the Azure Services Developer Portal. Select the appropriate project to deploy. Select Deploy, as shown in Figure 15.6.

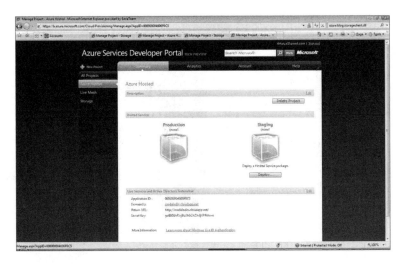

FIGURE 15.6   New Azure project.

3. Enter the appropriate app package and the appropriate configuration settings. Then click Deploy, as shown in Figure 15.7.

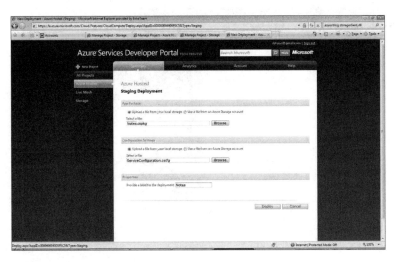

FIGURE 15.7   Uploading the newly built project.

4. Select Run. Then use the link below to test the application functionality (see Figure 15.8).

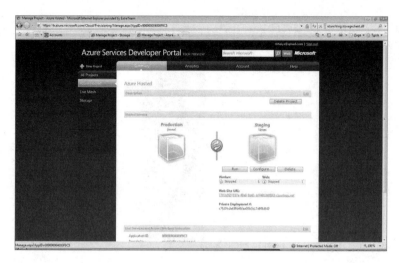

FIGURE 15.8   Starting the Azure application.

5. When you are happy with the functionality, use the two arrows to move the code into production, as shown in Figure 15.9.

FIGURE 15.9   Deploying the application, from staging to production.

6. Verify the application by browsing to the URL.

Viewing the Analysis of the Application

This is a great feature that enables developers and system administrators to monitor the resource usage of the application. Being able to do so greatly aids system administrators to allocate resources appropriately and to scale the application:

1. Log in to the Azure Services Developer Portal.

2. Click the appropriate project.

3. Click Analytics to view the usage of the application (see Figure 15.10). This helps developers scale the application appropriately.

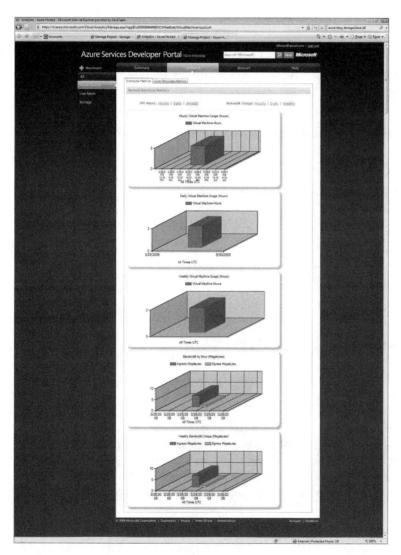

FIGURE 15.10   Viewing the performance of the application.

Deploying Azure Using IFrames

A common way to integrate the Azure application is by using IFrames (located within the main screen of the CRM) that use the Azure services. To set up this feature in Microsoft Dynamics CRM, complete the following steps:

1. Open Microsoft Dynamics CRM.

2. Click Customizations from the left navigation.

3. Click Customize Entities.

4. Open the Accounts entity.

5. Click Forms and Views.

6. Open the form.

7. Click Add a Tab from the Common Tasks located on the right side.

8. Give it a Name (for example, Azure), and then click OK.

9. Navigate to the new tab created.

10. Select Add a Section, and give it a friendly name (for example, AzureSection). Then click OK.

11. Click the newly created IFrame.

12. Click Add an IFrame with the following properties:

    Name: AzureIFrame

    URL: http://<SiteURL>/

13. Select the check box for Pass Record Object-Type Code and Unique Identifier as Parameters.

14. Click OK.

15. Click Save and Close to save the form modifications.

16. Click Save and Close to save the entity modifications.

17. Click the Accounts entity, and then select Publish.

Summary

Azure is a new up-and-coming technology that can provide access to data from nearly any location. The most appropriate use of this technology is to gather data from various locations. Consolidate that information to a singular location (for example, the Azure data storage). After the data has been consolidated into a singular location, we can flow that information to the CRM system for further analyses and thus enhance business decision making.

Azure also allows remote applications to have an application proxy layer in the cloud for gathering data from various sources and for making the application available globally.

CHAPTER 16

Scribe Integration

Throughout this book, we discuss a variety of components and methods for integrating systems, data, and applications with Microsoft Dynamics CRM 4.0. In this chapter, we discuss a Microsoft independent software vendor (ISV) that focuses on data integration: Scribe Software.

Introduction

Although you have several options and solutions for integration, including Microsoft options such as BizTalk (see Chapter 14, "BizTalk Server Integration"), the Scribe Software toolsets offer a solution that we've found to be "best of breed." Their products offer a level of customization that we've not found anywhere else, and their support for scaling means they work for implementations with only a few users and enterprise customers.

Benefits from using Scribe, which we explain further in this chapter (and the next two chapters), include the following:

▶ Use of Microsoft Message Queuing (MSMQ), which provides a mechanism for messages (in the form of data updates) to reliably reach their destination.

▶ Intuitive and easy-to-use graphic interface for development.

▶ Existing templates and adapters that allow for quick deployment, with minimal coding. The current templates and adapters include all the Microsoft Dynamics enterprise resource planning (ERP) products (AX, SL, NAV, GP), Salesforce, SalesLogix, and a few others.

Although we have extensive experience working with the Scribe products (and in fact have worked with them to develop some of the material in this chapter), it would be impossible to describe every integration option or solution. So instead, our goal in this chapter (as in the entire book) is to outline the toolsets and explain how the various tools work. We hope this clear outline explains the setup and configuration of the toolsets so that you can realize their benefits within your organization.

Integration Options

Generally speaking, companies implement three distinct levels of integration:

▶ **Data replication:** Moving data "one way," into *or* out of CRM

▶ **Data synchronization:** Moving data "two ways," into *and* out of CRM

▶ **Process integration:** Facilitating business processes that rely on consistent data across a broad range of business applications

Each category has its own characteristics, implementation requirements, benefits, risks, and costs.

With regard to costs (we cover the benefits, risks, and requirements in each section), there are varying levels, both during the initial project and on an ongoing basis. As a general rule, the complexity and resulting costs associated with an integration project will be exponentially greater for two-way or multidirectional integration projects versus one-way integrations. Complexity also rises dramatically as more and more dependencies between applications (and their respective user bases) are expanded. Costs tend to break down into two major categories: the technical implementation and support costs, and the organizational disruption costs (with the latter in many cases greatly underestimated).

Figure 16.1 illustrates the relationship between value versus cost/disruption for companies across the three levels of integration.

The following list summarizes the costs you should consider when embarking on a CRM integration project:

▶ **Technical implementation and support**

    ▶ Integration requirements analysis and design

    ▶ Integration software (including maintenance, support, training, and upgrades), whether purchased from a vendor or developed internally

    ▶ Application "adapters," particularly when applications are targets in the integration (another reason why one-way integrations can be simpler and less costly)

    ▶ The costs of ensuring data integrity across systems (especially costly with synchronization and process integration because of the need to maintain updatable data in multiple systems)

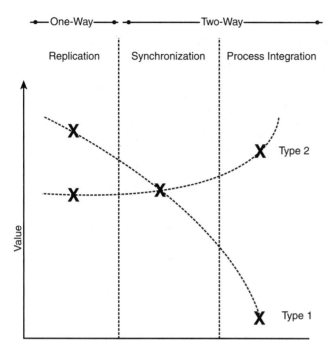

FIGURE 16.1   Cost/disruption with integration levels.

▶ **Organization disruption costs**

    ▶ User training and orientation around the use of the newly integrated systems (sometimes referred to as reengineering).

    ▶ Risks and costs of creating dependence between mission-critical transaction systems and CRM

    ▶ The political barriers of data ownership and coordinating activities across functional areas of the business (one of the most common being CFOs who don't want salespeople messing with their back-office data)

The following table maps the three levels of CRM integration against the preceding criteria to represent the relative cost of each option.

Cost and Disruption	Data Replication	Data Synchronization	Process Integration
Integration requirements and design	Low	Med	High
Integration software	Low*	Low*	Low*
Application adapters	Low	Med**	High**
Maintaining data integrity	Low	High	High

Cost and Disruption	Data Replication	Data Synchronization	Process Integration
Training and orientation	Low	Low	High
System interdependence	Low	Med	High
Political barriers	Low	Med to High	High

*Assumes the purchase of a full-function CRM integration platform.
**Although two-way, synchronization involves much simpler application touch points.

It becomes apparent that as we move from one level to the next, the cost and disruption of each grow exponentially.

So now that we understand the relative costs of the three different types of integration, how do we make sense of the relative benefit of each? To answer this question, it is important to understand how your company markets and sells its products. To illustrate how a company's sales and marketing process impacts the value side of the equation, let's define two types of companies at opposite ends of the spectrum. We refer to one category of company as Type 1 and the other as Type 2:

▶ **Type 1:** These companies have intensive, relationship-focused sales processes. They generally need to educate their buyers about their products, have longer sales cycles, and have direct and indirect sales teams skilled in the "art" of relationship, value-based selling. Industries that tend to fall in this category include financial services, professional services, health care, capital goods manufacturing, and much of high technology. These types of companies generally benefit the most when you provide their knowledge workers with information that enables them to target customers better and to more effectively manage customer relationships. Given that the transaction side of the customer relationship is generally an occasional event in the sales process that does not dominate the lion's share of the sales team's efforts, they tend to gain diminishing value from additional levels of integration. This is particularly true for process integration.

▶ **Type 2:** In these companies, the majority of the sales process is centered on transactions. Their customers generally require less information about the features and benefits of products and are more concerned about things such as quantity on hand, price, and availability. Industries that fall in this category include consumer goods, distribution, process manufacturing, and commoditized high technology. These types of companies generally benefit the most from integrated, coordinated, and efficient management of customer transactions. Type 2 companies still benefit from data replication and data synchronization, but ultimately realize the greatest strategic advantage through process integration.

After you've decided on the appropriate level of value versus cost, integration can be expanded to include additional data replication, data synchronization, or for Type 2 companies, expanded to include process integration.

With the right long-term plan implemented on a technology platform that can expand with your changing business, your CRM investment will be well positioned to deliver meaningful and sustainable competitive advantage.

Figure 16.2 summarizes the key capabilities required to support the integration requirements previously outlined.

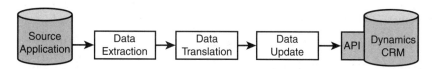

FIGURE 16.2   Ongoing monitoring and management in batch and real-time automation.

As shown in this figure, you need five major capabilities to perform these data aggregations.

▶ **Data extraction:** You must have direct access to your source applications via a database or a proprietary application programming interface (API) from enterprise applications such as Microsoft Dynamics GP, JD Edwards, SAP, MAS 90/200/500, and Siebel. You must also be able to capture net changes either through source queries or via published messages from the source where available.

▶ **Data translation:** The semantics and format of many fields of your source data will likely differ from those in Microsoft Dynamics CRM. Important capabilities include parsing and concatenating text fields, performing date and numeric calculations, executing conditional logic, and performing lookups to resolve synonym values. You also need to maintain a cross reference of primary key values, to apply updates from one record in your source to the corresponding record in Dynamics CRM.

▶ **Data update:** This capability is the most crucial, yet complex area of your integration task. Capabilities you should look for include the following:

    ▶ Avoiding duplicates using fuzzy logic (like comparing elements of the company name and ZIP code to look for an account match) for record lookup

    ▶ Performing insert and update operations against multiple objects within Microsoft Dynamics CRM when processing a single source record

    ▶ Performing all target processing against the Microsoft Dynamics CRM integration API to ensure that all data imported has been validated by Microsoft Dynamics CRM's application rules

▶ **Automation:** This is where using a customizable template model that incorporates a one-step process from source to target proves very useful. After you have designed your business process, you need to implement an automated event-detection mechanism to initiate an update to Microsoft Dynamics CRM. Look for a solution that supports both batch and message-based processing; each approach is appropriate in different integration scenarios.

16

▶ **Monitoring and management:** After you have developed and implemented your data aggregation solution, you need to consider the ongoing management of the solution. Look for a technology that

  ▶ Enables you to remotely support the solution (including start and stop processes, diagnose errors, and so on) via your web browser

  ▶ Automatically alerts an administrator via email when processes fail, error, or produce abnormal data conditions

  ▶ Can scale across multiple processors to support high-volume data scenarios

Traditional approaches to data aggregation for CRM cover a broad spectrum from custom development to the use of sophisticated technologies such as Microsoft's BizTalk Server. Unfortunately, these choices represent approaches that are either way too little or way too much. In the case of custom development, someone has to code all the functionality outlined previously to deliver a workable solution. More often than not, these custom solutions are lacking in functionality, unreliable, or difficult to manage. In addition, they are inflexible to changes in your business.

BizTalk Server, on the other hand, may include some of the functionality required but is designed as more of an infrastructure backbone to support a wide range of integration scenarios. This poses two challenges. First, BizTalk Server lacks quite a bit of the specific CRM-focused functionality needed, forcing you to fill in the blanks with custom coding (with all the challenges of custom coding mentioned earlier). Second, it tends to be very complex to install, configure, and manage, and generally requires significant additional hardware and software infrastructure investments. You can quickly lose track of the fact that you just want to get customer data to the sales team.

For more information about BizTalk Server, see Chapter 14.

Data Replication

Data replication is by far the simplest and least interdependent type of integration. With replication, a copy of certain customer data that resides in one system is added to the customer records in the CRM application, with data moving in only one direction. Typically, the replicated data is "view-only" in CRM; that is, it cannot be modified by the user but provides more complete customer data to increase the effectiveness of CRM.

Figure 16.3 illustrates data replication.

The following table outlines common replication scenarios and the benefits of each.

Source	Data	Description	Value
Website, marketing lists	Leads	Load leads on real-time or ad-hoc basis into CRM	Increase lead conversion rate and reduce administrative costs

Source	Data	Description	Value
ERP	Orders/invoices Product line items	Copy and update order and invoice data along with product details into CRM	Increase revenue through product-based sales targeting Improve customer service
Call center	Support incidents	Provide real-time support call history and status to CRM	Improve customer service
Field service	Service tickets	Provide real-time service ticket history and status to CRM	Improve customer service
Call center ERP	Support contracts	Copy and update customer support agreements in CRM	Increase contract renewal rates
ERP Data providers	Credit history	Provide company credit history in CRM	Increase revenue by targeting creditworthy customers Reduce collection costs

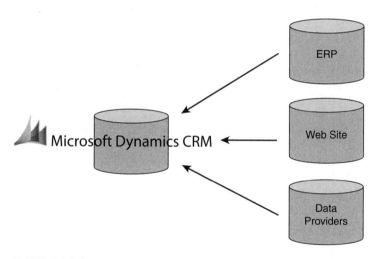

FIGURE 16.3   Data replication.

Bear in mind that implementing a replication scenario may involve extending the data model of a packaged CRM application if the key data elements you want to share do not exist in the base configuration of CRM.

By providing this additional information about customers within the CRM system, sales users can improve the quality of customer interactions and more effectively target customer opportunities.

Replication has another benefit that is not so obvious: It dramatically improves the adoption of CRM by users. CRM is one of those odd business applications where adoption by its "users" is difficult to mandate in most cases. It is rare to find a case where sales reps who were 200% of quota lost their job because they didn't put their sales activities in a

CRM system. So how do you get these individuals to adopt your CRM system? You provide them information in CRM that will help them sell more—information they couldn't otherwise get. In many cases, this type of quid pro quo has formed the basis for successful CRM implementations.

Data Synchronization

The objective of synchronization is to maintain the same set of customer information in multiple systems, reflecting changes made in one system across the others. Synchronization typically focuses on the more basic demographic customer information that is common to multiple systems, such as company contacts, addresses, phone numbers, and so forth. Figure 16.4 depicts a typical customer synchronization scenario between a company's ERP and CRM system.

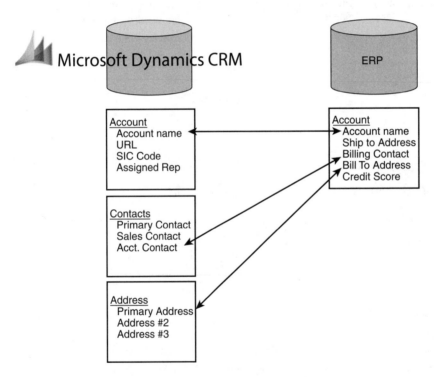

FIGURE 16.4   Typical customer synchronization scenario.

As you can see in Figure 16.4, only certain subsets of data within each system are being synchronized. Given the varying structures of these systems, it is not uncommon to see multiple integration "touch points" between systems to support a synchronization scenario.

Because changes made in one customer database are reflected across all customer databases, data entry effort is dramatically reduced, errors are eliminated, and your entire organization is working from the same information.

Process Integration

With process integration, data is shared from one system to the next based on each system's role in an integrated customer process. The most commonly discussed customer process related to CRM systems is the "quote-to-order" process.

The following table outlines the integration steps required to support quote-to-order activities between a CRM system and a back-office system.

Step	From	To	Data	Description
1	ERP	CRM	Product catalogue	Provide CRM with latest available products and pricing
2	CRM	ERP	Quote	Provide ERP with quote for demand planning and calculate "available to promise"
3	ERP	CRM	Quote	Provide CRM with product availability for quote
4	CRM	ERP	Order	Place order with ERP
5	ERP	CRM	Order	Provide order confirmation
6	ERP	CRM	Order Invoice	Provide ongoing order deliver status and final calculated invoice, including shipping and taxes

One thing to consider in process integration is that the order of the steps is extremely important. In the example shown here, if the quote is created from an invalid or out-of-date item from the product catalogue, the ERP system will not be able to support later steps of providing product availability dates or processing the order. In addition, in most cases, data replication and data synchronization are prerequisite integration requirements for implementing process integration.

Typically, process integration relates to those activities in the sales cycle that involve an event or transaction, such as a sales quote, an order, an invoice, a credit verification, a contract renewal, a product return, and so on. By coordinating these activities more efficiently across the users and systems involved in these processes, companies can accelerate revenue and cash flow, eliminate redundant effort, and provide a better experience to their customers.

Scribe Toolset Explained

Scribe Insight for Microsoft Dynamics CRM is a solution that has been specifically built for aggregating customer data into Microsoft Dynamics CRM from other applications. Its powerful, graphical design and management environment enables you to rapidly create solutions within your current infrastructure to provide your salespeople with one complete view of their customers within Microsoft Dynamics CRM.

Scribe Insight provides the following built-in technology capabilities that ensure a successful integrated solution:

▶ Change capture and event automation

▶ Support for varying latency

▶ Conflict detection and resolution

▶ Maintain relational integrity

▶ Duplicate detection and resolution

▶ Data mapping and transformation

▶ State management

▶ Security and record ownership

▶ Diagnostics, monitoring, and remediation

Change Capture and Event Automation

The sharing of data and initiation of processes across multiple CRM tenants begins when a change is made to specified data elements within any one of the CRM databases. As discussed in earlier chapters, Microsoft Dynamics CRM uses plug-ins that can "publish" this data in the form of XML for processing. The capability to configure these plug-ins with a few mouse clicks and to organize these XML documents for processing across the other CRM tenants is important. When these changes are published, an automated, fault-tolerant, queue-based process can then be automatically initiated to apply the changes to the other CRM tenants. It is also important that the plug-ins be configured to ignore changes that come from another "federated" process, to avoid the endless bounce back of changes across the CRM tenants.

Support for Varying Latency

Different integration processes are going to have very different latency requirements. For example, in the case of synchronizing data in multiple directions between CRM tenants, latency should be as close to zero as possible, especially if the volume of changes to the data is high. This minimizes the chances that changes to the same record will pass by each other in process and thus create inconsistent updates across CRM tenants. In cases where data is being replicated in one direction and the time sensitivity of the data is not high (for example, the sharing of past activities across CRM tenants), it might be much more efficient to process these records in large batches during off hours. In any event, Scribe Insight enables you to dial the latency of individual integration processes up or down depending on the business need.

Conflict Detection and Resolution

As mentioned earlier, ownership of data is an important consideration for any federated CRM deployment. There might be certain data elements that can be updated only by specified CRM tenants. Scribe Insight enables you to compare a date and time stamp to ensure that only more recent changes are updated (which can mitigate the issue of changes passing by each, as mentioned previously). There might be a requirement to update only null values in the target application, so that another CRM tenant does not overwrite existing data, for instance.

Maintaining Relational Integrity

The relationships within each CRM tenant (for multiple-tenant implementations) are maintained by a series of unique primary keys for each record. When the same record (an account record, for example) is maintained across different CRM tenants, each instance of that record will have its own unique primary ID. Maintaining a cross reference of these keys for all instances of the record across the CRM tenants is critical to ensure the relational integrity of records within each CRM instance. For example, in the case where a new opportunity is created in one CRM tenant, when that opportunity is processed within another CRM tenant, the foreign key that identifies the account in the source needs to be replaced with the foreign key for the account record in the target to ensure relational integrity in the target. Dynamically maintaining the primary ID relationships across CRM tenants is essential and is an inherent feature in the Scribe Insight toolkit.

Duplicate Detection and Resolution

There is no bigger enemy to user adoption than duplicate records. Users will quickly get frustrated with a CRM application if they have to hunt through a significant number of duplicate records to use the system. When new master records are created in one CRM tenant, it is important to be able to ensure that the record does not exist in the other CRM tenants before a new record is inserted. The use of "fuzzy" logic to identify duplicate account and contact records is an important capability here.

Data Mapping and Transformation

The most obvious need here is the mapping and translation of data elements across the different CRM tenants. Another important requirement is the mapping and cross referencing of different pick-list values across different CRM tenants. For example, one CRM tenant may have a different set of sales stages than another, requiring a "best fit" mapping between the two tenants. In some cases, multiple CRM tenants can have different database designs requiring some level of structural remapping of data. For example, one tenant might have designed a many-to-many relationship between contacts and accounts, whereas the other tenant does not have this design. Object-level mapping, as provided by Scribe Insight, is required to resolve the design differences between the two.

State Management

The integration process needs to be able to dynamically update the state of records and transactions within each of the CRM tenants in real time. For example, a record that was changed in one CRM tenant could have a state value of "updated, not yet synchronized" until all other CRM tenant subscribers to that data have been successfully updated. At that point, the integration process could modify the value of the record to "synchronized." The result is that Scribe Insight can be used to maintain state at the endpoints, and greater fault tolerance can be designed into the integration processes.

Security and Record Ownership

The integration process should fit within the existing security model of Microsoft Dynamics CRM, taking advantage of the predefined roles, permissions, and data ownership. This ensures data access is controlled and data integrity is maintained. With the ability to initiate data integration processes using the privileged user option, Scribe Insight supports predefined security roles and permissions already in existence within the Microsoft Dynamics CRM environment.

Diagnostics, Monitoring, and Remediation

Integration of data and business processes across multiple CRM tenants involves dependencies on network and application availability and the potential for user actions that were not designed into the integration processes. These are two common scenarios that can lead to exceptions and errors in even the best-designed integration processes. Having the capability to proactively monitor for exceptions, anomalies, or inconsistent data conditions and raising alerts to administrators when they occur, as Scribe Insight provides, is essential.

Scribe Insight Architecture

Scribe Insight is designed to support the effective deployment of a number of market-leading business applications, including Microsoft Dynamics CRM, Microsoft Dynamics GP, Microsoft Dynamics NAV, Salesforce, and SalesLogix.

Scribe Insight is the core technology that forms the basis for the migration and integration solutions using a unique and open template model that enables companies to quickly and efficiently configure any data integration or migration to meet their specific needs, all without having to write a single line of code. (See Figure 16.5.)

Because each customer configures their business applications differently and has different requirements for how the integration itself will work, Scribe Insight is designed to provide highly functional integration solutions that meet the specific needs of each customer.

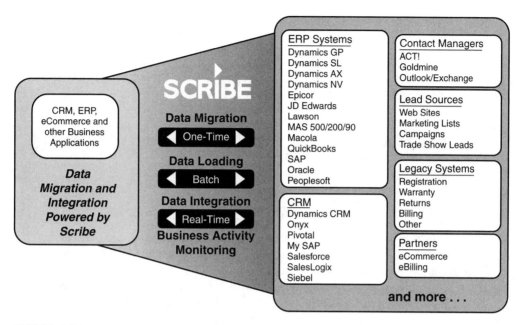

FIGURE 16.5   Data migration and integration.

Scribe Insight has five major design points:

- ▶ **No programming required:** The tool has a graphical user interface that enables business or data analysts (the people who know the issue best) to design and deploy sophisticated integration solutions.

- ▶ **A single point of management:** Companies can support and maintain the integration solution after it has been deployed.

- ▶ **A consistent adapter model:** The core Insight design environment views all applications in the same way, while presenting to the designer information about each application that is important to the integration task.

- ▶ **Open connectivity:** Lets companies integrate these core business systems with the wide variety of applications and data stores that are unique to their business.

- ▶ **A template model:** Users can quickly assemble reusable integration components and configure them for each deployment's unique needs. After the initial deployment, required changes in the integration can be accommodated with a simple reconfiguration.

The core components of Scribe Insight are built using the Microsoft Visual Studio development platform for the Windows family of operating systems. The Scribe Server is the core engine that provides connectivity to the various applications, databases, and messaging systems within the integration environment. Communications between the Scribe components and the applications being integrated is provided using the appropriate technology. For example, Scribe adapters to those applications that support web services, such as

Salesforce or Microsoft Dynamics CRM, use Simple Object Access Protocol (SOAP), whereas other on-premise APIs are worked with using Component/Distributed Component Object Model (COM\DCOM).

Figure 16.6 shows the topology of Scribe Insight components. These items represent the five major Scribe Insight components:

▶ Scribe Server

▶ Scribe Workbench

▶ Scribe Console

▶ Adapters

▶ Templates

Scribe Insight is based on a loosely coupled, yet tightly integrated architecture that is highly adaptable to each customer's unique and constantly changing business environment. For example, each adapter communicates to the Scribe Server in precisely the same way regardless of the application or database to which it is connecting. This abstraction of the application or database details provides for a highly productive design environment; once users learn to use the Workbench, they can design integrations with a wide variety of applications and data stores. This abstraction also means that templates (representing

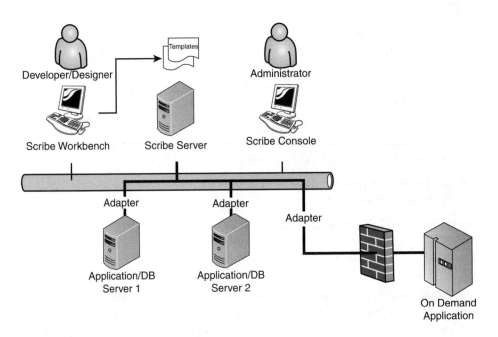

FIGURE 16.6 The Scribe topology.

specific integration processes between applications or databases) are insulated from most changes/updates to the application or database interface. The same template that works with version x of an application will continue to work with version y, requiring no reconfiguration except to accommodate substantive changes in the schema or functionality of that application.

The Scribe Server

The Scribe Server is the core of Scribe Insight–supported integration processes and facilitates the exchange of data between two or more applications or databases. Because Scribe Insight, in essence, brokers a conversation between these applications and databases, it can support a highly heterogeneous server environment of Windows, UNIX, Linux, on-demand applications, and so on. All that it requires is a "connection" to these applications via a Windows client, a non-platform-specific middleware protocol such as Open Database Connectivity (ODBC), or via a Microsoft Message Queuing (MSMQ) message queue.

Underlying the Scribe Server are a number of Windows services designed to monitor and detect events, process messages, raise alerts, and provide an access point for the Scribe Console to the other services. The Scribe Server also includes its own internal database that stores all execution and error logging, persisted integration settings, cross-reference tables, and important integration statistics. The Scribe internal database can be configured to support the Microsoft SQL Server Express database (provided with Scribe Insight) or the other Microsoft SQL Server editions.

For more information about the Scribe Server, see Chapter 17, "Scribe Integration Components."

The Scribe Workbench

The Scribe Workbench provides a rich graphical environment where users design and configure the data mappings and business rules that define the integration solution. All work completed in the Scribe Workbench is "saved" in a lightweight file that is referenced by the Scribe Server at runtime. This self-documenting, metadata-driven model allows for easy debugging during the deployment phase and rapid modification as the application environment or business needs change.

The Scribe Workbench enables you to connect to your applications, define a source result set, configure object-level target processing, and then just point and click to modify or add data mappings.

One of the key capabilities in the Scribe Workbench is the ability to "normalize" source data on-the-fly as it processes against the target application. In other words, single- or multi-row "source" data can have multiple operations executed per row on "target" data objects. These operations, referred to as *steps*, can be conditionally executed based on user-defined logic, allowing complex, transaction-enabled, multiple-object operations. (See Figure 16.7.)

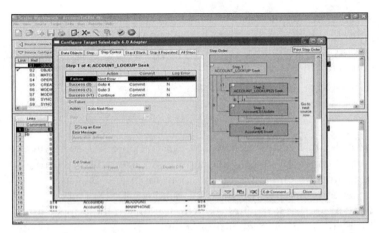

FIGURE 16.7   The Scribe Workbench.

With the Scribe Workbench, designing complex data transformations is a simple task. The Scribe Workbench provides more than 150 Microsoft Excel-like functions for data translation, including the following:

▶ Parsing functions for names and addresses

▶ Date and time conversions

▶ String manipulation

▶ Database and file lookups for processing synonym values

▶ Logical if/then/else functions to support conditional processing

In the rare case where there is a need for data transformation beyond what is included in the Scribe Workbench, additional functions may be created using COM and simply added to the function list.

The Scribe Workbench was designed to support many advanced integration needs beyond data transformation and mapping and includes these additional capabilities:

▶ A Test window that shows the results of processing test data without committing the data to the target system. Users can view the results of data translations and object-level transaction processing for easy and efficient debugging of integration processes.

▶ Built-in system key cross reference and management, designed to dynamically maintain data integrity between records across two or more loosely coupled applications.

▶ Built-in support for foreign key value reference management, designed to dynamically maintain data integrity between related records within an application.

▶ Net change tracking by updating or deleting successfully processed source records or by comparing a source-side update stamp against a variable last run date/time in the source query.

▶ Conflict detection and resolution to support bidirectional data synchronization.

▶ Formula-based lookups for "fuzzy" record matching logic.

▶ Value cross-reference and lookup support.

▶ Automatic data type mismatch resolution.

▶ Transactional support for Header-Detail type data sets.

▶ Configuration of target-side commit and rollback.

▶ Rich error handling and logical flow control, including support for user-defined errors.

▶ Rejected row logging to support automated repair and recovery processes.

For more information about the Scribe Workbench, see Chapter 17.

The Scribe Console

The Scribe Console is a Microsoft Management Console snap-in that provides the user interface to an array of powerful features used to set up, organize, and manage key aspects of any number of integration processes. The Scribe Console is the main user interface to the capabilities underlying the Scribe Server.

The Scribe Console can be installed independently from the Scribe Workbench, and can be configured to connect to the Scribe Server using either COM/DCOM technology over a LAN or a provided SOAP-based web service connection hosted by Microsoft Internet Information Services (IIS).

The Scribe Console (shown in Figure 16.8) provides a single point of management for a company's various integration points, organizing them as discrete units of work or collaborations. Each collaboration is a series of related integration processes and instructions for how and when these processes should be automatically executed. Collaborations are organized in a graphical, user-defined tree and can be managed as independent objects with their own reporting, monitoring, and diagnostic functions. The Scribe Console also provides easy access and control of all integration processes running on the system, through controls implemented at the integration server level.

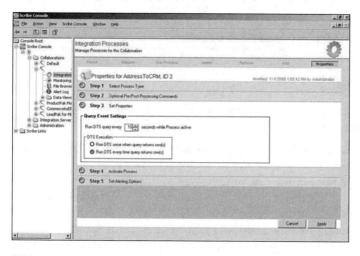

FIGURE 16.8   The Scribe Console.

At the core of the Scribe Console are its sophisticated event management capabilities. The Scribe Console allows each company to precisely define the proper latency for each integration process, from scheduling batch processes to run on a predefined time period, to establishing near real-time polling intervals based on a file drop in a directory or the results of a source-side query, to the real-time processing of messages arriving in an in queue.

The Scribe Server is built with a modular, multithreaded architecture that allows for scaling of integration processes based on the available CPU processing strength. It also features efficient connection sharing to maximize performance, where possible.

Additional capabilities of the Scribe Console include the following:

▶ Access to the files on the Scribe Server that may need to be moved, copied, renamed, or deleted.

▶ Automated system monitoring of business-level events or integration errors with configurable alerts via email, page, and net send notification.

▶ For those data sources that do not have a built-in net change mechanism (including event-based message publishing, time and date stamps for updates, or other forms of update stamps), the Console provides a Query Publisher that compares time-based "snapshots" of a source system and publishes the differences as an XML message.

▶ Settings to launch an executable file to run before or after an integration process. One example where this pre- or post-execution processing can be useful is the ability to move files into an archive directory after the process is executed.

▶ Onscreen editable views of predefined queries that can be displayed in chart or list format.

▶ User interface for MSMQ management providing message viewing, moving, copying, and deleting.

▶ Review execution history of what processes succeeded or failed, including detailed error reporting.

For more information about the Scribe Console, see Chapter 17.

Scribe Adapters

Scribe adapters enable Scribe Insight to communicate seamlessly to a variety of applications, databases, messages, and files.

Scribe adapters present rich levels of schema information, which is available through the application interface (via a "declare" type function in an application API or in a Web Service Definition Language [WSDL] in the case of web services interfaces) to the Scribe Server and Scribe Workbench. This schema information includes object properties and interrelationships and detailed field attributes such as labels, data types, lengths, restrictions, and default/pick-list values. Combined with the rich features in the Scribe Workbench, this information provides for unparalleled control over integration processes and eliminates the "last-mile" coding required with other integration tools.

Scribe adapters are classified in two ways: enterprise application adapters and connectivity adapters.

Enterprise Application Adapters

Enterprise application adapters are adapters that have been designed and developed to optimize Insight for use with Scribe-targeted CRM and ERP applications, including Microsoft Dynamics CRM, Microsoft Dynamics GP, Microsoft Dynamics NAV, Microsoft Dynamics AX, Salesforce, and SalesLogix. Scribe's enterprise application adapters are sold as add-ons to Scribe Insight. Key features of these application adapters include the following:

- ▶ The automation of common data loading tasks such as assigning primary ID values, setting default values, validating input data, and setting object relationships—all designed to eliminate runtime errors and provide for greater data integrity.

- ▶ Dynamic discovery that presents the unique configuration of each application or database instance to the Scribe Console and Scribe Workbench at runtime and adjusts to changes in the application or database schema without requiring recoding or recompiling.

- ▶ The seamless integration of application and database error messages to provide detailed exception reporting and handling from the Scribe Console's single point of management.

Connectivity Adapters

Connectivity adapters are included in core Scribe Insight product. They are designed to complement the enterprise application adapters by providing a wide variety of integration options to support connectivity to the varied applications and data stores within each company's computing environment. These connectivity adapters enable Scribe Insight to communicate with applications and databases in the following ways:

- ▶ Direct communication with database tables, views, and stored procedures through ODBC 3.0 or later and natively to SQL Server. Scribe leverages all the filtering and querying capability of these databases when employing this approach.

- ▶ The exchange of flat files or XML documents via a directory or FTP/HTTP location.

- ▶ The asynchronous exchange of XML messages via an industry-standard message queue, email, or integration broker.

- ▶ SOAP Messages via web-based transport protocols, such as http/https.

A common use of Scribe's connectivity adapters is to support integration between the targeted applications served by Scribe's application adapters and a wide variety of other packaged enterprise applications. These other enterprise applications include the following:

- ▶ ERP and CRM systems from SAP, Siebel, Oracle (Oracle, PeopleSoft, JD Edwards,) Sage (MAS 90/200/500,) Epicor, and so on

- ▶ Packaged applications that serve a particular niche or vertical market

- ▶ Custom in-house-developed systems

16

Scribe provides a number of approaches to integrating with these applications, depending on the business requirements and available technical resources, including the following:

▶ **Directly to the database:** This is a simple, straightforward approach if you are migrating from an application or your project is limited to a one-way feed of data from that application. Scribe Insight provides a number of methods using this approach to extract "net change" data from the application.

▶ **Via interface tables:** Many applications support a set of interface or staging tables that provide for a safe way to integrate data into that application. After data is passed into the interface tables, an application process is initiated that validates the data and applies appropriate application rules. With Scribe Insight, you can write to these tables and initiate the application process automatically.

▶ **Via an XML/messaging interface:** Many enterprise applications provide an XML interface that is incorporated into the workflow engine within the application. Using this method, Scribe Insight can publish XML messages into a message queue for real-time integration with the other application. Scribe Insight can also receive XML transactions published by the application's workflow engine into a message queue in real time.

▶ **Via the application's API:** Many applications expose a web services- or COM-based API where transactions can be passed to the application. Data can also be queried via this API. Out of the box, Scribe Insight cannot "natively" integrate with this API; however, custom code can be written to convert these calls into an intermediate format. This intermediate format can be an XML message, a flat file, or a record in a database staging table.

Scribe Insight also includes connectivity adapters for data migration from/to certain leading desktop applications, including ACT!, GoldMine, and Microsoft Outlook/Exchange.

Scribe Templates

Scribe templates represent complete or partial data integration or migration processes that have been developed using Scribe Insight technology. Scribe provides a number of these templates as free downloads from the Scribe Web Community to support the successful deployment of Scribe Insight.

Templates consist of the building blocks of a fully functional migration or integration solution as configured with Scribe Insight, including the following:

▶ Source-side "net change" processes and filtering

▶ Event and process automation

▶ Data mappings

▶ Record matching for updates and duplicate avoidance

▶ User/owner mappings

▶ Field ownership and update rules

- ▶ System key cross referencing and management
- ▶ Connection validation and security
- ▶ Data ownership and customizations
- ▶ Application customizations
- ▶ Transaction management
- ▶ Commit and rollback settings
- ▶ System monitors and alerts
- ▶ Business monitors and alerts

There are two distinct styles of Scribe templates: solution templates and component templates.

Solution Templates

Solution templates represent a complete, fully functional integration or migration solution between two applications. Examples of these include migration solutions for ACT! into Microsoft Dynamics CRM, SalesLogix, or Salesforce and "front to back-office" integration solutions between Microsoft Dynamics GP and Microsoft Dynamics CRM or Salesforce. Scribe's unique template model provides out-of-the-box functionality for these integration scenarios, built over its industry-leading integration tool. Because most customers have business needs unique to them, these standard templates can be quickly extended and customized via the GUI-based mapping and development environment.

The component architecture of these solution templates also enables customers to implement templates in phases or pick and choose the elements of the templates that they require. In the front to back-office integration example, a customer might not want to implement order integration initially (or in some cases never) but can still synchronize customer activity (accounts, contacts, invoices) between the two systems. This modularity enables customers to implement an integration solution tailored to their exact needs.

Component Templates

Component templates are starting points for common integration processes used by customers that are implementing an integration solution for which Scribe has not developed a solution template.

For example, Scribe provides templates that integrate customers, products, orders, and invoices between a Scribe-developed sample ERP system and Scribe's targeted CRM applications, including Microsoft Dynamics CRM, Salesforce, and SalesLogix. A customer that is looking to integrate one of these applications with their own ERP application can use the appropriate component template as a significant starting point. Typically, these component templates provide the bulk of the end solution, with the remainder easily configurable with Scribe Insight.

16

For more information about Scribe templates, see Chapter 17.

Summary

This chapter explained what integration means and when and how to consider different options related to integration options. The basics of the Scribe toolset were reviewed at a high level, as was the value of working with them. In the next few chapters, we delve deeper into the toolset to show and explain it in further detail.

Scribe Integration Components

In this chapter, we examine common integration scenarios and how the Scribe Workbench and Scribe Console toolsets can be used for each of them.

The scenarios we review are migration (or data replication), integration (or data synchronization), and process integration. While the scenarios and the examples provided cover a majority of situations, we have found that every integration is unique in some way, and the solutions presented should provide enough illustration for integration challenges particular to your organization.

As mentioned, the three most common integration scenarios are as follows:

▶ **Migration, or data replication:** A common and straightforward integration use case is the need to replicate data from one application to other applications in one direction. For example, a company may want to replicate contract expiration data from its contracts management system into its CRM application. By having up-to-date contract data, users can conduct effective marketing and sales campaigns targeted at renewing customers and designed to increase renewal rates and recurring revenue. Identifying those records that change in the contracts system and updating the CRM application with those changes is the most efficient way to ensure that the CRM users have the most current information.

▶ **Integration, or data synchronization:** In this scenario, a company has two or more applications that contain the same information, and it wants to ensure that all copies of that information are consistent. For example, a company may have information on customers (contact names, addresses, phone numbers, and so on) in both a CRM and enterprise resource planning (ERP) application. If a customer notifies the billing department of an address change and that change is made in the ERP application, it is important that the new address be reflected in the CRM application, too. This consistency of data drives more efficiency and avoids embarrassing missteps with customers. Given that changes may occur to data in any of the applications, updates will be moving in multiple directions. This type of bidirectional integration process places significant pressure on the timeliness and reliability of the net change capture mechanism.

▶ **Process integration:** In many cases, the actions of a user within a business application can trigger a business process that spans multiple applications. The most common example of a process type integration is the quote to order process that spans across a company's CRM and ERP application. A typical process initiation is the submission of the sales order by a salesperson within the CRM application. This new order transaction needs to be captured and delivered to the ERP application for processing by the back-office operation. As with data synchronization, these types of integrations are bidirectional and underscore the need for a timely and reliable net change approach.

The Scribe product line addresses these three scenarios through two different toolsets: the Scribe Workbench and the Scribe Console.

Table 17.1 outlines the various features of each tool and how they map to the previously outlined integration scenarios.

TABLE 17.1   Integration Options

	Integration Scenario		
	Data Migration	Two-Way Synchronization	Process Integration
Scribe Workbench			
Create integrations	X	X	X
Test run an integration	X	X	X
Update the source upon integration completion	X	X	X
Siphon rejected and failed rows to a separate data source	X	X	X
Manage key cross-reference fields between source and target applications	–	X	X
Manage "bounce back"	–	X	X

TABLE 17.1   Integration Options

	Integration Scenario		
	Data Migration	Two-Way Synchronization	Process Integration
Scribe Workbench			
Scribe Console			
Configure real-time and event-driven integrations	–	X	X
Administer the Scribe integration server	–	X	X
Configure system notifications (for example, alerts when an integration fails)	–	X	X
Configure business notifications (for example, alerts when there are unfulfilled orders)	–	–	X
Define system and business data views and monitors	–	–	X

In this chapter, we also review the consequences associated with changed data and the impact across the integration design.

> **NOTE**
>
> This concept of changed data across an integrated environment is referred to as the *net change pattern*.

Data Migration (Replication)

Data migration, or data replication, is, as you might expect, the least complex scenario. That doesn't mean that it is any less significant, or easier to perform correctly than the other scenarios. In fact, it is common to perform a migration multiple times as part of the overall validation process.

In this section, we review how to perform a migration using the Scribe toolset.

Scribe Workbench

The Scribe Workbench (shown in Figure 17.1) is the main Scribe tool for managing migrations. The Scribe Workbench enables users to define both source and target data sets. Either or both of these may be a specific application (such as Microsoft Dynamics CRM,

Microsoft Dynamics NAV, Salesforce, or other applications) or may be a more generic data set (such as SQL Server, XML, ODBC, and others).

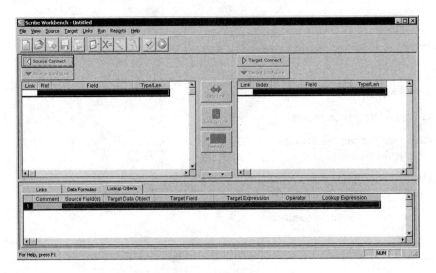

FIGURE 17.1   The Scribe Workbench.

After defining both a source and a target, users can relate the two systems together using a linking/mapping window. Linked fields can incorporate formulas (custom formulas and 180+ functions that ship with the product) to calculate or transform data in the mapping window, too.

Choosing the source and target, linking fields, and creating formulas all combine to create what is referred to as an *integration definition*. Users can choose to run the integration manually through mouse clicks in the Scribe Workbench.

Other options are also configured in the Scribe Workbench and are considered part of this integration definition, including the following:

▶ Source and target definitions

▶ Mapping and linking options

▶ Additional functions

Source and Target Definitions

As part of the definition of an integration, users define both source and target data. When possible, using one of the Scribe application adapters is the best option because each adapter is built to work with its respective application and is optimized based on that application's API. However, connecting to data via generic connection types (such as ODBC, XML, and others) is also supported.

Adapters also act as a layer of indirection between your integrations and the application. Scribe adapters keep a consistent development interface that will insulate the integration creator from changes in the applicable system. The differences between Microsoft Dynamics CRM 3.0 and 4.0 provide a good example of this. Although the technical differences between these two releases are significant, the Scribe adapter for Microsoft Dynamics CRM looks and acts essentially the same for both versions. For Scribe integrations, upgrading to Microsoft Dynamics CRM 4.0 is as easy as upgrading the Scribe adapter.

Source Configuration   Defining the source data begins with choosing how to connect to the data (using an application adapter, ODBC, or XML). After you choose the connection parameters, a series of prompts helps you define the query set for the source data. This can be a single "object" or can be a custom query joining multiple objects together.

When you join multiple objects, the syntax is much like SQL. You can define calculated values in the Scribe Workbench (referred to as variables) that filter on a static or dynamic values.

Figure 17.2 shows the Source Connection Wizard that prompts for the source connection method.

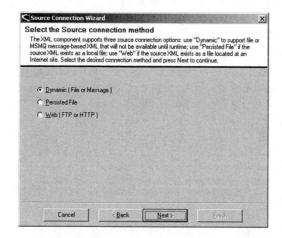

FIGURE 17.2   The Scribe Source Connection Wizard.

Target Configuration   Choosing the target system is nearly identical to choosing the source data, but the process varies after you have provided the necessary connection parameters.

Figure 17.3 shows the Scribe target connection options.

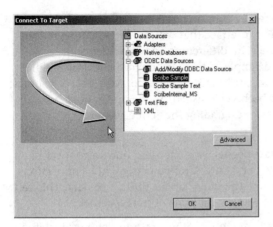

FIGURE 17.3   The Scribe target connection options.

A "target" in the Scribe Workbench consists of both the locations in the target system and how the target data is structured (including transaction integrity).

Suppose, for example, that you are integrating sales orders into a target system. Often, the sales header will be a different location than the sales lines. Therefore, you define the target system as both places. Furthermore, you most likely attempt to integrate the lines after the header has been successfully integrated.

In this example, integrating into the sales header and sales lines would be represented as steps. A step has an action (for example, an insert or update) and a workflow of what you want to happen as each step passes, and what you want to happen should the step fail. You can chain these steps together based on the result of a given step. The Scribe Workbench contains a graphical representation of this flow, showing the workflow of behaviors based on various results of the steps defined. When you preview or test an integration, you will see the steps, or route, each record being integrated follows, as shown in Figure 17.4.

Mapping and Linking Options

Scribe Insight makes some intelligent decisions about data transformation and management based on how you relate the source and target data sets to each other. For example, Scribe retains the cross-referential integrity between two systems based on key fields defined in the two systems. To accomplish this, there are two ways to link fields in the Scribe Workbench:

- ▶ Links

- ▶ Formulas

Links   A data link is the traditional mapping relationship between two fields in two separate systems. By choosing to relate to fields using a data link, you are stating that you want to change the value in the target to the value in the source.

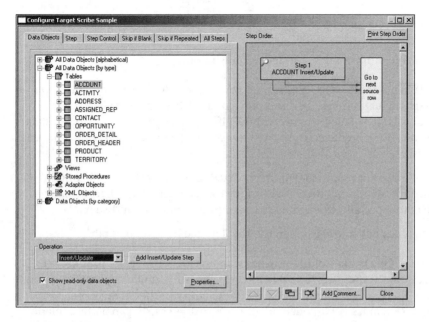

FIGURE 17.4   Configuring a target example.

A lookup link defines the relationship between the source and target fields a bit differently. A lookup link tells Scribe that the two fields (or, more specifically, the relationship between the two fields) define how the two data sets relate to each other. You can customize how these two fields relate to each other; for example, the first four characters of the source key field should align to the last four characters of the target key field.

Formulas   You can choose to use any of the 180+ formulas included with the product to transform data as it moves from source to target. Alternatively, you can create your own formulas in Visual Basic 6.0.

Many of the core formulas are data driven, so you can modify or extend their behavior by adding content to the appropriate Scribe database table (specifically the SCRIBE.FunctionList table). Applications for this feature include modifying the data used by fuzzy logic functions available within Scribe and adding permutations for lookup.

Additional Functions
Although not in direct support of the migration of data, the Scribe Workbench allows some other functionality worth mentioning.

Test Window   The Test window lets you to step through each record being integrated. This preview includes the original source content, the target value (including any transformation or formula applied to the link), and the step control.

To open the Test window, on the Run menu, click Test.

Update Source   Upon successfully integrating a given record, a value can be written back to a field in the source. This feature is commonly used to mark a row as having been successfully integrated. This value can be a string literal or a calculated value (using a formula).

The feature is available in the Source Configuration window.

Rejected Rows   When a record fails to integrate, you can opt to have a copy of the source data saved in a separate data source. This can prove useful when there are larger sets of data and you want to review failed records without sifting through the entire source data set. Furthermore, by redirecting rejected source rows to a different location, you can focus solely on those rows.

For example, if 150 rows fail out of 20,000, the rejected source rows table will contain only the 150 failed rows. Working with a set of 150 rows is much easier than working with a row of 20,000 (especially when you are trying to troubleshoot an issue).

On the Run menu, click Edit Settings. Then use the Rejected Source Rows tab.

Key Cross Reference   One of the common issues when trying to integrate data between disparate systems is that values that uniquely identify an entity in one application do not match up nicely with values used to identify that same entity in the other system. For example, Microsoft Dynamics GP uniquely identifies a customer using an alphanumeric quasi-"human-readable" string; whereas Microsoft CRM uses a globally unique identifier (GUID). Scribe offers the Key Cross Reference feature as a way to coordinate these unique/"key" values across disparate systems.

Over time, these unique identifiers (databases refer to them as a "key"; hence the feature name) are collected in a Scribe table. The more identifiers tracked, the more efficient your integrations become. The efficiency comes in Scribe's capability to resolve an alphanumeric value to a GUID without having to make calls in to CRM, for example.

These unique values can be leveraged in formulas, too. For example, if you want to use the key value of the Microsoft Dynamics GP customer as a note on the account in Microsoft CRM, you can reference the unique GP customer ID as a formula on the account's Note field.

To manage key cross references, on the Links menu, click Cross-Reference Keys.

Data-Migration Example

Life will be easier for you if you create a CRM Adapter publisher as the first step, because the CRM Adapter publisher is responsible for capturing changes that occur in CRM, and uses that change event to trigger an integration to occur (for example, integrate a new account into the ERP system.)

The publisher will publish data in a specific schema, however. Creating the publisher first will allow you to get that schema for use when creating the actual integration.

NOTE

Depending on your version of Microsoft Dynamics CRM, you may need to customize CRM to publish changes before creating a Scribe CRM adapter publisher.

▶ CRM 3.0 uses the "call-out" functionality.

▶ CRM Live uses workflow to publish changes.

▶ Microsoft Dynamics CRM 4.0 makes use of "plug-in" technology.

The Scribe CRM adapter Help outlines how to configure these various versions of Microsoft Dynamics CRM.

This section assumes you have already made any necessary customizations to Microsoft Dynamics CRM based on the version.

Creating a CRM Adapter Publisher

1. Open the Console and go to the Publisher and Bridges node under Integration Server.

2. Create a new publisher, and make its type Microsoft Dynamics CRM Publisher. You will be prompted for connection information when you move to the next step of the creation process.

3. After the connection to CRM has been established, you need to indicate what CRM entities you want to monitor for change; where a change in an entity of that type (add/delete/update) triggers some event in your integration solution (for example, starts an integration). To indicate which entities you want to use as indicators of change, go to step 4 of the publisher-creation process and click the Add button.

4. Select Account as your Dynamics CRM entity that will be used to start an integration. Select the Insert operation to indicate that when new accounts are created you want Scribe to publish information about the related account. Select the Update operation to indicate that when existing accounts are changed you want Scribe to publish information about the related account.

   Figure 17.5 shows the publisher entry that is created at this step.

   Although not required, we have created a message label for continuity with other examples in this chapter.

NOTE

Be sure to remember this label because you will need it when creating the integration process that gets started when a new CRM account is created (or updated)

5. While still on step 4 of the publisher-creation process, click the XML Schema's button and save the XDR someplace you can get to later. This is the schema that you can use to create integrations against (for example, create an integration definition for what should happen when a new account is created).

Now that you've created the CRM adapter publisher, we'll create a data migration.

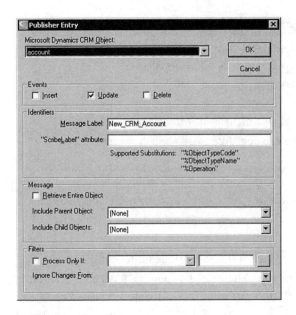

FIGURE 17.5   Scribe publisher entry.

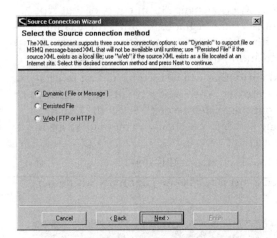

FIGURE 17.6   Scribe Source Connection Wizard.

Creating a Data Migration

1. Open the Workbench and select XML as a source.

2. Use the Dynamic (File or Message) option, as shown in Figure 17.6.

   You'll be prompted for both a schema and a sample file.

NOTE

Although you don't need the sample file to create the integration definition, you won't be able to run the integration without real data.

Because we have already created a CRM publisher (our first step), we can get an XML file with real data by just creating an account in Microsoft Dynamics CRM.

If your publisher is showing as active (not paused), after a short time you will have a message in your ScribeIn queue. In the Scribe Console, you can open this Microsoft Message Queuing (MSMQ) message and opt to Save Body. This option will create an XML document that conforms to the schema as defined by the publisher and will contain "real" data based on the CRM entity you created.

NOTE

If the message does not show up in the ScribeIn queue, make sure your Integration Process is active (e.g., not paused). The message may have been routed to the ScribeDeadMessage queue as well.

---

3. Link to the schema file that defines what your source data will look like. The "sample" file is optional, but you will not be able to run the integration if there is only a schema (that is, no data).

4. Connect to the target application by using the Scribe Sample ODBC database connection, as shown in Figure 17.7.

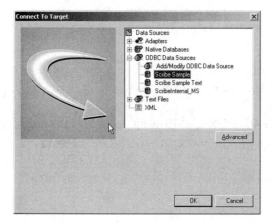

FIGURE 17.7   Connect to Target dialog box.

17

The Scribe Sample uses SCRIBE as the user ID and integr8! as the password.

5. After the target has been defined, select the Account table.

   With Operation set to Insert/Update, click Add Insert/Update, as shown in Figure 17.8.

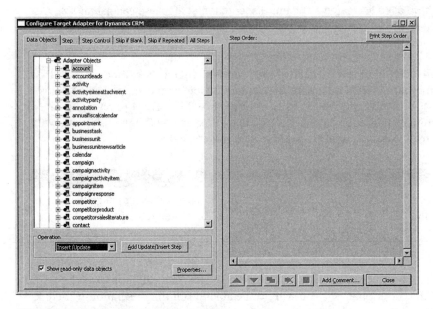

FIGURE 17.8   Scribe target configuration sample.

NOTE

By defining the target in this way, you are stating that for each new source record you want to insert a new record in the Account table in the target. If that record already exists, update it instead.

6. After the source and target have been defined, map the following fields from source to target:

   Map source field Name to target column ACCOUNTNAME using the Data Link button.

   Map source field accountnumber to target column ACCOUNTID using the Data Link button.

   Map these same source and target fields (accountnumber and ACCOUNTID) using the Lookup Link button.

NOTE

A lookup link is used to test if a record exists. (And in this case, ACCOUNTID is a primary key field on the target table Account.) A data link maps the value in the source to the target field.

7. Save and run the integration. After it has completed, your new row should be in your target.

8. While still in the Workbench, select the PHONE target column.

9. Click the Formula button and make the formula read as `"(xxx) 123-1234"`. You will need quotes here because this is a string literal.

10. Save and run the integration again. The row should be updated with this new value in the PHONE column.

> **NOTE**
>
> If you receive Primary Key violations on this second run, ensure that the lookup links defined previously are accurate with respect to the constraint being violated.

Data Integration (Synchronization)

This section provides more information about the Scribe tools and describes how they work in data-synchronization scenarios. This section introduces the major features of each tool, including how they can be used

Scribe Console

Creating event-driven integrations begins with using the Scribe Workbench to define the integration (for example, what should happen when the integration commences based on some event). The Scribe Console is used to configure integrations to run automatically when one or more conditions are met (as opposed to starting the integration manually from the Scribe Workbench).

Collaborations

Integrations are aligned with a logical collection of jobs called a collaboration in the Scribe Console. You might configure one collaboration to process sales lead events. Then you might configure a second collaboration to process order events.

It makes sense to store these collaboration files in a logical folder structure. For example, create a folder named Sales and a second folder named Orders.

By compartmentalizing integrations and related items, you will be able to manage and report against your integrations more easily.

Each collaboration has these parts:

- ▶ **Integration processes:** A collection of integration definitions, each keyed to run off of a specific event (see later in this chapter for specific examples).

- ▶ **Monitoring:** Monitors work hand in hand with alerts. Monitors are used to measure and report system health indicators (for example, unhandled message in an MSMQ, or unfulfilled sales orders). Monitors and alerts are covered in more detail in the "Process Integration" section.

▶ **File browser:** A direct view in to the folder associated with this collaboration.

▶ **Alert log:** A history of alerts over time. This log has some useful workflow management capabilities, too (such as being able to mark alerts as being "acknowledged" or as having been "handled").

▶ **Data views:** A data view is a report based on a query written against an adapter. The data views result set can be represented in tabular or graphical form. For a collaboration, you may want to see representations of the number of sales orders integrated over time, for example.

For real-time and two-way integrations, the integration processes node is where you will spend much of your time. One of the first decisions you need to make is choosing the event that will trigger when an integration is run:

▶ **File:** Periodically checks for the existence of a particular file in a particular location. If that file is detected, the integration is run. You can choose to rename or even delete the file after the integration has finished.

▶ **Time:** Runs the integration based on a time event. Time-based events can be repeating.

▶ **Query:** Runs the integration when a particular query returns a result set.

▶ **Queue:** Runs the integration when a message is received in a specific MSMQ. A single MSMQ can serve multiple integrations, and you can use the message header or the root node of the incoming XML document to refine which integrations are run. Queue-driven integration processes and related parts are covered later in this chapter.

Integration Server

Although a particular Scribe deployment can have many Scribe Consoles and Workstations on a variety of computers, one computer must be designated as the integration server (see Figure 17.9). It is this computer that coordinates real-time integrations and from which you monitor overall system health. In fact, when using the Scribe Console from a separate computer, you are actually pointing to resources on this central integration server.

This allows you to manage who has access to the integration resources (for example, the Scribe application) apart from who has access to Scribe. Suppose, for example, you are integrating into an ERP system that contains payroll information. You might not want users who have access to Scribe to have access to the payroll information. (And therefore the Scribe application does have access, but users might not.)

Within the Scribe Console, there is an additional node for the integration server. The options here let you manage and monitor resources used by various integrations:

▶ **Integration processes:** Nearly identical to the option of the same name under a specific collaboration. This view rolls up all integration processes across all collaborations rather than a single collaboration.

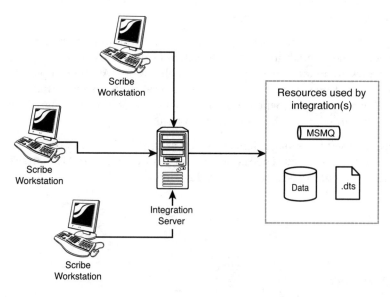

FIGURE 17.9　Integration server.

▶ **Publishers and bridges:** Publishers and bridges are used to manage net change between two applications. Publishers and bridges are covered in more detail in the "Process Integration" section.

▶ **Monitoring:** Monitors found under the Integration Server node are technically identical to monitors listed under each collaboration node. The monitors listed here, however, are meant to be used for integration server monitoring (whereas the monitors listed with a given collaboration are meant to be used for monitoring business activities related to the specific collaboration).

▶ **Queue browser:** Lists the MSMQs currently available to the Scribe server to the Scribe Console. Unlike the MSMQ view in MSC, you can resubmit failed messages by dragging them from the ScribeDeadMessage queue and dropping them into the ScribeIn queue.

▶ **File browser:** Exposes file system resources available to the Scribe server to the Scribe Console.

▶ **Services:** Exposes windows services available to the Scribe server to the Scribe Console.

Administration

Scribe system administration is also managed through the Scribe Console. Scribe system administration consists of reviewing results of integrations over time, responding to and managing Scribe system alerts, choosing system-level resources that the Scribe system should have access to, and more:

▶ **Execution log:** Review a list of integrations over time. The list can be filtered by integration process or result (failure, success).

▶ **Alert log:** Similar to alert logs in collaborations, alerts in the administration alert log should reflect an alert pertaining to overall system health (whereas alert logs in collaborations represent an alert that affects that collaboration). As an example, an alert on the administration side may be used to signal that there are more than 1,000 items in the execution log, whereas an alert in a collaboration may signal that there are unfulfilled orders older than a predefined term.

▶ The alert log can be used to manage alerts, too. You can mark an alert as being acknowledged and then resolved. The Scribe alert log, shown in Figure 17.10, tracks timestamps and comments associated with these changes.

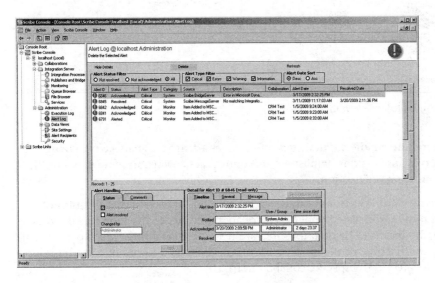

FIGURE 17.10   Scribe alert log.

▶ **Data views:** Much like data views at the collaboration level. As with alert logs, data views on the administration side part of the Scribe Console report on overall system health as opposed to a business-related collaboration activity. For example, a data view at the administration level may be the number of failed integrations over time, whereas a collaboration data view might be the number of new orders over time.

▶ **Site settings:** The Scribe system administrator can define some system-level options, including email server location (for alert delivery) and system sleep options (so that integrations are paused during a predefined backup period, for example).

▶ **Alert recipients:** Used to define recipient users, recipient groups, or recipient maps of users to be alerted. A recipient user has some sort of address (such as an email address) to which the notification will be sent. A recipient group is a collection of one or more users.

▶ A recipient map lets you create abstract groups. An example best demonstrates this feature: You create a monitor based on a SQL query. One of the columns contains the values A, B, or C. In the definition of that query monitor, you can bind that column such a recipient map, where the elements of that recipient map are titled A, B, or C. If the value of the query is A, the users and groups associated with element A in the map will be notified.

▶ **Security:** The Scribe system administrator needs to explicitly designate a system resource to be listed in the file browser, queue browser, and services nodes described earlier. This node helps facilitate that process.

MSMQ-Driven Integration Processes

For queue-driven integration processes, you should be aware of some intrinsic predefined message queues. To help with context, let's assume you are looking to create new customers in the ERP/back-office system whenever a new account is created in Microsoft Dynamics CRM. Therefore, this event begins when a new account is created in Microsoft Dynamics CRM. A piece of Scribe technology called a publisher oversees this change management process.

In this case, the Microsoft Dynamics CRM adapter has a few different publishers (depending on whether you are using Microsoft Dynamics CRM On-Line, Microsoft Dynamics CRM Hosted, or Microsoft Dynamics CRM On Premise). The publisher's duty, at this point, is to recognize that the change occurred and to signal to Scribe that an entity in Microsoft Dynamics CRM has been modified, inserted, or deleted. To accomplish this, a lightweight message is dropped into a publisher-specific MSMQ. Scribe often refers to this as the PubIn queue. (You can have many publishers monitoring Microsoft Dynamics CRM, with each potentially using its own MSMQ—so the exact MSMQ name is determined at publisher creation time.) The "lightweight" message includes the entity changed, the nature of the change, and enough information to uniquely identify the specific entity or entities that changed.

Messages on the PubIn queue are picked up by a publisher, and the information required to perform the integration is retrieved. By using this two-step process when creating a publisher, you can define the process so that changes to one entity (such as an account in Microsoft Dynamics CRM) actually retrieve information from other entities (all addresses for that account) in addition to the entity that changed. In this way, the first step serves as a generic handler to signal to the publisher that a change has occurred, while the second step is the publisher retrieving all the information necessary based on its definition.

After the complete information is retrieved from the source application (in this case, Microsoft Dynamics CRM), a message is added to ScribeIn MSMQ. Unlike the PubIn queue, the ScribeIn queue is an MSMQ named ScribeIn and is created when you install Scribe. All queue-based integration processes will be listening on this queue. (Note how you do not specify a specific MSMQ when creating an MSMQ-driven integration process.) For what it is worth, if you are opposed to using ScribeIn as the default MSMQ and want to use a different MSMQ, you can define the Scribe input queue in the Administration's Site Settings node.

17

After a message is in the ScribeIn queue, Scribe finds and runs the correct integration definition based on the settings used when creating the integration process.

Finally, when creating an integration in the Scribe Workbench, you mark the integration to be automatically retried should it fail. (For example, you are integrating customers and orders in real time across many queues; on the off-chance that an order comes through before the customer, you may want to automatically retry versus having it fail with a "customer does not exist" error.)

To do this, on the Target Configure window's Step Control tab, choose the Failure option. In the list of results, change the On Failure control from Goto Next Row to End Job. Make sure that the Exit Status is set to Retry.

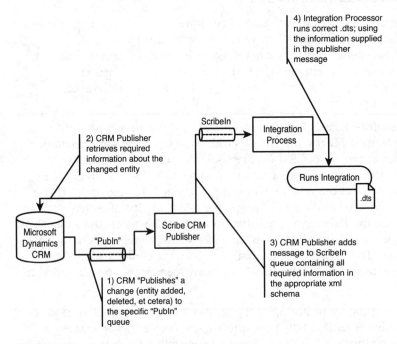

FIGURE 17.11   Publish process flow.

Data-Integration Example

To create an event-driven integration in the Console, follow these steps:

NOTE

We are assuming that you have followed the steps outlined previously in this chapter to create a CRM adapter publisher. (During that process, you will have defined a message label, which will be used when creating an integration process in this example.)

---

1. Open the Console, and move to the Integration Processes node for a specific collaboration.

2. Click the Add button.

3. Select Queue as the event type, give the integration process a name, and then select a DTS that should be invoked.

4. At step 3 of the integration process creation, change the message label from a wild-card (*) to match the message label you defined when creating your publisher, as shown in Figure 17.12.

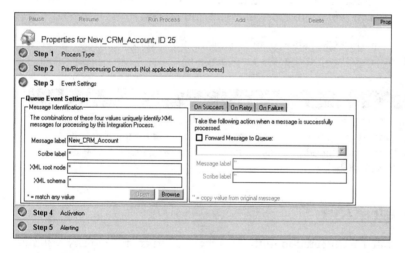

FIGURE 17.12   Scribe properties, event settings.

5. Moving to another step of the integration process creation will allow you to save the integration process.

6. After you have finished creating the integration process, select the integration process you just created and click the Pause button.

> **NOTE**
>
> Pausing the integration process will enable you to see (and diagnose) various steps in the integration pipeline. Normally, you keep the integration unpaused.

7. Create a new account in CRM. If you've configured your publisher, you will see a new message in the ScribeIn queue.

> **NOTE**
>
> If you don't see a message in the ScribeIn queue, ensure that your publisher was created according to the "Creating a CRM Adapter Publisher" section.

8. Select the integration process you just created and click the Resume button. The integration process will remove that new message and process it.

   A new account created in CRM should automatically flow straight through to your target application (as defined in the .dts you created).

> **NOTE**
>
> If the message remains in the ScribeIn queue, make sure the integration process is set to use a queue (versus time, file, or query events). If it is, confirm the message label associated with this integration process matches the message label being placed on the message by the publisher.

Process Integration

Now that you have created an integration in the Workbench and configured any real-time integration requirements in the Console, there are a number of features of Scribe that will help you manage some of the common issues that arise in real-time integration solutions.

Bounce-Back

One of the frequent issues integrators need to resolve is bounce-back. Bounce-back occurs in two-way integrations when changes in one application trigger an integration in a second application and the changes in this second application trigger changes back in the first. Ultimately, the same change bounces back and forth between the two systems.

To avoid this bounce-back, you define the integration solution such that changes should not be published out of the second integration if they are from a specific user. Scribe refers to this user as the integration user. Configuring this is a two-step process:

1. When defining an integration in the Scribe Workbench, open the Settings - Adapter window (found under Source, Adapter Settings or under Target, Adapter Settings), as shown in Figure 17.13. In the Run As tab, choose the user you want to be tagged as having performed this integration.

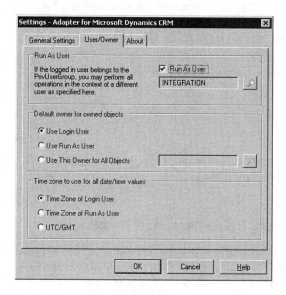

FIGURE 17.13   Scribe adapter settings.

2. When configuring your publisher, choose to ignore messages from a certain user and choose the same user you chose to "run as," earlier.

NOTE

Currently, only two adapters support this functionality: the Scribe Adapter for Microsoft Dynamics CRM and the Scribe Adapter for Microsoft Dynamics NAV.

Monitors

There are two different types of monitors that behave similarly:

▶ **System monitors:** System monitors are monitors that report on overall Scribe system health. System health indicators may be items such as the number of integrations over a period of time or they could be the number of failed integrations over time.

▶ **Business activity monitors:** Business activity monitors use the same technology but are more focused on business goals than on system health. Examples of business activity monitors may include the number of customers added in CRM over time or the average time to fill an order grouped by date.

A Scribe user can create a monitor through the Scribe Console. Monitors can be set up to work off of a "query" or a "queue." For query monitors, you write SQL-like syntax to form a query. Query monitors "alert" when the result set meets or exceeds a certain row count or based on the value of a field.

Queue monitors listen in on an MSMQ queue. You can define which messages will be monitored by customizing the message label, the XML schema of the message contained in a particular MSMQ message, and other similar message traits. Like query monitors, alerts can be tied to a number of messages in the queue. A common use for queue monitors is to ensure that communications between systems are happening efficiently (for example, by setting a monitor to alert the Scribe administrator if the number of messages in the ScribeIn MSMQ climbs over 100).

Data Views

Data views are meant to present information in tabular or graphical forms. Think of data views as key performance indicator (KPI) reporting meters. Users can create a data view to report on a metric.

Scribe Application Publishers, Query Publishers, and Bridges

A key part of process integration is the capability for the extended system to respond to a user-driven event in one part of the system. For example, the system needs to be able to respond to a user adding an account in Microsoft Dynamics CRM to drive the relevant information into the ERP/back-office system. Scribe supports a variety of ways to accommodate this need:

▶ **Query publishers:** A query publisher is a mechanism where the Scribe user would define a query. Results from this query represent items to be managed. An example is returning all the CRM accounts that have not been brought over to ERP. Each row of the result set should be then brought over. Alternatively, you can take a "snapshot" of the results of a query and publish only those items that differ from the snapshot.

▶ In either case, the resulting rows can be grouped if you routinely expect large result sets and want to optimize the integration event.

▶ This mechanism is a "poll" type of approach, where Scribe periodically (at a time interval configured by the user) runs the query and reacts to the result set returned.

▶ **Adapter publishers:** Query publishers operate on a "poll" basis, where periodically a change is made to see whether new data exists to be published. Some applications, however, signal themselves when a change has occurred.

▶ In these cases, instead of making periodic checks, the application signals when new content is ready. This approach is useful when you are concerned with the amount of unnecessary network chatter a query publisher may produce, or if "near real-time" integration is not good enough. Real-time is when the event of the changing data initiates the process, near real-time is when a periodic check is made and the events age could be equal to the period of that check. (That is, if your query publisher checks once a minute, changes found may be up to a minute old.)

▶ To use an adapter publisher, you must complete some additional configuration in the application in question. For Microsoft Dynamics CRM, for example, you might need to configure a workflow. Scribe has preconfigured units (SQL triggers, sample workflows, or custom call-outs depending on the technology at hand) that make this configuration as easy as possible.

▶ **Email bridges:** Email bridges are similar to publishers in concept but differ in implementation. Email bridges listen to an email alias at a specific email server for incoming email messages. When an email message is received, the bridge adds a message on the ScribeIn MSMQ queue with the body contents (or an attachment) as the source data.

Net Change Patterns

In all three integration scenarios previously described, capturing changed data from a source application is a fundamental component of the integration design. This section reviews some of the key considerations for net change capture and their impact on the overall integration process. Then we present four "best practice" design patterns for net change, outlining the pros and cons of each pattern, along with some design tips to ensure the effectiveness of each pattern.

The following are some of the important considerations when designing a net change capture mechanism:

▶ **Efficiency:** The most efficient net change approaches minimize the number and size of messages based on the needs of the integration process. This minimizes the burden on the network and the applications involved in the integration. When messaging and communications are minimized, integration processes perform better, are less prone to error, and are simpler to troubleshoot.

▶ **Reliability:** Robust integration processes require that all record modifications and business events that meet the criteria defined in the process are captured and published. Failure to capture everything results in data integrity issues and broken business processes.

▶ **Bounce-back prevention:** Bounce-back or echoing occurs most often when synchronizing data between two applications. Let's say that a net change mechanism is in place for a CRM application that will send an account change to an ERP application for processing. If ERP receives a change from CRM, and ERP's net change mechanism has no way to ignore that change, the change initiated in CRM will be bounced back and processed against CRM. If CRM also has no way to ignore changes from ERP, the change would be trapped in an endless loop. Bounce-back prevention depends on the ability to ignore any changes created by the integration process.

▶ **Real-time processing:** Many integration processes require that changes be processed within seconds or minutes. This is particularly important when the business users require minimal latency in synchronized data or where time-sensitive business processes are involved.

▶ **Transaction sequencing:** Business processes across multiple applications often involve dependency across multiple transactions, where the sequence in which the transactions are processed is critical. Take the example of order processing between a CRM and ERP application. Let's say a user within the CRM application creates an order for a new customer. To process that order in the ERP application, a customer record must first be created in ERP before the order can be processed. CRM will need to publish both the new customer transaction and the order transaction to ERP. Ensuring the proper sequencing of these transactions avoids unnecessary errors and minimizes "retry" processing.

▶ **On-demand application support:** On-demand or Software as a Service (SaaS) applications by design do not allow access to the database layer, thereby limiting options for establishing net change mechanisms. Many on-demand application providers impose limits on the number of information requests each customer may make within a time period, thereby placing a premium on highly efficient processing.

▶ **Delete support:** Certain design patterns provide little or no support for capturing the deletion of records.

▶ **Guaranteed message delivery:** Just publishing a changed record or business transaction is not enough. Mechanisms need to be built in to the end-to-end integration process to ensure that all records are processed fully.

▶ **Multicast support:** Many integration processes involve more than two applications. In these cases, changed records or transactions may need to be published and processed against two or more applications.

The remainder of this chapter discusses four common net changes patterns used in integration processes today. Note that this is not an exhaustive list; these are just the more prevalent approaches. These four patterns are as follows:

▶ **Pattern 1:** Application publisher

▶ **Pattern 2:** Modified flag

▶ **Pattern 3:** Modified date/timestamp

▶ **Pattern 4:** Snapshot comparison

Pattern 1: Application Publisher

This pattern leverages functionality available within the source application to proactively publish changes based on the occurrence of a specific event within the source application. The application publisher approach generally leverages workflow capabilities within the application, and in many ways can behave similarly to database triggers, yet function at the application level.

Figure 17.14 shows a typical application publisher scenario.

Whereas Microsoft Dynamics CRM supports notifications, most application architectures do not support this capability. Therefore, the cases where this pattern can be applied are limited. However, when available, this pattern combines the best real-time support with

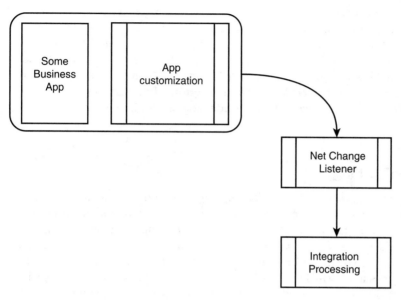

FIGURE 17.14 Typical application publisher scenario.

the greatest efficiency because an action is initiated only in the event of a specified data change or application event.

Pattern 1 Pros

▶ Provides real-time, event-driven notification of changes. There is no polling burden or overhead cost to either the application or database server.

▶ Usually supports deletes.

▶ Normally a highly reliable method with little chance of overlooking data changes or events.

Pattern 1 Cons

▶ Requires special application- and adapter-specific publisher support. This capability can be used only if the application architecture provides a change notification or call-out capability. Most application architectures do not support or provide change notification or call-out capability. The trend within the application industry is toward adding publisher mechanisms, particularly in the on-demand market given the pressure to limit the number of calls that each customer can make against his or her application instance within a 24-hour period.

▶ This pattern may not support filtering by user to prevent bounce-back.

Pattern 1 Implementation Tips

Changes tend to be queued in the order in which they occur, but this is not guaranteed. You might need to design your integration processes to handle out-of-sequence messages, including building in retry mechanisms to account for the potential of out-of-sequence messages.

17

If you are trying to send header/line-item (or master/detail) changes together, you will need to determine whether required line-item changes will always trigger a header notification. If not, account for notification of line-item changes, too. You might be able to configure both header/line-item and line-item-only changes to return messages with the same structure. The preferred method for capturing header/line-item changes is to wait for a specific user-requested action (like clicking a Submit button). This will prevent the system from sending multiple messages when a header and several line-items are entered or modified.

Pattern 2: Modified Flag

This pattern enables the tracking of changes by toggling off and on a synchronized flag or field; off when a change is made to the data in the source application, and on when the change has been processed against the target application. This approach depends on application (or source system) logic to toggle the synchronized flag off whenever a change is made (see Figure 17.15). The most common way to enable this synchronized flag is by creating database triggers and a shadow table within the source application database to perform this function. Triggers are added to each application base table for which you need to track changes. The triggers add or update a record in the shadow table to track the change.

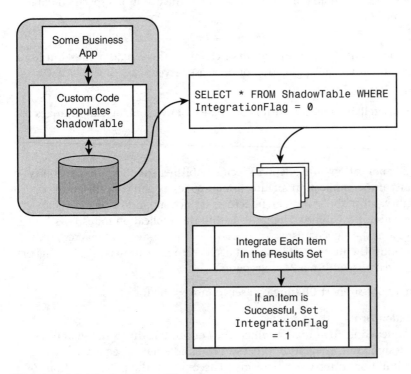

FIGURE 17.15   Typical modified flag scenario.

The most efficient way to implement this pattern is to create one shadow table that tracks changes to records in multiple application tables by using a combination of an object (table) name field and the object key (record primary key). If the base table uses a compound primary key, the fields may be concatenated in the shadow table object key field. The shadow table record and the base table record have a one-to-one relationship. When a base table record is created, the shadow table record is also created. After that, when the base table record is updated or deleted, the corresponding shadow table record is updated. To synchronize changes to another system, a query can be executed that joins the shadow table to the base tables to get all the current field values. The shadow table may contain multiple synchronization status fields that toggle back and forth when a record is modified and when it is processed against the target application.

Pattern 2 Pros

▶ Supports deletes by keeping the shadow table record after the base table record is deleted.

▶ Supports two-way integrations and prevents bounce-back by including a reliable ignore-user mechanism, further explained later.

▶ Supports multicast of changes by providing multiple synchronization status fields.

▶ A retry mechanism is inherent because records are not toggled as synchronized until successfully processed against the target application. This pattern doesn't require separate rejected row tables and integration processes.

Pattern 2 Cons

▶ If the application cannot be configured to toggle a field value on every insert and update, database engine triggers will probably be required. To do this, the database engine must support triggers.

▶ The database trigger approach requires detailed knowledge of the physical database schema to develop the script and triggers. Also knowledge of trigger coding is required.

▶ This approach is a polling mechanism that is inherently inefficient because the query process will execute whether there are source changes or not.

▶ If you are using the trigger and shadow table approach, a direct connection to the database is required.

▶ Triggers can be affected or dropped when an application upgrade is performed. The trigger script must be saved so that it can be reapplied if this happens.

Pattern 2 Implementation Tips

Application logic or trigger code should be designed to ignore the change (don't toggle the synchronize flag) if the change was applied by a specified "integration user."

You may build a retry timeout into your source query. This retry timeout can be configured to stop after greater than x minutes by comparing a record modified date/timestamp to the current time minus x minutes.

Pattern 3: Modified Date/Timestamp

This pattern uses a modified date/timestamp field in the base table or object to identify records that have been changed. When a record in the source application is added or changed, the date/timestamp is updated to reflect the time of the modification. A query can be run against the source database to return records that have been updated since the last time the query was executed. The query requires a "bind variable" of the source system time at the time of last execution to identify the changed records.

Figure 17.16 outlines a typical modified date/timestamp scenario.

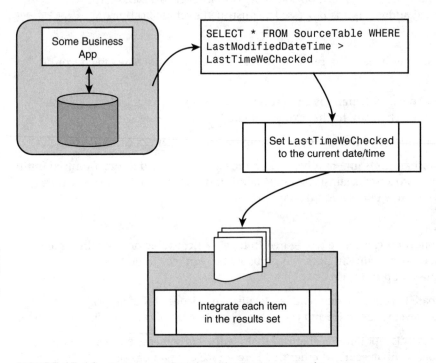

FIGURE 17.16   Typical modified date/timestamp scenario.

Date/timestamp fields are quite common elements of an application's database design today. If your application table does not have a modified date/time field, you may be able to add one, but this will generally require application modifications, database triggers, or both.

Make sure the date/timestamp includes time information (not just date).

This pattern is subject to a few different reliability problems (outlined later). If the synchronization will be done only one way, one of the issues is avoided. Integrations that use a modified date/timestamp are therefore best suited for one-way environments (and not two way).

Pattern 3 Pros

▶ Supports multicast of changes to multiple systems, because the bind variables can be tracked independently for multiple source queries. Each of the distinct integration processes must maintain the date and time of its last query execution.

▶ Setup is simple if the application tables already include a modified date/time field.

▶ This pattern can be used with any application API, or data source that supports filtered queries, without requiring a direct connection to the SQL database. This makes this pattern generally useful in on-demand application environments.

Pattern 3 Cons

▶ This pattern might not be completely reliable for two-way synchronization processes. To prevent bounce-back, an "ignore user" filter needs to be implemented. Many applications that have a modified date/timestamp often include a ModifiedBy or ModifiedUser field, too. This field can be used to ignore updates that bounce back but can result in missed updates. When one user makes a change, and the "ignore user" filter changes the same record before the source query detects the change, the first change is ignored.

▶ This method presents significant challenges with clock synchronization if the ModifiedDate field is not set using the clock of the source database server (or application server, if appropriate).

▶ This pattern requires you to build additional functionality to support retry of rejected records against the target application.

▶ This pattern typically does not support deletes. If the application performs "soft deletes," deletes may be accessible. However, deletes can be unreliable in this case because the cleanup of soft deletes is usually unpredictable.

▶ Source queries can get complex if you are tracking changes on parents and children together (joining them as one result set). In this case, the modified stamps on the parent and child records need to be checked.

Pattern 3 Implementation Tips

Integration processes that use this pattern must include a mechanism to capture records that are not successfully processed against the target application for retry. This can be accomplished by either processing records through a message queue or maintaining a rejected row table or file.

Be sure the Modified field includes both date and time. (If only the date is available, the frequency of synchronizations cannot be greater than daily.)

Be sure the Modified field is database (or application) server-based. Sometimes the modified stamp field will be set using the clock on the network client computer, and this will cause significant problems when changes are made by clients with clocks that are out of sync. If the application supports remote or intermittent synchronization of laptops, sometimes the modified stamp field is the time entered or modified on the remote laptop. To capture changes accurately and reliably, this field must be set using the server clock.

17

> **NOTE**
>
> Microsoft Dynamics CRM data timestamps are coordinated universal time (UTC) based.

Your source query relies on maintaining the date of the last time the query was run. Right before executing your query, get the date/time from the same database or application server clock used to set the modified date/time for use in your next query.

For better performance, be sure that the modified date/time field is an indexed field within the database. If it is not indexed individually, but only as part of a multisegment index, make sure it is the first segment (in at least one index).

If you are implementing a two-way synchronization, investigate whether the updating of the modified stamp field can be suppressed for changes coming from other applications. If so, a ModifiedBy field is not required to prevent bounce-back, and the missed updates problem will be eliminated.

If capturing changes to parent and children records together (header and line items), check to see whether all child required record changes result in a change to the parent modified stamp. If so, the parent stamp can be used exclusively.

Pattern 4: Snapshot Comparison

This pattern uses an exact replica of the source application's data set to identify changed records. By comparing a copy made at point A in time with the latest source data at point B in time, changes between point B and point A can be identified (see Figure 17.17). This process needs to compare all source data row by row and field by field, to identify new, modified, and deleted records. After those changes have been identified, a new replicated copy of the source data is made to be used as the point of comparison for the next time the process is run.

This pattern can be used by querying the source data directly, or by processing data that has been exported to a file or staging table.

Pattern 4 Pros

▶ This pattern can be used with almost any data source. Special system and application requirements are minimal. This approach works equally well when accessing source data directly and when processing an extracted copy of the source data.

▶ This pattern can be used with any application API or data source that supports ordered queries and does not require a direct connection to a SQL database. If the data source does not support ordered queries, the data must have been presorted.

▶ This pattern is not prone to the missed update problem that can occur when filtering on user to avoid bounce-backs.

▶ Supports reliable delete detection.

▶ Processing can be timed or sequenced to prevent dependent record sequencing issues.

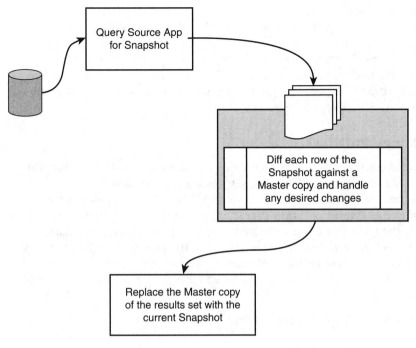

FIGURE 17.17   Typical snapshot comparison scenario.

▶ If a change is made to a source field that is not included in the integration, no processing is performed. This reduces the number of no-change messages that are processed, and thus reduces the potential for update conflicts.

▶ Header and line-item records can be grouped together into one message (and one comparison) to detect any changes to the group, and generate a single header and line-item message or transaction.

▶ This mechanism is reliable and ensures that no changes are missed.

Pattern 4 Cons

▶ This approach can be complex to create, involving significant coding.

▶ This approach is an inefficient way to detect changes and can take many minutes of processing to find just a few changes.

▶ Because of the long time required to process all source records, the frequency support is low (usually only daily).

▶ This pattern does not include any mechanism to prevent bounce-back. Therefore, all changes originating in the target system will make a complete cycle back to the target system. However, the cycle will end there, even if this same net change pattern is used to synchronize changes from the target system. The bounce-back messages can cause update conflict issues when competing changes happen in a short time frame and in a specific sequence.

Pattern 4 implementation Tips

The processing time required, and the inefficiency of this approach, is determined by the number of records in the source and the percentage of records that typically change within the scheduled time. To maximize the efficiency of this process, this pattern requires that the source result set be ordered by a unique key field (or set of fields). The snapshot data can then be retrieved from the shadow tables in the same order, and the result sets are traversed in lockstep.

Which Net Change Pattern?

The best net change for any project is determined by a number of factors, including the overall integration requirements, available skill sets within the company's IT organization, and the limitation imposed by the applications involved. Table 17.2 summarizes the four patterns discussed in this chapter and how they stack up against the key design considerations, with 5 being the most and 1 being the least. In most real-time, bidirectional integration scenarios, the application publisher pattern is clearly the preferred method but may not be useful given that very few applications support these capabilities today. Support for this pattern is growing within contemporary, packaged business applications and should be strongly considered if it is available.

Table 17.2 outlines key net change considerations.

TABLE 17.2   Key Net Change Considerations

Key Considerations	Pattern 1: Application Publisher	Pattern 2: Modified Flag	Pattern 3: Modified Date/Timestamp	Pattern 4: Snapshot Comparison
Efficiency	5	3	3	1
Reliability	5*	4	2	3
Bounce-back prevention	5*	5	3*	1
Real-time processing	5	3	3	1
Transaction sequencing	3	3	2	4
On-demand support	5*	1	3	3
Delete support	5*	3	1	5
Guaranteed delivery	5**	5**	3**	3
Multicast support	5	4	5	2

Limited by the functionality of the source application or database.
**Using message queues significantly enhances capabilities.*

Summary

This chapter covered methodologies and approaches available when using Scribe integration components (specifically migration, synchronization, and process integration options).

We reviewed both the main features of Scribe Workbench and Console, and worked through a number of integration and migration examples. Then, we covered the key concept of net change (and looked at several examples).

It is important to note that this chapter illustrated the high-level components of data integration (both in approach and concept) but is by no means exhaustive, and your specific business needs may well exceed what is outlined here.

17

The Role of Templates in the Scribe Solution

Templates represent a starting point toward creating an integration solution and play a major role within Scribe. The template model is based on the premise that although each integration problem is different, many customers will require similar integration needs as some part of the integration solution. Therefore, templates maximize reuse by allowing integration solution designers to capture core integration needs into a reusable starting point.

Templates should be designed to balance both breadth and depth. If you are consistently solving the same integration problem over and over, that is a good candidate for a template solution. On the other hand, if you find that you are continuously removing or reworking parts of a template to redo at each client, you should consider how that part of the template is implemented.

Introduction to Templates

Scribe does have many free templates available for download, many of which leverage the full set of tools available in Scribe outlined in the preceding chapter. Templates can be created by anyone, however, and the process of doing so is really not that much different from creating integrations, as described in Chapter 16, "Scribe Integration."

Templates in Scribe can consolidate all parts of the integration solution that work together (integration definitions, data views, monitors, publishers, and so on) to enable integration between two applications. Many Scribe consultants use the import/export utility (as described later in this chapter) to move an integration solution from one server to another at a specific client. For example, when moving from a test server to a production server, many Scribe consultants create a "template" that contains all the various parts of the integration solution. Importing that "template" will redeploy the solution on a brand new system. Although not necessarily conforming to the "maximize reuse" message of templates, this is an efficient use of the tool to automate what could be a large manual process.

After all these various Scribe items that are going to be included in the template have been created, you can engage the Scribe Import/Export utility, via Scribe Console, Import/Export (see Figure 18.1).

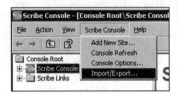

FIGURE 18.1   Import/Export from the Scribe Console menu item.

This utility asks which items you want to include in the template (for example, which integration definitions, data views, monitors, publishers). In addition, you can choose to non-Scribe items (such as text files on your file system). The utility then creates a single file that includes all the selected items and a list of the various connections that are required to support the selected items. This file can be easily transported/downloaded and "imported" on a system.

Implementing Templates

If creating a template involves "exporting," then implementing a template involves "importing" the template. You can initiate the import by double-clicking the exported file or using the same Scribe Import/Export utility you used to create the template (Scribe Console, Import/Export).

The import process prompts you for connection information between the two applications (among other things) and then deploys the various parts throughout the Scribe system. Any non-Scribe items (such as text files) are copied into the relative location they were exported from.

To run the Import Wizard, complete the following steps:

1. Select the Import option from the first screen of this wizard, as shown in Figure 18.2.
2. Browse to the template file (*.spkz extension), as shown in Figure 18.3. The Backup option on this screen enables you to create a copy of this template. Because templates are meant to be customized, this second copy can be used to revert parts

of the template (so that if a customization did not go the way you intended, you don't have to reimport the whole template and start over).

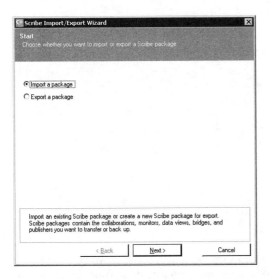

FIGURE 18.2   Import Wizard.

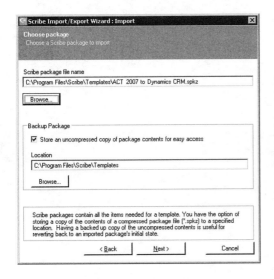

FIGURE 18.3   Choose a package.

3. Select which parts of the template you want to import (you may only want the DTS files or just the data views), as shown in Figure 18.4. By default, all artifacts of the template are selected to be imported.

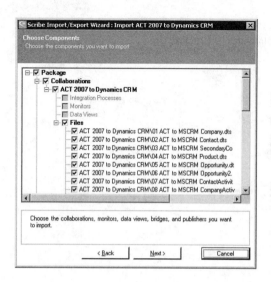

FIGURE 18.4   Choose components.

4. Acknowledge any missing prerequisites (for example, if you are importing a template for MS CRM to MS NAV, you will probably want the Scribe NAV adapter installed), as shown in Figure 18.5.

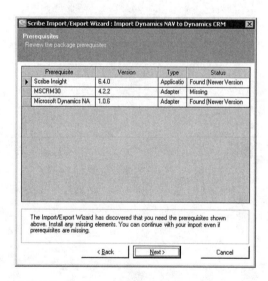

FIGURE 18.5   Package prerequisites.

5. Define required connections, as shown in Figure 18.6. For example, the MS NAV to MS CRM template has DTS files that require a connection to MS NAV and MS CRM. It is at this point that you define your connections to each application. Scribe often includes "hints" as to what this connection is for in the Name column. (For example

if there is an additional connection to SQL Server for whatever reason, it will give additional information as to the purpose of that connection.)

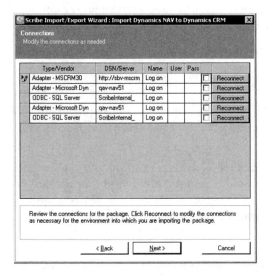

FIGURE 18.6   Define the required connections.

Although the username and password information is not required at this point in time, if you opt to not supply the username and password information during "import," you will be prompted for this information at the time you open a DTS and the connection information is missing. This goes for publishers, views, and other parts of the template that require connection information.

6. Click the Commit button on the final screen to perform the import.

More often than not, however, the import of the template is only the first step in solving the integration problem. If the customer has customized either of the applications the template was designed to support, the template will most likely need to be modified to accommodate this customization.

Customizations

Once deployed, a template is meant to be changed to meet the unique needs of each different customer, which is why they are referred to as templates versus solutions unto themselves. For templates created and deployed by Scribe, the goal is to get the two out-of-the-box systems communicating, leaving any customizations to either application to be accommodated by the implementing consultant.

Customizations for the template can be as varied as types of customizations that one can do to one of the applications supported by the template. Common examples include adding custom fields to integration points already supported by the template, changing the frequency at which polls are taken to look for net change, and even adding additional integration points that the template does not offer.

See Chapter 16 for more information about how to perform these customizations.

Go-Live Pipeline

Deploying an integration solution often has three stages to it: a preparation phase, an initial synchronization of data between the discrete systems, and a test run of the real-time portion of the solution.

If you are basing your solution on a Scribe-created template, you can find information about performing both of these stages in the template Help (usually found near the end of the chapter titled "Implementing the Template"). However, if you have grown your own solution, these stages are outlined here (albeit more generically).

Preparation

When getting ready to deploy and stabilize the integration solution, you should attend to a few things (depending on your integration needs and the business applications involved) before running integrations:

▶ Ensure consistent use of codes (currency codes, country codes, price lists, and so forth) between the systems involved. These are usually few in number and can often be manually modified/added to systems (instead of creating an integration to handle this). You should work with the application users for this (so that they understand the new codes and can validate that changing any existing codes will not break reports or processes they currently have in place).

▶ If using time-based triggers, be sure to set the default date-/timestamp. For instance, if you are using a Query-based publisher, the filter will (usually) be tied to a time-stamp variable. You need to ensure that timestamp has the correct value before running your integrations for the first time.

NOTE

If you did not develop the solution on the production system (best practice is to use a development or test server), be sure to make any changes to the production applications required for your integration to run. For Microsoft CRM, you may need to enable integration mode (which is a Registry hack for Microsoft CRM v4.x and earlier) so that CRM users can submit orders to a back-office system. Note that you can start and stop integration mode in Microsoft Dynamics CRM 4.x by running the following DTS files:

EnableIntegrationMode.dts (starts integration mode)

DisableIntegrationMode.dts (stops integration mode)

These files are installed in C:\Program Files\Scribe\Samples\MicrosoftDynamicsCRM.

Initial Synchronization

The initial sync is mainly a migration event. Before actually executing, you need to understand the entities that your solution has dependencies on. (For example, if your integration solution synchronizes customers, you may need currency codes in both systems to match.) Once you have a list of these entities and have ensured that they are consistent between the systems in question, the sync event itself is much like a data migration.

Often the sync event involves many hundreds if not thousands (or tens of thousands) of rows. Therefore, Scribe recommends using the Rejected Source Rows feature of the Scribe Workbench (outlined in the preceding chapter) to make debugging/resolving failed records easier.

Upon completion of the initial synchronizations, Scribe recommends that you have the application users review the synchronization before putting the real-time elements of the solution into place.

> **NOTE**
>
> Each Scribe-created integration template has different initial synchronization steps, and the template Help outlines these steps. These steps vary based on which integration template you are using.

Test Run

When the initial synchronization is complete, you can start deploying the real-time elements of your integration solution. To do that, Scribe recommends enabling each step of the integration process/pipeline individually to confirm each step is working before enabling the next step. This approach should be done for each integration process used by the solution.

This example extends the examples you worked with in Chapter 17, "Scribe Integration Components":

1. Pause both the Microsoft CRM publisher and integration process you created in the preceding chapter, as shown in Figure 18.7.

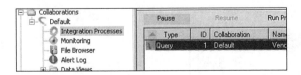

FIGURE 18.7   Paused integration process.

2. Create an account in Microsoft CRM. After a pause (no longer than a minute or two), you should have an MSMQ message in the applicable PubIn queue similar to the one shown in Figure 18.8.

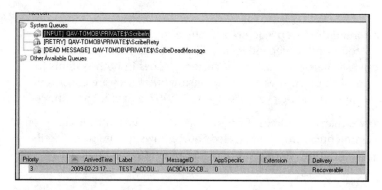

FIGURE 18.8   Message in the Scribeln queue (message shown at the bottom of the figure).

If you don't see a message in the PubIn queue:

a. Check that the Scribe CRM adapter plug-in publisher (or workflow, depending on the version of CRM you are using) is installed and configured.

Or

b. From the CRM server, send a message to the PubIn queue outside of Scribe. (A utility in the Scribe Install folder called TestMessageQueueUtility.exe enables you to do this; you can copy this EXE to your CRM server and use it to send a test message to a message queue.) To use this utility, specify the target queue and click the Send Test Message button. You should see a simple test message in the target queue.

3. Once the message is visible in the PubIn queue, resume the Microsoft CRM publisher. You should see that message disappear from the PubIn queue and a related message show up in the ScribeIn queue.

If the message doesn't leave the PubIn queue:

a. Make sure you resumed the correct Microsoft CRM publisher. Clicking the Settings button (as shown in Figure 18.9) on step 4 of the publisher properties view will show the connection settings in use by the selected publisher.

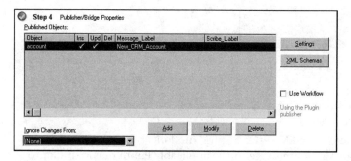

FIGURE 18.9   Publisher/bridge properties.

b. On this connection dialog, double-check the MSMQ names at the bottom of the connection dialog.

> **NOTE**
>
> If you don't see the message show up in the Scribeln queue:
>
> a. Check to see whether the message moved to the ScribeDeadMessage queue. If it did, you probably have another integration process that is not paused and is catching the message. (As explained previously, all integration processes monitor the same Scribeln queue.) To remedy this, change the event settings of the active integration process so that it filters on something unique in step 3 of the Integration Process Configuration screen, as shown in Figure 18.10.

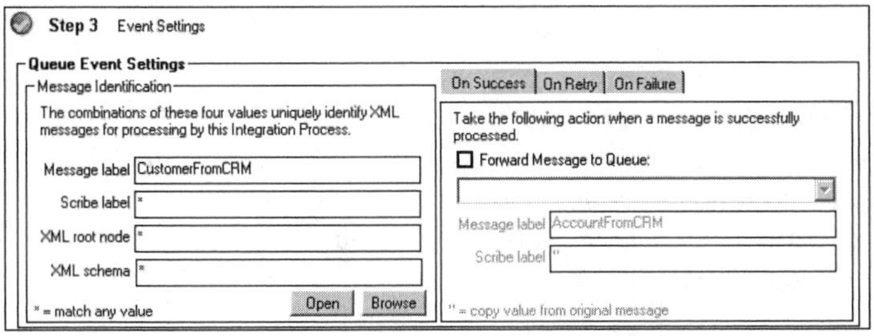

FIGURE 18.10   Event settings.

b. Check to see whether the message went into the PubFailed queue. If it did, the body of the message in the PubFailed queue will outline why it failed. You review contents of a message by double-clicking the message in the Scribe Console, as shown in Figure 18.11.

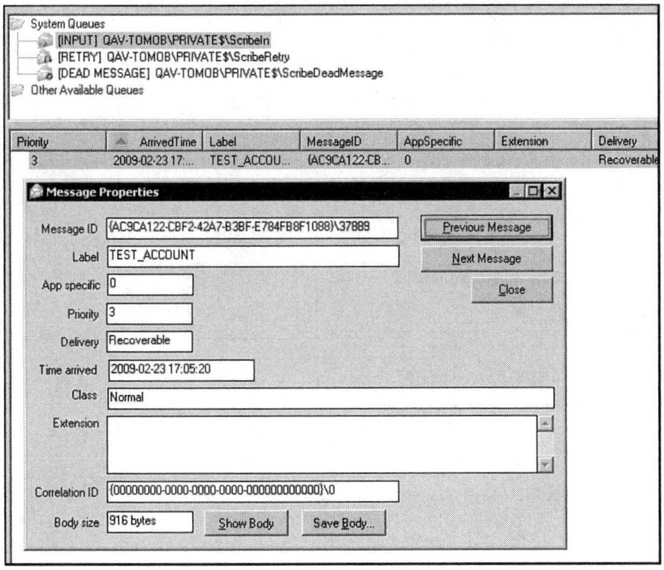

FIGURE 18.11   Message properties of a failed message in the queue.

4. Once the message is in the ScribeIn queue, enable the integration process associated with this integration. You should see the message disappear and the associated DTS run. Once completed, there will be an entry in the execution log (under the Administration node in the Scribe Console), as shown in Figure 18.12.

If the integration did not run:

Check the execution log. The integration may have failed to run for some reason (and the log entry will give you additional information).

5. Have users of the target system validate that the integration meets their needs. Having the target system owners' review will often uncover previously undefined use cases, which may or may not affect the integration solution.

Tips and Tricks

▶ Use monitors to alert when messages go in PubFailed and other queues. Scribe will divert messages to PubFailed or ScribeFailed queues when appropriate. Associate a monitor with these queues so that someone is notified in these cases (you can automatically notify someone by associating a recipient group or name in step 3 of the monitor properties dialog), as shown in Figure 18.13.

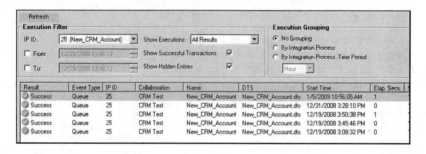

FIGURE 18.12   Execution log.

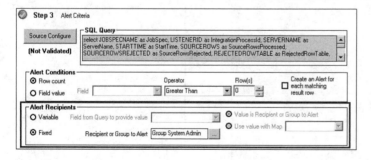

FIGURE 18.13   Alert criteria.

▶ Use source field and target field properties to ensure you are mapped to the correct field. When creating an integration in the Scribe Workbench, it isn't always obvious which fields in the Workbench represent a specific field in the source/target application. You can use the target field properties to cross reference the "label" of a CRM field, as shown in the Workbench for the label in the CRM user interface. The CRM field label can be found by right-clicking a field and selecting Field Properties (see Figure 18.14).

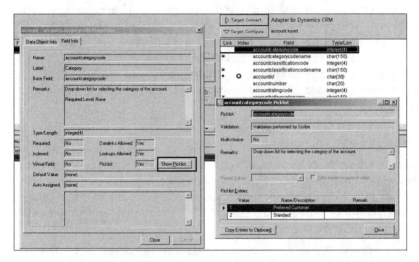

FIGURE 18.14 Field properties. The values shown on the right are the values from the drop-down list.

▶ If the CRM field is a drop-down list, you can cross reference the drop-down list values on the Field Properties dialog, too. Clicking the Show Picklist button will list the name-value pairs for the drop-down list. To accommodate internationalization scenarios, it is best to use the numeric "value" versus the text "name" of the pair.

▶ Figure 18.15 shows the corresponding value in Microsoft Dynamics CRM.

FIGURE 18.15 Microsoft Dynamics CRM Category drop-down.

▶ Use the Test dialog. To verify that you are using the appropriate source fields and any functions you may have used, you can use the Test window in the Scribe Workbench. This will show the source value, the ultimate value pushed to the target (including

18

the formula associated with the link), and the step control flow for the particular integration document (so that you can review what step control logic path was traveled based on how you configured the step control for the target application).

▶ Create custom functions or use Scribe variables to encapsulate complex logic. When linking between source and target in the Scribe Workbench, you may be required to create a relatively complex formula to represent the data transformation between two systems. Although you could do this in the formula on the link itself, the formula would be executed each invocation of the mapping logic (for example, each source row to target). Alternatively, you should create a compiled function in Visual Basic 6.0 *or* use a calculated variable in Scribe. Using a calculated variable will allow you to reuse the complex formula without having to re-create it; and creating the function in VB will bring greater flexibility to your approach and will have the added benefit of being compiled rather than interpreted (thereby having a marginal increase in performance).

 ▶ A document in the %SCRIBE%\Samples\VBFunctions\ folder outlines how to create and register VB 6.0 functions.

▶ Extend fuzzy logic. A few "fuzzy" logic type functions that ship with Scribe enable you to avoid creating duplicate entries For example, source data collected from various places may refer to the same logical organization as The Jones Group, Inc., The Jones Group, and Jones Group (and so on). As they are shown here, they would be integrated as three different organizations.

 ▶ By using the STRIPCOMPANY([...]) formula, you can strip out some of the extraneous parts of this (for example, the "The" and ", Inc." if they exist) to remove some of these duplicates. Furthermore, you can extend the behavior of the STRIPCOMPANY([...]) function by adding rows in the STRIPCOMPANY table in the SCRIBEINTERNAL database. You can add/modify the behavior of this function to suit any specific needs you have.

▶ Periodically purge the execution log and alert log. Over time, these logs can grow fairly large. You can periodically run a SQL script that ships with the Scribe product (%SCRIBE%\ScribeMaintenance.sql) to purge older entries. The SQL script enables you to define the term (for example, how long you want to keep entries around).

 ▶ This script can be run manually, or you can set up a SQL job to run it periodically.

Scribe Templates

Scribe has a few templates specific to Microsoft Dynamics CRM. The most popular templates include the following:

▶ Scribe ERP to Microsoft Dynamics CRM

▶ Microsoft Dynamics GP to Microsoft Dynamics CRM

▶ Microsoft Dynamics NAV to Microsoft Dynamics CRM

Scribe ERP to Microsoft Dynamics CRM

The Scribe ERP (Enterprise Resource Planning) to Microsoft Dynamics CRM template provides a working integration between the ScribeERP sample application and Microsoft Dynamics CRM that integrates customer, product, order, and invoice data.

The template can be used for demonstration purposes or as a framework for building an integration between Microsoft Dynamics CRM and another ERP system.

You can create a simple working integration by using the sample elements and then modifying them as necessary to work with your target application. After using the sample application to build and test your framework, you can strip out the ScribeERP sample elements and swap in your target ERP application.

To use this framework, you can strip out the ScribeERP application and swap in a different ERP application. You need to create two components to make the new integration work. One component needs to capture the changes in the ERP application to put them into a message queue where Scribe will integrate that data with Microsoft Dynamics CRM. The other component needs to take changes from Microsoft Dynamics CRM that Scribe provides as XML messages and put them into the ERP system.

Information about swapping another ERP system for the ScribeERP is provided as you create your integration.

The goals of this template are as follows:

1. Provide the interactive ERP user with order and invoice history for customers.
2. Enable users to create and submit orders that originate in Microsoft Dynamics CRM.
3. Provide for the creation of reports that key off of the relationship between products ordered or invoiced and customers. By extension, this supports reporting on product purchase trends and detail by items related to account such as region/territory and sales representative.
4. Provide business activity monitors that notify key business users of events related to their customers' purchases of the company's products (for example, orders over certain dollar value, orders shipping late).
5. Keep customer data in sync.
6. Synchronize the master products in the ERP system into Microsoft Dynamics CRM.

To support these objectives, the template provides two-way data integration from ScribeERP to Microsoft Dynamics CRM for the touch points listed in Table 18.1.

Process Flow

The template is designed to support the following business processes and flow of data between the ERP system and Microsoft Dynamics CRM (see Figure 18.16). The framework is in place for you to use this as a starting point for building an integration with another ERP system. With a new integration, the business processes and the data flow supported depends on the capability of your ERP system and your ability to adapt this template for your purposes.

TABLE 18.1   ScribeERP to Microsoft Dynamics CRM Integration Touch Points

ScribeERP Object	Microsoft Dynamics CRM Object
Customer + primary address	Account + primary address
Address	Customer address, contact
Order + items	Order + products (existing, write-in)
Invoice + items	Invoice + products (existing, write-in)
Product, price lists/levels	Product + price list item

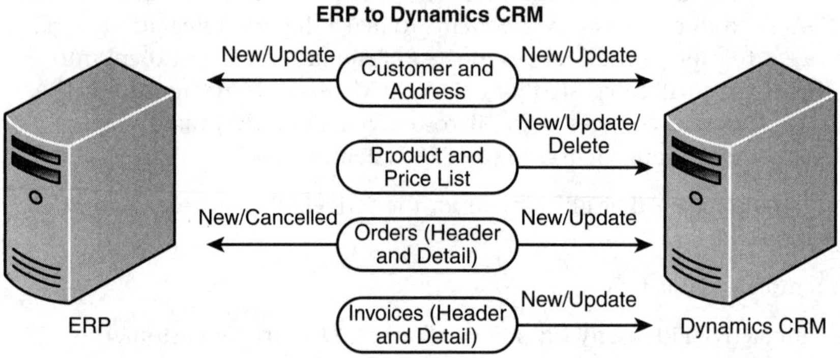

FIGURE 18.16   Process flow.

▶ **Customer and address:** This data can be created or modified in either the ERP system or Microsoft Dynamics CRM (except for certain fields owned by a system, such as credit limit or credit authorization), and the additions or changes will be synchronized with the other application. The company matching components provide fuzzy account matching to avoid the creation of duplicate accounts and to facilitate an initial synchronization of the existing ERP and CRM environments.

▶ **Items and price list (master product schedule):** This data is mastered in the ERP system and replicated to Microsoft Dynamics CRM to support the order process needs in Microsoft Dynamics CRM.

▶ **Orders:** Orders are created in Microsoft Dynamics CRM and may be modified in Microsoft Dynamics CRM until that order is submitted to the ERP system. Updated information about the order is provided to Microsoft Dynamics CRM from the ERP system. Orders that originate in the ERP system are provided to Microsoft Dynamics CRM in a submitted state. Orders that are canceled in Microsoft Dynamics CRM are voided in the ERP system and vice versa. Transferred orders in the ERP system are also included.

▶ **Invoices:** Invoices are created in the ERP system and replicated to Microsoft Dynamics CRM. Updates can only be made from the ERP system. Posted invoices in the ERP system are also included.

ERP to CRM Integration Processes
Integration processes automate the processing of the DTS files by detecting events such as a message in a queue, the results of a query, a file placed in a folder, or a specific time. The events are the trigger for the integration process to run its associated DTS file.

Some integration processes in this template are set up to forward the message back into the ScribeIn message queue with a different message label so that the message can be processed by another integration process. This technique enables an integration designer to trigger multiple integrations off of one event. For example, when an order is created in CRM, a message is added to the ScribeIn queue and routed to a DTS, which circles back to CRM to ensure that the account associated with the order exists in the ERP system. When that is completed, the same message is then resubmitted back into the ScribeIn queue with a different message label. This second message label causes the message to be routed to a different DTS, which actually integrates the relevant order data into the ERP system.

TABLE 18.2   DTS Components

Component	Purpose
AccountToCRM	Runs AccountToCRM.dts
AddressToCRM	Runs AddressToCRM.dts
InvoiceToCRM	Runs InvoiceToCRM.dts
OrderToCRM	Runs OrderToCRM.dts
ProductToCRM	Runs ProductToCRM.dts

CRM to ERP Integration Processes
The integration processes automate the processing of the DTS files.

TABLE 18.3   DTS Components

Component	Purpose
AccountToERP	Runs AccountToERP.dts
AddressToERP	Runs AddressToERP.dts
CascadeAccountToERP	Runs CascadeAccountToERP.dts, forwards message to OrderToERP
CascadeAddressesToERP	Runs CascadeAddressesToERP.dts
OrderToERP	Runs OrderToERP.dts, forwards message to OrderToERP_Result
OrderToERP_Cancel	Runs OrderToERP_Cancel.dts, forwards message to OrderToERP_Result
OrderToERP_Result	Runs OrderToERP_Result.dts

18

DTS Files

The DTS files contain the field mappings, data transformation formulas, and data processing rules used to integrate data from the source to the target. Table 18.4 lists the DTS files used in the template.

TABLE 18.4 DTS Components

Component	Purpose
AccountToCRM.dts	Sends new and updated customers from ScribeERP to Microsoft Dynamics CRM.
AccountToERP.dts	Sends new and updated customers from Microsoft Dynamics CRM to ScribeERP.
AddressToCRM.dts	Sends new and updated addresses from ScribeERP to Microsoft Dynamics CRM.
AddressToERP.dts	Sends new and updated addresses from Microsoft Dynamics CRM to ScribeERP.
CascadeAccountToERP.dts	Triggered when an order is submitted. Its purpose is to make sure that the account is shared between Microsoft Dynamics CRM and ScribeERP. If the account is not shared, it updates the type to customer in Microsoft Dynamics CRM, causing the account to be sent.
CascadeAddressesToERP.dts	Touches all the addresses in Microsoft Dynamics CRM for a newly shared account. This causes all the addresses to be sent to ScribeERP.
InvoiceToCRM.dts	Sends all invoices (including posted) from ScribeERP to Microsoft Dynamics CRM.
OrderToCRM.dts	Sends all orders (including transferred orders) from ScribeERP to Microsoft Dynamics CRM.
OrderToERP.dts	Sends submitted orders from Microsoft Dynamics CRM to ScribeERP.
OrderToERP_Cancel	Sends a request to cancel/void an order from Microsoft Dynamics CRM to ScribeERP.
OrderToERP_Result.dts	Updates CRM with the results of an order submit or cancel. Sets the submit status description and the last submitted date.
ProductToCRM.dts	Sends new and updated products from ScribeERP to Microsoft Dynamics CRM.

Publishers

The publishers are responsible for gathering changes in the ScribeERP and Microsoft Dynamics CRM systems and publishing those changes as XML messages in the ScribeIn message queue (see Table 18.5).

TABLE 18.5   Publishers

Component	Purpose
Dynamics CRM	Interacts with callout mechanism on Microsoft Dynamics CRM server to track changes to accounts, addresses, and sales orders. Publishes these changes as XML messages in the ScribeIn message queue.
AccountFromERP_UpdateSource	Collects ScribeERP customer changes from the Scribe shadow table and publishes them as XML messages in the ScribeIn message queue.
AddressFromERP_UpdateSource	Collects ScribeERP address changes from the Scribe shadow table and publishes them as XML messages in the ScribeIn message queue.
InvoiceFromERP_UpdateSource	Collects ScribeERP invoice changes from the Scribe shadow table and publishes them as XML messages in the ScribeIn message queue.
ProductDeleteFromERP_UpdateSource	Collects ScribeERP deleted products from the Scribe shadow table and publishes them as XML messages in the ScribeIn message queue.
ProductFromERP_UpdateSource	Collects ScribeERP product changes from the Scribe shadow table and publishes them as XML messages in the ScribeIn message queue.
SalesOrderFromERP_UpdateSource	Collects ScribeERP sales order changes from the Scribe shadow table and publishes them as XML messages in the ScribeIn message queue.

Order-History Monitors

The order-history monitors create alerts based on business activity in the Microsoft Dynamics CRM database. When you add alert recipients to the Sales Managers group, these alerts can be sent to individuals by the Scribe Insight server (see Table 18.6).

TABLE 18.6   Order-History Monitors

Component	Purpose	Notification
Accounts Placed on Credit Hold	Raises an alert to the account manager with a list of any accounts updated that day and on credit hold	MSCRMUsers recipient map
Accounts with No Recent Orders	Raises an alert with a list of accounts that have not placed an order within 30 days	Sales Managers recipient group
Large Orders	Alerts when an order with a total amount > $25,000 is entered or modified	Sales Managers recipient group
New Order from Preferred Customer	Alerts when an order from a preferred customer is entered or modified	Sales Managers recipient group

18

TABLE 18.6   Order-History Monitors

Component	Purpose	Notification
New Orders	Alerts when a new order is entered	MSCRMUsers recipient map
Newly Linked Accounts	Alerts with a list of accounts added or linked from ERP	Sales Managers recipient group
Order Rate High	Raises an alert when the number of new orders for the day is more than 30	Sales Managers recipient group
Order Rate Low	Raises an alert when the number of new orders for the day is fewer than 5	Sales Managers recipient group
Order Shipping Late	Raises an alert with a list of orders with items that have not shipped and today >= requested delivery date	MSCRMUsers recipient map

Order-History Data Views

The order-history data views report on information about orders and summarize them in different ways, including by time period, salesperson, and territory.

TABLE 18.7   Order-History Data Views

Component	Purpose
Order Rate by Day	Order inserts/updates from ERP in the past 30 days.
Product Cross-Sell	Counts number of customers of product A, product B, and both.
Sales of Products by Quarter	Product quantity sold by quarter (within the last 12 months).
Sales of Products by Rep	Product quantity sold by rep (within the last 12 months).
Sales of Products by Territory	Product quantity sold by territory (within the last 12 months).
ERP Alerts by Type	Alert counts by type within the last 12 weeks. Update the SQL query to include the name of the ERP to CRM collaboration you have implemented.

Audit Data Views

The audit data views show data that is not shared that should be shared. The SQL queries for the data views use outer joins between the Scribe internal database, the ScribeERP database, and the Microsoft Dynamics CRM database to determine whether a record should be shared. A record is shared when it exists in ScribeERP, Microsoft Dynamics CRM, and in the Scribe internal database in the KEYCROSSREFERENCETWOWAY table.

These views can be helpful initially setting up the template to make sure that the initial synchronization process was successful. These views are also a good resource for monitoring the status of the data being integrated and for troubleshooting.

Figure 18.17 shows a listing of the products in the ERP that have not been shared with CRM, and Figure 18.18 shows a chart representing the number of each type of object that is shared between CRM and ERP.

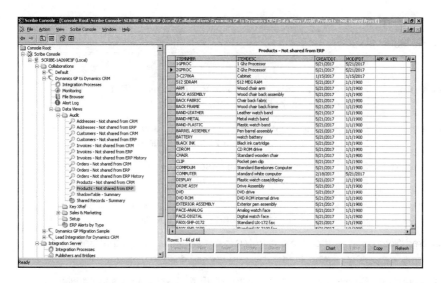

FIGURE 18.17   Products not shared.

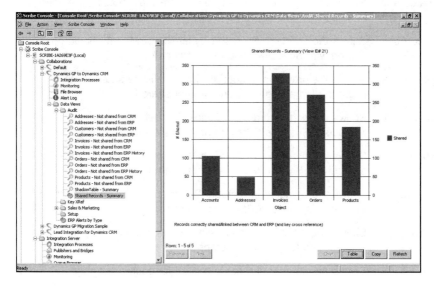

FIGURE 18.18   Chart showing shared objects.

If a record shows up in one of the audit data views and it has no data in the APP_A_KEY and APP_B_KEY columns, it means that the record was never sent from the source system, *or* the record was sent from the source system, but it failed to be inserted into the target system.

If a record shows up in one of the audit data views and it has data in the APP_A_KEY and APP_B_KEY columns, it means that the record used to be shared and is now not in both systems.

TABLE 18.8   Audit Table Views

Component	Purpose
Addresses – Not shared from CRM	Shows the addresses in Microsoft Dynamics CRM that should be shared with ScribeERP and are not shared
Addresses – Not shared from ERP	Shows the addresses in ScribeERP that should be shared with Microsoft Dynamics CRM and are not shared
Customers – Not shared from CRM	Shows the customers in Microsoft Dynamics CRM that should be shared with ScribeERP and are not shared
Customers – Not shared from ERP	Shows the customers in ScribeERP that should be shared with Microsoft Dynamics CRM and are not shared
Invoices – Not shared from CRM	Shows the invoices in Microsoft Dynamics CRM that should be shared with ScribeERP and are not shared
Invoices – Not shared from ERP	Shows the invoices in ScribeERP that should be shared with Microsoft Dynamics CRM and are not shared
Invoices – Not shared from ERP History	Shows the history invoices in ScribeERP that should be shared with Microsoft Dynamics CRM and are not shared
Orders – Not shared from CRM	Shows the orders in Microsoft Dynamics CRM that should be shared with ScribeERP and are not shared
Orders – Not shared from ERP	Shows the orders in ScribeERP that should be shared with Microsoft Dynamics CRM and are not shared
Orders – Not shared from ERP History	Shows the history orders in ScribeERP that should be shared with Microsoft Dynamics CRM and are not shared
Products – Not shared from CRM	Shows the products in Microsoft Dynamics CRM that should be shared with ScribeERP and are not shared
Products – Not shared from ERP	Shows the products in ScribeERP that should be shared with Microsoft Dynamics CRM and are not shared
ShadowTable – Summary	Shows counts of the various sync status values by object. Provides connect info for your ERP database
Shared Records – Summary	Shows the number of records shared for each object

Key XRef Data Views

The key XRef data views show you what is in the KEYCROSSREFERENCETWOWAY table in the Scribe internal database. Records in this table indicate that a record is shared or was once shared. The KEYCROSSREFERENCETWOWAY table stores the primary ID of the shared records from ScribeERP and Dynamics CRM.

For example, for a ScribeERP customer who is shared with Microsoft Dynamics CRM, the table stores the customer number from ScribeERP and the accountid from Microsoft Dynamics CRM.

TABLE 18.9   Key XRef Data Views

Component	Purpose
Key XRef – Accounts	Shows accounts
Key XRef – Addresses	Shows addresses
Key XRef – Invoices	Shows invoices
Key XRef – Orders	Shows orders
Key XRef – Orphans	Shows records in the KEYCROSSREFERENCETWOWAY table that no longer have a corresponding record in ScribeERP and Microsoft Dynamics CRM
Key XRef – Products	Shows products
Key XRef – Summary	Shows a summary

Setup Data Views

The setup data views provide lists of data from ScribeERP as an aid to help you entering those values in your Dynamics CRM setup (see Table 18.10).

TABLE 18.10   Setup Data Views

Component	Purpose
ERP Price Levels	Shows a list of price levels configured in ScribeERP. It is helpful when configuring your Microsoft Dynamics CRM system to match.
ERP Units of Measure	Shows a list of the units of measure (and the corresponding schedule) configured within ScribeERP. It is helpful when configuring your Microsoft Dynamics CRM system to match.

18

Microsoft Dynamics GP to Microsoft Dynamics CRM

The Scribe Microsoft Dynamics GP to Microsoft Dynamics CRM template provides a working integration between Microsoft Dynamics GP and Microsoft Dynamics CRM that integrates customer, address, product, order, and invoice data (see Figure 18.19).

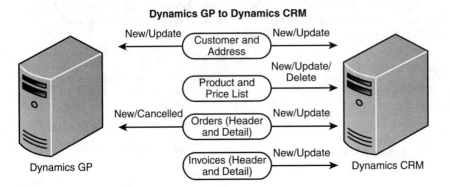

FIGURE 18.19   Process flow.

The template can be used for demonstration purposes or as a framework for building an integration between Microsoft Dynamics GP and Microsoft Dynamics CRM.

The goals of this template are as follows:

1. Provide interactive Microsoft Dynamics CRM users with customer order and invoice histories.

2. Let users create and submit orders that originate in Microsoft Dynamics CRM.

3. Provide data for creating reports that key off of the relationship between products ordered or invoiced and customers. By extension, this supports reporting on product purchase trends and detail by items related to account such as region, territory, or sales representative.

4. Provide business activity monitors that notify key business users of events related to their customers' purchases of the company's products (for example, orders over certain dollar value, orders shipping late).

5. Keep customer data in sync.

6. Synchronize the master products in Microsoft Dynamics GP into Microsoft Dynamics CRM.

To support these objectives, the template provides two-way data integration from Microsoft Dynamics GP to Microsoft Dynamics CRM for the touch points listed in Table 18.11.

TABLE 18.11   Integration Touch Points

Microsoft Dynamics GP	Microsoft Dynamics CRM
Customer	Account
Primary address	Primary address
Customer address	Customer address
Product (one-way to Microsoft Dynamics CRM)	Product ProductPriceLevel
Order	SalesOrder SalesOrderDetail
Invoice	Invoice InvoiceDetail

Process Flow

▶ **Customer and address:** This data can be created or modified in either Microsoft Dynamics GP or Microsoft Dynamics CRM (except for certain fields owned by a system, such as credit limit or credit authorization), and the additions or changes will be synchronized with the other application. The company matching components provide fuzzy account matching to avoid the creation of duplicate accounts and to facilitate an initial synchronization of existing Microsoft Dynamics GP and CRM environments.

▶ **Products and price list (master product schedule):** This data is mastered in Microsoft Dynamics GP and replicated to Microsoft Dynamics CRM to support the order process needs in Microsoft Dynamics CRM.

▶ **Orders (header and detail):** Orders are created in Microsoft Dynamics CRM and may be modified in Microsoft Dynamics CRM until that order is submitted to Microsoft Dynamics GP. Updated information about the order is provided to Microsoft Dynamics CRM from Microsoft Dynamics GP. Orders that originate in Microsoft Dynamics GP are provided to Microsoft Dynamics CRM in a submitted state. Orders that are canceled in Microsoft Dynamics CRM are voided in Microsoft Dynamics GP and vice versa. Transferred orders in Microsoft Dynamics GP are also included.

▶ **Invoices (header and detail):** Invoices are created in Microsoft Dynamics GP and replicated to Microsoft Dynamics CRM. Updates can only be made from Microsoft Dynamics GP. Posted invoices in Microsoft Dynamics GP are also included.

GP to CRM Integration Processes

Integration processes automate the processing of the DTS files by detecting events such as a message in a queue, the results of a query, a file placed in a folder, or a specific time. The events are the trigger for the integration process to run its associated DTS file.

TABLE 18.12   DTS Components

Component	Purpose
AccountToCRM	Runs AccountToCRM.dts
AddressToCRM	Runs AddressToCRM.dts
InvoiceToCRM	Runs InvoiceToCRM.dts
OrderToCRM	Runs OrderToCRM.dts
ProductToCRM	Runs ProductToCRM.dts

CRM to GP Integration Processes

The integration processes automate the processing of the DTS files (see Table 18.13).

TABLE 18.13   DTS Components

Component	Purpose
AccountToERP	Runs AccountToERP.dts
AddressToERP	Runs AddressToERP.dts
CascadeAccountToERP	Runs CascadeAccountToERP.dts, forwards message to OrderToERP
CascadeAddressesToERP	Runs CascadeAddressesToERP.dts
OrderToERP	Runs OrderToERP.dts, forwards message to OrderToERP_Result
OrderToERP_Cancel	Runs OrderToERP_Cancel.dts, forwards message to OrderToERP_Result
OrderToERP_Result	Runs OrderToERP_Result.dts

DTS Files

The DTS files contain the field mappings, data transformation formulas, and data processing rules used to integrate data from the source to the target. Table 18.14 lists the DTS files used in the template.

TABLE 18.14   DTS Purposes

Component	Purpose
AccountToCRM.dts	Sends new and updated customers from Microsoft Dynamics GP to Microsoft Dynamics CRM.
AccountToERP.dts	Sends new and updated customers from Microsoft Dynamics CRM to Microsoft Dynamics GP.
AddressToCRM.dts	Sends new and updated addresses from Microsoft Dynamics GP to Microsoft Dynamics CRM.
AddressToERP.dts	Sends new and updated addresses from Microsoft Dynamics CRM to Microsoft Dynamics GP.
CascadeAccountToERP.dts	Triggered when an order is submitted. Its purpose is to make sure that the account is shared between Microsoft Dynamics CRM and Microsoft Dynamics GP. If the account is not shared, it updates the type to customer in Microsoft Dynamics CRM, causing the account to be sent.
CascadeAddressesToERP.dts	Touches all of the addresses in Microsoft Dynamics CRM for a newly shared account. This causes all the addresses to be sent to Microsoft Dynamics GP.
InvoiceToCRM.dts	Sends all invoices (including posted) from Microsoft Dynamics GP to Microsoft Dynamics CRM.
OrderToCRM.dts	Sends all orders (including transferred orders) from Microsoft Dynamics GP to Microsoft Dynamics CRM.
OrderToERP.dts	Sends submitted orders from Microsoft Dynamics CRM to Microsoft Dynamics GP.
OrderToERP_Cancel.dts	Sends a request to cancel/void an order from Microsoft Dynamics CRM to Microsoft Dynamics GP.
OrderToERP_Result.dts	Processes orders going into the Microsoft Dynamics GP. Updates the sales order in Microsoft Dynamics CRM. For orders that failed to be inserted into Microsoft Dynamics GP, sets the state back to Active.
ProductToCRM.dts	Sends new and updated products from Microsoft Dynamics GP to Microsoft Dynamics CRM.
UofMToCRM.dts	Initializes the unit of measure settings in Microsoft Dynamics CRM to match Microsoft Dynamics GP.

Publishers

The publishers are responsible for gathering changes in the Microsoft Dynamics GP and Microsoft Dynamics CRM systems and publishing those changes as XML messages in the ScribeIn message queue (see Table 18.15).

TABLE 18.15   Publishers

Component	Purpose
Microsoft Dynamics CRM	Interacts with Microsoft Dynamics CRM server to track changes to accounts, addresses, and sales orders. Publishes these changes as XML messages in the ScribeIn message queue.
AccountFromERP_UpdateSource	Collects Microsoft Dynamics GP customer changes from the Scribe shadow table and publishes them as XML messages in the ScribeIn message queue.
AddressFromERP_UpdateSource	Collects Microsoft Dynamics GP address changes from the Scribe shadow table and publishes them as XML messages in the ScribeIn message queue.
InvoiceFromERP_UpdateSource	Collects Microsoft Dynamics GP invoice changes from the Scribe shadow table and publishes them as XML messages in the ScribeIn message queue.
InvoicePostedFromERP_UpdateSource	Collects Microsoft Dynamics GP posted invoice changes from the Scribe shadow table and publishes them as XML messages in the ScribeIn message queue.
ProductDeleteFromERP_UpdateSource	Collects Microsoft Dynamics GP deleted products from the Scribe shadow table and publishes them as XML messages in the ScribeIn message queue.
ProductFromERP_UpdateSource	Collects Microsoft Dynamics GP product changes from the Scribe shadow table and publishes them as XML messages in the ScribeIn message queue.
SalesOrderFromERP_UpdateSource	Collects Microsoft Dynamics GP sales order changes from the Scribe shadow table and publishes them as XML messages in the ScribeIn message queue.
SalesOrderTransferred_UpdateSource	Collects Microsoft Dynamics GP transferred sales order changes from the Scribe shadow table and publishes them as XML messages in the ScribeIn message queue.

Order-History Monitors

The order-history monitors create alerts based on business activity in the Microsoft Dynamics CRM database. When you add alert recipients to the Sales Managers group, these alerts can be sent to individuals by the Scribe Insight server (see Table 18.16).

TABLE 18.16   Order-History Monitors

Component	Purpose
Accounts Placed on Credit Hold	Raises an alert to the Account Manager with a list of any accounts updated that day and on credit hold
Accounts with No Recent Orders	Raises an alert with a list of accounts that have not placed an order within 30 days

TABLE 18.16 Order-History Monitors

Component	Purpose
Large Orders	Alerts when an order with a total amount > $25,000 was entered or modified
New Order from Preferred Customer	Alerts when an order from a preferred customer is entered or modified
New Orders	Alerts when a new order is entered
Newly Linked Accounts	Alerts with a list of accounts added or linked from ERP
Order Rate High	Raises an alert when the number of new orders for the day is more than 30
Order Rate Low	Raises an alert when the number of new orders for the day is fewer than 5
Order Shipping Late	Raises an alert with a list of orders with items that have not shipped and today >= requested delivery date

Order-History Data Views

The order-history data views report on information about orders and summarize them by different ways including time period, salesperson, and territory (see Table 18.17).

TABLE 18.17 Order-History Data Views

Component	Purpose
Order Rate by Day	Order inserts/updates from ERP in the past 30 days.
Product Cross-Sell	Counts number of customers of product A, product B, and both.
Sales of Products by Quarter	Product quantity sold by quarter (within the past 12 months).
Sales of Products by Rep	Product quantity sold by rep (within the past 12 months).
Sales of Products by Territory	Product quantity sold by territory (within the past 12 months).
ERP Alerts by Type	Alert counts by type within the past 12 weeks. Update the SQL query to include the name of the ERP to CRM collaboration you have implemented.

Audit Data Views

The audit data views show data that should be shared but is not shared. The SQL queries for the data views use outer joins between the Scribe internal database, the Microsoft Dynamics GP database, and the Microsoft Dynamics CRM database to determine whether a record should be shared. A record is shared when it exists in the Microsoft Dynamics GP,

18

the Microsoft Dynamics CRM, and in the Scribe internal database in the KEYCROSSREFER-
ENCETWOWAY table.

These views can be helpful when initially setting up the template to make sure that the
initial synchronization process was successful. These views are also a good resource for
monitoring the status of the data being integrated and for troubleshooting.

If a record shows up in one of the audit data views and it has no data in the APP_A_KEY
and APP_B_KEY columns, it means that the record was never sent from the source
system, *or* the record was sent from the source system, but it failed to be inserted into the
target system.

If a record shows up in one of the audit data views and it has data in the APP_A_KEY
and APP_B_KEY columns, it means that the record used to be shared and is now not in
both systems.

Because audit data views require direct access to the database in order to run queries, audit
data views cannot be used with Microsoft Dynamics CRM Online.

Reconfiguring the Default Views

The template includes a set of data views. Some of these views perform joins across databases. By default, these views use the database names of the standard CRM sample databases that ship with Microsoft Dynamics CRM (Microsoft_CRM_MSCRM) and Microsoft
Dynamics GP (TWO) in their join clauses. You'll want to reconfigure these views to
connect to the databases in your system.

In the Scribe Console, replace the default CRM database names in the SQL query (on the
Configure Source tab of the view in the list shown in Table 18.18) with the database
names used in your system.

TABLE 18.18   Default CRM Database Names

Component	Purpose
Addresses – Not shared from CRM	Shows the addresses in Microsoft Dynamics CRM that should be shared with Microsoft Dynamics GP and are not shared.
Addresses – Not shared from ERP	Shows the addresses in Microsoft Dynamics GP that should be shared with Microsoft Dynamics CRM and are not shared.
Customers – Not shared from CRM	Shows the customers in Microsoft Dynamics CRM that should be shared with Microsoft Dynamics GP and are not shared.
Customers – Not shared from ERP	Shows the customers in Microsoft Dynamics GP that should be shared with Microsoft Dynamics CRM and are not shared.
Invoices – Not shared from CRM	Shows the invoices in Microsoft Dynamics CRM that should be shared with Microsoft Dynamics GP and are not shared.
Invoices – Not shared from ERP	Shows the invoices in Microsoft Dynamics GP that should be shared with Microsoft Dynamics CRM and are not shared.

TABLE 18.18   Default CRM Database Names

Component	Purpose
Invoices – Not shared from ERP History	Shows the history invoices in Dynamics GP that should be shared with Dynamics CRM and are not shared.
Orders – Not shared from CRM	Shows the orders in Microsoft Dynamics CRM that should be shared with Microsoft Dynamics GP and are not shared.
Orders – Not shared from ERP	Shows the orders in Microsoft Dynamics GP that should be shared with Microsoft Dynamics CRM and are not shared.
Orders – Not shared from ERP History	Shows the history orders in Microsoft Dynamics GP that should be shared with Microsoft Dynamics CRM and are not shared.
Products – Not shared from CRM	Shows the products in Microsoft Dynamics CRM that should be shared with Microsoft Dynamics GP and are not shared.
Products – Not shared from ERP	Shows the products in Microsoft Dynamics GP that should be shared with Microsoft Dynamics CRM and are not shared.
ShadowTable – Summary	Shows counts of the various sync status values by object. Provide connect info for your GP database.
Shared Records – Summary	Shows the number of records shared for each object.

Key XRef Data Views

The key XRef data views show you what is in the KEYCROSSREFERENCETWOWAY table in the Scribe internal database. Records in this table indicate that a record is shared or was once shared. The KEYCROSSREFERENCETWOWAY table stores the primary ID of the shared records from Dynamics GP and Dynamics CRM.

For example, for a Microsoft Dynamics GP customer who is shared with Microsoft Dynamics CRM, the table stores the customer number from Microsoft Dynamics GP and the accountid from Microsoft Dynamics CRM (see Table 18.19).

TABLE 18.19   Key XRef Data Views

Component	Purpose
Key XRef – Accounts	Shows accounts
Key XRef – Addresses	Shows addresses
Key XRef – Invoices	Shows invoices
Key XRef – Orders	Shows orders

TABLE 18.19   Key XRef Data Views

Component	Purpose
Key XRef – Orphans	Shows records in the KEYCROSSREFERENCETWOWAY table that no longer have a corresponding record in Microsoft Dynamics GP and Microsoft Dynamics CRM
Key XRef – Products	Shows products
Key XRef – Summary	Shows a summary

Setup Data Views

The setup data views provide lists of data from Microsoft Dynamics GP as an aid to help you entering those values in your Microsoft Dynamics CRM setup (see Table 18.20).

TABLE 18.20   Setup Data Views

Component	Purpose
GP Price Levels	Shows a list of price levels configured in Microsoft Dynamics GP. It is helpful when configuring your Microsoft Dynamics CRM system to match.
GP Units of Measure	Shows a list of the units of measure (and the corresponding schedule) configured within Microsoft Dynamics GP. It is helpful when configuring your Microsoft Dynamics CRM system to match.

Microsoft Dynamics NAV to Microsoft Dynamics CRM

The Scribe Microsoft Dynamics NAV to Microsoft Dynamics CRM template provides a working integration between Microsoft Dynamics NAV and Microsoft Dynamics CRM that integrates customer, address, product, order, and invoice data.

The template can be used for demonstration purposes or configured to meet your business requirements.

The goals of this template are as follows:

1. Provide interactive Microsoft Dynamics CRM users with customer order and invoice histories.

2. Let users create and submit orders that originate in Microsoft Dynamics CRM.

3. Provide data for creating reports that key off of the relationship between products ordered or invoiced and customers. By extension, this supports reporting on product purchase trends and detail by items related to account such as region, territory, or sales representative.

4. Provide business activity monitors that notify business users of events related to their customers' purchases of the company's products (for example, orders over certain dollar value, orders shipping late).

5. Keep customer data in sync.

6. Synchronize the Microsoft Dynamics NAV master product list and prices with Microsoft Dynamics CRM.

To support these objectives, the template provides data integration between Microsoft Dynamics NAV and Microsoft Dynamics CRM for the types of data listed in Table 18.21.

TABLE 18.21   Data Integration Points

Microsoft Dynamics NAV	Microsoft Dynamics CRM
Customer	Account
Customer address	Primary address
Ship to addresses	More addresses
Currency exchange rate	Currency conversion
Customer price group and currency code combinations	Price lists
Items	Products
Item variants	
Item unit of measure	Unit group/units
Sales price	Product price lists
Order	Order
Order lines	Order products
Invoice	Invoice
Invoice lines	Invoice products

Process Flow

The Scribe Microsoft Dynamics NAV to Microsoft Dynamics CRM template provides the high-level functionality shown in Figure 18.20.

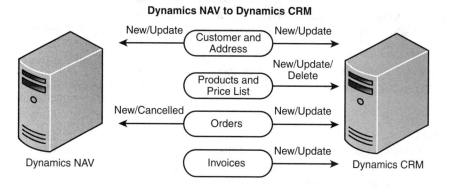

FIGURE 18.20   NAV to CRM process flow.

▶ **Customer and address:** This data can be created or modified in either Microsoft Dynamics NAV or Microsoft Dynamics CRM (except for certain fields owned by a system, such as credit limit or credit authorization), and the additions or changes will be synchronized with the other application. The company matching components provide fuzzy account matching to avoid the creation of duplicate accounts and to facilitate an initial synchronization of existing Microsoft Dynamics NAV and Microsoft Dynamics CRM environments.

▶ **Products and price list (master product schedule):** This data is mastered in Microsoft Dynamics NAV and replicated to Microsoft Dynamics CRM to support the order process needs in Microsoft Dynamics CRM.

▶ **Orders (header and detail):** Orders are created in Microsoft Dynamics CRM and may be modified in Microsoft Dynamics CRM until that order is submitted to Microsoft Dynamics NAV. Updated information about the order is provided to Microsoft Dynamics CRM from Microsoft Dynamics NAV. Orders that originate in Microsoft Dynamics NAV are provided to Microsoft Dynamics CRM in a submitted state.

▶ **Invoices (header and detail):** Invoices are created in Microsoft Dynamics NAV and replicated to Microsoft Dynamics CRM. Updates can only be made from Microsoft Dynamics NAV. Posted invoices in Microsoft Dynamics NAV are also included.

Audit Data Views

Audit data views show data that should be shared but is not shared. The SQL queries for the data views use outer joins between the Scribe internal database, the Microsoft Dynamics NAV database, and the Microsoft Dynamics CRM database to determine whether a record should be shared. A record is shared when it exists in the Microsoft Dynamics NAV, the Microsoft Dynamics CRM, and in the Scribe internal database in the KEYCROSSREFERENCETWOWAY table.

These views can be helpful when initially setting up the template to make sure that the initial synchronization process was successful. These views are also a good resource for monitoring the status of the data being integrated and for troubleshooting.

If a record shows up in one of the audit data views and it has no data in the APP_A_KEY and APP_B_KEY columns, it means that the record was never sent from the source system, *or* the record was sent from the source system, but it failed to be inserted into the target system.

If a record shows up in one of the audit data views and it has data in the APP_A_KEY and APP_B_KEY columns, it means that the record used to be shared and is now not in both systems.

Reconfiguring the Default Views

The template includes a set of data views. Some of these views perform joins across databases. By default, these views use the database names of the standard CRM sample databases that ship with Microsoft Dynamics CRM and Microsoft Dynamics NAV in their join clauses. You must reconfigure these views to connect to the databases in your system.

In the Scribe Console, replace the database names listed in Table 18.22 with the database names used in your system.

TABLE 18.22   Default Views

Component	Purpose
Addresses – Not shared from CRM	Shows the addresses in Microsoft Dynamics CRM that should be shared with Microsoft Dynamics NAV and are not shared
Addresses – Not shared from ERP	Shows the addresses in Microsoft Dynamics NAV that should be shared with Microsoft Dynamics CRM and are not shared
Customers – Not shared from CRM	Shows the customers in Microsoft Dynamics CRM that should be shared with Microsoft Dynamics NAV and are not shared
Customers – Not shared from ERP	Shows the customers in Microsoft Dynamics NAV that should be shared with Microsoft Dynamics CRM and are not shared
Invoices – Not shared from CRM	Shows the invoices in Microsoft Dynamics CRM that should be shared with Microsoft Dynamics NAV and are not shared
Invoices – Not shared from ERP	Shows the invoices in Microsoft Dynamics NAV that should be shared with Microsoft Dynamics CRM and are not shared
Orders – Not shared from CRM	Shows the orders in Microsoft Dynamics CRM that should be shared with Microsoft Dynamics NAV and are not shared
Orders – Not shared from ERP	Shows the orders in Microsoft Dynamics NAV that should be shared with Microsoft Dynamics CRM and are not shared
Products – Not shared from CRM	Shows the products in Microsoft Dynamics CRM that should be shared with Microsoft Dynamics NAV and are not shared
Products – Not shared from ERP	Shows the products in Microsoft Dynamics NAV that should be shared with Microsoft Dynamics CRM and are not shared
Shared Records – Summary	Shows the number of records shared for each object

Key XRef Data Views

The key XRef data views show you what is in the KEYCROSSREFERENCETWOWAY table in the Scribe internal database. Records in this table indicate that a record is shared or was once shared. The KEYCROSSREFERENCETWOWAY table stores the primary ID of the shared records from Dynamics NAV and Dynamics CRM.

For example, for a Microsoft Dynamics NAV customer who is shared with Microsoft Dynamics CRM, the table stores the customer number from Microsoft Dynamics NAV and the accountid from Microsoft Dynamics CRM (see Table 18.23).

TABLE 18.23   Key XRef Data Views

Component	Purpose
Key XRef – Accounts	Shows accounts
Key XRef – Addresses	Shows addresses
Key XRef – Invoices	Shows invoices
Key XRef – Orders	Shows orders
Key XRef – Orphans	Shows records in the KEYCROSSREFERENCETWOWAY table that no longer have a corresponding record in Microsoft Dynamics NAV and Microsoft Dynamics CRM
Key XRef – Products	Shows products
Key XRef – Summary	Shows a summary

Summary

In this chapter, we explained what templates are and how they work. It is critical to realize that templates represent a starting point and are then often modified to fit the needs of particular integrations.

It is important to note that while there are specific adapters for products such as GP and NAV, the base Scribe ERP template is the source of these templates. They have been modified to the predefined requirements for the particular system.

Scribe continues to add new functionality and define new templates, so be sure to check their resource center for new versions.

CHAPTER 19

Direction of Microsoft Dynamics CRM

The fact that Microsoft has committed to the Microsoft Dynamics CRM application should be readily apparent from your reading of this book. They continue to position Microsoft Dynamics CRM as a platform and are continuing to leverage not only the partner community but also customers for new and interesting solutions that use Microsoft Dynamics CRM as a backbone technology. In addition, with the ongoing releases of accelerators, service updates, and related technologies for CRM 4.0, the current version continues to offer new and exciting feature enhancements.

So, the question is this: What does the next version of Microsoft Dynamics CRM hold?

> **NOTE**
>
> The information in this chapter is based on pre-beta and development builds and should not be considered definitive.

CRM v.Next

Because of the way Microsoft handles product releases, the question of what is included in the next version is as difficult to answer as guessing what the next version will be called. (Currently, it is known as CRM v.Next or CRM5.)

However, Microsoft has indicated that the following are possibilities for inclusion (as of this writing):

- Native SharePoint integration
- Easier deployment and upgrade options
- A way to protect intellectual property (IP) of installed code, consisting of solution management options
- User interface enhancements, including
  - Better integration with Outlook, including performance, stability, and features
  - Filtered lookups (called related records lookup)
  - Label positioning
  - Subgrids
  - Smarter lookups
  - Multiple-option sets
  - Enhanced form editor, including drag and drop
  - Context-sensitive menu bars
  - Fewer screens open at a time
  - Field-level security and auditing options
- Azure options
- Unstructured relationships for enhanced collaboration
- Team ownership options
- Native data analysis and data charting, including inline charting with drill-down capabilities

The concept of solution management is an important change that should significantly increase template and vertical applications, because the customizations can be versioned, published, and protected.

From a developer's standpoint, the code base for all versions (on-premise, partner hosted, and CRM Online) should be the same, and the addition of a "sandbox" for custom code (via a new server role) will allow custom code to run on any version. In addition, there is talk of transactional support for plug-ins (allowing for platform event management) and plug-in profiling, which will allow for detailed management of the component.

One feature we're hoping for is role-based forms. One of our earliest implementations crossed not only business units, but also business organizations, and a custom form based on role membership would have gone a long way toward managing complex implementations such as these. (Currently, the only way to deal with this issue is through JavaScript and by showing/hiding fields or using a third-party component.)

Platform, Platform, Platform

There is much talk (in this book, among the development community, and from Microsoft) about CRM as a platform via xRM (*anything* relationship management). We discuss the concept of xRM in Chapter 1, "Extending Microsoft Dynamics CRM Explained." The main point here is that the next version of Microsoft Dynamics CRM may extend xRM to the next level via the server role that has no graphical user interface (GUI).

What this means is that we can load Microsoft Dynamics CRM and not have anything other than web services that interact with the CRM database. This has great value for organizations that want to use CRM-type functionality but have little use for the actual CRM interfaces.

By using this role, organizations will leverage the benefits of CRM (business processes, security model, and structure) and develop robust applications that have nothing in common with the existing Microsoft Dynamics CRM look and feel.

> **NOTE**
>
> The "server" role exists in the current version of CRM (available via the advanced deployment options during install) and supports scaled-out deployments. However, the proposed role is a packaging of a "platform only" or "UI-less" server option.

Microsoft CRM Statement of Direction

Microsoft has provided a greater level of transparency around what the future holds for Microsoft Dynamics CRM through its Statement of Direction (SOD) documentation, which is periodically updated and made available for customers and partners.

The SOD is a good guide, but it is not a definitive promise of delivery. What this means is that although the documentation includes the overall goals of where Microsoft would like the product to go, and can include specific examples and integration goals, there is no guarantee on timeline or actual delivery.

However, this documentation is valuable for organizations that want to plan around investments in the technology of Microsoft CRM with a relative assurance that Microsoft has at least thought of, if not formally promised, integration point delivery.

19

> **NOTE**
>
> The Statement of Direction is available for download from https://partner.microsoft.com/40086846, or you can just search for "Microsoft Dynamics CRM Statement of Direction."

Summary

The next version of Microsoft Dynamics CRM should exhibit considerable improvements in both form and functionality and offer even more choices to consumers of Microsoft Dynamics CRM.

As stated from the latest Microsoft SOD, the primary goals of the next version of CRM include

- Driving maximum user productivity

- Delivering business insight and collaboration regardless of the user's role

- Enriching the sales, service, and marketing capability of Microsoft Dynamics CRM

- Providing a flexible and scalable business solution platform

Microsoft is clearly listening to user requirements/input surrounding the next version, and we've already seen several necessary improvements incorporated into the overall design.

If you would like to be involved in helping shape the next version of CRM, register for its Connect website located at http://connect.microsoft.com. This site provides a mechanism where feedback about its product is managed by Microsoft and can significantly affect product release functionality.

CHAPTER 20

Other Integration Tools

This book has delved into many different integration options for Microsoft Dynamics CRM. This chapter now focuses on other products in the Microsoft Dynamics ecosystem that can and should be evaluated as potential integration options.

This chapter is divided into two sections. The first section is a high-level overview of the Microsoft Dynamics integration product that integrates CRM to GP (project code named Rockwell). The second is an overview of some of the companies that offer integration products and services. Note that this list of companies is neither exhaustive nor conclusive. We see new and interesting products and companies all the time, and it would be difficult to include everything and everyone in this book.

Microsoft CRM to GP Connector

At the 2009 Microsoft Convergence event in New Orleans, Microsoft finally announced a dedicated integration component for CRM to Great Plains (GP).

This has been long in coming and desired by many customers.

In an attempt to overcome some of the difficulties associated with its previous CRM to GP connector, Microsoft created from the ground up a middleware component that that uses adapters, templates, and a dedicated database to handle the data movement. The difficulties addressed by the previous component included the requirement (in both setup and configuration and management) of Microsoft BizTalk Server (which is now not required), problems encountered in configuration and resource usage/management, and a variety of other issues that occurred in both small and enterprise environments. Figure 20.1 shows the service architecture at a high level.

> **NOTE**
>
> The information in this chapter is based on pre-beta and development builds and should not be considered definitive.

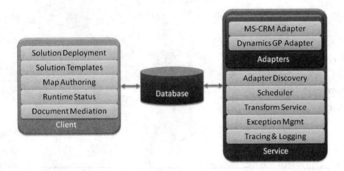

FIGURE 20.1   Microsoft CRM to GP connector architecture.

The Microsoft CRM to GP connector will provide the following integration benefits:

- Simplicity and ease of use
- High reliability and fault tolerance
- Interval scheduling
- Logging for failure and success
- Rules-based retries of integration failures

Similar to Scribe, the CRM to GP integration product uses an abstract adapter pattern to identify source and destination systems. In fact, the product is technically unaware of exactly which systems it is integrating, because it communicates solely with the adapter at the source (which reads data) and the adapter at the destination (which writes data).

The product will provide system configuration and integration specialists with map templates that support the integration. Note that maps will be generic in nature and will invariably require configuration to meet each customer's particular business requirements.

The maps will represent the settings needed to integrate. An example of a map in CRM might be the products mapping to GP inventory items.

The product will support integration on either a pull (preferred) or a push model. The pros and cons of each are outlined as follows:

▶ **Pull**

▶ Leverages resources more efficiently

▶ Requires source system to track changes using dates and times

▶ **Push**

▶ Uses document keys to transform and integrate with the specified mapping

The final configuration options for the CRM to GP product remain to be seen. In addition, although the product is designed initially for CRM to GP integration, there is no reason why it couldn't be expanded for use with any of the Dynamics products.

At this point, it is impossible to say for sure how or if it will compete with more mature products already available (Scribe, for example). We anticipate that it will provide a new option to customers for Dynamics integration, if nothing else.

Other Tools

This section covers some of the third-party plug-ins available for Microsoft Dynamics CRM. These plug-ins play a vital role in various industry-specific implementations. Microsoft Dynamics CRM provides a strong foundation layer, which works for most companies, but the third-party products are required to optimize many business flows.

c360

c360 offers many add-on products and solutions for the Microsoft Dynamics CRM platform. The c360 products facilitate the management (on most levels) of Microsoft Dynamics CRM. c360 understands the importance of managing, monitoring, and maintaining Microsoft Dynamics CRM systems and therefore makes available various solutions to enable the same. In addition, it provides tools that enable individual enterprises to customize their Microsoft Dynamics CRM environments (see Figure 20.2).

A variety of c360 plug-ins may be purchased individually. c360 has also packaged these products into three packs (Core Productivity pack, Sales Productivity pack, and Service Productive pack):

▶ The **Core Productivity pack** provides tools beneficial for all CRM users in an enterprise. This pack provides add-on packages such as Record Editor, Relationship Explorer, SharePoint Integration, Multi-Field Search, Alerts, Console, and Summary. Combined, these packages provide Dynamics CRM users a great deal of flexibility:

▶ **Record Editor:** Edit/modify multiple CRM records within a single screen wherever in the CRM database.

▶ **Relationship Explorer:** Shows existing relationships between CRM records.

20

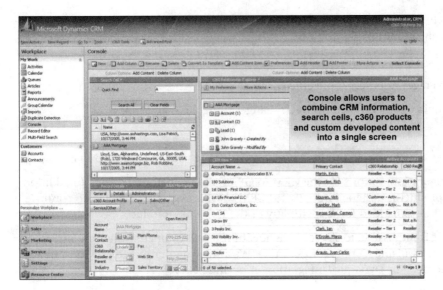

FIGURE 20.2   Sample c360 products.

▶ **SharePoint Integration:** Designed to created SharePoint sites for any type of CRM records.

▶ **Multi-Field Search:** Provides a quick search screen for every CRM user.

▶ **Alerts:** Users will be notified whenever critical data is added to the CRM system.

▶ **Console:** Ability to create individual workspace based on preference.

▶ **Summary:** Displays open and closed activities.

▶ The **Sales Productivity pack** includes the following:

   ▶ **Forecast Manager:** Simplifies the process of assessing and updating all sales forecast and opportunities information.

   ▶ **Web Connect:** The enterprise CRM can integrate into Microsoft CRM for "web visitor activity capture."

▶ The **Service Productivity pack** includes the following:

   ▶ **Email to Case:** Supervises the conversion of inbound email into service cases from the Microsoft CRM queues

   ▶ **My Workplace:** Enhances the Workplace screen of Microsoft CRM users

Semantra

Semantra, Inc., is a software company that provides natural-language search within application databases. It focuses on providing easier access to information from large, complicated database systems. Most critical business decisions are made on structured data, and Semantra delivers a new solution that extends traditional business intelligence in a way that empowers employees by enabling them to access information from massive databases. (Figure 20.3 shows a sample Semantra data flow.) Moreover, Semantra solutions improve the value of Microsoft CRM and its business intelligence, so that nontechnical users can easily handle relational databases and use a more self-service approach. Furthermore, information retrieval is improved with the use of conversational (natural) language.

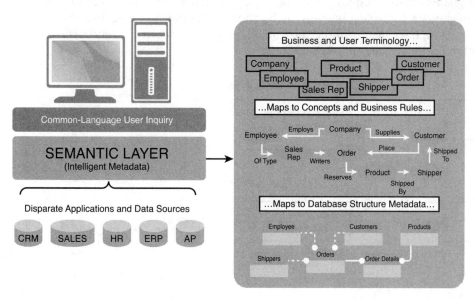

FIGURE 20.3   Sample Semantra data flow.

Consider this example. Semantra drove improvement within the Wyoming Department of Environmental Quality by proving it the relevant platform that helped the department's inspectors to more quickly identify and eliminate pollutants. The water-monitoring program is now more effective and efficient in terms of accessing compliance data, performing sophisticated real-time reporting, and analyzing exiting reports.

NOTE

For more information about this Wyoming Department of Environmental Quality solution provided by Semantra, refer to http://www.semantra.com/library/Semantra-CaseStudy-WDEQ-2008-08-18.pdf.

Nolan

Nolan Computers created the Integration Bridge for Microsoft CRM and Microsoft Dynamics Great Plains. The Integration Bridge enables you to interface both packages, perhaps to enhance the management console for mapping and customization, for instance. In addition, it enables standard data mappings and automatic schema changes to

Microsoft Dynamics CRM. The purpose of the Integration Bridge is to allow multiple Microsoft Dynamics CRM and GP business units to integrate with each other. The most intricate integration requirements can be dealt with by user-defined field mappings of the Integration Bridge. Enterprises that desire complete, complex integrations can use the Integration Bridge and can get help from Nolan as they design, install, and support those complex requirements.

The Integration Bridge's custom plug-in technology facilitates the addition of various other integrations. Individual plug-ins, such as a Sales Document plug-in and a Service Module plug-in, have their own specific features. Figure 20.4 shows the server, client, and Integration Bridge mechanism relationships.

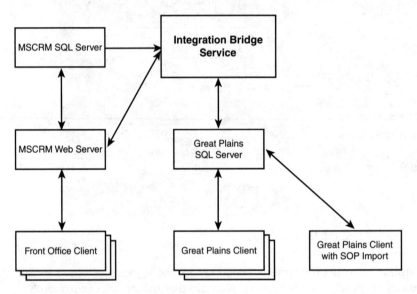

FIGURE 20.4   Sample Nolan integration.

The Integration Bridge works as follows:

1. Users add/create data in the source system.
2. This action is caught by the server-side events on the source system, in which integration records are then created in the integration queue.
3. The Integration Bridge monitors the queues on both systems and administers the next process accordingly.
4. The Integration Bridge determines the right process, and information is taken from the source system and mapped across to the destination system.
5. All integration activity is recorded.

eOne Integrated Business Solutions

eOne Integrated Business Solutions is a solutions-based developer of add-on products. eOne adds value to Microsoft CRM and GP applications. eOne offers a range of products, including the eXtender, SmartConnect, and Flexicoder. (A sample eOne screen is shown in Figure 20.5.)

The eXtender enables end users to modify and customize their solutions or create new applications to meet specific requirements. SmartConnect is more integration-based, as it provides a user interface that eliminates the involvement of developers in the Dynamics GP integration work. Moreover, the interface provides mapping solutions between various types of source data and the eConnect nodes. Real-time triggers, CRM-based web services, and the drag-and-drop interface automatically remove the necessity of having a developer integrate Microsoft Dynamics CRM and Microsoft GP. Flexicoder, on the other hand, brings the efficiency of one enterprise resource planning (ERP) solution to Microsoft Dynamics GP users: This interface can deal with the complexity of a general ledger.

eOne developed SmartConnect as an end-user tool so that it can be used by consultants or individual "department" teams. SmartConnect provides an easy-to-use interface for leveraging powerful tools (by combining eConnect nodes and out-of-the-box web services for Microsoft Dynamics CRM, coupled with a simplified architecture). The SmartConnect solution is more flexible and provides a higher degree of Dynamics CRM to Dynamics GP integration. (For example, no form of Dynamics CRM and GP integration requires the writing of complex code.) In addition, SmartConnect enables users to detect duplicate information and rectify it automatically with foolproof record-correlation design.

Faster mappings, automated data entry, processing bulk transactions quickly, and the creation of intercompany transactions—these are some of the highlights of SmartConnect.

FIGURE 20.5   Sample eOne screen.

20

Summary

This chapter provided an overview of some third-party products that can help streamline the Microsoft Dynamics CRM application.

The Microsoft CRM to GP connector tool should be released in Q3 or Q4 of 2009, so we can safely assume enhancement to and further unification of the Microsoft Dynamics family.

Locale ID (LCID)

Locale Description	Short String	Hex Value	Decimal Value	Locale Description	Short String	Hex Value	Decimal Value
Afrikaans	af	0x0436	1078	Icelandic	is	0x040F	1039
Albanian	sq	0x041C	1052	Indonesian	id	0x0421	1057
Arabic - United Arab Emirates	ar-ae	0x3801	14337	Italian - Italy	it-it	0x0410	1040
Arabic - Bahrain	ar-bh	0x3C01	15361	Italian - Switzerland	it-ch	0x0810	2064
Arabic - Algeria	ar-dz	0x1401	5121	Japanese	ja	0x0411	1041
Arabic - Egypt	ar-eg	0x0C01	3073	Korean	ko	0x0412	1042
Arabic - Iraq	ar-iq	0x0801	2049	Latvian	lv	0x0426	1062
Arabic - Jordan	ar-jo	0x2C01	11265	Lithuanian	lt	0x0427	1063
Arabic - Kuwait	ar-kw	0x3401	13313	Macedonian (FYRO)	mk	0x042F	1071
Arabic - Lebanon	ar-lb	0x3001	12289	Malay - Malaysia	ms-my	0x043E	1086
Arabic - Libya	ar-ly	0x1001	4097	Malay - Brunei	ms-bn	0x083E	2110
Arabic - Morocco	ar-ma	0x1801	6145	Maltese	mt	0x043A	1082
Arabic - Oman	ar-om	0x2001	8193	Marathi	mr	0x044E	1102
Arabic - Qatar	ar-qa	0x4001	16385	Norwegian - Bokmål	no-no	0x0414	1044
Arabic - Saudi Arabia	ar-sa	0x0401	1025	Norwegian - Nynorsk	no-no	0x0814	2068
Arabic - Syria	ar-sy	0x2801	10241	Polish	pl	0x0415	1045

Locale Description	Short String	Hex Value	Decimal Value	Locale Description	Short String	Hex Value	Decimal Value
Arabic - Tunisia	ar-tn	0x1C01	7169	Portuguese - Portugal	pt-pt	0x0816	2070
Arabic - Yemen	ar-ye	0x2401	9217	Portuguese - Brazil	pt-br	0x0416	1046
Armenian	hy	0x042B	1067	Raeto-Romanic	rm	0x0417	1047
Azeri - Latin	az-az	0x042C	1068	Romanian - Romania	ro	0x0418	1048
Azeri - Cyrillic	az-az	0x082C	2092	Romanian - Republic of Moldova	ro-mo	0x0818	2072
Basque	eu	0x042D	1069	Russian	ru	0x0419	1049
Belarusian	be	0x0423	1059	Russian - Republic of Moldova	ru-mo	0x0819	2073
Bulgarian	bg	0x0402	1026	Sanskrit	sa	0x044F	1103
Catalan	ca	0x0403	1027	Serbian - Cyrillic	sr-sp	0x0C1A	3098
Chinese - People's Republic of China	zh-cn	0x0804	2052	Serbian - Latin	sr-sp	0x081A	2074
Chinese - Hong Kong SAR	zh-hk	0x0C04	3076	Tswana	tn	0x0432	1074
Chinese - Macau SAR	zh-mo	0x1404	5124	Slovenian	sl	0x0424	1060
Chinese - Singapore	zh-sg	0x1004	4100	Slovak	sk	0x041B	1051
Chinese - Taiwan	zh-tw	0x0404	1028	Sorbian	sb	0x042E	1070
Croatian	hr	0x041A	1050	Spanish - Spain	es-es	0x0C0A	1034
Czech	cs	0x0405	1029	Spanish - Argentina	es-ar	0x2C0A	11274
Danish	da	0x0406	1030	Spanish - Bolivia	es-bo	0x400A	16394

Locale Description	Short String	Hex Value	Decimal Value	Locale Description	Short String	Hex Value	Decimal Value
Dutch - Netherlands	nl-nl	0x0413	1043	Spanish - Chile	es-cl	0x340A	13322
Dutch - Belgium	nl-be	0x0813	2067	Spanish - Colombia	es-co	0x240A	9226
English - Australia	en-au	0x0C09	3081	Spanish - Costa Rica	es-cr	0x140A	5130
English - Belize	en-bz	0x2809	10249	Spanish - Dominican Republic	es-do	0x1C0A	7178
English - Canada	en-ca	0x1009	4105	Spanish - Ecuador	es-ec	0x300A	12298
English - Caribbean	en-cb	0x2409	9225	Spanish - Guatemala	es-gt	0x100A	4106
English - Ireland	en-ie	0x1809	6153	Spanish - Honduras	es-hn	0x480A	18442
English - Jamaica	en-jm	0x2009	8201	Spanish - Mexico	es-mx	0x080A	2058
English - New Zealand	en-nz	0x1409	5129	Spanish - Nicaragua	es-ni	0x4C0A	19466
English - Philippines	en-ph	0x3409	13321	Spanish - Panama	es-pa	0x180A	6154
English - South Africa	en-za	0x1C09	7177	Spanish - Peru	es-pe	0x280A	10250
English - Trinidad	en-tt	0x2C09	11273	Spanish - Puerto Rico	es-pr	0x500A	20490
English - United Kingdom	en-gb	0x0809	2057	Spanish - Paraguay	es-py	0x3C0A	15370
English - United States	en-us	0x0409	1033	Spanish - El Salvador	es-sv	0x440A	17418
Estonian	et	0x0425	1061	Spanish - Uruguay	es-uy	0x380A	14346
Farsi	fa	0x0429	1065	Spanish - Venezuela	es-ve	0x200A	8202

Locale Description	Short String	Hex Value	Decimal Value	Locale Description	Short String	Hex Value	Decimal Value
Finnish	fi	0x040B	1035	Southern Sotho	st	0x0430	1072
Faroese	fo	0x0438	1080	Swahili	sw	0x0441	1089
French - France	fr-fr	0x040C	1036	Swedish - Sweden	sv-se	0x041D	1053
French - Belgium	fr-be	0x080C	2060	Swedish - Finland	sv-fi	0x081D	2077
French - Canada	fr-ca	0x0C0C	3084	Tamil	ta	0x0449	1097
French - Luxembourg	fr-lu	0x140C	5132	Tatar	tt	0X0444	1092
French - Switzerland	fr-ch	0x100C	4108	Thai	th	0x041E	1054
Gaelic - Ireland	gd-ie	0x083C	2108	Turkish	tr	0x041F	1055
Gaelic - Scotland	gd	0x043C	1084	Tsonga	ts	0x0431	1073
German - Germany	de-de	0x0407	1031	Ukrainian	uk	0x0422	1058
German - Austria	de-at	0x0C07	3079	Urdu	ur	0x0420	1056
German - Liechtenstein	de-li	0x1407	5127	Uzbek - Cyrillic	uz-uz	0x0843	2115
German - Luxembourg	de-lu	0x1007	4103	Uzbek – Latin	uz-uz	0x0443	1091
German - Switzerland	de-ch	0x0807	2055	Vietnamese	vi	0x042A	1066
Greek	el	0x0408	1032	Xhosa	xh	0x0434	1076
Hebrew	he	0x040D	1037	Yiddish	yi	0x043D	1085
Hindi	hi	0x0439	1081	Zulu	zu	0x0435	1077
Hungarian	hu	0x040E	1038				
Yoruba	yo	0x046A	1130				

Index

A

How can we make this index more useful? Email us at indexes@samspublishing.com

L

M

How can we make this index more useful? Email us at indexes@samspublishing.com

V

validation

data validation example, 93-96

of form types, 14-15

schema validation, 84

versions

of BizTalk Server, 406-407

of Microsoft Dynamics CRM, customization options, 82

of MOSS (Microsoft Office SharePoint Server 2007), 115

features, 116-122

viewing analysis from Azure web services sample application, 450-449

Virtual Earth, 237

Visual Studio, Microsoft Silverlight Tools for Visual Studio 2008, 101

VoIP (Voice over IP), 202

VSTS (Visual Studio Team System), 343-347

environment requirements, 347-348

integration example, 348-403

customization requirements, 349-350

deployment stage, 393-399

TFS Automation solution, 351-381

TFSAutomationConsumer solution, 381-393

walkthrough, 404-403

W

web parts

Business Data Actions web part, 149

Business Data Item Builder web part, 149

Business Data Item web part, 149

Business Data List web part, 149

Business Data Related List web part, 149

List web part, displaying data in SharePoint, 127-129

web service connections, properties for, 132-136

web service programming, extending Microsoft Dynamics CRM, 9

web services. *See also* **Microsoft Dynamics CRM web services**

Azure web services

distributed machinery example, 440

Live Services, 438-437

Microsoft .NET Services, 437

Microsoft SQL Azure Database, 436-437

overview, 435-436

real estate industry example, 440

sample application, deploying, 450

sample application, deploying with IFrames, 450-451

sample application, developing, 441-448

sample application, testing, 450-446

sample application, viewing analysis, 450-449

Windows Azure, 436, 438-439

creating for Microsoft Dynamics CRM and GP10 integration, 428-424

CrmDiscoveryService web service, 16

CrmService web service, 17

defined, 16

MapPoint web services, 250-258

MetadataService web service, 16

social network integration. *See* social network integration

TFS Automation web services, deployment stage, 393-392

Windows Azure, 436, 438-439

Windows Resource Kit, debugging Kerberos, 43-44

How can we make this index more useful? Email us at indexes@samspublishing.com

X

UNLEASHED

Unleashed takes you beyond the basics, providing an exhaustive, technically sophisticated reference for professionals who need to exploit a technology to its fullest potential. It's the best resource for practical advice from the experts, and the most in-depth coverage of the latest technologies.

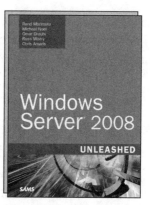

Windows Small Business Server 2008 Unleashed
ISBN-13: 9780672329579

OTHER UNLEASHED TITLES

Microsoft Exchange Server 2007 Unleashed
ISBN-13: 978-0-672-32920-3

Microsoft Office Project Server 2007 Unleashed
ISBN-13: 978-0-672-32921-0

Microsoft SharePoint 2007 Development Unleashed
ISBN-13: 978-0-672-32903-6

Microsoft Small Business Server 2008 Unleashed
ISBN-13: 978-0-672-32957-9

Microsoft SQL Server 2008 Unleashed
ISBN-13: 9780672330568

Microsoft SQL Server 2008 Analysis Services Unleashed
ISBN-13: 9780672330018

Microsoft SQL Server 2008 Integration Services Unleashed
ISBN-13: 9780672330322

Microsoft SQL Server 2008 Reporting Services Unleashed
ISBN-13: 9780672330261

Windows Server 2008 Hyper-V Unleashed
ISBN-13: 978-0-672-33028-5

ASP.NET 3.5 Unleashed
ISBN-13: 978-0-672-33011-7

C# 3.0 Unleashed
ISBN-13: 978-0-672-32981-4

Microsoft Visual Studio 2008 Unleashed
ISBN-13: 978-0-672-32972-2

Microsoft XNA Unleashed
ISBN-13: 978-0-672-32964-7

VBScript, WMI and ADSI Unleashed
ISBN-13: 978-0-321-50171-4

Windows Communication Foundation Unleashed
ISBN-13: 978-0-672-32948-7

Windows Presentation Foundation Unleashed
ISBN-13: 978-0-672-32891-6

Windows Server 2008 Unleashed
ISBN-13: 9780672329302

Windows PowerShell Unleashed
ISBN-13: 9780672329883

SAMS

informit.com/sams

FREE Online Edition

Your purchase of **Microsoft® Dynamics CRM 4 Integration Unleashed** includes access to a free online edition for 45 days through the Safari Books Online subscription service. Nearly every Sams book is available online through Safari Books Online, along with more than 5,000 other technical books and videos from publishers such as Addison-Wesley Professional, Cisco Press, Exam Cram, IBM Press, O'Reilly, Prentice Hall, and Que.

SAFARI BOOKS ONLINE allows you to search for a specific answer, cut and paste code, download chapters, and stay current with emerging technologies.

Activate your FREE Online Edition at www.informit.com/safarifree

> **STEP 1:** Enter the coupon code: UKLUQGA.

> **STEP 2:** New Safari users, complete the brief registration form.
> Safari subscribers, just log in.

If you have difficulty registering on Safari or accessing the online edition, please e-mail customer-service@safaribooksonline.com